WORKERS
and the
STATE
in TWENTIETH CENTURY
NOVA SCOTIA

Gorsebrook Studies in the Political Economy of the Atlantic Region

General Editor: Ian McKay

1. Gary Burrill and Ian McKay, eds., *People, Resources, and Power: Critical Perspectives on Underdevelopment and Primary Industries in the Atlantic Region* (1987).

2. Michael Earle, ed., *Workers and the State in Twentieth Century Nova Scotia* (1989).

The Gorsebrook Research Institute for Atlantic Canada Studies was formed in 1982 to encourage and support interdisciplinary research concerned with a variety of socio-economic, political, environmental, and policy issues specific to Canada's Atlantic region. Closely allied to the Atlantic Canada Studies program at Saint Mary's University, Halifax, the Gorsebrook Research Institute encourages interdisciplinary co-operation across the Atlantic region.

WORKERS
and the
STATE
in TWENTIETH CENTURY
NOVA SCOTIA

Edited by Michael Earle
with an introduction by Michael Earle and Ian McKay
and an afterword by Craig Heron

GORSEBROOK
RESEARCH
INSTITUTE

FOR ATLANTIC CANADA STUDIES

Published for the Gorsebrook Research Institute of
Atlantic Canada Studies by Acadiensis Press,
Fredericton, New Brunswick.

Canadian Cataloguing in Publication Data

Main entry under title:

Workers and the state in twentieth century Nova Scotia
(Gorsebrook studies in the political economy of the
Atlantic region; no. 2)

Co-published by: Gorsebrook Research Institute.

Includes bibliographical references.

ISBN 0-919107-21- 4

1. Industrial relations -- Nova Scotia -- History -- 20th
century. 2. Trade-unions -- Nova Scotia -- History -- 20th
century. I. Earle, Michael J. (Michael John) II. Gorsebrook
Research Institute for Atlantic Canada Studies. III. Series.

Printed in the Maritimes by union labour.

Contents

Acknowledgements

Thanks to all the contributors and the Gorsebrook Research Institute for making this book possible, Ken MacKinnon and Anders Sandberg at Gorsebrook for their help and encouragement, and Fraser Ross of Cardinal Communications, the cover designer. Five of the articles in this book have been published in *Acadiensis*, and benefitted considerably from the fine editorial skills of Phillip Buckner. Finally, Ian McKay, the general editor of the series, contributed very substantially to the original conception of this book and to all phases of the editorial process.

M. E.

MICHAEL EARLE and IAN McKAY

Introduction: Industrial Legality in Nova Scotia

What we have to decide is whether contracts are a help or a hurt to us. Whether we gain or lose by them. I am convinced that they tie our hands and restrict our liberties and are not a good thing to any union....

— Delegate to the Grand Council of the Provincial Workmen's Association (PWA), 1905, on the question of signing a three-year contract with the Dominion Coal Company.[1]

THERE WAS NO EASY ANSWER to this coal miner's question in 1905, and there can be no easy answer eight and a half decades later. The dominant trend among Canadian labour historians has been, however, to give a very easy answer indeed: legally binding contracts, free collective bargaining, certification hearings, conciliation, the check-off of union dues, grievance procedures — all these formalized, state regulated laws and procedures governing industrial life are Good Things. They are Good Things because they give workers written and guaranteed rights and their unions legal and financial security. According to this optimistic "Whig Interpretation" of Canadian Labour History, the workers began their long march towards legal recognition in the dark, oppressive mines and mills of the 19th century; they arrived at the far gentler and fairer world of modern collective bargaining only after fierce battles and tremendous sacrifices. Today's workers, we are told, are freer and more secure than those of the past. Where once there was only a ragged army of beleaguered unions, we now find an imposing array of duly certified bargaining units.[2]

---

1   Department of Labour Library, Ottawa, Minutes of the Grand Council of the Provincial Workmen's Association, September 1905, p. 528. A typographical error in the original has been corrected.
2   See Desmond Morton with Terry Copp, *Working People: An Illustrated History of Canadian Labour* (Ottawa, 1980); Harold Logan, *State Intervention and Assistance in Collective Bargaining: The Canadian Experience, 1943-1954* (Toronto, 1956). There is also more than a touch of the Whig approach in Laurel Sefton MacDowell's very useful article "The Formation of the Canadian Industrial Relations System During World War Two", *Labour/Le Travail*, 3 (1978), pp. 175-96. Among industrial relations writings, Paul Weiler, *Reconcilable Differences: New Directions in Canadian Labour Law* (Toronto, 1980) stands out. For an excellent alternative viewpoint on the system during the Second World War, see Jerermy Webber, "The Malaise of Compulsory Conciliation: Strike Prevention During World War II", *Labour/Le Travail*, 15 (Spring 1985), pp. 57-88. There is a growing international literature

The stimulating essays in this collection raise important and illuminating questions about the complex network of laws, systems, and procedures (now often called "industrial legality") which structures bargaining relations between workers and employers in Canada. Some of the articles that touch on this matter suggest that legally-binding contracts could mean a drastic reduction in the direct power of the workers. They underline the immense ideological power of the *idea* of the contract and the *idea* of conciliation — ideas which have conservative implications for the proper activities of "responsible" trade unionism. Some of the articles also show how industrial legality could turn trade-union leaders into bureaucrats for whom the smooth functioning of the system meant more than the needs of the average worker. They also suggest the inherent fragility of trade-union rights that come from above — for concessions made to workers when labour was perceived to be strong could be dispensed with when labour was considered to be weak.

In fact, what is often documented here is the opposite of a "Whig Interpretation" of Canadian Labour History. The Nova Scotia coal miners provide the most graphic example. The miners in the 1880s could, and did, go on strike when they wanted to. If they found conditions unsafe or wage payments unfair, they would go on strike. No laws impeded them. True, they also enjoyed no legal guarantees that the coal companies would not fire them all, but since these companies required their specialized skills and could not readily replace them, their unions and their "managing committees" were often recognized by the coal companies. Individual members who brought grievances to the attention of the local union frequently found prompt action being taken, and their union was more a loosely-knit collection of democratically managed local lodges than a top-down centralized organization.

Slowly, however, this flexible formula for trade unionism in a large and expanding industry was changed, and bargaining relations in the coalfields were formalized. This did not initially entail state intervention. What appears to be the first written contract in the coalfields was between Pioneer Lodge of the Provincial Workmen's Association (PWA) and the Cumberland Railway and Coal Company in 1885. The contract was written in legal language, but it carried no legal penalties for either side. In this early agreement, the management promised to keep their mines in active operation at least five days per week on an average, to take all the coal the miners could mine, not to employ any more workmen provided the existing

critical of industry legality.   See in particular three articles by Karl Klare: "Judicial Deradicalization of the Wagner Act and the Origins of Modern Legal Consciousness, 1937-1947", *Minnesota Law Review,* 62 (1978), pp. 265-339; "Critical Theory and Labour Relations Law", in David Kairys, ed., *The Politics of Law: A Progressive Critique* (New York, 1982); and "Labor Law and Liberal Political Imagination", *Social Review,* 62 (March-April 1982). See as well Christopher L. Tomlins, *The State and the Unions: Labour Relations, Law, and the Organized Labor Movement in America, 1880-1960* (Cambridge, 1985) and Katherine Van Wezel-Stone, "The Post-War Paradigm in American Labour Law", *The Yale Law Journal,* 90 (June 1981), pp. 1509-80.

workforce could keep the slopes running, and to observe seniority rights in discharging surplus employees. In exchange, the miners agreed to a wage reduction.[3]

After this modest beginning, the miners' union became more and more wedded to industrial legality. It supported Canada's first compulsory arbitration legislation, the Nova Scotia Mines Arbitration Act of 1888, and in 1905 signed a three year contract with the largest company in the industry, the Dominion Coal Company. By 1909-11, what had been a relatively decentralized union whose essential operations were local and based on rank-and-file activism, had become an organization dependent on the check-off of union dues, long-term contracts, and the armed force of the state, which it needed to fend off a challenge from the more militant United Mine Workers of America (UMW) in a bitter 22-month period of labour insurgency. The memory of the PWA's experience with long-term contracts explains some of the caution with which the radical socialists in the UMW approached contracts after they in turn assumed leadership of the miners' movement in 1917. The first district-wide agreement between the UMW and the employers contained a clause that provided that the one year contract could be re-opened for revision after just four months. Yet, in this 1920 contract, the UMW officers traded off the right to strike during the life of the agreement (except in cases of danger to life and limb or an unexplained refusal to pay wages on the regular payday) in exchange for a favorable wage settlement. Their gamble was that by making this concession on the right to strike the union would preserve the economic gains the miners had made during the First World War. As the miners' most influential spokesperson, J.B. McLachlan, was later ruefully to observe, even the wages provision of this new structure — seemingly the most attractive feature of this trade-off — left the worker unprotected against reductions in rates affecting a wide range of mining work and allowed the coal company to lay off "surplus" miners as it chose.[4] Since the local right to strike had been bargained away, the local lodges had no legitimate means of redressing such grievances. Rank-and-file coal miners did sometimes engage in "wildcat" or illegitimate strikes, but these were clearly supplementary to the "proper channels" of official collective bargaining. Under the authorized system, grievances could be brought up by union members, but they often took months, or even more than a year, to wind their weary way through the intricate bureaucratic channels the union and the company had devised.[5]

In the years that followed the UMW became even more committed to industrial legality, as the rank-and-file coal miners lost control over their own union. The

3   This important early document in the history of collective bargaining in Nova Scotia is preserved in the file on the Springhill Arbitration of 1889, RG 21, series "A", vol. 11, Public Archives of Nova Scotia (PANS).

4   Nova Scotia, Royal Commission to Inquire into the Coal Mining Industry of the Province of Nova Scotia, Minutes of Evidence, 1925, Evidence of J. B. McLachlan, p. 258, microfilm, PANS.

5   See Ian McKay, "Industry, Work and Community in the Cumberland Coalfields, 1848-1927", Ph.D. thesis, Dalhousie University, 1983, pp. 800-28 for a discussion of the impact of industrial legality on grievance procedures.

height of bureaucratic domination was attained in 1923 and 1924. First, John L. Lewis, international head of the UMW, suspended the autonomy of District 26 on the grounds that the Nova Scotia miners had broken their contract by engaging in a sympathy strike in support of the Sydney steelworkers. Then, in 1924, came the negotiation of the first genuine collective agreement in the coalfields, governing rates, working conditions and rules. This agreement contained remarkable restrictions on the union's right to freedom of political expression, outlawing the financial support locals of the UMW had given to the radical newspaper, *The Maritime Labour Herald*. Some of this agreement's provisions (although not the most outrageous) would be echoed in collective agreements in the coalfields for the next four decades. Here was a savagely ironic history. By the 1930s the UMW found itself in the same position as the PWA, the union it had replaced in 1917-18: it was sustained as the bargaining agent only through the efforts of the state and the coal company, which preserved it from a radical alternative supported by a majority of the coal miners. Predictably enough, the key ingredients in this conservative victory were the compulsory check-off of union dues and company recognition of union committees.

It was thanks to the coal miners — who were unusual in the Canadian context in having organized a large, militant, industrial union — that Nova Scotia could justifiably claim, in both the 1880s and 1930s, that its labour legislation and collective bargaining mechanisms were far more sophisticated and "advanced" than those of other provinces. Nova Scotia's coal miners have had union organization since 1879, and throughout the first half of this century had a record of militant strikes and a leaning towards political radicalism unsurpassed by any other workers in Canada.[6] As Kirby Abbott shows in his contribution to this volume, "The Coal Miners and the Law in Nova Scotia", in the latter decades of the 19th century a separate and more interventionist labour law was applied to coal miners, much of which was contained in successive revisions of the Coal Mines Regulation Act. The Nova Scotia coal miners were unusual in the Canadian context: they had a powerful industrial union from the earliest years of the 20th century, and they contributed to making industrial Cape Breton one of the few areas in the country where the Communist Party, and later the Co-operative Commonwealth Federation, were influential for many years (as documented in "The United Mine Workers and the

---

6   A more extensive literature exists on the history of coal miners than any other aspect of Nova Scotia's labour history. See David Frank, "The Cape Breton Coal Industry and the Rise and Fall of the British Empire Steel Corporation", *Acadiensis*, VII, 1 (Autumn 1977), pp. 3-34; and "Class Conflict in the Coal Industry; Cape Breton, 1922", in G.S. Kealey and Peter Warrian, eds., *Essays in Canadian Working Class History* (Toronto, 1976); Donald MacGillivray, "Military Aid to the Civil Power; The Cape Breton Experience in the 1920's", *Acadiensis*, III, 2 (Spring 1974), pp. 45-64; Michael Earle, "The Coalminers and their 'Red' Union: The Amalgamated Mine Workers of Nova Scotia, 1932-1936", *Labour/Le Travail*, 22 (Fall 1988), pp. 99-137; among numerous other titles. The popular accounts written by Paul MacEwan, *Miners and Steelworkers* (Toronto, 1976) and John Mellor, *The Company Store* (Toronto, 1983) should be treated with caution.

Coming of the CCF to Cape Breton", by Michael Earle and Herbert Gamberg, in this volume).

The reaction of the state to the strength of the miners' union movement went through various stages in the inter-war years. The most famous, and most visible, stage was outright repression. In 1910-11 and in the early 1920s police and military were sent in to help break strikes, and the most militant leader, J. B. McLachlan, was sent to prison. But this open coercion did not provide a long term solution to the problem of labour relations in the mining industry, and in the 1925 provincial election public sympathy with the miners helped to end the long ascendancy of the Liberal party in Nova Scotia. The Conservative government that followed adopted a more conciliatory approach to the coal union, granting concessions such as the legal right to the check-off privilege, and helping moderates in the union leadership against the militants and radicals.

This more sophisticated form of industrial legality is often regarded as a "consensual" (as contrasted to "coercive") system of labour relations, but this is an oversimplification. The state's use of open force, as exemplified in the 1920s in Cape Breton, was a clumsy reaction to the massive strikes. The state assisted the coal company in imposing wage cuts on the miners, but only after prolonged disruptions of production, and at the cost of strengthening the workers' political radicalism, and undermining the governing party's general electoral support. Such directly repressive tactics did not result in destroying the miners' union, nor did they provide any long-term solution to labour militancy among the miners. Offering concessions to the miners' union in the period after this was in part an attempt to return to the relationship late 19th century Liberal governments had with the PWA, and depended on finding union leaders amenable to a consensual system of labour relations. But the system of union legality that began to take form explicitly for the miners, and which later was extended to all industrial workers' unions, did not mean the abandonment of coercion by the state. Instead, the sporadic use of force, military occupations and the like, was replaced by the more systematic and all embracing coercion of workers by the legally binding regulations imposed in return for the guarantee of certain union rights, sometimes against the resistance of employers. A central element in the consensual system of union legality is that it legitimized the coercive power of the state in the minds of unionized workers.

Under industrial legality, a worker in his union activity is subjected to more coercion from the state, not less, than a striking coal miner in a time in which soldiers or police occupied his town. Laws dictate when strikes are permissible, how the grievance procedures are to operate, how negotiations with the employer are to be conducted, and what are the valid fields of union activity. Unions or union officials who defy these restrictions face almost certain fines or imprisonment. Wildcat rank-and-file strikers rarely have any public sympathy even from other workers. The difference from earlier times is not that there is less control over workers, but that the legal controls have been internalized by workers and union activists, who have accepted that it is fair for the state to intervene in this way, since the state also legally binds the employer to acknowledge the union in various ways and will correct certain glaring abuses at the workplace. Conditioned to accept the concepts of union legality, however, the unions and the workers have little ability to defend themselves against changes in the law which tilt the balance of relative power even more in favour of employers.[7]

The policies of industrial legality initiated by the Conservatives were continued and extended by the Liberals under Angus L. Macdonald, who came to power in 1933. Provincial cabinets met annually with the union executive to discuss changes in the legislation affecting miners, a provincial Ministry of Labour was created (combined with the Mines Ministry in this period), and in 1933-6 the government threw its weight behind the efforts of the UMW to defeat a radical breakaway union. In 1936-7 the major upsurge of industrial unionism led by the Committee for Industrial Organization (CIO) was winning victories in the United States, helped by New Deal labour legislation, and labour activists in Canada began to call for similar laws. In Nova Scotia the state had already largely adopted a policy directed towards the miners of attempting to contain labour militancy within a legally recognized union, possessing privileges and rights, but limited and constrained by regulations. Under pressure from the miners and steelworkers the government extended this policy to the workers of Nova Scotia in general, through the 1937 Trade Union Act. This was the first law passed in Canada that required employers to recognize and bargain with unions supported by a majority of their employees, and to provide the check-off of dues. (In vivid contrast, in the same week this law was passed, Premier Mitchell Hepburn of Ontario, cheered on by Premier Maurice Duplessis of Quebec, was using the coercive power of the state against striking automobile workers in Oshawa in an effort to prevent the coming of CIO industrial unionism to Central Canada.[8]) The principal practical effect of the Nova Scotia law was to bring about the unionization of the province's steelworkers. Inspired by the miners, and facing the same giant corporation, workers in the steel industry had long fought to build a union and win union recognition. The workers at the Sydney and Trenton plants achieved this in 1937, establishing the earliest Steel Workers' Organizing Campaign locals in Canada.

Because most of the elements of industrial legality were first articulated in Nova Scotia, the province's record can be used as a fascinating laboratory for all Canadian labour historians. Here they have a sufficiently long period and abundant sources to test various hypotheses concerning the formalization of collective bargaining. Some conventional ideas are certain to be challenged in the process. In the 1940s, some historians have confidently told us, industrial unionism made its triumphant breakthrough with federal recognition of collective bargaining rights in PC 1003 and the Industrial Relations and Disputes Investigation Act of 1948. But in fact

---

7   See Leo Panitch and Donald Swartz, *The Assault on Trade Union Freedoms* (Toronto, 1988).

8   See Irving Abella, *Nationalism, Communism, and Canadian Labour* (Toronto, 1973); and "Oshawa 1937" in Irving Abella, ed., *On Strike. Six Key Labour Struggles in Canada 1919-1949* (Toronto, 1974).

there was little in the industrial relations system that emerged from the Second World War that had not long since been tried in the Nova Scotia coalfields. Indeed, many industrial unionists in Ontario were to learn the rudiments of "modern collective bargaining" at the knees of Silby Barrett, the Nova Scotia miner-turned-CIO-organizer, who had profited most directly from the 1923 suspension of democracy in District 26, and who was identified by rebellious miners in the early years of the Second World War as the very epitome of the undemocratic industrial unionism they opposed, as Mike Earle suggests in this volume in "Down With Hitler and Silby Barrett".

Were the laws that established the workers' right to form unions, modelled on the wartime federal Order-in-Council, PC 1003, the breakthrough they are often thought to be? With these laws, and the Rand Formula, which established a right to the check-off of union dues, a system entrenched in the coal industry of Nova Scotia was extended across the country. The state granted certain rights to unions that were legally enforceable against employers, but also set limits on the timing of strikes, established the inviolability of contracts, and sought to eliminate spontaneous militant activity on the part of workers. The very complexity of the laws and regulations through which the state achieved these aims facilitated the bureaucratization of unions, as professional union business agents and labour lawyers became the key players in union affairs. Further, the officials of unions often came to be placed in a position of enforcing legally binding contracts on workers, so that the alienation between union memberships and leaders was accentuated. Bureaucracy, not democracy, was thus almost mandated within unions by the laws, "progressive" as many of them at first appeared to be.

None of this would have surprised an observer of industrial legality in Nova Scotia since the 1920s. Had various left-wing CIO enthusiasts, or the historians who most closely represent their views today, studied the Nova Scotia record more carefully, they would have had a far more realistic grasp of what to expect from the system of industrial legality they hailed as a decisive working-class victory. There was a tragic ambivalence to the breakthrough to industrial legality whose undemocratic effects, had they been understood at the outset, might well have been mitigated. Once in place, however, the system imposed its logic upon every union and every union member: it was impossible for any union to live outside the ever-expanding corpus of rules, regulations, and procedures through which the state now regulated labour. In effect, the labour movement was "nationalized" and would never again have the same relationship with its membership, nor with society as a whole.

Yet it would be a mistake equivalent to the "Whig Interpretation" of industrial legality as a Good Thing to see it as an unadulterated Bad Thing. Even in the case of the coal miners, where the logic of bureaucratization and dis-empowerment is unmistakable and instructive, it would be wrong to overlook other factors — the economic eclipse of coal, the impact of outmigration, the general context of regional dependence — which also contributed to the demise of the miners' radical movement. Furthermore, in the case of workers who lacked the miners' capacity for collective action, industrial legality cannot be linked with a decline in working-class power. For some workers, such as longshoremen and steelworkers, modern industrial legality, with all its problems, represented the first effective collective challenge to the power of capital.[9] The record is not simple, and the terrain is not even.

And here we find another major contribution of these essays: to provide us with a map, far from comprehensive, but the best to date, of the remarkably uneven provincial record in industrial relations outside the coalfields in 20th century Nova Scotia. It thus gives us a vivid impression of the remarkable dichotomy in state policies towards labour. Although 19th century Nova Scotia did experience a considerable surge of widely-dispersed industrial development, this was followed by the decline of much of this industry in the first half of the 20th century, in an historical process that saw most of Canada's manufacturing become concentrated in the provinces of Quebec and Ontario.[10] Nova Scotia's pattern of dependent development entailed the emergence of industrial enclaves, associated primarily with the coalfields of Cape Breton, Cumberland and Pictou counties and the steel plants in Sydney and Trenton. These enclaves tended to buy their equipment and capital goods from the outside, and thus did not become the engines of general economic transformation. Outside them much of Nova Scotia was dominated by such primary industries as fishing, agriculture, and lumber. The steel and coal industries, although beset with financial difficulties, remained among the province's largest employers in the period between the First and Second World Wars. In the years following 1945, these industries declined rapidly, private capital withdrew, and today coal and steel in the province survive as government controlled and supported industries with greatly reduced workforces. Nova Scotia and the Atlantic provinces in general had little share in the economic boom of the 1950s and 1960s, and since the Second World War the region's industrial disparity with central Canada and its economic dependency have grown steadily.

This starkly uneven economic and social record has produced an equally uneven labour history. The fisherman and the coal miner, symbolic figures of labour in Nova Scotia, each faced hard work, harsh conditions, and danger at the workplace for low wages, but the experience of fishermen and coal miners with regard to collective action has been at opposite poles. Nova Scotia's workers in the inshore and offshore fishery engaged in sporadic struggles through the years, but failed to win any long

9   John Foster, "On the Waterfront: Longshoring in Canada" in Craig Heron and Robert Storey, eds., *On the Job: Confronting the Labour Process in Canada* (Kingston and Montreal, 1986), pp. 281-308; Craig Heron, "The Great War and Nova Scotia Steelworkers", *Acadiensis*, XVI, 2 (Spring 1987), pp. 3-34.
10   See T. W. Acheson, "The National Policy and the Industrialization of the Maritimes, 1880-1910", *Acadiensis*, I, 2 (Spring 1972); "The Maritimes and 'Empire Canada'" in David Jay Bercuson, ed., *Canada and the Burden of Unity* (Toronto, 1977); Ernest R. Forbes, "Misguided Symmetry: The Destruction of Regional Transportation Policy for the Maritimes" in *ibid.*; David Alexander, "Economic Growth in the Atlantic Region, 1880 to 1940", *Acadiensis*, VIII, 1 (Autumn 1978).

lasting organization or trade union rights until the 1970s.[11] The local state, when forced to pay attention to the fishery, has generally sought to prop up the outdated traditional operation of the industry and defined fishermen as small independent operators or "co-adventurers", even though a blatantly exploitative relationship frequently existed between vessel owners or fish-buyers and the fishermen. Inshore fishermen are still legally denied the rights of collective bargaining extended to almost all other workers in Canada. In its labour history Nova Scotia presents two images: one of the ineffectual bargaining power of labour in a backward economy, symbolized by the fishing industry; the other of a powerful union movement and intense class struggle, symbolized by the history of the mining industry.

Thus, outside the coal and steel industries from the 1880s to the 1940s, and apart from a pioneering experiment in state-supported technical education,[12] the record of the state in Nova Scotia suggests *at best* an effort to keep up with the workers' compensation schemes, minimum wage laws, industrial standards legislation, or health and safety regulations that had been passed elsewhere. At its not infrequent *worst*, however, it suggests a conscious effort (especially since 1947) to weaken labour's position in the province as part of a strategy of economic development. Thanks to these efforts and the legacy of dependent development, Nova Scotia in recent decades can be seen as a Maritime backwater, characterized by political and social conservatism, its economy propped up by federal transfer payments, with a dominated and impoverished workforce whose main avenue of entry into the affluent North American lifestyle has been migration out of the region. The province's depressed economy has helped to enfeeble the labour movement, and successive provincial governments, preoccupied with attracting industrial investment from outside, have sought to keep unions weak through legislation favouring capital. If Nova Scotia's early 20th century labour history is significant in that it represented a "trial run" for forms of industrial legality that were subsequently generalized across Canada, its post-1945 history is significant in that it suggests a "trial run" for the forms of de-legitimization that have forced labour to acquiesce before the logic of de-industrialization, "international competitiveness", and dependent development. As such, unfortunately, it may also have general lessons for other Canadians.

It will certainly not do to read the present *debacle* back into the historical record and present the workers of Nova Scotia as die-hard conservatives. Western Canadian historians have legitimately drawn attention to the distinctive radical traditions and institutions of their region, but they have overstated their case in attempting to

11   See L. Gene Barrett, "Underdevelopment and Social Movements in the Nova Scotia Fishing Industry to 1938" in Robert J. Brym and R. James Sacouman, eds., *Underdevelopment and Social Movements in Atlantic Canada* (Toronto, 1979), pp. 127-60; Rick Williams, "Inshore Fishermen, Unionization, and the Struggle against Underdevelopment Today" in Brym and Sacouman, *Underdevelopment and Social Movements*, pp. 161-75; Wallace Clement, *The Struggle to Organize, Resistance in Canada's Fishery* (Toronto, 1986).
12   Janet Guildford, "Coping with De-industrialization: The Nova Scotia Department of Technical Education, 1907-1930", *Acadiensis*, XVI, 2 (Spring 1987), pp. 51-84.

contrast this dynamic record with the supposedly static conservatism of the East.[13] In the early 20th century Nova Scotia unions of urban skilled workers turned, as did their fellow workers across Canada, toward "labourism" in politics, a vague ideology seeking labour representation in government and fair play for workers.[14] The Socialist Party of Canada had supporters in Nova Scotia, and Amherst, as well as Winnipeg, had a general strike in 1919.[15] In 1920 11 Farmer-Labour members were elected to the provincial Assembly, and for a brief period formed the official opposition. Until the 1920s, industrial growth had created an urban working-class movement which responded similarly to that of Ontario in the expansion of trade unionism, frequency of strikes, and the beginnings of working class political action. With respect to the skilled tradesmen and workers in manufacturing in Nova Scotia, government intervention in labour relations and in regulating conditions at the workplace also followed reasonably closely developments in Central Canada — as Suzanne Morton suggests in this volume in "The Halifax Relief Commission and Labour Relations during the Reconstruction of Halifax, 1917-1919".

But through most of the inter-war years, in keeping with the general Canadian pattern, the labour movement expanded very little. The divergence of the experience of the miners and steelworkers from that of the rest of the Nova Scotian workforce became more pronounced. The decline of industry in the province caused the union movement to languish in urban centres such as Halifax or Amherst where it had previously held considerable strength. Indeed, in a worsening climate for labour, significant past achievements were reversed, as Fred Winsor shows in his contribution to this volume, "'Solving a Problem': Privatizing Worker's Compensation for Nova Scotia's Offshore Fishermen, 1926-1928".

The startling difference between state policies towards miners and fishermen respectively surfaced even more dramatically after the passage of the Nova Scotia Trade Union Act in 1937. Thanks to the pressure applied on the government by miners and steelworkers, Nova Scotia could point to this provincial replica of the American Wagner Act as the most progressive labour legislation in Canada. But the government had no real intention of allowing this pathbreaking law to lead to the widespread growth of unions in the province — and certainly not in the fishing

---

13   For Western radicalism see A. Ross McCormack, *Reformers, Rebels and Revolutionaries: The Western Canadian Radical Movement, 1899-1919* (Toronto, 1977); David Jay Bercuson, *Confrontation at Winnipeg: Labour, Industrial Relations and the General Strike* (Montreal, 1974); *Fools and Wise Men: The Rise and Fall of the One Big Union* (Toronto, 1978); Paul Phillips, *No Power Greater: A Century of Labour in B.C.* (Vancouver, 1967). The most exaggerated claims for a conservative East and a radical West are made by David Bercuson, "Labour Radicalism and the Western Industrial Frontier: 1879-1919", *Canadian Historical Review*, 8 (Summer 1978), pp. 44-51.

14   For Labourism, see Craig Heron, "Labourism and the Canadian Working Class", *Labour/Le Travail*, 13 (Spring 1984), pp. 54-9; Suzanne Morton, "Labourism and Economic Action: The Halifax Shipyards Strike of 1920", *Labour/Le Travail*, 22 (Fall 1988), pp. 67-98.

15   David Frank and Nolan Reilly, "The Emergence of the Socialist Movement in the Maritimes, 1899-1916", *Labour/Le Travail*, 4 (1978), pp. 85-114; Nolan Reilly, "The General Strike in Amherst, Nova Scotia, 1919", *Acadiensis*, IX, 2 (Spring 1980), pp. 56-77.

industry. In early 1938 the government helped to defeat the effort of fish plant workers in Halifax to unionize.[16] In 1939 coercive tactics and red-baiting by government officials were used to defeat fishermen and fish plant workers in Lockeport, and one of the organizers, Charles Murray, was among the Canadian communists interned early in the war.[17] Provincial and federal governments were keenly aware that more deep seated political radicalism existed in the miners' and steelworkers' unions than in the union of Lockeport fishermen, yet no communists from Cape Breton were interned. Even in the repression of communists, the state seemed aware of the very distinct labour traditions it confronted.

The 1940s were the golden years of industrial unionism in Canada. Many Nova Scotians also seized the opportunities provided by the country's wartime expansion to organize. As Jay White shows in his contribution to this volume, "Pulling Teeth: Striking for the Check-off in the Halifax Shipyards, 1944", shipbuilding workers were not slow to respond to this moment of opportunity, and they did so by demanding the same official guarantees of union security that other workers were winning across Canada. But the 1940s in Nova Scotia do not have the same significance as they do elsewhere. Where breakthroughs were made, as in shipbuilding, rapid post-war de-industrialization meant drastic reductions in the power of unions. Elsewhere in post-war Canada we find big industrial strike victories; in Nova Scotia, disastrous defeats.

Thus the Nova Scotian 1940s was not the era of the triumph of "industrial unionism", but the decisive decade in the triumph of conservative strategies of repression, incorporation, and business unionism. In the 1940s the labour movement in Nova Scotia lost most of its broader social vision. As elsewhere, communists and radicals were purged from positions of influence in the labour movement in the early years of the Cold War. This was carried out, where such radicals had widespread support among the workers, by a three pronged attack from the state, the right-wing leadership of the parent American international unions, and the bureaucratic business unionists within the unions, who were frequently closely allied to the national leadership of the CCF.[18] Nova Scotia saw some of the most ruthless actions in this destruction of union radicalism. As Jean Nisbet shows in her article, "'Free Enterprise at Its Best': The State, National Sea, and the Defeat of the Nova Scotia Fishermen, 1946-1947", the judiciary, the politicians, and the employers relied on a combined strategy of legalistic hair-splitting and vintage red-baiting to smash the organized fishermen and their dreams of a less exploitative fishing industry. In the same years, huge defeats in the coalfields spelled the decline of militancy among steelworkers and miners. The region's merchant seamen faced thugs, beatings, and bullets in their efforts to save the Canadian Seamen's Union in 1949 from the gangster-led Seamen's International Union, brought to Canada courtesy of the Canadian government. (The gun battle for the *Lady Rodney* in

16 Barrett, pp. 148-50; K. Dane Parker, interview, May 1985.
17 Sue Calhoun, *The Lockeport Lockout* (Halifax, 1983).
18 See Abella, *Nationalism, Communism, and Canadian Labour.*

Halifax harbour is a well-remembered episode in this story.)[19] State sponsored anti-communism continued apace in 1952, with the refusal of the Nova Scotia Labour Board to grant certification to locals of the Maritime Shipping Federation on the sole grounds that its Secretary, J.K. Bell, was a Communist Party member. This decision was later overturned in the Supreme Court, but not before the growth of the union had been greatly disrupted. When the Nova Scotia government combined classic red-baiting strategies with a wide range of specious arguments regarding the special status of fishermen to break the Canso fishermen's strike of 1970,[20] it was simply continuing a long, dishonourable tradition. The post-war political compromise through which labour's influence was acknowledged and the welfare state implemented was, in Nova Scotia, imposed in terms far less favorable to workers than in other regions.

Labour's defeat in the 1940s established disadvantageous terms for workers that have not since been successfully challenged. The power of the union movement in the province, once greater than, or on a par with, that of the movement in the rest of Canada, is now much reduced in relative terms. This has been true since the Second World War. The period since the late 1950s can be portrayed as one of fundamental continuity with the late 1940s. As C. J. H. Gilson and A. M. Wadden show in their contribution, "The Windsor Gypsum Strike and the Formation of the Joint Labour/Management Study Committee", one union's attempt in 1957 to put a union security provision in its contract initiated an explosive labour struggle. The defeat in Windsor placed the Nova Scotia labour movement even more on the defensive. Through the 1960s and 1970s much of the attention of the Nova Scotia Federation of Labour was devoted to efforts to find common ground with local businessmen and so find solutions to the problems of industrial relations through such agencies as the Joint Labour/Management Study Committee, based on the premise of a fundamental compatibility of interests of employees and employers. The Nova Scotia government looked benignly on this co-operation between business and labour, so long as it appeared useful. But in 1979 the government did not hesitate to enact the notorious "Michelin Act", which, by requiring a joint certification vote in widely separated localities, enabled the Michelin Tire Company to prevent unionization of its workers.[21] By this time the government was able to pass such an act — the very epitome of conservative backwardness — without fearing any militant upheaval or adverse political effect.

This was because the labour movement in Nova Scotia had long, in its relations with employers and the state, operated from a position of growing weakness, not strength, and its leaders had embraced the framework of industrial legality as the

---

19   See the account of this incident in Jim Green, *Against the Tide. The Story of the Canadian Seamen's Union* (Toronto, 1986), pp. 222-9.

20   For the Canso strike, see Silver Donald Cameron, *The Education of Everett Richardson* (Toronto, 1977); Lorna Darrach and Rosilind Belland, "The Canso Fishermen's Strike 1970-71" in C. H. J. Gilson, ed., *Strikes. Industrial Relations in Nova Scotia 1957-1987* (Hantsport, 1987), pp. 56-73.

21   See Ken Clare, "Michelin. The Fortess that Didn't Fall", *New Maritimes*, July/August 1986.

major prop of unions, rather than relying on the collective strength of workers' solidarity and militancy. One effect of this system, here and elsewhere, is that rank-and-file union members themselves become alienated from the bureaucratic leadership of their unions. Unions are often regarded by their members merely as service agencies, and the spirit of solidarity is undermined. In recent years in Nova Scotia there have been local examples of strong worker militancy in the strikes of the miners, Scott Paper workers, school bus drivers, hospital workers, steelworkers and others, but the weakness of the movement as a whole is undeniable.

Notwithstanding the continuity of trends since the 1940s, the period since 1960 represents an interesting shift in labour's position. Working people in the region demanded better living standards and came to expect the benefits of the welfare state. They have also been able to obtain certain changes to legislation affecting them, such as the extension of unemployment insurance to seasonally employed fishermen. State industrialization policies in the fishing industry have concentrated capital and damaged the resource base, but they have also prompted the growth of the region's most significant new union, the Newfoundland Fishermen, Food and Allied Workers' Union, which has transformed conditions in the offshore fishing fleets, and which now, as an affiliate of the Canadian Automobile Workers, represents many workers in Nova Scotia as well.[22]

The state now occupies a position in the economy of the Atlantic region that would have been unthinkable in the 1940s and which is unusual in Canada. Average levels of public sector investment as a proportion of total fixed capital formation in Nova Scotia far outstrip the national average. Even more striking is the expansion of the state in the province as an employer. State employees now represent about 27 per cent of the total employed persons in Nova Scotia, and earn close to one third of all taxable income. A far higher percentage of Nova Scotians are government employees than is the case in Canada as a whole.

As Anthony Thomson shows in his contribution to this volume, "From Civil Servants to Government Employees: The Nova Scotia Government Employees Association, 1967-1973", public sector employees in Nova Scotia, the majority of whom are women, were relatively late in unionizing. It has nonetheless been in the public sector that the most vigorous recent growth of union militancy has occurred. Perhaps in the coming years employees in the state sector will be able to break the tradition of defeat that extends back to the 1940s. The unanticipated consequence of the massive extension of the state has been that the state itself has been "colonized" by various social interests, a fact which greatly impedes the ability of government (as one part of a now massive and cumbersome state) to set policy. As state and society have become more and more interlocked, it becomes less appropriate to see the state simply as guarding the interests of a particular class. Rather, as Claus Offe has put it, "it sanctions the general interests of all classes on the basis of capitalist

---

22   See Gordon Inglis, *More Than Just a Union: The Story of the NFFAWU* (St. John's, 1985).

exchange relationships".[23] The capitalist state is oriented, in this understanding, towards putting private actors in a position to increase their efficiency and effectiveness according to the criteria of private exchange and accumulation. The extraordinary growth of the postwar state in the province, and its dramatic failure to find a successful strategy for economic development, places it in some respects in the position of a helpless giant, incapable of legitimizing its position or changing its fundamental direction. The fiscal crisis of the state in the 1980s carries some dire implications for this "embedded state", among which may well be an unprecedented degree of turmoil in the public sector. (This has certainly been the record in Newfoundland.) As the coal miner defined so much of the province's labour history before the 1950s, the state employee may well be the deciding element in the period after the 1960s. If, as seems likely, the weakening of the welfare state entails serious cutbacks and layoffs in the province, it will fall to workers in the state sector to put forward an alternative agenda. Their future is certainly an open one, and effective and radical alliances with new social movements (such as those of the feminists and environmentalists) and with the traditional blue-collar labour movement, could provide new energy for the province's left. It is at least possible that the sentence passed upon the Nova Scotia labour movement in the 1940s may finally be appealed.

This book represents the work of a community of critical labour scholars over the past 15 years. Almost all of these essays are drawn from previously unpublished research on aspects of Nova Scotia's labour history. (A number appear simultaneously with this volume in *Acadiensis*, the region's leading history journal.) Most of them represent the work of a new generation of labour historians, many of whom are at present in graduate school. No claim, of course, can be made that the historical episodes dealt with here provide a comprehensive account of the province's labour history. Most emphasize struggles of organized labour and the development of state intervention in the collective bargaining process. Little is included about working-class cultural traditions or about conditions in the unorganized workforce. A traditional focus is maintained on the miners and fishermen, those great symbolic figures of the province's labour movement: a truly comprehensive collection would explore the conditions and struggles of workers in the woods, in the service sector, or in the manufacturing industries. There is very little here on women and work (an absence to be addressed in a future volume on work and gender in this series, the Gorsebrook Studies in the Political Economy of the Atlantic Region). One pressing need is for greater understanding of the relations between the workers and primary producers — for the prospects for genuine social change hinge on effective alliances between city and country, office worker and woodsworker. Nova Scotia's labour historiography is relatively new. Large topics remain to be explored

---

23   Claus Offe, *Contradictions of the Welfare State* (Cambridge, Mass., 1985), p. 123.

Within these limits, there is strength. With varying ideological approaches, the authors all share a lively sympathy with the labour movement, and an equally vigorous concern for accuracy and fairness. They have pushed the existing labour historiography well beyond its earlier conventional stopping-place of 1925. In documenting, with sober accuracy and vivid liveliness, the record of the provincial labour movement, they have suggested important lessons for both scholars and trade unionists, as we confront, and struggle to change, the legacy of industrial legality today.

KIRBY ABBOTT

The Coal Miners and the Law in Nova Scotia: From the 1864 Combination of Workmen Act to the 1947 Trade Union Act

THE COAL INDUSTRY of Nova Scotia early saw a large industrial union engaged at times in sharp conflict and at other times in relatively peaceful negotiation with a huge corporation. There was always intense government concern when labour strife occurred in this key industry, and state intervention at times took the form of coercive measures and at other times attempts to conciliate the miners through the granting of substantive rights to their unions. The history of legal intervention in labour relations in the coal industry therefore provides an excellent avenue through which to examine the development of the modern framework of collective bargaining law. It also permits some evaluation of two conflicting theoretical perspectives on the overall role of labour legislation. These differing perspectives can be termed the "mainstream" and the "critical legal studies" outlooks on labour law.

The mainstream or "pluralist" perspective holds that while labour and capital have distinct legitimate interests, these interests need not be irreconcilable, and there is a third legitimate interest, the public interest represented by the state. The purpose of collective bargaining law is to promote industrial peace in the public interest, and at the same time allow both parties to bargain freely. Whereas historically employer-employee relations were characterized by extreme economic inequality and workers had few rights, the modern law intervenes in such a way as to create rights for workers, while at the same time guaranteeing that the legitimate managerial rights of the employer are preserved. Thus the law provides a framework for stable and democratic industrial relations.[1]

---

1   For literature which represents the mainstream perspective see *Woods Task Force Report on Canadian Industrial Relations* (Ottawa, 1968); S. Hameed, ed., *Canadian Industrial Relations* (Toronto, 1975); J. D. Muir, "Highlights in the Development of the Legal System", in Hameed, *ibid.*, p. 83; S. Jamieson, *Times of Trouble — Labour Unrest and Industrial Conflict in Canada* (Ottawa, 1968); J. Crispo, *Industrial Relations* (Toronto, 1966); H. Arthurs, "Challenge and Response in the Law of Labour Relations", in Crispo, *ibid.*, p. 91; H. Arthurs, "Developing Industrial Citizenship", *Canadian Bar Review* (1967), p. 786; P. Weller, *Reconcilable Differences* (Toronto, 1980); P. Weiler, "The Remedial Authority of the Arbitrator", *Canadian Bar Review*, 52 (1974), p. 79; E. Finn, "The Adversary System is Dead, But It Won't Lie Down", *Labour Gazette* (1974), p. 767; C. B. Williams, "Notes on the Evolution of Compulsory Conciliation in Canada", *Industrial Relations*, 19 (1964), p. 298; M. Chartland, "The First Canadian Trade Union Legislation: An Historical Perpective", *Ottawa Law Review*, 16 (1984), p. 267; G. W. Adams, "Industrial Democracy: A Canadian Perpective", *Cambridge Lectures* (1983), p. 280.

The critical perspective holds the central premise that employers and employees within a capitalist society have interests which are fundamentally and structurally opposed to one another. These distinct interests are materially based on the respective positions of workers and capital in the production process, and form the basis of the most fundamental conflicts within society as a whole. Existing labour law is basically a mechanism of domination that hinders workers' aspirations for a democratic workplace. In attempting to control the irreconcilable conflict between capital and labour the state intervenes through law to maintain social order and stability, and thus reproduces the existing inequality. Specifically, collective bargaining law attempts to integrate labour within the objectives of capital, and to control and structure conflict, by reducing the use of strikes and by formalizing dispute resolution procedures.[2]

Does the mainstream perspective appreciate the real structural differences in interests between employee and employer displayed in the history of labour relations? Has the state ever been a neutral representor of the "public interest?" But, if labour legislation is so one-sided, dominating, and anti-democratic as the critical perspective declares, why did rank and file workers struggle so hard for laws upholding trade union rights? Attempts to answer such questions require an analysis of historical experience, and no industry in Nova Scotia experienced as much state intervention as mining.

One reason for this was the direct interest the provincial state had in mining after the mid-19th century, when it successfully petitioned the British Crown for full legal ownership of Nova Scotian mining and mineral rights.[3] This gave the province legal jurisdiction to regulate the industry and acquire revenue from royalties. Thus economic, political and legal interdependence between the provincial state and the industry was established, and this interdependence grew as the provincial government increasingly became more dependent on royalties as revenue. In 1872 the coal royalties comprised seven per cent of provincial revenue; by 1900 they were 41 per cent.[4]

In 1825 the British owned General Mining Association (GMA) acquired exclusive mining rights in the province and by 1840 had established 12 mines.[5] In 1858 the GMA signed an agreement ending the monopoly in exchange for lower

---

2   For examples of the critical perspective see: Karl Klare, "Labour Law as Ideology: Towards a New Historiography of Collective Bargaining Law", *Industrial Relations Law Journal*, 4 (1981), p. 450; "Judical Deradicalization of the Wagner Act", *Minnesota Law Review*, 62 (1978), p. 265; Lynd, "Government Without Rights", *Industrial Relations Law Journal*, 4 (1981), p. 483; "Workers Control in a Time of Diminished Workers' Rights", *Radical America* (September 1976), p. 5; Stone, "The Post-War Paradigm in American Labour Law", *Yale Law Journal*, 90 (June 1981), pp. 1509-80.
3   Ian McKay, "Industry, Work and Community in Cumberland Coalfields, 1848-1927", Ph.D. thesis, Dalhousie University, 1983, note 16, p. 10.
4   *Ibid.*, p. 195.
5   Sharon Reilly, "The Provincial Workmen's Association of Nova Scotia", M.A. thesis, Dalhousie University, 1979, p. 9. The GMA acquired the mining rights from the Duke of York in partial payment of a debt.

royalties. This, along with Reciprocity with the United States and the Civil War in that country, resulted in a brief mining boom, and by Confederation 87 new pits had been opened. In 1858 also, the Province had established the Inspector of Mines Office, the first piece of bureaucratic apparatus that was established solely for the industry. While initially concerned with the task of collecting royalties the office later increasingly concerned itself with safety issues in the mines.[6]

Up to this time coal mining labour relations were basically paternalistic, and operated through tradition and unwritten convention, not law. The labour process was little mechanized, and miners usually worked unsupervised with a partner in their own section of the mine and were paid by piecerates, based on the amount of coal sent to the surface. Piece rates and grievances were usually negotiated individually with the employer or manager whose authority received considerable deference and extended "beyond the confines of the workplace to take in many aspects of social and political life".[7]

A significant effect of the mid-century mining boom was the erosion of the stable economic conditions in which such paternalism best operated. In the more turbulent work environment many old assumptions and traditions were swept away. Between 1864 and 1876 there were at least four strikes at Sydney Mines and one in 1868 at Cow Bay, Cape Breton. While little is known about them they appeared to have occurred in response to miners' dissatisfaction with wage fluctuations and the influx of large numbers of unskilled miners into the mines.[8]

In the 1864 strike the provincial militia intervened under the justification of a new Combination of Workmen Act. This Act prohibited forcing anyone "by violence to person and property...[or by] anyway obstructing another" to strike or join an association in order to advance wages or working conditions, or to influence the way the industry was regulated. The Act did not prohibit collective workers' associations or the collective negotiation of wages, only the use of force in these activities.[9]

The effect of this law was ambivalent, since its passage relieved trade unions of the earlier notion that their very existence was illegal. Yet the wording does not make clear precisely what type of activity constituted "forcing", and the sporadic usage of the Act seems to have rested more on the degree of concern an employer had that workers would hinder his business than on the occurrence of violence. The Act itself arose during the 1864 strike in response to a request made by the GMA manager at Sydney Mines for aid to assist in the eviction of striking miners from company houses. The government found there was no statutory basis upon which to

6   D. MacLeod, "Mines, Mining Men and Mining Reform: Changing the Technology of Nova Scotia Gold Mines and Collieries, 1937 — 1960", Ph.D. thesis, University of Toronto, 1981, p. 379.
7   S. Martell, "Early Coal Mining in Nova Scotia", *Dalhousie Review*, 25 (1945), p. 171; McKay, "Industry, Work and Community", pp. 691, 694.
8   MacLeod, "Mines, Mining Men and Mining Reform", p. 435.
9   *An Act Relating to the Combination of Workmen*, Statutes of Nova Scotia (S.N.S.), 1864, c. 11. An offence under the Act was punishable by imprisonment of up to one year hard labour.

do this, so the bill was written and passed all three readings before lunchtime.[10] The troops were organized and ready to go before the Act was passed.

In 1873 the Coal Mines Regulation Act was introduced. The Act regulated the general engineering requirements of a coal mine. It gave the Inspector of Mines the power to enter and inspect mines; and gave mine owners and management, but not workers, the power to make additional rules, subject to the Inspector's approval. In keeping with the laissez-faire economic and political philosophy of the times, little attention was paid to labour relations. Nevertheless, the Act provided that no boy under the age of ten was to be employed in any mining operation. No boys between ten and 12 years of age could work in a mine over sixty hours a week or ten hours a day. Another provision was that no wages were to be paid within any public house that sold alcohol. The wages themselves were to be dependent upon the amount of coal mined, which was to be weighed by a "weighman".[11] In general, however, the Act intervened minimally in the sacred terrain of an employer's relations with his workmen.[12]

In 1879 miners at Springhill formed a union named the Provincial Miners' Association, which was subsequently renamed the Provincial Workmen's Association (PWA). In 1881, the union began to organize Cape Breton miners who complained of low wages, a long work day, high prices at the company store and dishonest weighmen.[13] After only six months of unionizing about half of the Cape Breton miners were organized.[14] The major conflict in the organizing drive occurred at the GMA's Lingan Mine in New Waterford where a long strike occurred. The strike arose over the firing of workers who joined the PWA and soon evolved into an all out struggle by the company to break the union. The provincial militia was sent to the area and the leaders of the strike were blacklisted. Despite this the PWA was not crushed out of existence, and by 1887 it was strong enough to win a non-compulsory check-off of union dues in some of the mines.[15]

---

10   K. G. Pryke, "Labour and Politics: Nova Scotia at Confederation", *Histoire Sociale/Social History*, 6 (1970), note 24, p. 34.

11   *Coal Mines Regulation Act*, S. N. S. 1873, c. 10. With respect to the provision of shorter hours for boys, the minister responsible came under attack for imposing such a restriction but defended it by responding that allowing children to work longer than 60 hours per week would interfere with their right to have access to an education.

12   Reilly, "The Provincial Workmen's Association", pp. 28-9. This point is emphasized by the fact that although the Act was based on a similar British statute of 1872, those sections in the British Act which covered the salary rights of the miners were missing in its Nova Scotia version. When questioned about this the minister responsible stated that the Nova Scotian miner, unlike his British counterpart, "was not under the control of a master and therefore needed no protection in law". Pryke, "Labour and Politics", note 24, p. 45, citing 1873 Nova Scotia House of Assembly Debates.

13   Reilly, "The Provincial Workmen's Association", note 15, p. 37.

14   Robert Drummond, *Recollections and Reflections of a Former Trade Union Leader* (Stellarton, 1926), pp. 62-72.

15   The check-off came into being unevenly in the mines in Nova Scotia in the 1880s, and the exact details of this are worth further research. It even seems possible that miners in Nova Scotia were the first workers anywhere in the world to have the check-off of union dues, although this would be almost impossible to prove.

The establishment of a union gave the miners a power which allowed them to influence the content of the laws that affected them. The PWA leader, Robert Drummond, pursued an active style of lobbying before and after his appointment to the Government's Legislative Council in 1891. The lobbying power of the miners was strengthened in 1889 when unpropertied miners, living in company housing, won the right to vote by way of amendments to the Nova Scotia Franchise Act.[16] By 1892 mining interests were complaining that Drummond was "the little man who legislates without check or hinderance in the provincial parliament in return for a pledge of the labour vote".[17] But Premier Fielding informed mine managers that "the law could no longer be molded at the will of the mine owner".[18] Even before this, following 44 deaths caused by an explosion at a mainland mine in 1881, the PWA successfully demanded a "place in the regulatory apparatus" of the Coal Mines Regulation Act.[19] The Act was amended to include increased inspections of mines by a committee which included miners as well as managers and Inspectors. Significantly, amendments were made which gave miners the power to file charges against management.

In 1888 the province passed the Mines Arbitration Act setting up a mechanism to resolve disputes in the mining industry by a process of binding arbitration. Either the employer or the miners could apply for an Arbitration Board. If the employees had made the initial request for arbitration, the employer could retain the wages of all the employees for the 14 days before the application, to become payable upon the Board's decision. If the decision favored the employer the employees had to submit at once to the decision or risk forfeiting the retained wages. If the decision favored the employees, the employer had to submit or become liable for an amount equal to the amount of wages held. The Act also contained a statutory freeze of wages and dismissals, and employees were barred from drinking while the dispute was being arbitrated.[20]

When contrasted to the 1864 Act Against the Combination of Workmen this Act shows the changed ideological climate that had come about with the existence of the union. The earlier legislation exemplified the laissez-faire approach and almost total deference to the idea of "management's right to manage". On this the Attorney General of 1871 stated the prevailing view: "the servant was always under the authority of the master. The man who paid another wages had the right to control his actions as a general rule".[21] A notable change is reflected in the speech by the Attorney General of 1888 when he introduced the arbitration legislation:

> ...the principle of the bill is one which is extremely radical; far more so than in any principle which is ordinarily introduced in measures which pass

16   *Nova Scotia Franchise Act*, S. N. S. 1889, c. 1.
17   *Canadian Mining Reports*, 11 (1892).
18   In *Canadian Mining Reports*, 3 (1893), p. 38.
19   MacLeod, "Mines, Mining Men and Mining Reform", note 15, p. 442.
20   *The Mines Arbitration Act*, S. N. S 1888, c. 3.
21   Nova Scotia House of Assembly, *Debates*, 25 March 1871.

the Assembly. It is an effort, or an attempt on the part of the State to interfere with private contract between employers and employed and in that respect it is a very important principle, and one which is to be considered in every possible consequence not only in the relation of mere matter of contract between coal mine owners and employers, but in all the relations of life because if you once introduce the principle that the legislature can counsel parties to be guided by any other principle than that of free contract, you at once open the door for the legislature to interfere in all matters of that character.[22]

The speech noted that this was an historic moment in Nova Scotia labour legislation, yet it is significant that the Act saw little use.[23] Neither employers or employees were willing to risk applying for binding arbitration since both sides considered its usage too risky; and while the provincial state was willing to interfere with freedom of contract, it would do so only upon invitation.

The emergence of a modern system of industrial relations had thus begun with the formation of the PWA and these state interventions, and a more complete break with the traditional paternalistic labour relations occurred between 1893 and 1907. In 1893 the Province passed An Act For Further Encouragement of Coal Mining which established the Dominion Coal Company (Domco) into which most Cape Breton coal companies were merged.[24] The creation of such a large corporate employer proved a significant step in breaking down paternalism. The coal union and companies had already had signed contracts in some cases, the earliest perhaps being at Springhill in 1885. Formal contracts between Domco and the union now became standard practice. Also following the establishment of Domco a rapid expansion of the mining industry took place. Between 1893 and 1913 provincial coal production increased from 1,682,713 to 7,203,913 long tons. In 1900 Domco employed 3,109 miners, and by 1913 the number had risen to 6,452.[25] On a national scale the consumption of coal tripled from 1902 to 1913. Cape Breton mines accounted for almost half of coal produced in Canada up to the 1920s and therefore held a strategic place.[26]

At about this same time the federal state was becoming involved in labour relations through the 1900 Conciliation Act[27] and the 1907 Industrial Dispute

---

22   Cited in Drummond, *Recollections and Reflections,* note 31, p. 117.
23   In 1901 the Glace Bay PWA made an application in their bid for a wage increase. The arbitration ruled in the company's favour. Eugene Forsey, *Economic and Social Aspects of the Nova Scotia Coal Industry* (Montreal, 1926), note 32, p. 19.
24   Donald MacGillivray, "Henry Melville Whitney Comes to Cape Breton: The Saga of a Gilded Age Entrepreneur", *Acadiensis,* IX, 1 (Autumn 1979); *An Act for Further Encouragement of Coal Mining,* S. N. S. 1893, c. 1.
25   Nova Scotia, *Journals of the House of Assembly,* Mine Reports (1900 and 1914).
26   Donald MacGillivray, "Industrial Unrest in Nova Scotia, 1919-1925", M.A. thesis, University of New Brunswick, 1971.
27   *Conciliation Act,* 1900.

Investigation Act (IDIA).[28] The Conciliation Act provided a procedural mechanism for the conciliation of disputes upon the application of either party. Upon receiving the request the federal Minister of Labour would construct a tripartite board. There were no statutory freeze provisions nor any remedies should one party refuse to conciliate. The IDIA was able to intervene more effectively than the earlier law as it required compulsory conciliation of disputes before any strike or lockout could legally be called. The Act applied to designated key national industries, including the coal industry. It set a compulsory limit on a union's strike weapon by establishing a "cooling out" period before a strike could take place. In this sense the IDIA was the first piece of labour legislation to actively shape the nature of negotiations.

While the IDIA was an immediate product of Mackenzie King's experience with the 1906 Lethbridge coal strike, the Act was more fundamentally a reaction to the increased unionization of strategic national industries throughout the country.[29] It was soon to be used in Nova Scotia where many miners, dissatisfied with the PWA, had begun to demand a new and more militant union in the form of the United Mine Workers of America (UMW). By 1909 District 26 of the UMW had been formed and roughly half of the miners were members of the new union. Domco began firing all miners suspected of UMW membership, and when the UMW applied under the IDIA to have these workers rehired, the Wallace board was established. Domco refused to participate in the proceedings and was subsequently forced by subpoena to attend and give evidence. In a two to one decision the board's majority found "no evidence" to support UMW claims of discrimination, although the evidence showed Domco, in anticipation of a UMW strike, was firing miners who would not pledge that they would continue working during a possible strike. The board's majority reasoned:

> As this question was asked irrespective of whether the person...was a member of the PWA or UMW, there is no evidence of any discrimination against the members of the latter organization, the only men who were laid off being men whose answers or conduct showed that they could not be relied upon to continue work.[30]

Concerning the question of recognition, the majority cited as legitimate Domco's refusing to recognize the UMW on the grounds that it was a "foreign" and "outside" force which could hinder the "local" industry:

> Without presuming to dictate as to which union the men should belong, or as to whether they should belong to any union, we think it is in the interest of the operators, the men and the whole community that our difficulties, which will always be with us, should be settled amongst

28 *Industrial Disputes Investigation Act,* 1907, c. 20.
29 R. Whittaker, "The Liberal Corporatist Ideas of Mackenzie King", *Labour/Le Travail,* 2 (1971); W. Baker, "The Miners and the Mediator: The 1906 Lethbridge Strike and Mackenzie King", *Labour/Le Travail,* 11 (1983).
30 *Labour Gazette* (1909), p. 1229.

ourselves, and not subject to the control of any outside party. The men must see that their interests are bound up with those of the Coal Company...anything that tends to hamper materially the operations of the company must in the end prejudicially affect themselves.[31]

When following this the UMW went on strike, Domco, which had initially been reluctant to accept the IDIA, now claimed the strike was "illegal" on the grounds that notice of the walk-out had not been given or IDIA conciliation procedures followed. Under a provision of the IDIA one UMW official was successfully prosecuted for providing food for strikers' families, and his conviction was upheld on appeal to the Nova Scotia Supreme Court.[32] All UMW miners and families were evicted from company houses, credit at company stores was cancelled, and strike-breakers were brought in. In anticipation of violence Domco electrified its gates at various pit heads, erected bunkhouses within the gates for scabs, and hired 625 men to act as company police.[33] After skirmishes at a number of pitheads, Domco successfully petitioned for the federal militia under the Militia Act. In a matter of days the militia arrived to protect PWA and scab miners and within two weeks Domco mines were operating at 70 per cent capacity.[34] Though the strike continued, it was a losing battle. Despite a union expenditure of over one million dollars and families spending the winter in tents, the UMW miners in Cape Breton began to go back to work by April 1910. While most were rehired, several activists were blacklisted. In 1913 District 26's charter was revoked for lack of membership.[35]

While the Cape Breton coal fields would be the site for other hard fought strikes, this 1909 strike was perhaps the most brutal of all, since it divided the miners and the community and left bitter memories in the minds of all who experienced it. For miners on both sides it was also an education as to the biased nature of the role of the law and the state in labour disputes. Within a period of four months the miners had experienced both the consensual (IDIA) and coercive (militia) sides of the state's approach to maintaining industrial peace. This was an experience that destroyed belief in the state's legitimacy as an "impartial umpire".

The irony of 1909 was that the activities of Domco and the state, aimed at maintaining "order" and preventing a militant force from shaping the nature of industrial relations, had the effect of radicalizing the miners. This formed the basis for the UMW's re-emergence in 1917, when the leaders of the 1909 UMW formed the United Mine Workers of Nova Scotia (UMWNS) and were successful in

31 *Ibid.*, p. 1231. Apart from the ideological bias in this decision it was remarkable given that Domco was owned by Montreal and U.S. interests.

32 Ian McKay, "Strikes in the Maritimes, 1901-1914" in P.A. Buckner and David Frank, eds., *Acadiensis Reader: Volume Two. Atlantic Canada After Confederation* (Fredericton, 1988), pp. 274-5.

33 Paul MacEwan, *Miners and Steelworkers* (Toronto, 1976), note 51, pp. 28-9; Forsey, *Economic and Social Aspects,* note 32, p. 23.

34 MacEwan, *Miners and Steelworkers,* p. 33; Forsey, *Economic and Social Aspects,* p. 25.

35 M. Logan, *Trade Unions in Canada* (Toronto, 1948); Forsey, *Economic and Social Aspects,* p. 26.

recruiting a majority of miners. Upon receiving applications from both the UMWNS and the PWA for an IDIA board the Chisholm Royal Commission was appointed. Fearing a repetition of the 1909 strike and loss of production during the war, the commission pressed the unions to unite for "the advantage of both employers and employees as well as the community".[36] Emerging from the Chisholm Commission was the unification of the unions into the Amalgamated Mine Workers of Nova Scotia which in 1919, after a pithead vote, became District 26 of the UMW.

IDIA boards were involved in the first contract the UMW negotiated in 1919 with Domco, but during the life of this contract Domco was taken over by the British Empire Steel Corporation (Besco) which merged the Sydney Steel Plant, all Domco holdings in Cape Breton and the mainland, Nova Scotia Steel and Coal and the Halifax Shipyards within one giant corporation.[37] Despite its size, Besco was financially weak from the beginning, so weak that its watered down stock was in excess of its existing assets by $54 million. [38]Besco's strategy was to use revenues from its coal sector as the major source of the large profits necessary to meet its responsibilities to shareholders; and this profit was to be gained at the expense of the miners, by reducing their wages.[39] Following the inability of an IDIA board and a Royal Commission to bring about a settlement, the Minister of Labour called Besco and UMW officials to Montreal in an attempt to prevent a strike. A series of meetings occurred between October 1920 and January 1921 and a tentative agreement was reached.[40] This was the "Montreal Agreement", which was remarkable for the formal "peace obligation" it included. During the one year life of the agreement there was to be "no stoppage of work...owing to any dispute arising at any mine under the jurisdiction of District 26 except for refusal of employers to pay wages...or danger to life and limb". Additionally there was to be no hearing of grievances if miners did suspend work. The UMW officials were bound to "guarantee fulfillment of the agreement and pledge their co-operation and support in every legitimate way to maintain and encourage increased output". Any grievances were to be submitted to District 26 executive and the company superintendent, and if the dispute could not be settled it was to be referred for "binding arbitration". If parties could not agree upon an arbitrator, one was to be selected by the Premier.[41] In exchange for the "peace obligation" the miners received the highest rates of pay that they would experience until World War II. Despite the favorable wage settlement, the rank and file were extremely hesitant about the agreement and feared

36   *Labour Gazette* (1917), "Chisholm Report", pp. 453-5.
37   D. Schwartzman, "Mergers in the Nova Scotia Coal Fields", Ph.D. thesis, University of California at Berkeley, 1953.
38   *Ibid.*, pp. 151-73.
39   See David Frank, "The Cape Breton Coal Miners 1917-1926", Ph.D. thesis, Dalhousie University, 1979; "The Cape Breton Coal Industry and the Rise and Fall of the British Empire Steel Corporation", *Acadiensis*, VII, 1 (Autumn 1977).
40   See *Labour Gazette* (1920), pp. 831-3, 116-84.
41   *Labour Gazette* (1921), "Montreal Agreement", pp. 36-71.

that they would lose control of working conditions in the mine. Only after days of public debate were the leaders able to convince the miners that the agreement would not strip them of their independence.[42]

The 1921 agreement can be said to be the high water mark of consensus for the industry during the period. The miners had relatively high wages, the union had recognition and the check-off of union dues, and the company had a guarantee of continued production throughout the life of the contract. Never before had an agreement provided a procedural mechanism to resolve disputes arising from the contract. This seems very like the stable and consensual agreements reached between large industrial unions and corporations in the period following the Second World War. Yet this was the prelude to the period of the most violent confrontations between the Cape Breton miners and the forces of the coal company and the state.

In late 1921 Besco announced a wage reduction of 33 1/2 per cent.[43] The UMW applied for a conciliation board under the IDIA, and also applied to the Nova Scotia Supreme Court for an injunction against Besco to maintain work conditions as required pending IDIA board deliberations. The union was successful at the Trial Division but the decision was overturned on appeal. Three judges, including Justice Mellish, former counsel for Besco, ruled that as the Montreal agreement had expired prior to the IDIA application there were no longer "existing work conditions" and therefore nothing required to be frozen.

After the IDIA Gillen Board's recommendation of 29 per cent wage cuts was rejected by the UMW, all parties were called to Montreal by the Minister of Labour and a second Montreal agreement, similar to the Gillen Report, was proposed. This agreement was overwhelmingly voted down by the Cape Breton miners.[44] A significant aspect of this second Montreal Agreement was that some of the District 26 officers supported it. This was the first visible sign of what was to become a long lasting left-right split within the union, the right being led at this time by President Robert Baxter and International Board Member Silby Barrett, and the left led by Secretary-Treasurer J.B. McLachlan.

In March 1922 the radical majority of the District 26 executive called on all Cape Breton miners to begin a slowdown strike. This new strategy was labeled "un-British" by the Minister of Labour [45]and an emergency debate in Parliament was called. Prime Minister King set up another IDIA board, the Scott Board,[46] which also recommended wage cuts that were rejected by the UMW.[47] The militancy and radicalism of the miners continued to rise and at the District 26 convention a resolution was passed to regain the wage rates of the First Montreal Agreement, and

---

42   The agreement was accepted by a vote of 6,499 to 4,490. Frank, "Cape Breton Coal Miners", note 15, p. 331.
43   Forsey, *Economic and Social Aspects*, p. 55; Frank,"Cape Breton Coal Miners", pp. 255, 332.
44   Forsey, *Economic and Social Aspects*, note 32, p. 58.
45   Frank, "Cape Breton Miners", note 15, p. 257.
46   Forsey, *Economic and Social Aspects*, note 32, p. 58.
47   *Labour Gazette* (1922), "Scott Report", p. 579.

another calling for the "complete overthrow of the capitalist system, peacefully if we may and forcibly if we must".[48] In the district election the miners voted in officers who were from the radical wing; the President, "Red" Dan Livingstone, the Vice-President, Alex S. MacIntyre, and the Secretary-Treasurer, J.B. McLachlan were all members of the Workers Party of Canada.[49]

The strike that began on August 15 was a "100 per cent strike" meaning that maintenance and pump men left the pits during the strike along with the other mineworkers, thus threatening the destruction of mines through flooding or gas build-up. Both the federal and provincial states responded immediately. Under the authority of the Militia Act, 950 troops were called into Cape Breton and the provincial government created a 1000 member special police force and declared Cape Breton County a police zone.[50] After the strike had lasted several weeks, the provincial government successfully negotiated a truce which allowed a 17 per cent increase in the wages above the level to which they had been reduced before the strike began. Significantly the "peace obligation" was dropped from the two year contract. Vice-President Dan Livingstone later referred to accepting the terms of this settlement "under the muzzle of rifles, machine guns and gleaming bayonets with the further threatened invasion of troops".[51]

The industrial peace realized through this contract was short lived. In early 1923, when the steelworkers in Sydney were seeking recognition of a union, the militia and the provincial police were once again sent to the area, where rather than maintaining order they seemed to instigate violence. After a particularly violent police attack on some Sydney citizens the Cape Breton miners went on a 100 per cent strike in sympathy.[52] Almost immediately miners' leaders McLachlan and Livingstone were arrested on charges of seditious libel, on which charge McLachlan was subsequently imprisoned. At the same time John L. Lewis, head of the International UMW, expelled all District 26 officers from union membership, revoked the District 26 charter, and appointed a provisional executive headed by right-winger Silby Barrett.[53] The presence of the militia and provincial police, the arrests of the leaders, and the revoking of the charter proved successful in getting the miners back to the pits.

In early 1924 Besco announced another 20 per cent reduction in wages and the Cape Breton rank and file immediately walked out of the mines. Taken by surprise the provisional union executive, federal Department of Labour representatives, the Premier and Besco began to negotiate in the midst of another "illegal" strike. Based on a partial disclosure of the terms of a new agreement the miners went back to

---

48   MacEwan, *Miners and Steelworkers*, pp. 85-6.
49   Frank, "Cape Breton Miners", p. 339.
50   Forsey, *Economic and Social Aspects,* note 32, p. 58.
51   MacEwan, *Miners and Steelworkers,* p. 89.
52   Donald MacGillivray, "Military Aid to the Civil Power: The Cape Breton Experience in the 1920's" in D. MacGillivray, and Brian Tennyson, eds., *Cape Breton Historical Essays* (Sydney, 1980), pp. 104-6.
53   Frank, "Cape Breton Miners", note 15, p. 350.

work on 11 February 1924. Later it was revealed that miners would get a six per cent increase; the UMW would get a closed shop; and Besco in return would receive the reinstitution of the "peace obligation", an express prohibition on 100 per cent strikes, and the withdrawal of union funding for the radical periodical the *Maritime Labour Herald*.[54] As was the case with the first Montreal Agreement, Besco attempted to "buy" industrial peace and stability. Although the contract was rejected by the Cape Breton miners by a vote of 3614 to 1747 the provisional executive signed the agreement.[55] In response to this the rank and file held an independent convention at the same time J.B. McLachlan was released from imprisonment. Fearing a revolt the international UMW reinstated District 26 autonomy, and a new slate of radically supported officers was elected to replace the provisional executive.[56]

Following the elections negotiations were entered into with Besco for a 1925 contract. Again Besco announced a 20 per cent cut in wages and then applied for an IDIA board to make any immediate walkouts "illegal". But while the Winfield Board was sitting its legitimacy was undermined by a decision of the Privy Council, which ruled in Snyder v. Toronto Electric Commission that the IDIA was unconstitutional as ultra vires the federal government. Labour relations matters were held as a general rule to be within provincial jurisdiction.[57] From the miners' point of view the IDIA procedure in general had long lost any credibility. The UMW refused to participate in the Winfield Board and argued that its members were biased, since two of the three members were businessmen with strong connections to Besco.[58] The miners' perception of the role of the IDIA was articulated by the following letter from the District 26 President to Prime Minister King:

> We do not doubt your sincerity...but we have been through this experience frequently and the procedure is familiar to us...Eventually we will be confronted with the batons of the Provincial Police and the bayonets of the Canadian Militia as the final reason for us to accept a cut, when we ask for no more than human treatment for our workers and their women and children...Yet whoever criticizes this corporation is termed "Red" and he must walk with great concentration to avoid the jails of our country...We have long since abandoned the effort to obtain a fair hearing before the public.[59]

Boards having failed, Besco began to cut credit at company stores and to reduce shifts at the most militant Cape Breton mines. In response, on 6 March 1925, the Cape Breton miners began a 100 per cent strike.[60] Negotiations during the

54   *Ibid.*, pp. 262, 359.
55   *Ibid.*, pp. 263, 359.
56   *Ibid.*, p. 361.
57   *Toronto Electric Commission* v. *Snider* (1924), 55 o. LR. 454 (S. C. App. Div.), revd (1925) 2 D.L.R. 5 (P.C.).
58   *Labour Gazette* (1925), "Winfield Report", p. 124.
59   Cited in MacGillivray, "Military Aid to the Civil Power", note 46, p. 176.
60   Frank, "Cape Breton Miners", note 15, p. 264.

subsequent three months produced no settlement and by the end of this time mining families were near starvation. It was estimated that 31,986 people in the Cape Breton mining areas were on government, church or Red Cross relief. On June 11 the strike reached its climax in a clash in which one miner was killed by company police. Throughout that night many of Besco's properties were torched, all the company stores were looted, and military occupation of the mining towns followed.[61] In July the newly elected Conservative Premier E. N. Rhodes managed to bring about a settlement of the strike. The contract consisted of a six per cent wage reduction, with the government providing a rebate of royalties for Besco, and promising a Royal Commission on conditions in the coal industry.[62] But this commission, the 1926 Duncan Commission, did nothing for the miners. Its report recommended a ten per cent wage reduction and declared bad management practices and communist union leaders were the source of the conflict in the industry.

There were also repercussions of these struggles in the provincial laws. In the midst of chaos during the 1925 strike and the Snider decision the provincial government had scrambled to draft its own legislation to replace IDIA. The result was the Industrial Peace Act which reproduced the procedures that existed within the now unconstitutional IDIA. The Act, however, allowed for binding arbitration upon the application of either party, and it gave the Minister of Mines very broad authority, in the "public interest", to establish a Board of Conciliation upon application of a municipality, regardless of whether either party wanted it.[63] This Act was never used, for while the statute reflected what the government would have liked to do, both Besco and the UMW strongly criticized the notion of binding arbitration. Faced with a refusal to use this new legislation the province did what most other provinces did, and passed some enabling legislation. The Industrial Disputes Investigation Act (Nova Scotia) of 1926 allowed the Province to adopt the entire IDIA and let the federal state regulate industrial relations in sectors defined in the Act.[64]

In 1927 a minor concession was given to the UMW when the provincial government amended the Coal Mines Regulation Act to provide that every employer must, when required by a miner, check off his union dues.[65] While the UMW, and the PWA before it, had the check-off for many years, the coal companies had never previously been legally obliged to do this. This was the first substantive right which any Nova Scotia union received from either provincial or federal legislation.

In the confrontations of the 1920s the miners' solidarity had saved their union organization from destruction, and had no doubt modified the amount of wage reductions that would otherwise have been forced upon them. But by 1931 real

---

61 *Ibid.*, pp. 222-68.
62 *Ibid.*, p. 374.
63 *Industrial Peace Act*, S. N. S., 1925, c. 1.
64 *Industrial Disputes Investigation Act (Nova Scotia)*, S. N. S., 1926, c. 5.
65 *Coal Mines Regulations Act*, S. N. S., 1927, c. 1.

wages were only 58 per cent of what they had been in 1921. [66]The strikes and Besco's other financial problems led to the corporation's collapse in 1928, to be reorganized with new financing as the Dominion Steel and Coal Corporation (Dosco). During the thirties the Depression added to the crisis within the industry, and by 1932 the average miner was working 102 days while in 1926 he had worked 230.[67] In late 1931 Dosco called for wage reductions ranging from ten to 19 per cent and for the closure of four mines. The response from the provincial government was the appointment of the second Duncan Commission, which recommended a wage reduction of ten per cent and closure of the mines specified Dosco, and stressed the need to come to grips with a declining coal market and to establish a controlled strategy of de-industrialization of the coal industry.

The miners' reaction to this situation was a burst of renewed radicalism. Critical of the response of the UMW executive to this crisis, many miners joined an alternative union formed in June 1932 by communist influenced miners who advocated militant resistance to mine closures and wage cuts. This was the Amalgamated Mine Workers of Nova Scotia (AMW), named after the union into which the UMW and PWA had temporarily united in 1917.[68] At its peak the AMW had a majority of the miners, particularly in Cape Breton, but the UMW remained the union recognized by the coal company. The threat to industrial peace posed by the division in the miners' union movement was a major concern when a new provincial government, the Liberal government of Angus L. MacDonald, was elected in 1933. One of this government's first actions was to set up a provincial department of labour. This was a separate department, but under a joint ministry with the mines department. Michael Dwyer, who had formerly been and was to become again a Dosco official, was the first Minister of Mines and Labour. The new administration at first made a display of neutrality on the union issue; after AMW appeals, Dosco was instructed in December 1933 that it was required by the Coal Mines Regulation Act to check off AMW as well as UMW dues. However, in May 1934 the provincial government amended the Coal Mines Regulation Act so that the employer was only obliged to check off union dues for the union whose members presented the largest number of signed check-off request cards. A card count was to be held annually to determine which union had the majority.[69] The AMW protested that the lack of a secret ballot would prejudice the results, but card counts were held in November of 1934 and 1935. In both counts the AMW were only able to retain the check-off at the Sydney Mines collieries. Although they held the majority in the Cape Breton mines, the addition of mainland results meant they

66   M. J. Earle, "The Rise and Fall of a 'Red' Union: The Amalgamated Mine Workers of Nova Scotia, 1932-1936", M.A. thesis, Dalhousie University, 1984, p. 36.
67   William White, "Left Wing Politics and Community: A Study of Glace Bay, 1930-1940", M.A. thesis, Dalhousie University, 1977, p. 45.
68   See Earle, "The Rise and Fall of a 'Red' Union", pp. 71-7; White, "Left Wing Politics", p. 59.
69   *Coal Mines Regulations Act*, S. N. S., 1934, c. 45.

lost the check-off in all the Domco mines, and the union's finances suffered accordingly.[70]

The government claimed it had no bias in the matter, and was acting merely to clarify a situation in which an employer might be called upon to deduct union dues for an unlimited number of unions. But clearly, given the timing of the bill and the government's refusal to allow a secret ballot, the amendment was aimed at finessing the more militant AMW out of any opportunity to acquire power. Thus the state was intervening, through the regulation of a substantive legal right it had previously granted, to favour one type of union over another. This intervention helped in the defeat of the AMW, which reunited with the UMW in early 1936.

The reunified UMW gave considerable support in 1936 and 1937 to the efforts of steelworkers in Sydney and Trenton to organize a union, and participated with the steelworkers in lobbying the provincial government and Premier Angus L. MacDonald to enact law guaranteeing workers the right to form unions and engage in collective bargaining. Also, the national Trades and Labour Congress (TLC), inspired by the 1935 U.S. Wagner Act, in 1936 sent out a draft "Workers' Right to Organize Bill" to all provincial political parties. In March 1937, Col. Gordon S. Harrington, the leader of the Conservative opposition, introduced a bill modelled on the TLC draft in the Nova Scotia legislature. Harrington was the member for the Sydney riding, and presumably hoped to regain support for his party through this action.[71] The Liberal government claimed they had intended to introduce such a bill themselves, and passed an amended version including a check-off provision. [72] This was the 1937 Trade Union Act, the first in a wave of such legislation passed by most Canadian provinces in the years 1937 to 1943.

The Act stated that "it shall be lawful for employees to form themselves into a trade union, and to join the same when formed", and that "every employer shall recognize and bargain collectively with the members of a trade union representing the majority choice of employees eligible for membership in said trade union, when requested so to bargain". Further, employers who already had a system of checking off deductions for any purpose were required to check off union dues after a vote was conducted "under conditions fixed by the Minister of Labour". On the other hand, the Act contained provisions which prevented union intimidation of employees who refused to join the union. It also stated that nothing in the Act was to "detract from or interfere with the right of an employer to suspend, transfer, lay off or discharge employees for proper and sufficient cause". Unions were required to submit their constitutions and annual financial reports to the Provincial Secretary. [73]

---

70   Earle, "The Rise and Fall of a 'Red' Union", p. 224 and Appendix B, pp. 281-90.
71   In spite of this, Harrington lost his seat in the election that quickly followed the passing of the Trade Union Act.
72   See Brian MacLean, "Who's Protecting Whom? Capital, Labour, the State and Collective Bargaining Legislation In Nova Scotia, 1937-1960", B.A. Honours thesis, Dalhousie University, 1979, pp. 51-60.
73   *Trade Union Act*, S. N. S., 1937, c. 6.

The check-off provision was not included in the other provincial acts that were passed about this time, and in this respect the Nova Scotia act was more useful to the union movement than other provincial laws. The steady flow of dues from the Sydney steelworkers greatly helped the Steel Workers Organizing Campaign (SWOC) in organizing steelworkers in other parts of the country. [74]The fact that the UMW had the legal right to the check-off under the Coal Mines Regulation Act no doubt helped in bringing this clause into the Trade Union Act. It is also likely that the experience of using the check-off privilege to assist in the defeat of the radical AMW predisposed the government to include it in the Act. The 1937 Act gave the legal right to join a trade union but set up no procedural rights of certification, bargaining, unit determination or of negotiating contracts. Only minor protections and limited penalties against unfair labour practices by employers were included in the Act, and no form of provincial labour relations board was set up. Thus the Act did not create a legal context that sustained en masse unionization as occurred under subsequent wartime legislation. Its main practical effect was that it enabled the steelworkers to force Dosco to recognize their union and provide the check-off, although the first contract was not signed with Dosco until 1940.

In UMW contracts with Domco signed during the AMW/UMW split the "peace obligation" had re-emerged. The 1937 contract contained a clause entitled "No Stoppage of Work" which stated that work was to continue in the case of all disputes and grievances "of every nature arising under this contract". If a sophisticated multi-tiered grievance system failed to resolve a grievance, it was to be referred to an Umpire whose decision was to be final and binding.[75] However, in the years that immediately followed the UMW executive found it impossible to force the rank and file's compliance with the "peace obligation". One reason for this renewed militancy was the fear of mechanization leading to loss of jobs. Coal mining in Nova Scotia had remained very labour intensive; with the exception of the introduction of coal cutting machines at the turn of the century almost all work was done by hand. In 1938, when the new No. 20 mine was opened in Glace Bay, Domco attempted to introduce a mechanical loading process which would scoop up coal and automatically load it unto a conveyor belt and subsequently into awaiting cars. Domco argued that over 50 per cent of the coal consumed in Canada was imported from U.S. mines which were wholly mechanized and to survive in the market mechanization was essential.[76] Fearing this was the beginning of mechanization of all the mines leading to widespread loss of jobs, the miners walked out of No. 20 until January 1939 when the machinery was taken out. After this defeat, Domco did not attempt to mechanize its mines until 1948.

---

74 Irving Abella, *Nationalism, Communism, and Canadian Labour* (Toronto, 1973), p. 55.
75 *Agreement Between the Dominion Coal Company and District 26 of the United Mine Workers of America*, February 1937.
76 A. Cameron, "The Coal Resources of Nova Scotia and Their Future", *Transactions,* XLVII (1944); F. Gray, "The Development of the Coal Industry in Canada From 1920 to 1935", *Transactions* (March 1936); *Sydney Post,* 25, 26, 30 May 1938.

Through 1938, 1939 and 1940 the number of wildcat strikes in the individual mines became a matter of great concern to the union officials, as well as the company and the government. This was probably what led to the passage of the 1941 Nova Scotia Conciliation Service Act, which empowered the Minister of Labour to appoint conciliators "wherever in his opinion the interests of industrial peace may require it to be done".[77] This act was never used, presumably being unnecessary in view of the heavy wartime involvement of the federal government in labour relations.

In 1940 and again in 1941 IDIA boards chaired by Ontario Justice McTague were appointed to conciliate negotiations between District 26 and Domco. The 1940 Board recommended modest increases, but the miners voted down the offer and worked without a contract throughout the year. Prior to the formation of the second McTague Board in 1941, the federal government introduced PC 7440 which stated that wages received between 1926-1929 would be assumed "fair and reasonable" and any increases above these levels would only be wartime bonuses based on the cost of living. Despite the miners' arguments that their 1926-29 wage levels were exceptionally low, the McTague Board granted only very limited wage increases. In April 1941 the District 26 executive signed the agreement without having it ratified by the customary rank and file pithead vote. The miners throughout the Cape Breton pits responded with a four month slowdown strike. Apart from demanding a wage increase the miners also sought the resignation of the District 26 executive. After months of fruitless efforts by the union officers and both federal and provincial governments to coerce or cajole the men to end the slowdown, the company began to fire miners at all Cape Breton pits. By late September 1400 men were out of their jobs, and the miners were forced to capitulate.[78] The executive was not forgiven, however. In the 1942 District elections the executive was replaced by a slate of "left" officers.

Throughout the war years the federal government took the lead in industrial relations, through a series of Orders in Council issued under the emergency powers given by the War Measures Act. Most of the state intervention in the early part of the war was aimed at controlling labour and preventing strikes. Through PC 3495 the IDIA jurisdiction was extended to cover all essential war industries; PC 7440 was aimed at limiting wage settlements in war related industries; PC 8253 extended these controls to all workers; and PC 7307 required the workers take a strike vote both before and after a conciliation board before they could legally strike. One measure of 1940, PC 2685, was aimed at placating workers' dissatisfaction by calling on employers to recognize the right of employees to join trade unions. This was, however, an unenforced recommendation, not a legal requirement.[79]

77 *An Act Respecting the Appointment of Commissioners of Conciliation,* S. N. S.,1941.
78 MacEwan, *Miners and Steelworkers,* pp. 233-6.
79 See Laura Sefton MacDowell, "The Formation of the Canadian Industrial Relations System During World War Two", *Labour/Le Travailleur,* 3 (1978), pp. 175-96.

Industrial strife, particularly in the steel industry, brought increasing pressure on the Mackenzie King government to change these policies, and the government also found the rise of popular support for the CCF alarming. This led to an extremely significant legislative intervention into industrial relations with the introduction of PC 1003 in 1944. In contrast to the IDIA, which it superceded, PC 1003 was more sophisticated procedurally and substantively. It granted similar rights to join trade unions to those in the 1937 Nova Scotia Trade Union Act, but unlike the Nova Scotia Act it included procedural mechanisms for certification. There were also some prohibited employer unfair labour practices. No employer was permitted to interfere with the "formation or administration of a trade union...or contribute financial or other support to it". Additionally, the employer could not refuse to employ an employee because of trade union membership. Like the 1937 Act it was expressly stated that nothing in PC 1003 was to restrict the "right of an employer to suspend, transfer, layoff or discharge employees for appropriate and sufficient cause"; and it was made unlawful for an employee to compel or influence a person to join a trade union or for a trade union representative to solicit members at the place of employment during working hours. Most significant, from the perspective of workers already unionized like the miners, were the sections which concerned the procedural requirements of negotiations and the content of collective agreements. Both parties were required to engage in collective bargaining in "good faith with...every reasonable effort to conclude a collective agreement". If negotiations remained unresolved after thirty days either party could apply to the Wartime Labour Relations Board for intervention. A conciliation officer would then confer with the parties and make a report to the Minister of Labour. If the conciliation officer failed a tripartite conciliation board would be appointed and a strike would not be legal until 14 days after the board reported. The contract itself was "binding on every employee" and had to be at least a year in length. One of the most significant clauses required that all collective agreements contain a "provision establishing a procedure for final settlement, without stoppage of work, on the application of either party, of differences concerning its interpretation or violation". If an agreement did not contain such a provision the Board was to establish one. The requirement of the absolute peace obligation was further emphasized by a statement that "slowdowns" were prohibited, and further that no "employee...shall go on strike during the term of the collective agreement". Clearly PC 1003 was more encompassing than the province's 1937 Act. Not only did it grant the same substantive right to join a trade union but established a procedural and remedial framework that could help to establish those rights. Like the IDIA it included procedural mechanisms for dispute resolution but added a longer "cooling out" period with the possible introduction of a conciliation board to follow the work of an officer. Additionally it created, for the first time, an absolute peace obligation during the life of a contract. Thus the strike weapon was greatly curtailed by the new law.

This federal law was still in effect when a district-wide strike of Nova Scotia miners began in January 1947. The UMW had entered negotiations with a demand for a $2.50 per day increase and a rank and file strike resolution if this was not achieved. Domco's counter offer of $1.00 and a wage scale for mechanized mining was refused and the strike began. Immediately the Federal Minister of Labour appointed a conciliation officer (Justice Carroll) and warned the District that no strike could occur until the conciliation officer had made his report. District President Freeman Jenkins complied and called the miners back to work after two days, arguing that he was preventing "an illegal strike".[80] The conciliator's report suggested a $1.40 per day increase and did not recommend a conciliation board. The miners walked out again and remained out until 26 May 1947. Unlike the 1920s, when the industry was extremely strategic and Cape Breton a major producer of coal and royalties, the coal strike of 1947 did not produce economic crisis, so there was no extreme state concern about the duration of the strike. Dosco and its subsidiary Domco were in a good position to wait out the strike. The Emergency Coal Production Board had granted Domco a guaranteed subsidy should its coal production and sales drop below a defined level. The original purpose of the subsidy was to encourage the company to expand production during the war, but it was most useful to Domco in avoiding losses during the post war strike. In the end the miners had to accept a guaranteed $1.00 per day increase and an additional 40 cents per day should production rise to a specified level. Thus ended the first major district coal strike in 22 years; and it would be the last until 1981, 34 years later.

The acceptance of legal restraints by the union during this strike, as well as the absence of coercive state machinery, show a markedly different situation than existed in the big strikes of the early 1920s. The most fundamental difference was the general crisis of the coal industry, which by the end of the war had brought most of the miners, as well as union officials, the company and the government, to accept the necessity of mechanization in the mines if any coal industry was to survive. In 1945 the federal government had sponsored a Royal Commission on Coal, also chaired by Justice Carroll. The Report clearly stressed the necessity of increasing production in the Cape Breton mines if the industry was to exist in the 1950s. It cited that the Domco pits produced 1.6 tons of coal per manshift while the mechanized U.S. pits produced six tons a manshift. The Report further estimated that mechanization of the Cape Breton mines would cost $8,000,000.[81]

Therefore "productivity", not surprisingly, was stressed in the settlement of the 1947 strike, and unlike earlier periods, neither the union nor any group among the miners opposed mechanization of the mines. Announced at the same time as the strike settlement was an $8,000,000 federal grant to fund the mechanization, and union President Jenkins spoke of the need for "joint co-operative action by both parties to bring about increased production which is vital and necessary for the

---

80 *Sydney Post*, 3 March 1947.
81 *Royal Commission on Coal*, 1945, Ottawa.

stability and prosperity of the industry, the communities and people affected".[82]
Between 1947 and 1951 the mines were mechanized. This soon led to a large decline
in the number employed in the industry, as the miners had feared. Further, the entire
workplace both in terms of the type of activity performed and culture sustained by it
was completely transformed. All aspects of mining which were previously done by
hand were now done in part, if not completely, by machines. The workplace became
an integrated production line of machines and miners, whereas in the traditional
system the miners had largely worked unsupervised. Thus with the reorganization of
the mines came the loss of the miners' considerable power to define their labour
process. With this transfer of control at the point of production went also the
transfer of a set of rights which would later be given legal effect and ironically be
assumed to be "traditional management rights".

From the perspective of the law the 1947 strike was interesting, as the authority
of PC 1003 expired in March 1947 with the ending of the "National Emergency"
and no legislation replaced it until the introduction of the amended Nova Scotia
Trade Union Act on 12 May 1947. The problem was more theoretical than practical,
however, as the UMW complied with the law as it existed when the strike began.

The 1947 Trade Union Act was similar in most respects to PC 1003. The Act
applied to all "employees" within Nova Scotia, with the exception of public
employees. The definition of an employee was slightly extended from that under PC
1003 and included those in "professional" occupations, although it did not include
fishermen. The Act restated the previously existing right to join and participate in a
trade union and outlined a prohibition against unfair labour practices by the
employer. These rights were balanced against other sections which stated that no
trade union should support or encourage the limitation of production, and which
allowed the employer to manage his firm and operations in any way which did not
create a lockout. In collective bargaining both parties were to make "every
reasonable effort" to conclude an agreement. Throughout the negotiation period the
old contract was to remain in force and no strike or lockout could occur. Either party
could apply to the Minister of Labour for the assistance of a conciliation officer,
who could call for a board. The board was tripartite in nature and had 14 days to
effect a settlement. The board's decision could become binding if both parties agreed
to be bound any time during its sitting of the board. Prior to going on strike, after
all these conciliation procedures were exhausted, a mandatory strike vote was
required. As in PC 1003 some of the terms of any agreement were legally defined.
The agreement had to be for at least one year, binding on all employees, and contain
a grievance procedure. The general administration of the Act was undertaken by the
Labour Relations Board of Nova Scotia which was created at that time.

The 1947 Trade Union Act established what, with relatively minor
modifications, became the modern legal framework which regulates labour relations.
Now established was the distinctively Canadian system which severely curtailed the

82   *Halifax Herald*, 20, 21, 28 May 1947.

legal use of the strike by instituting strike votes, timeliness requirements and conciliation proceedings in the interim. In 1947 left wing unionists still had considerable prominence in the Nova Scotia Federation of Labour and the UMW, and protested sections of the bill before it was passed, particularly the limitations on the right to strike.[83] But the unions themselves were at this time undergoing a transformation as communists and left-wingers were purged, and a leadership took full control which was perhaps happy with laws restraining spontaneous militant action by workers. However this may be, union leaders since, either reluctantly or willingly, have had to live with this basic system.

This survey of the historical relationship of the mining industry with the law does not give much support to one idea implicit in both the mainstream and the critical perspectives on the role of labour law. This is the notion that the law itself was the decisive force in defining the nature of industrial relations. At least with regard to the Nova Scotia coal industry before 1947 the law was never a consistent or controlling force. Through most of the period there was an overlapping of provincial and federal legal jurisdiction, and interwoven within this chaotic legislative framework were constant extra-legal interventions by Premiers, Mayors, Prime Ministers, provincial and federal Royal Commissions, provincial police and the federal militia. The development of law occurred within a dynamic context that witnessed both the union and the company, at various periods, questioning the legitimacy of the provincial or federal state to intervene and thus rendering the legislation inoperative. Additionally the changes in the law must be understood within the backdrop of what the parties had negotiated between themselves. Often it was the legislation which followed rather than led, particularly with regard to establishing "peace obligations", grievance systems and union rights.

In this regard the critical perspective seems weak in viewing labour legislation as the major leading force which initiates a procedural and ideological mechanism whereby conflict is contained. If the law is the source of this process of domination, one must ask for an explanation of why the UMW negotiated a "peace obligation" in 1921 and then consistently onwards through the 1930s, long before one was legally required in 1944?

A conceptualization of labour legislation as primarily a structure that hinders, restricts and subordinates workers' power fails to recognize that the law provides some protection for certain rights for which workers have fought fiercely. Through struggle in the late 1880s and early to mid 1900s the miners won and maintained recognition of their trade union as their bargaining agent. In the 1920s Besco was quite open in its desire to see District 26 crushed, but failed to achieve this due to the miners' solid resistance. When in 1937 the right to join and participate in a trade union was given legislative effect this obviously gave extra protection to the UMW

---

83   The longest submission to the public hearing of the Committee on Law Amendments was made by C. B. Wade, the research director of the UMW. Another fruitless submission was made by Capt. Ben MacKenzie of the Canadian Fishermen's Union, protesting the exclusion of fishermen from the Act. MacLean, "Who's Protecting Whom", pp. 104-5.

and helped Sydney steelworkers to form a union. The critical perspective, focussing on how workers are dominated, fails to understand, or fully appreciate, the real impact that such rights have on the nature of the workplace. If the positive aspects of collective bargaining are even acknowledged by some who hold the critical perspective, the "victory" is quickly contrasted to the remaining inequality which exists within capitalist society. The reality of the situation is that workers, for better or worse, have had to live with capitalism. While this is so workers and their unions have sought practical legal rights to enable them by collective bargaining to realize better wages, to improve health and safety at work, and to make the workplace a little more democratic.

At the same time labour law is not a vehicle of democracy and fairness instituted by the state to force bilateral negotiations of work conditions, as the mainstream perspective would have it. The motive force behind progressive labour legislation was never a neutral state wishing to establish fair play. It was without assistance from law that miners won recognition, the right to collective bargaining and the check-off. The Industrial Disputes Investigation Act did not further the rights of workers, but only compelled those unions powerful enough to threaten key industries to enter into a conciliation process. Despite all of Mackenzie King's liberal ideology of capital and labour as partners, and the state as an "impartial umpire", the IDIA did nothing to help workers assert their interests. In the decisions of IDIA boards "legitimate" demands were invariably defined in accordance with the laws of classical capitalist economic theory. And the wartime transformation of labour law that compelled employers to recognize their employees' right to form unions was the result of the pressure brought by workers on provincial and federal governments.

Based on the history it is clear that the miners and the company were never "equal partners" in the coal industry. The industry was based on private ownership and by its inherent structure all bargaining occurred within a structure of inequality. Obviously the miners did have tremendous bargaining power at various historical moments. This did not mean that they had equal bargaining power, but rather that they had the ability to narrow the company's ability to define the wage scale. After a contract was negotiated the owners still owned, the workers still worked and the profits flew beyond the geographical boundaries of coal towns.

The modern Canadian legal framework for collective bargaining remains based on stabilizing a system of unequal power and economic disparity. It has, however, been relatively successful in achieving this stability, partly because it has provided some substantive rights and material advance to workers, while establishing regulations aimed at confining workers' collective action into forms that do not threaten the capitalist system. This required, in the case of the Cape Breton miners at least, a change above all in the nature of the miners' union movement from its class struggle outlook of the 1920s to a more moderate and compromising acceptance of the unavoidability of working within the capitalist system in the post-war era. In a sense, this meant that "irreconcilable differences" had become reconcilable. The history of the coal mining industry indicates that legislation in itself played only a minor role in transforming the broad economic, social, ideological and political context of labour relations to the point that it could sustain a law such as the 1947 Trade Union Act. Yet the establishment of such laws was certainly to contribute to the stability of industrial relations in the years that followed.

SUZANNE MORTON

The Halifax Relief Commission and Labour Relations during the Reconstruction of Halifax, 1917-1919

ON 6 DECEMBER 1917, an explosion ripped through the north end of Halifax killing nearly 2,000, injuring even more, and rendering approximately 10,000 people homeless. The immediate task which lay before the city was to identify and bury the dead and to treat the injured; the daunting longer term task was to reconstruct the large residential section levelled by the explosion. The rebuilding of a large section of the city required a vast industrial army of labour, which in 1918 would number over 10,000 men, and a central agency capable of organizing and directing the reconstruction operations. At first responsibility for reconstruction was placed in the hands of an *ad hoc* citizen's committee but in late January 1918, the federal government established under an Order-in-Council a three man commission consisting of two Halifax judges, the chairman T. Sherman Rogers and William B. Wallace, and Frederick Luther Fowkes, a former mayor of Oshawa, Ontario.[1] In the spring of 1918 the Halifax Relief Commission (HRC) Act was passed in the Nova Scotia legislature. Under the Act the Commission was given responsibility for investigating enquiries regarding losses, damages and injuries and for awarding reasonable compensation. It had the power to enforce attendance at its courts and boards, to set wages for its employees, and to avoid municipal and provincial taxation. Within a defined region it also had the right to expropriate land, create zoning regulations, rebuild, repair and carry out a town planning scheme.[2] The HRC was thus responsible for both the physical and financial rehabilitation of the explosion's victims and for the reconstruction of the devastated area. Because of the sweeping nature of Commission's powers, post-explosion Halifax provides a unique situation in which to examine trade unionism as it encountered new forms of state intervention at the end of World War One. Of course, labour across Canada felt excluded from war-time consulsion and influence, and the "1919 Labour Revolt" was a national and international phenomena, but in Halifax, labour experienced this isolation more intensely, as it was shut out from decisions regarding the redevelopment of its own city and the predominantly

---

1   Privy Council Minutes, P.C. 112, 22 January 1918, National Archives of Canada [NAC].

2   See "An Act to incorporate the Halifax Relief Commission", *Statutes of Nova Scotia 1918*, 8-9 Geo. V, Chapter 61; Samuel H. Prince, *Catastrophe and Social Change Based Upon a Sociological Study of the Halifax Disaster* (New York, 1920), p. 105.

working-class neighbourhood which had been destroyed.[3] The post-explosion experience of Halifax organized labour cannot therefore be regarded as simply a microcosm of the national experience.

Unfortunately, the subject of labour relations during the reconstruction of Halifax has been virtually ignored by historians.[4] Urban historians concerned with reconstruction have concentrated on the Hydrostone housing development, Canada's first public housing experiment built to provide homes for dislocated Halifax families under radical town planning legislation. John Weaver, in a 1976 article, explored such important themes as the role of outside experts and the imposition of their decisions on a "client" community.[5] In 1985 John Bacher discussed the significance of the reconstruction of Halifax in the evolution of Canadian policy toward public housing.[6] But the experience of the trade unions was peripheral in both studies. Yet the reconstruction efforts of the Commission dramatically affected the Halifax building trade unions and led to a struggle by labour to maintain the pre-war and war-time *status quo*. Moreover, labour in Halifax found that it was ideologically and organizationally incapable of dealing with the powers of the HRC.

Before the explosion, the Federal and Nova Scotian governments had tampered with the operation of the local labour market in three ways. Strikes in Cape Breton had been brought under control by military intervention; protective

---

3 Gregory Kealey, "1919: The Canadian Labour Revolt", *Labour/Le Travail*, 13 (Spring 1984), pp. 11-44.

4 The refusal of the government to grant restitution to explosion victims meant that Haligonians were largely dependent on private donations for relief. In order to sustain these contributions, relief efforts required a good public image. It is impossible to determine the extent to which the attempts to project this image and the role of war-time propaganda and censorship affected the reporting of reconstruction activities. What Russell Hann has described as an "artificial void in the record" can certainly be applied to Halifax. Advertisements for labour needed in Halifax appeared in the region's daily press but the labour press was remarkably silent about the massive reconstruction efforts in Halifax. The only mention of reconstruction in Sydney's *Canadian Labor Leader* was a campaign to donate a day's pay to relief efforts. This silence was primarily a result of the absence of a local labour paper in Halifax. Government labour documents are also lacking as the Department of Labour left most reconstruction efforts to the Department of Militia and Defence. Therefore, this study will depend too heavily on the available sources: the records of the Halifax Relief Commission and the local press. As a result the thousands of migrant workers will remain as faceless to the reader as they were to contemporary Haligonians. Russell Hann, "Introduction" in Daphne Read, ed., *The Great War and Canadian Society: An Oral History* (Toronto, 1978), p. 29; *The Daily Times* (Moncton), 23 December 1917; *Canadian Labor Leader* (Sydney), 15 December 1917. The importance of press censorship in isolating labour disputes is discussed in Myer Siemiatycki "Munitions and Labour Militancy: The 1916 Hamilton Machinists' Strike", *Labour/ Le Travailleur*, 3 (1978), p. 147.

5 John Weaver, "Reconstruction of the Richmond District in Halifax: A Canadian Episode in Public Housing and Town Planning, 1918-1921", *Plan Canada*, 6, 1 (March 1976), pp. 36-47.

6 John Bacher, "Keeping to the Private Market; The Evolution of Canadian Housing Policies", Ph.D. thesis, McMaster University, 1985.

legislation had been passed which was designed to acquire the political allegiance of the workman; and government had acted as a mediator, adopting the appearance of an independent arbitrator between the interests of labour and capital.[7] The pressure of the war and in particular the organizational efforts required to rebuild Halifax created a significant departure from the past. The quest for efficiency, primarily demonstrated by the use of outside expert management, meant that government had its own objectives, quite distinct from those of both local contractors and organized labour. Government began acting on behalf of what it defined as the community's public interest, in ways which did not necessarily coincide with how individual citizens perceived their own interests.[8] But government regulations aimed at efficiency and rationalization clashed with the interests of Halifax skilled labour.

In 1918, organized labour in Halifax was primarily composed of skilled craft unionists, who had a perception of their own importance and a definite understanding of their place in the wider local community. Members of the building trades generally adhered to the vague political philosophy of labourism. They saw the liberal democratic state as a viable political and economic system and believed that skilled labour played a central and essential role in the operation of the community.[9] Their worldview was moulded by craft exclusivity and, while they accepted the hierarchical nature of society, they saw themselves firmly in the middle, below the capitalists and above the mass of unskilled workers. Craig Heron has pointed out that labourites held a "liberal view of the state" and saw government as "a neutral apparatus which could serve an undefined common good".[10] This view of the state was increasingly at odds with war-time realities. The commitment of labourites to libertarian and egalitarian democracy conflicted with a government characterized by authoritarian rule. Moreover, skilled labour was always most vulnerable from the bottom and the

---

7   Desmond Morton, "Aid to the Civil Power: the Canadian Militia in Support of the Social Order, 1867-1914", *Canadian Historical Review*, 51, 4 (December 1970), pp. 407-25. Examples of protective legislation include the Nova Scotia Factory Act of 1901 and the Nova Scotia Workmen's Compensation Act of 1910. The Industrial Disputes Investigation Act of 1907 gave the government the authority to act as mediator.

8   According to John English the growth of war-time patriotism fostered "a real or imagined sense of solidarity". John English, *The Decline of Politics: The Conservatives and the Party System 1901-20* (Toronto, 1977), pp. 110, 106.

9   Suzanne Morton, "Labourism and Independent Labour Politics in Halifax, 1919-1926", M.A. thesis, Dalhousie University, 1986; Suzanne Morton, "Labourism and Economic Action: The Halifax Shipyards Strike of 1920," *Labour/Le Travail*, 22 (Fall 1988), forthcoming; James Naylor, "Ontario Workers and the Decline of Labourism", in Roger Hall, William Westfall and Laurel Sefton MacDowell, eds., *Patterns of the Past: Interpreting Ontario's History* (Toronto, 1988), pp. 278-300.

10 Craig Heron, "Labourism and the Canadian Working Class", *Labour/Le Travail*, 13 (Spring 1984), pp. 54, 59.

tremendous influx of unskilled and unorganized workers into Halifax wreaked chaos in the operation of the local trades by jeopardizing craft exclusivity.

Labour problems grew serious in late January 1918 when the Commission took over from the *ad hoc* citizen's organization which had been in place since the explosion. The immediate post-explosion housing needs were met by the construction of temporary apartments on the Commons and Exhibition Ground but the most lasting evidence of the Commission's work would be the 70 wooden houses and the 326 row houses that composed the Hydrostone housing district in the north end of the city.[11] The construction of the Hydrostone district and the Commission's decision that long-term pensions would be financed by the development's rental revenue meant that the HRC had contact with organized labour not only as an employer, but also as a landlord, community planner, and claims court. The government appointed body, reflecting the approach of the federal Unionist Government, outraged unionized labour with its military style and undemocratic methods, as it sought, with the use of outside professionals, to rebuild Halifax as quickly and as efficiently as possible.

The HRC, like the Unionist Government, was criticized for simultaneously lacking direction and arbitrary decisiveness. In his biography of Prime Minister Borden, R. Craig Brown has described the war-time government as "trying to maintain the tenets of non-intervention in a situation where compulsion was increasingly necessary".[12] This strain was demonstrated in Halifax by the federal government's refusal to compensate victims of the explosion, although it was willing to regulate the local labour market and the reconstruction in the devastated area.[13] In May 1917, the Trades and Labour Congress accused the Imperial Munitions Board of lowering established wage schedules, eliminating the eight hour day, diluting skill, substituting "cheap semi-skilled labor from rural districts for construction work because of their willingness to accept less than Trade Union rates", and finally refusing to recognize trade union leadership.[14] These charges would be mirrored in Halifax.

The building trades formed the core of organized craft unionism in Halifax. Although no single construction union reached the size of the longshoremen, collectively the building trades exerted considerable influence and their leadership was prominent in the Halifax Trades and Labour Council and in the

11 Graham Metson, *The Halifax Explosion: December 6, 1917* (Toronto, 1978), p. 158.

12 Robert Craig Brown, *Robert Laird Borden: A Biography* (Toronto, 1975), p. 94; John Herd Thompson, *Harvest of War: The Prairie West, 1914-1918* (Toronto, 1978), pp. 164-5.

13 *Statutes of Nova Scotia 1918*, 8-9 Geo. V, Chapter 61, Sections 8, 11, 28.

14 Report of Proceedings of Thirty-Third Annual Convention of Trades and Labor Congress of Canada, Ottawa, Ontario, 17-22 September 1917, p. 32; See also Myer Siemiatycki "Munitions", pp. 131-51; David Bercuson "Organized Labour and the Imperial Munitions Board", *Industrial Relations*, 28 (July 1973), pp. 602-16.

pre-war Labour Party.[15] In *The Craft Transformed*, Ian McKay argues that by 1914, in response to changing economic conditions, the construction unions had adopted a new approach to industrial action and had united under one umbrella organization known as the Building Trades Council.[16] In May 1914, the secretary of the Building Trades Council notified employers that "no union man in the following trades — carpenters, painters, plumbers, electrical workers, steamfitters or plasterers — will work on any job unless all workmen in those trades working on the job are furnished with building trades cards for the then current quarter".[17] The implementation of a closed shop on all city building sites reflected and encouraged a growing militancy within the construction trades. In 1910 and 1914 Halifax plumbers struck, in 1913 carpenters went out, and in 1917 electricians left their jobs. A strike in 1914 encompassed all of the building trades.[18] The employers responded to the creation of the Building Trades Council by forming the Constructive Mechanical Trades Exchange in June 1914.[19] Since both sides were organized and met on terms of near equality, the construction industry was normally able to negotiate annual city-wide contracts, lending some stability to a volatile situation. But the Commission's refusal to adhere to rates approved by the Exchange and the Building Trades Council deprived the Halifax building trades, during their busiest period in history, of their traditional means of affecting minimum wages and conditions of employment.

The influx of a new group of largely unskilled and unorganized workers compounded the sense of crisis among the building trades.[20] Migrant labour

15 In the *Seventh Annual Report on Labor Organizations in Canada, 1917* (Ottawa, 1918), the Halifax Longshoremen reported 1,000 members, composing nearly half of the city's reported union membership (p. 207). See also Ian McKay "Class Struggle and Mercantile Capitalism: Craftsmen and Labourers on the Halifax Waterfront, 1850-1902", in Rosemary Ommer and Gerald Panting, eds., *Working Men Who Got Wet: Proceedings of the Fourth Conference of the Atlantic Shipping Project* (St. John's, 1980); Ian McKay, "The Working Class of Metro Halifax 1850-1889", Honours essay, Dalhousie University, 1975; Catherine Waite, "The Longshoremen of Halifax 1900-1930: Their Lives and Working Conditions", M.A. thesis, Dalhousie University, 1977.

16 The timing of the formation of the Building Trades Council is not entirely clear. The *Halifax District Trades and Labor Council Journal 1928* (Halifax, 1928) claims that the Building Trades Council was formed on 27 June 1913 (p. 43).

17 Quoted in Ian McKay, *The Craft Transformed: An Essay on the Carpenters of Halifax, 1885-1985* (Halifax, 1985), p. 62.

18 Government of Canada, *Labour Gazette* (June 1910), p. 1441; (May 1913), p. 1301; (June 1913), p. 1416; (June 1914), p. 1463; (August 1917),p. 613; McKay, *The Craft Transformed*, pp. 56-8.

19 McKay, *The Craft Transformed*, p. 61. The Constructive Mechanical Trades Exchange was incorporated on 10 June 1914. *Statues of Nova Scotia*, 1914, 4 Geo V, Chapter 173, p. 354.

20 While most of the migrant labour was unskilled, skilled, unionized workers also came to Halifax. Striking plumbers from Saint John were able to use excellent employment conditions created by

broke down the closed union shop in Halifax and thereby curtailed the chief means which Halifax labour had used to control the local labour market. In April 1918, the HRC estimated that since the disaster, it had daily employed between 2,000 and 3,000 men and had registered a total of 9,124 names, excluding those employed by local contractors.[21] Since most local union men worked for city contractors, over 10,000 workers connected with the building trades must have passed through the city. The instability and high turnover associated with construction explains the extraordinary number of men employed by the HRC.[22]

Although the vast amount of labour recruited to Halifax may appear remarkable in light of the national labour shortage in 1918, the war-time labour shortage in Canada did not protect all workers from the irregularities of the labour market. Seasonal production, technological change, and local factors such as fires, war-time shortages and strikes created unemployment at various times and places among both the skilled and unskilled. The building trades were particularly vulnerable as construction projects by their nature were dependent on good weather and non-military construction was often postponed until the war's end. As a result, the building trades seem to have been excluded, to some extent, from the tight labour market and many men were available to come to Halifax. In February 1918 an Ontario labour paper, the *Industrial Banner*, referred to a group of Chinese labourers who had frozen to death *en route* to Halifax and criticized the injustice of employing foreign labour when "Hardly a day passes but news comes of men and women being notified that their services are no longer required".[23] In fact, the national crisis of available labour did not affect operations in Halifax until the late spring and summer of 1918. Even then, the industry, characterized by uneven construction techniques and a dependence on fair weather for outside work, required a tremendous pool of manpower because of the large daily fluctuations in the number of labourers employed.[24]

Halifax labour leaders were quick to blame migrant workers for their problems. Antagonism against migrant workers was encouraged by newspaper reports of their fights in construction camps, thefts in which they refused to

the explosion to prolong a strike against employers. *American Federationist* (Washington D.C.), February 1918, p. 155.

21 *Morning Chronicle* (Halifax), 13 April 1918; *Daily Echo* (Halifax), 13 December 1918.

22 In a contemporary examination of life and conditions on railway and lumber camps, Edmund Bradwin described the tendency of migrant workers to "jump" or move on. In one extreme example Bradwin points to a turnover of 160 men in a three month period to maintain a work force of 25. Edmund Bradwin, *The Bunkhouse Man: A Study of Work and Pay in the Camps of Canada, 1903-14* (Toronto, 1972 [1928]), pp. 79, 226.

23 *Industrial Banner* (London), 15 February 1918.

24 "Summaries of Daily Labour Reports", Halifax Relief Commission, MG 36, Series R, 1731, Public Archives of Nova Scotia [PANS].

come to the assistance of their bunkmates, and cases of fraud.[25] The housing crisis was also magnified by the presence of migrants, for while many of those employed by the HRC were housed in special construction camps, others successfully competed with native Haligonians for housing.[26] The high concentration of native-born Nova Scotians in Halifax probably made local workers particularly susceptible to xenophobia. Cavicchi and Pegano, a railroad contracting firm which employed 1,250 unskilled largely foreign-born and alien labourers recruited in Montreal, came under particular criticism. Their men represented a significant number of those employed in the reconstruction of Halifax, but there was little evidence of their presence.[27] Not only were they separated in housing from other workers, in shacks erected on Longard Road known as "Cavicchiville"; they were also isolated by language and culture. Local union members also played upon racism and war-time hostility by emphasizing the number of French-Canadians in the city. Prejudices aroused during the conscription debates outside Quebec saw French-Canadians labelled as "slackers" and their visible presence in Halifax probably reinforced the idea that their non-participation in the war was self-serving.[28]

There was some justification for the resentment directed against the outsiders. The world of the migrant worker was exclusively male. Married men left their families behind as they found work where it was available. The financial burden of supporting two households in two different locations made the offer of unlimited working hours difficult to decline, despite established craft practices which defined the number of working hours in a day without overtime. Moreover, hard feelings by native Haligonians were not unrequited and occasionally the usually silent migrant labour voice spoke out in the press:

> On Monday last, while working on Water street, I heard a Halifax bricklayer speak of the men from Montreal as a lot of "hoboes" and the sooner they were back home the better it would be for the city. Now if it were not for the strangers here, would this work have been done? What have the bricklayers of Halifax done to help in this distress for I believe that not more than two members of the Halifax union have worked on the reconstruction job, preferring to work for local contractors because of a few cents an hour increase in pay.[29]

25 *Acadian Recorder* (Halifax), 5 June, 2 October 1918; *Evening Mail* (Halifax), 24 August 1918. This type of behaviour seems characteristic of migrant or temporary construction workers and is discussed by Rex Lucas in *Minetown, Milltown, Railtown: Life in Canadian Communities of Single Industry* (Toronto, 1971), pp. 40-1.

26 *Evening Mail*, 15 March 1918.

27 *Acadian Recorder*, 8 January 1918; *Morning Chronicle*, 13 April 1918.

28 Thompson, *Harvest of War*, p. 148.

29 *Evening Mail*, 20 March 1918.

The issue of skill was always central in discussions surrounding wages. Halifax workers, in an attempt to defend their established practices, criticized and condemned the quality of work performed by outsiders.[30] The Building Trades Council and the Trades and Labour Council claimed that "The man who knew his work was worth three times as much as the unskilled man and it was the skilled mechanic who would be wanted by the people of the north end".[31] While Halifax workmen stressed the importance of skill and economy, the HRC undertook a public education campaign on the ways and means of modern building. In announcing the plans for the development of new permanent housing, the HRC explained that "The public will also understand how important it is that a large amount of work be carried on at one time, so that materials can be purchased more cheaply, and houses — particularly those of the less expensive class — be standardized and money saved".[32] It was becoming increasingly evident, in a world of mass production, speed, and standardization, that the value placed on skill had indeed changed.[33]

In this new, unfamiliar environment characterized by migrant unskilled labourers and the interference of a third party between labour and capital, Halifax organized labour made a number of challenges to the act which gave the HRC its power. The fight was led by the Halifax Trades and Labour Council, an umbrella organization which represented most Halifax trade unions. The president of the Council and of the carpenters' union, Ralph Eisnor, criticized the power given to the HRC which permitted it to set wages, claiming that wages should be a matter of negotiation between the employer and employee. Another prominent Council man, Joseph Garnett, argued that, if the Commission set the wage scale, it could "secure labor from Montreal, laborers of foreign element who could work for wages which the ordinary workman could not live on".[34] The non-assessment of employees of the HRC was also considered unfair to local workmen. While local plumbers were required to pay a municipal license fee, the outside workmen under the employ of the HRC were exempt. Although the Council unsuccessfully lobbied for the establishment of a head tax, it did secure an amendment to the HRC Act which provided that all workmen engaged in work for the HRC were exempted from any special taxes, rates, or levies.[35] Although this section continued to benefit outsiders, this change prevented the

---

30 *Acadian Recorder*, 15 March 1918.

31 *Morning Chronicle*, 4 June 1918.

32 *Acadian Recorder*, 7 May 1918.

33 For changes in construction see Michael J. Doucet and John C. Weaver, "Material Culture and the North American House: The Era of the Common Man, 1870-1920", *Journal of American History*, 72, 3 (December 1985), pp. 560-87.

34 *Morning Chronicle*, 6 April 1918.

35 *Morning Chronicle*, 26 April 1918.

direct discrimination of the initial draft against local craftmen who were required to pay for special licenses.

The greatest public outcry was aroused by the attempt of the HRC to exclude itself and those injured during the explosion from falling under the terms of the Nova Scotia Workmen's Compensation Act. This decision seems to have been the result of the dire financial condition of the Workmen's Compensation Board at the time of the explosion. In January 1918, W.C. Urluier wrote to Prime Minister Borden that "Mr. Premier Murray has rather burned his fingers in his manipulation of the Labor vote through the Workmen's Compensation Act. The Institution has $100,000 in the treasury with liability estimated at $150,000 when adjusted. Mr. Paton, the Chairman of the Board, declared the whole thing utterly bankrupt".[36] Unionized labour regarded tampering with workmen's compensation awards as a direct assault on the rights of the workingman. The Halifax Typographical Union unanimously condemned the HRC's power "as employers of labor to fix wages of employees, yet desire to escape responsibility in cases of accident or fatal injury to workmen in the course of their employment". It warned that any exceptions made to the operation of the Workmen's Compensation Board "establishes a precedent which cannot fail but to seriously endanger the future working out of the Compensation Act".[37] In this case, Labour successfully persuaded the Nova Scotia Government to amend the Halifax Relief Commission Act so that any person who after 10 June 1918 was entitled to Workmen's Compensation benefits and did not receive equivalent benefits from the HRC would be provided for under the Compensation Act.[38]

Through intense united opposition Halifax organized labour thus brought about minor amendments to the original act, but it did not succeed in altering the HRC's right to set wages. From its creation, the HRC refused to acknowledge the legitimacy of the Building Trades Council and the Exchange. It refused to comply with the Exchange standards, recognize unions, or enter into collective bargaining, although it frequently met with the union's leadership in appealing for labour's cooperation.[39]

The single most influential person in reconstruction operations was Colonel Robert S. Low, the general manager of a prominent Ottawa construction company. Born in Michigan, Low was educated in Halifax where he also entered his father's contracting company. Responsible for many major projects in Cape

36 W.C. Urluier to Borden, 7 January 1918, Borden Papers, MG 26H, Vol. 90, OC 445 (2) (A), p. 46753, NAC.

37 *Acadian Recorder*, 8 April 1918.

38 *Morning Chronicle*, 26 April 1918; *Acadian Recorder*, 26 April 1918.

39 One of the Reconstruction Committee's initial actions was to arrange a meeting with local labour leaders "pointing out to them the great necessity of everyone 'putting his shoulder to the wheel', and bespeaking their kind co-operation". HRC Minutes, 10 December 1917, PANS.

Breton, he attained national fame as the military builder responsible for Valcartier, Camp Borden, Camp Hughes, and Sacree Camp. In 1914, Low was appointed Honourary Lieutenant-Colonel Officer Commanding the 4th Pioneers Canadian Expeditionary Force and in 1916 was promoted to full Honourary Colonel.[40] The day after the explosion, Low was called by the military to Halifax "to organize and superintend the work of emergency repairs and to provide temporary accommodation for the homeless as quickly as possible".[41] On 9 December 1917, only three days after the explosion, a contract was negotiated with Colonel Low's Ottawa firm Bate, McMahon and Company to begin building on the Halifax South Commons at a 7 1/2 per cent commission.[42] After being awarded the initial contract, Low was named director of all reconstruction operations efforts in Halifax, a relationship which continued after the HRC was established in January 1918. The close association between Low, the manager of reconstruction, and his company, Bate, McMahon and Company, the recipient of a large contract under the jurisdiction of the Commission, established a precedent for unusual business practices. The HRC followed Public Works procedures and issued most contracts on a commission basis. Under this system, contractors hired all the labour and the HRC paid the wage bill and the salary of one overseer. The contractor received a set percentage of the wage bill which ran very high when thousands of labourers were battling difficult winter conditions.[43] This system placed contractors in a dilemma. High wages were in their interest after the contract was awarded but their reputation and good relations with government were important if they wanted to be awarded another project.

With its head office in Ottawa, Bate McMahon maintained its connections with government and the ear of the Department of Labour over disputes which arose over issues such as the fair wage clause.[44] Newspapers and local

---

40 Upon Low's death in January 1919, his estate was valued at $68,599 independent of his interests in Bate, McMahon and Company which were thought to exceed the value of the estate. *Acadian Recorder*, 16 and 19 January 1919; *Daily Echo*, 19 January 1919; *Evening Mail*, 16 January 1919.

41 The plan provided for the construction of tenements which could be used by the Relief Committee until the spring when they would be taken over by the military during demobilization. Thomas Benson to Secretary Militia Council Ottawa, 15 December 1917, Department of Militia and Defence, RG 24, Vol. 6359, File HQ, 7126.99.11, NAC; W. Hallick, Director of Stores, to R.T. MacIlreith, Halifax, 16 December 1917, Department of Militia and Defence, RG 24, Vol. 6358, File 7126.99, Vol 2, NAC; HRC Minutes, 7 December 1917, PANS.

42 District General Staff memo to Militia General Officer, 17 December 1917, Department of Militia and Defence, RG 24, Vol. 6358, File 7126.99, Vol 2, NAC.

43 Cynics would later question whether the desire to clean up before spring emanated from the advice of health professionals and their fear of an epidemic or was an opportunity for contractors to increase the labour bill as labourers continually shovelled snow and ice before getting to their work. *Herald*, 20 February 1918.

44 The fair wage clause, included in all federal government contracts since 1900, was designed to

contractors also continually complained that no tenders were publicly issued for the temporary housing or the clearing of the devastated area and on 15 March 1918, the *Evening Mail* complained that "large amounts of work, particularly in painting, plumbing and wiring, are said to be going otherwise than by tender".[45] These claims were supported by the absence of tender notices appearing in local papers. Resentment also arose as outside contractors who were given large projects completed all of their hiring out of town.[46] One of these large outside contracting companies, with admittedly a local connection, was the Montreal firm of Cavicchi and Pegano, which in July 1918 became known as the Bedford Construction Company. It received the lucrative contract to clear the debris from Richmond on the commission of 6 1/2 per cent.[47]

Many of the conflicts which emerged between the HRC and the Building Trades Council can be traced to the conflict between Low and the unions. In 1917, the Trades and Labour Congress convention heard complaints about Low's activities when building Camp Borden in Ontario which were similar to those later expressed in Halifax; construction work had been based on 10 to 16 hour days, seven days a week, with no recognition of overtime rates.[48] The Halifax president of the carpenters' union, Ralph Eisnor, informed the Commission in February 1918 that Low had "been a thorn in our flesh for a year, or more back. This is not the first time we have had trouble with the Colonel". In the same meeting with the HRC, the president of the Canadian Trades and Labour Congress, J.C. Watters, supported the local carpenters, stating that Low had a "reputation that did not meet with the approval of the Labor Congress and the treatment accorded organized workers by Col[onel] Low is not calculated to bring out the best results".[49] Both Watters and John W. Bruce, president of the Canadian Plumbers and Steamfitters Union, commented on the large number of complaints they had received during their visits to Halifax.[50] Nevertheless, Low

---

prevent abuses in sub-letting by contractors and to ensure that employees on government contracts received the going rate "for competent workmen in the district". Government of Canada, *Labour Gazette* (September 1900), p. 15; Bradwin, *Bunkhouse*, p. 207.

45 *Evening Mail*, 5 February 1918; *Morning Chronicle*, 9 April 1918.

46 *Morning Chronicle*, 22 July 1918.

47 *Herald*, 15 February 1918; *Acadian Recorder*, 5 July 1918. Vincent J. Cavicchi appears to have been associated with some dubious practices since evidence was presented at the Nova Scotia Highway Inquiry of 1921 that he had attempted to bribe the chief engineer of the Highways Board. *Evening Mail*, 21 February 1921. See Gregory Cooper, "Politics and Fraud in Nova Scotia Road Policy: The Highways Scandal of 1920-21", Honours Essay, Dalhousie University, 1983.

48 *Report of Proceedings of Thirty-Third Annual Convention of Trades and Labor Congress of Canada, Ottawa, Ontario, September 17-22, 1917*, p. 33.

49 HRC Minutes, 20 February 1918, PANS.

50 *Ibid.*

remained the undisputed master of Halifax reconstruction until June 1918 when he returned to his regular position at the Bate, McMahon Ottawa office.

Although the problems between the Commission and the local unions were magnified by the involvement of a non-cooperative manager such as Low and by large contractors such as Cavicchi with his foreign work-force, the central issue in the conflict was organized labour's desire to sustain past union victories. Hard fought battles over wages and hours were placed in jeopardy as the Commission claimed that emergency conditions should override past agreements. The issue of wages arose even before Christmas 1917 with the carpenters, who had the least control over the skill level of their craft. But wages were not the only issue at stake. Plumbers, bricklayers, and plasterers all quickly realized that the power of the HRC threatened old victories won over the number of hours which constituted a day's work, the principle of overtime, and most importantly the closed shop. In response to attacks by these unions, the Commission repeatedly claimed that its disregard for union rules and regulations was an excusable response to emergency conditions.

In February 1918, when the plumbers approached the HRC over the matter of overtime, the Chairman of the Commission, T.S. Rogers, threatened a campaign of public opinion against the union.[51] Plumbers were portrayed in the Halifax *Herald* as unpatriotic, monopolistic, and tyrannical for defending the practice of an overtime rate for Sunday labour.[52] While middle-class spokespersons almost consistently sided with the *Herald*, Alderman John E. Godwin, who was not associated with the labour movement but represented the ward most affected by the explosion, pointed to the inconsistency of denying overtime rates while paying the transportation costs and supplying the tool kits of out-of-town workers.[53] Ignoring public opinion, the plumbers refused to work overtime without proper compensation and effectively held up construction during the initial two months of construction. Their firm resolve to boycott Sunday work without overtime only weakened in mid February when Colonel Low threatened to bring in "200 Frenchmen".[54] Since migrant plumbers were permitted to operate without the necessary municipal license, and rules governing plumbing regulations were suspended, the plumbers faced the prospect of losing all control over the local labour market. The fear of permanent changes after the period of emergency led the plumbers to compromise and work without extra compensation until 1 May 1918.[55] Halifax plumbers thus sacrificed an important principle

51 *Ibid.*, 23 February 1918.

52 *Evening Mail*, 4 February 1918.

53 *Ibid.*, 23 February 1918.

54 HRC Minutes, 20 February 1918, PANS.

55 *Ibid.*, 27 February 1918.

to maintain their local monopoly over the local labour market and some control over the standard of work.

The building trades agreed to postpone any labour disruptions until 1 May, the traditional date for establishing new wage rates in Halifax, which was also to coincide with the commencement of the second stage or permanent building of the Hydrostone housing development. To the disappointment of the unions, however, in May 1918 the *Labour Gazette* published a fair wage schedule approved by the HRC, which was considerably below the existing city union standards.[56] According to the HRC schedule, carpenters were to receive 40 cents, glaziers and plumbers 45 cents, stone masons and bricklayers 50 cents, and labourers 30 cents an hour. At the time of this notification, the Building Trades Council and the Exchange had entered into a new agreement for 1918, which increased the rate for carpenters to 50 cents an hour for a nine hour day, and time and a half for Saturday afternoons throughout the summer. Painters and bricklayers also received increases to 55 and 60 cents an hour respectively for an eight hour day. The new agreement with the plumbers was more complicated as it gave the plumbers 50 cents an hour for a nine hour day until November when the length of the day would return to eight hours.[57]

The determination of the bricklayers to uphold Building Trades Council union rates may have been a factor in the decision that brick would not be the primary material used in reconstruction efforts. The HRC desired an inexpensive non-combustible building material and selected "hydrostone", a cement block-like material composed of pressurized sand, crushed stone and gravel which did not require the use of skilled bricklayers. The bricklayers were able to place pressure on the Commission because of the high level of expertise involved in their trade and their relative scarcity in Halifax. In early April, they met with the Commission and requested that the HRC scale fall into line with the 60 cents an hour agreed on by local contractors.[58] A second delegation returned on 30 April and repeated their request for the union rate for HRC employees. Although not a single member of their local union was actually employed by the HRC, the return to a standard wage across the city was regarded as vital in maintaining the strength of labour when the period of emergency had passed. Rogers, who had previously agreed to consider the increase, postponed any decisions until permanent building began. At the beginning of May, no final decision concerning the building material to be used in new construction had been made, for the HRC Chairman asked the delegation "the rate the bricklayers would charge if brick was to be taken into consideration in building the

56 *Labour Gazette* (May 1918), p. 354.
57 *Acadian Recorder,* 1 May 1918; *Evening Mail,* 1 May 1918.
58 HRC Minutes, 8 April 1918, PANS.

houses".[59] The bricklayers' response of the standard union city rate probably decided once and for all that hydrostone, not brick, would be the principal material used in the new houses. Although brick works were not well developed in Nova Scotia, hydrostone had to be manufactured in a factory constructed specifically for that purpose in Eastern Passage and connected to the north end of Halifax by a temporary railway. This factory was owned and managed by the assistant manager of reconstruction, Hamilton Lindsay.[60]

The 1 May deadline given to the Commission by the building trades almost passed without any response. Out-of-town union bricklayers employed by the HRC decided to continue working under existing conditions until 1 June. The plasterers, however, pointed out that another delay gave no assurance that the HRC would come to terms with the unions.[61] From the beginning, the plasterers had willingly worked long hours with no overtime, but on 1 May stopped all work and demanded that the Commission fall in line with union regulations. With the plasterers out on strike and work on reconstruction falling further behind schedule, the Commission met with Low and the architects to discuss the local labour situation. The increasing difficulty in securing sufficient manpower led the HRC to adopt the practice of the Imperial Munitions Board which coordinated agreements among local employers to set wage rates and "avoid wage competition for scarce labor".[62] It therefore approached the Exchange to guard their mutual interests and prevent excessive wage demands. Cooperation with the exchange also guaranteed a stable wage until the next contract in May 1919. It was a labour shortage not the power of the unions that led to the signing of an agreement of 4 June to set a uniform standard of wages and hours across the city.[63] In fact, as Table One shows the explosion did not affect minimum union wage levels and wages did not rise dramatically until a year and a half later, in June 1919 with the settlement of the building trades strike.

The shortage of men during the summer of 1918 continued to affect wages and delayed the construction of the Hydrostone development.[64] Unable to find sufficient labour to build its massive housing project, the Commission issued appeals that only emergency repairs to existing buildings be undertaken throughout the rest of the city.[65] The lack of skilled plasterers put all work behind

59 *Ibid.*, 30 April 1918.

60 Halifax Relief Commission, Second Report to Privy Council, 2 July 1918, NAC; Weaver, "Reconstruction", p.40.

61 *Evening Mail*, 3 May 1918. The strike by the Plasterers does not appear in the Department of Labour's Strike and Lockout files.

62 Cited Naylor, "The Canadian State", p. 37 from D. Carnegie, *The History of Munitions Supply in Canada 1914-1918* (London, 1925), p. 252.

63 HRC Minutes, 4 May 1918, PANS.

64 *Morning Chronicle*, 11 December 1917.

65 *Acadian Recorder*, 12 August 1918.

Table One

Wages Set for Halifax Building Trades, 1917-19;
Building Trades Council/Constructive Mechanical Trades Exchange
and
Halifax Relief Commission

	May 1917 BTC/EXC	May 1918 HRC	May 1918 BTC/EXC	June 1918 HRC	June 1919 BTC/EXC
carpenters	.40	.40	.50 9hr	.50 9/10hr	.66
painters	.40		.55 8hr	.55 8/10hr	.66
plumbers	.45	.45	.50 9/8hr	.50 9/10hr	.70
electricians				.60 9/10hr	.70
masons	.50	.50	.60 8hr	.60 8/10hr	.65
plasterers	.50			.60 8hr	.75
labourers	.30	.30		.35 9/10hr	
glaziers		.45		.55 8hr	
pipefitters	.45		.50 9/8hr	.50 9/10hr	
bricklayers	.50	.50	.60 8hr	.60 8hr	.65

Source: *Herald*, 29 December 1917; *Evening Mail,* 1 May 1918; *Acadian Recorder,* 23, 27 March, 1 May, 12 June 1918; *The Citizen* (Halifax), 20 June 1919; J.D. Reid, Deputy Minister Railways and Canals to General Mewburn, Minister of Militia and Defence, 4 March 1918 and Benson, Commanding Officer Military District 6 to Secretary Militia Council, 6 May 1918, RG 24, Vol. 6358, File HQ 71-26-99, Vol. 4, NAC; *Labour Gazette* (May 1918), p. 354; (August 1918), p. 639.

schedule and a statement in the *Echo* on 13 August proclaimed that 500 more men could be used in addition to the 2,400 employed.[66] By the autumn, conditions were critical and the HRC had to find a way around its agreement with the Exchange and pay above the set rate to attract the necessary manpower. With work plentiful, labour was reluctant to engage in particularly heavy work without "some special inducement".[67] The Commission therefore needed to find

66 *Evening Mail,* 11 July 1918.
67 HRC Minutes, 30 October 1918, PANS.

a way of attracting masons and labourers without actually violating its agreement with the Exchange, for to do so could increase the wage levels of all other trades. The HRC therefore evaded the intent of the agreement by sub-contracting stone setting to an outside contractor "who would bring in his own masons or stone setters and laborers, paying them whatever he pleased; the rate, however, not to be known to the Commission".[68] By this plan, the HRC was able to turn a blind eye to wages which exceeded the agreement and at the same time obtain the necessary labour. Another way of circumventing the "flat Rate" was by reclassifying stone setters, helpers, and labourers on the Hydrostone project under a separate and higher wage category from regular bricklayers and masons. If the intention of the Commission in its decision to use hydrostone blocks had been to keep wages low and avoid labour trouble by not being held hostage by the craft knowledge of the Bricklayers' Union, the commission was unsuccessful. Ironically, a situation was created where the need for labour was so great that demand was able to dictate wages more effectively than skill.

This change in the availability of labour and the use of a sub-contractor in the Hydrostone development encouraged the Commission to rid itself of the labour problem altogether. In January 1919, the reconstruction department of the HRC closed and all work completed thereafter was through a contractor.[69] The departure of the Commission from direct involvement in labour relations signalled a return to pre-explosion local conditions in which the Building Trades Council and the Exchange regulated labour standards. Organized labour, however, had changed since the explosion. While the Carpenters' business agent complained that not 60 per cent of the carpenters employed on the Hydrostone project were union members, the size of the Carpenters union had increased by nearly 425 per cent between the explosion and June 1919.[70] This new strength which was felt, though less dramatically, in other building unions would last until the economic collapse of 1920.

As the unions had changed, so had the consciousness of many of their members. The neighborhood most affected by the disaster had been the working-class suburb of Richmond, home to many of the city's skilled workers, railwaymen and shipyard employees.[71] The destruction of their homes, the loss of property, and the personal tragedy which resulted from the explosion created a shared experience. This shared loss was accompanied by the frustration that the skilled and semi-skilled working class were not receiving what they perceived as a fair deal. John Bacher, in his study of the state and housing, suggests that the

68 *Ibid.*, 30 October 1918.

69 *Echo*, 22 January 1919.

70 HRC Minutes, 26 August 1919, PANS; *The Citizen*, 6 June 1919.

71 Archibald MacMeecham, "The Halifax Disaster" in Metson, *Halifax Explosion*, p. 18; Waite, "Longshoremen".

explosion intensified "class conflict around housing".[72] Citing Halifax Trades and Labor Council pressure which secured rent controls in the HRC Act, Bacher concludes that the housing crisis galvanized "labour's class consciousness and political action".[73] The perceived injustice in the distribution of compensation by the HRC also encouraged the development of a collective consciousness among many of the city's skilled and semi-skilled workers. When the Commission classified pianos as luxury items and excluded them from any settlements, a "mechanic" from the north end saw the class bias in the decision and complained to the *Evening Mail* that

> Now most of us north end people managing to get pianos out of our hard earned savings feel such a necessity in cases where there are children to educate. Yet they [HRC] estimate the damage done to autos which are a luxury we mechanics cannot afford. Indeed they are a luxury of the rich. If they pay for an auto, why not pay for a piano? I ask this question because, I would like to know where we ring in.[74]

The demand for fair treatment was a prevalent theme as housing placements, reimbursements for tools, and the distribution of used clothing enraged north end residents.[75] HRC compensation policy created a sense of injustice as two different standards seemed to be used for the rich and the poor.

Frustration caused by perceived injustice in the dispersement of material compensation was augmented by the exclusion of labour from all community political participation. The absence of a working-class voice from the voluntary *ad hoc* Relief Committee seems highly unusual, not simply an oversight in the confusion. Precedent held that labour participated on municipal committees, occasionally sponsored political candidates, and was actively courted by both the Liberal and Conservative parties. Under these circumstances, it made little sense that labour should be forgotten when it was widely acknowledged that the geographic area most affected was inhabited by its constituents. There were people on the Relief Committee sensitive to the fact that the body should represent the entire community. After the initial organization was struck, there was an amendment that the Relief Committee be expanded to include some "ladies".[76] The exclusion of labour from participation in the post-explosion organizations which directly shaped the future of their community further

---

72 Bacher, "Keeping to the Private Market", p. 95.

73 *Ibid.*, p. 97.

74 *Evening Mail,* 19 February 1918.

75 *Evening Mail,* 5 January and 20 February 1918; *Acadian Recorder*, 15 March 1918; HRC Minutes, 14 January 1918, PANS.

76 HRC Minutes, 8 December 1917, PANS.

alienated labour from the Commission.

Finally, labour was frustrated by the inconsistency of the Commission's actions which waived union regulations during the emergency for the sake of expense and yet spent extravagantly on other non-labour items. The discrepancies between what was said and what was seen made it difficult for labour to accept restraint when $18,500,000 was spent in 1918 alone.[77] Aldermanic candidate James Rudge in 1919 questioned how government could borrow by the million for the war effort "but could not borrow enough to replace the houses destroyed in the explosion".[78] Examples of wasteful expenditures on building material, such as the extravagant use of pine for the framing of the temporary houses, and exorbitant contract commissions were contrasted with the unwillingness of the Commission to pay for quality workmanship.[79] This frustration, articulated in a letter to the editor of the *Evening Mail*, stated that since it was a mechanics' district that had been wiped out by the explosion and since the working-class had suffered the most from war-time inflation, it was only just that labour should somehow benefit from the catastrophe.[80]

Armed with the experience of dealing with a government agency which claimed to represent the community at the expense of the interests of some of its members, labour responded with both a series of concrete steps to enlarge its own constituency and a stronger committment to labourism and political action. In February 1919, the Halifax building trades were central in the organization of the Nova Scotia Federation of Labour.[81] Under the auspices of the Halifax Trades and Labour Council, in May 1919 Halifax trade unionists began publishing a weekly newspaper, significantly named *The Citizen*, capable of presenting labour's case to the public. The desire to be included in community affairs encouraged labour to sponsor two aldermanic candidates in the north end of the city. When the Halifax Labour Party was revived by the Halifax Trades and Labour Council after the war, the invitation for membership was extended to all "workers, whether organized or unorganized, mental or manual regardless of race, sex, creed or vocation".[82] The most important indication of this notion of an expanded community was the unified action taken by Halifax building trade unions when they closed down all city construction in May 1919. This building trades strike was particularly significant as it demanded a uniform wage across the skilled building trades and appealed for support from the entire

77 *Canadian Annual Review 1918* (Toronto, 1919), p. 651.

78 *The Citizen*, 6 June 1919.

79 *Evening Mail*, 2 February 1918; *Herald*, 9 February 1918.

80 *Evening Mail*, 4 February 1918.

81 *Morning Chronicle*, 1 March 1919.

82 *The Citizen*, 22 January 1920; Morton, "Labourism and Independent Labor Politics", one.

community, contemplating a General Strike across the city.[83]

On 1 May 1919, 2,000 men in the city's most active economic sector, the building trades, walked off the job in the largest strike action taken to this point in the city. Although the dispute had originally centred upon the issue of higher wages and the eight-hour day, once on strike the right to negotiate across the trades emerged as the principle issue.[84] This emphasis, according to Ian McKay, "marked a new unified state in the history of the building craftsmen" for negotiating as a single unit changed "craft unionism into something more like industrial unionism".[85] This very basic change in approach would not have been possible without both the negative experience of dealing with the HRC and the growth of construction unions which accompanied reconstruction. A departure from tradition in the building trades also appeared at the 14 May meeting of the Halifax Trades and Labour Council, when the Building Trades Council requested that the central organization organize a city-wide sympathetic strike.[86] Proposed before the Winnipeg and Amherst General Strikes, this decision was not a reaction to external circumstances.[87] Indeed, this action was possibly the only discussion of a General Strike in Canada in 1919 to be initiated outside the metal trades. While the strike illustrates the radical edge of the Halifax labour movement, its conclusion on 12 June with tripartite arbitration reveals the desire by the unions to reach beyond organized labour for support. The choice of Amherst businessman J.A. MacDonald as the union representative on the tribunal demonstrated labour's new desire to tie into the larger community.[88]

For many Canadian trade unionists, 1918 was a remarkable year of success and growth.[89] But, while unions in other parts of Canada were experimenting with power, the actions of the HRC left the Halifax labour unions aware of the

---

83 *Morning Chronicle*, 16 May 1919.

84 *The Citizen* claimed that the cost of living in Halifax was the highest in Canada, and according to figures published in *LG*, in May 1919, it cost $24.78 per week to feed, cloth and shelter a family in the city. At the existing scale of 50 cents and hour, a carpenter who was able to work a full 54 hours a week earned little more than basics and certainly not enough to save for seasonal layoffs, bad weather or emergencies. *Ibid.*, 13, 27 June 1919. See also Michael Piva, "Urban Working Class Income and Real Incomes in 1921: A Comparative Analysis", *Histoire Sociale/Social History*, 16 (1983), pp. 145-67.

85 McKay, *The Craft Transformed*, p. 69.

86 *Morning Chronicle*, 16 May 1919. The secretary of the HTLC was instructed to contact the affiliated unions for their opinions.

87 Nolan Reilly, "The General Strike in Amherst, Nova Scotia, 1919", *Acadiensis*, 9, 2 (Spring 1980), pp. 56-77.

88 The tribunal granted an increase but was unable to achieve a standardized wage of 75 cents. *Herald*, 12 June 1919.

89 Bryan Palmer, *Working-Class Experience. The Rise and Reconstitution of Canadian Labour, 1800-1980* (Toronto, 1983), p. 170.

tenuous position from which they operated. The Halifax building trades had barely been able to weather the pressures brought about by government involvement in post-explosion Halifax. Although membership increased and the HRC was eventually forced to comply with the standard wage because of pressures in the labour market, the actions of the Commission threatened skilled labour's most precious institution, the union. Employer-employee negotiations, which had appeared to be firmly established, were placed in great jeopardy. Trade unionists, excluded from positions of leadership, stood helpless as migrant workers with no commitment to the community or to individual unions swarmed into the city willing to forfeit long-contested restrictions and rights in exchange for making as much money as quickly as possible. The unwillingness of the HRC to recognize union rates and regulations encouraged this chaos. Eisnor reminded the Commission at one meeting that Halifax organized labour had "worked thirty or thirty-five years to complete our organization and to get what we have got, and while we regret as much as anybody in Halifax the calamity which has befallen our City, we cannot see any reason why people are coming in and running slipshod all over our trade regulations".[90] Rights, privileges, organizations and labour agreements were left untouched by the flying debris and flames of the catastrophe, but the actions of the Commission imperilled these hard won claims which had survived the original destruction only to be threatened in the rebuilding of the city.

The near collapse of organized labour under governmental pressure offered a tremendous boost to the creation of a temporary skilled and semi-skilled class awareness in the immediate post-war period. The attitude of the HRC to unions and the authoritarian methods of its manager, Colonel Low, caused considerable discontent among the skilled workers, who lived in the neighbourhood devastated by the explosion. The frustration over property settlements, disability compensation, and inadequate housing intensified the level of class consciousness in the community. At the same time, while encouraging the growth of a fragile and restricted class consciousness, clearly demonstrated in the building trades strike of 1919, the events of 1918 simultaneously encouraged labour to broaden its support in the wider community. Faced with the growing tendency of government to define and act upon the public interest, Halifax organized labour sought to maintain and increase its influence in the city through direct participation in the politics of the community. Organized labour's need to broaden support placed greater emphasis on the formalization and legitimization of labour's role and offered new importance to labourism. The election of candidates from the revived Labour Party of July 1919 was seen as vitally important.[91] While a labour party had existed before the war, the new face of Halifax labourism was

90 *Herald*, 15 February 1918.

91 *Morning Chronicle*, 10 January, 26 July 1919.

willing to form political coalitions outside the traditional craft elite to strengthen its electoral constituency. In this defensive effort to combat the encroachment of government, skilled labour's participation in community politics actually reinforced and sanctioned the emerging new role of the state. Futhermore, the temporary revival of labourism was almost anachronistic in the post-war era. As a grass roots movement concerned with egalitarian democracy, it seemed out of place with the increasing techno-corporatism of the 1920s.[92] Agencies such as the HRC with their expertise, planning, and central control were the real harbingers of things to come.

92 Guy Alchon, *Capitalism, Social Science and the State in the 1920s* (Princeton, 1985), p. 169.

FRED WINSOR

"Solving a Problem": Privatizing Worker's Compensation for Nova Scotia's Offshore Fishermen, 1926-1928

ON 6 AUGUST 1926 A LARGE portion of the Lunenburg schooner fleet was fishing off Sable Island. Catches were good as the vessels topped off their loads before the voyage home. What happened next is best described by two fishing captains present at the time:

> That's what you call a fishermen's luck. You're anchored in the middle of the ocean and you got to take it as it comes. When you take your clothes on the vessel, you never know if you're acomin' back. Yes, when you think it over you never know if you're acomin' back. Well the weather-glass gave no warning. It showed nothing at all. At nine o'clock there was an ordinary breeze but at ten o'clock the sea come ahead of the wind and you knew there was somethin' back of it driving it. We got everything below. By that time the breeze was here and you couldn't walk along the deck. You had to get a rope and haul yourself along. We had twenty-four hundred quintals of fish when the gale come and the vessel was like a log. At twelve o'clock she broke adrift and she went two to three hours in eighteen to nineteen fathoms of water. The riding sail filled on the lee side. That hove her down and she was very slow comin' back, so slow it looked kinda suspicious at one time if she was ever comin' back. We put out oil and that helped some, but I never see a worse blow at sea.

Describing what happened to his heavily laden vessel in the same storm another captain said:

> The sea would break from the bottom and strike us. The deck was swept clean by the gigantic sea. It took our boats and all our moveable gear. It smashed the skylight, the cabin doors and the cabin table. The stove and everything else was smashed. The cabin was half filled with water and the men washed around in the cabin and beat to pieces. Two men were washed overboard. We just saved them that was all. Nine men were injured with broken ribs and injured limbs and one man at the pump was half beaten to pieces with the terrific seas. George Locke, one of our best fishermen, was so badly injured that he has since died.[1]

1 *Herald* (Halifax), 9 October 1926.

The crews of the *Sylvia Mosher* and the *Sadie Knickle* were not so fortunate as these men. Both schooners went down in the storm and on these two vessels alone 47 men perished. It took more than two weeks to confirm that these vessels had been lost since, as was the case with all schooners, they did not have radios on board and could neither receive advance warning of storms nor send any distress signals.

The 1926 disaster was an immense tragedy for the men and women caught in its grip, but it sparked only minor changes in the fishery. Only William Duff, publisher of the Lunenburg *Progress-Enterprise*, argued for the installation of transmitting and receiving radio equipment aboard all the Lunenburg schooners.[2] There were a few requests that the federal government place a rescue ship out on the fishing banks to come to the aid of mariners in distress, but these were ignored. Even more telling was the absence of any investigation into the catastrophe. In the same storm, a Norwegian freighter, the *Ringhorn*, was lost off Scatarie Island on the east coast of Cape Breton, and five of the ship's crew died in the attempt to reach land. The loss of this foreign freighter gave rise to an inquiry within eleven days of the sinking, but no inquiry was ever held into the far larger disasters in the Nova Scotia schooner fleet.[3] The following year, the Lunenburg vessel owners sent the fleet out to the fishing grounds, having learned nothing from these events. Once again none of the schooners was equipped with radios or improved safety equipment. Consequently, although the disaster which followed was "natural", its magnitude was inevitable because of the failure of the industry or the government to respond to the lessons of 1926.

The storm that hit the Northeast Coast of North America on 24 August 1927 was not a normal gale, but a storm of exceptional force, the worst in the history of the 20th century schooner fishery. As it swept up the coast it devastated the Lunenburg fleet as well as fishing fleets from the other Maritime ports andNewfoundland, and also struck inland throughout the region. In Nova Scotia alone, damage was estimated at approximately a million dollars.[4] On 30 August, some six days after the storm, over 75 vessels from the Lunenburg fleet had still not been heard from. It was finally learned that four schooners had gone down, the *Mahalia*, the *Joyce Smith*, the *Clayton Walters*, and the *Una J. Corkum*. In the same vicinity as these vessels the *Columbia*, a banking schooner fishing out of Gloucester, Massachusetts, was lost with all hands, a crew of 20. In all 88 men belonging to the Lunenburg salt banker fleet lost their lives, while many others

2   *Progress-Enterprise* (Lunenburg), 1 September 1926.

3   *Herald*, 18 August 1926.

4   *Ibid.*, 26 August 1927. Cyril Robinson, in his *Men Against the Sea, High Drama in the Atlantic* (Hantsport, N.S., 1971), pp. 131-3, captures the savagery of this storm in his vivid description of the ordeal of Roland Knickle, captain of the *Andrava*, one of the Lunenburg schooners to survive the gale off Sable Island.

were maimed or severely injured. At least another ten small boat fishermen were lost along the coast of Nova Scotia and large numbers of men off the coast of Newfoundland, although newspaper accounts of the number conflict because of the lack of communication between the vessels and the land.[5]

It took up to a month before the fatalities were confirmed. The families of the men who died had then to face the loss of a loved one and the principal wage earner in the household. Fortunately, for most of the dependents, they were eligible to receive monetary compensation from the Nova Scotia Workmen's Compensation Board.[6] Offshore fishermen in Nova Scotia had been included under the Nova Scotia Workmen's Compensation Act since 1920. However, the government's response to the plight of the relatives of some who died in 1927 was miserly.[7] Widows received $30.00 a month for life or until they remarried and $7.50 a month for children under the age of 16 years. Many widows, whose husbands were Newfoundlanders, received nothing at all.[8] Moreover, there is a bitter irony to the fact that all the suffering and the loss of lives in the gales of 1926 and 1927 resulted in a worsening rather than an improvement in the compensation available to fishermen and in the safety conditions under which they worked. Inadequate as was the compensation given to the families after the deaths in 1926 and 1927, it required a large payment from the funds of the Workmen's Compensation Board. Because of the relations of production, economic conditions in the industry, and the political climate of the time, worker's compensation for offshore fishermen was privatized, thus removing any economic pressure on the Lunenburg fish merchants to improve their safety record.

Although European workers had successfully demanded worker's compensation at the turn of the century, in North America these programs did not gain general favour until the period after 1910. Before this time, damages for workers injured or killed could only be won through private costly court cases. Although accidents very often resulted from employer negligence, few workers or their heirs could succeed in proving the employer at fault and receive compensation.[9]

---

5 *Herald*, 29-30 August 1927.

6 The name of the Nova Scotia Workmen's Compensation Board was changed to the Nova Scotia Worker's Compensation Board in the mid 1970s. When not referring specifically to the Workmen's Compensation Board in the particular time period the author uses the term worker's compensation.

7 Workmen's Compensation Board of Nova Scotia, *Annual Report* (1921).

8 From the turn of the century, many of the crew members on the offshore fishing vessels operating out of Nova Scotia, and particularly Lunenburg, were residents of Newfoundland. As a result they were not covered by Workmen's Compensation if they were injured or killed while working aboard the vessel. At least 19 of those who died in the 1927 disaster were determined to be Newfoundland residents. The families of these men did not receive any compensation from the Workmen's Compensation Board in Nova Scotia and were relegated to receiving piddling relief payments from the Newfoundland Government.

9 James Weinstein, *The Corporate Ideal in the Liberal State* (Boston, 1968), p.41.

Michael Piva has pointed out that in Canada the establishment of Workmen's Compensation Boards was essentially an attempt to placate workers in the struggle between labour and capital.[10] Dianne Pothier has pursued a different tack, adopting the position that worker's compensation was essentially a compromise between capital and labour.[11] Under this compromise, workers were relieved of the responsibility of proving fault on the part of the employer; in return, they had to give up the right to sue both their own employer, and any other employer covered by the act. Employers, on the other hand, had to accept responsibility for injuries that occurred on the job. This responsibility included bearing the total cost of the insurance payments established for each industry or sub-class by the Workmen's Compensation Board. The employer then had an economic incentive to provide a safe workplace, since the rates set for each industry reflected the level of danger involved in that type of employment. Thus workers were offered a speedy remedy on a no fault basis in exchange for their acceptance of partial compensation.[12]

In Nova Scotia, a government administered worker's compensation program can be traced to the endeavors by organized labour in 1907-1908. Through the efforts of John Joy, leader of the Longshoremen's Union in Halifax, and a vigorous campaign by labour with the support of Dr. Kendall, a maverick Liberal Member of the Legislative Assembly from Cape Breton, the first Workmen's Compensation Act was enacted in 1911.[13] But offshore fishermen and most other industrial workers were not included until the revised act of 1915.[14] In 1914 the Meredith Commission in Ontario examined the question of worker's compensation and recommended the creation of a new worker's compensation act which was passed in 1915.[15] This Ontario act served as the basis for the revised

10 Michael Piva, *The Condition of the Working Class of Toronto 1900-1921* (Ottawa, 1979), pp.107-8.

11 Dianne Pothier, "Workers' Compensation: The Historical Compromise Revisited", *Dalhousie Law Journal*, 7, 2 (April 1983), p. 312.

12 Under the terms of the new act passed in Nova Scotia in 1916, workers would be eligible to receive "partial compensation" (a percentage of their wages) if unable to work due to an injury received on the job. This would be different from receiving "full compensation" which would mean receiving the same wage while injured as while working. The "partial compensation" received was based at that time on the industrial wages of the day, unlike present day workers' compensation rates which reflect current day social welfare rates.

13 Geoff Clare, "The Workmen's Compensation Movement in Nova Scotia", unpublished paper, Dalhousie University, April 1976, pp. 38-40.

14 *Ibid.*, p.49.

15 For an in-depth study of the Workmen's Compensation Act of Ontario and the Meredith Commission see R.C.B. Risk, "This Nuisance of Litigation: The Origins of Worker's Compensation in Ontario" in David Flaherty ed., *Essays in the History of Canadian Law, Vol. II* (Toronto, 1983), pp.418-91. The Workmen's Compensation Act of Ontario and the recommendations of the Meredith Commission served as the basis for similar acts in other Canadian provinces.

Workmen's Compensation Act in Nova Scotia. A board was established to administer the act in Nova Scotia similar to that in Ontario.[16]

There can be no question that fishermen needed some form of worker's compensation. The August Gales of 1926 and 1927 were dramatic events in which many men were lost at one time, but each year and every voyage brought brutally hard work, discomfort, and the dangers of death or disabling accidents. Fishermen who worked offshore during the early part of the 20th century usually worked aboard one of two types of vessels, a dory schooner or a "side" or "beam" trawler. On both types of vessels conditions were extremely dangerous. Dory schooners were 120-140 foot wooden sailing vessels with a crew of between 20-25. They usually carried six to eight "dories", small wooden boats approximately 16-18 ft. long, which put out from the schooner each day with one man or two men in each boat.[17] The fishermen tended "trawls", long lines of baited hooks, and while waiting for the fish (primarily cod) to come on the trawls, would also "jig" for cod. After the fish were caught, the catch was brought back to the schooner where it was gutted and split on the deck of the schooner, then salted in the hold. Conditions aboard were primitive. Living and working on a schooner as a dory fisherman meant sharing a very confined space for up to three or four months at a time with 20 to 25 other men. The limited storage facilities meant that crew members could only have one spare change of clothes with them for the duration of the voyage, and it was impossible to use any of the fresh water aboard for washing either oneself or one's clothes. All fresh water was required for cooking and drinking purposes.[18]

Trawling or handlining for cod in a dory left fishermen at the mercy of a hostile marine environment. To remain in contact with their schooners, dory fishermen could rely only on the foghorn in foggy weather, and without radios or any other means of communicating with the land, unexpected storms caught many schooner fishermen unprepared.[19] With no engines, the schooners were less able to operate safely in a storm than powered vessels. It was only after the disasters of 1926 and 1927 that Lunenburg schooners finally began using radios and auxiliary diesel engines.[20] But injured crew members were forced to wait until the return of

16 One of the three commissioners on this Board was John T. Joy, the President of the Halifax Longshoremen's Union, who had led the initial attempts to secure this kind of legislation.

17 Some of the schooners used a "one man" dory system with one man hauling trawl. Although this was found to be not as productive as the two man dories, some schooners used this method into the 1920s.

18 Interview with Fred Crouse, schooner fisherman, Audio Cassette tape, Fisheries Museum of the Atlantic, Lunenburg. For more information on living and working conditions on the fishing schooners, see Peter Barss, *Images of Lunenburg County* (Toronto, 1978).

19 Interview with Lewis Firth, schooner fisherman, Written Transcript, Lunenburg, Nova Scotia, Fisheries Museum of the Atlantic, p.4.

20 It is not clear if installing radios and engines aboard the schooners was done more to protect the investment (i.e. the catch and the vessel) than to aid the crew.

the vessel to port or they were transferred to another vessel heading into port, as there was no equivalent to modern air-sea rescue. With the schooners splitting and salting the catch, their captains had no incentive to come into port for weeks. The captains made their decisions on the fate of injured crew members with little if any medical training.[21] Fire-fighting and life-saving equipment on the schooners was non-existent. Unexpected fires were fought by throwing water on them and if this proved unsuccessful, the crew abandoned ship in the dories and hoped for the best.

Although living conditions on the trawlers were somewhat less severe than life aboard dory schooners, the dangers were almost as great.[22] Unlike dory schooners, which were seasonal and operated from March to December, the side trawlers fished throughout the year. In winter the severe icing up of the superstructure imperiled the stability of the craft. Nothing guaranteed that any fire-fighting and life-saving equipment would be on board, for no regulations required vessels to carry such equipment. In most cases the safety equipment on board the ship at the time of construction — a life ring, a couple of life boats, a few fire buckets, and some axes — was all the vessel carried. The individual safety of the crew members appears to have been of little importance. Hard hats, steel-toed boots or personal flotation devices were unheard of. Such devices were not beyond the level of existing technology; survival suits for pilots attempting trans-Atlantic crossings were then being manufactured by the Miner Rubber Company in Quebec. Yet none of their survival suits were available to schooner and trawler fishermen even though this same company produced wet gear and rubber boots for the fishing industry.[23]

The side or "beam" trawler was usually a steel-hulled, steam-powered vessel of British construction. It towed a net that was held open by two "doors". This type of gear was originally known as a "beam" trawl but had been modified for efficiency to become an "otter trawl".[24] The net of the otter trawl was set out, usually over the starboard side of the fishing vessel,[25] while it steamed port side to the wind. After the net was played out, the doors were let down, and the two ground warps — wire ropes or cables attached to the wings of the net — were let out at a distance that would permit the net to be towed along the bottom. After

---

21 Personal Interview with Loraine Weagle, schooner fisherman 1920-1927, Dayspring, Nova Scotia, July 1987.

22 *Progress-Enterprise*, 17 March 1920.

23 Unpublished "Background Testimony" to the *Royal Commission Investigating the Fisheries of the Maritime Provinces and the Magdalen Islands* (Ottawa, 1928), MG 6, vol. 7, p. 2610, Public Archives of Nova Scotia (PANS).

24 Ralph F. Symonds and Henry O. Trowbridge, *The Development of Beam Trawling in the North Atlantic* (Quincy, Mass., 1947), pp.2-5.

25 When on board a vessel and facing the bow "starboard" is the right side of the vessel and "port" the left side.

about two hours the crew hauled back the net using the huge winches on board to haul in the ground warps.[26] Then, two crew members knocked the pin out of the towing block which held the ground warps together near the aft gallows. Once this pin was removed the "doors" of the trawl were hauled up and the net was pulled aboard by hand until the wings and belly of the net were on board. A large strap was placed around the funnel shaped end of the net, known as the "cod end", and a hook attached to a wire cable, known as a "jilson", was placed through the large strap wrapped around the cod end and winched aboard. The knot in the cod end was then untied, and the fish dumped in the fish pens on board the deck of the trawler. The knot was then retied and the net reset over the side. This whole procedure of "hauling back" the trawl was done while the vessel was "side on" to the wind with the port side of the vessel in the wind and the starboard side in the lee.[27] In calm weather this procedure worked well. But in stormy weather, or while there was a considerable "swell" on, working on deck and hauling back the trawl were dangerous tasks. The cod end would swing back and forth in the air, usually with 2-3000 pounds of fish inside. The crew would scramble around on deck trying to control the net to get it lowered on deck and dumped. At the same time there was always the possibility (on a vessel broadside to the wind) of a wave coming in over the side and washing one of the crew members overboard.

A vivid sense of the fishermen's precarious work world emerges from newspaper accounts in the years 1915-1920. The number of vessels sinking, in trouble, running aground, or breaking down is staggering.[28] There are regular reports of persons being washed overboard, or crushed by cargo, and the loss of human life appears to have been accepted as part of the life of a sailor. Only with the large disasters, such as a large vessel going down with all hands, was there any outcry. Despite the dangers they faced, offshore fishermen in Nova Scotia initially did not receive coverage under the 1915 Workmen's Compensation Act because of a legal technicality; even though they were working for Nova Scotia employers, they were not working on Nova Scotia soil. The provincial government finally extended coverage to fishermen by passing an amendment in May 1919 stating that an employee-employer covenant made in Nova Scotia could permit the Compensation Act to apply beyond the province's borders.[29] This decision must

---

26 Frederick William Wallace, *Roving Fisherman (an Autobiography)* (Gardenvale, P.Q., 1955), pp. 310-32.

27 Personal Interviews with Ned Ingram, North Sydney, August 1987; Gerald Collins, Mulgrave, July 1987; and Lewis Riggs, Louisbourg, August 1987; all trawler fishermen who fished on side trawlers.

28 *Herald, Record* (Sydney) and *Progress-Enterprise*, November — April, 1915 to 1920. According to Jack Zinck in *Shipwrecks of Nova Scotia*, Vol. II (Hantsport, 1977), there were at least 83 schooners, ranging from 10 to 725 gross registered tons, and 24 other vessels of various types lost during this period.

29 Section 8 (8,a), Workmen's Compensation Act of Nova Scotia, *Statutes of Nova Scotia* (Halifax,

be understood as resulting from the general pressure from labour in the province, since the fishermen themselves had little power to affect government decisions.[30] Perhaps the Nova Scotia legislature was also influenced by the fact that the fishing fleet of Gloucester, Massachusetts, went on strike in July 1919, and activists from Gloucester had been in touch with fishermen in Yarmouth.[31]

The Nova Scotia Workmen's Compensation Act was essentially an insurance program. The Workmen's Compensation Board set insurance rates, based on the amount of risk, by type of industry or employment. These were known as sub-classes. The thinking behind creating these sub-class divisions was that they would act as an incentive for employers in a particular industry to provide a safer work place since by reducing the number of accidents the assessment rate was reduced.[32] In the fishing industry however, this concept was totally ignored and the vessel owners did not attempt to make their vessels any safer than they had been prior to their industry coming under Workmen's Compensation.[33]

In 1921 an amendment made to the Workmen's Compensation Act set the maximum yearly compensation for fishermen covered under the act at 55 per cent of $780 or $429 per annum,[34] considerably less than the figure of 55 per cent of $1200 per year, or $660 annually, which was the maximum set for workers in all other industries.[35] Despite these lower amounts of compensation, the numbers of men dying or suffering injury in the fishery caused the rates in that sub-class to be high ($5 for every $100 of wages paid). From 1920 to 1925, 54 people in the fishing sub-class died on the job. Another 123 were temporarily disabled and 13 were permanently partially disabled.[36] Following the 1926 gale, the considerable payments made to the families of the Nova Scotians who died or were injured

---

1919), ch. 61, pp.261-5.

30 At the same time the Nova Scotia Government was passing this amendment, both Halifax and Amherst were in the middle of major strikes (in Amherst it was a general strike) and the Winnipeg General Strike was in progress.

31 *Herald*, 26 July 1919.

32 David S. Beyer, *Industrial Accident Prevention* (Boston, 1917), p. 2.

33 Interview with Lewis Firth, Lunenburg schooner fisherman, Written Transcript, Fisheries Museum of the Atlantic; personal interview with Loraine Weagle, Dayspring, Lunenburg County, retired schooner fisherman; personal interview with Ellsworth Greek, Blue Rocks, Lunenburg County, retired schooner and scallop dragger fisherman.

34 The reasons for the amendment to the Workmen's Compensation Act reducing the amount of compensation for fishermen is not clearly spelled out, but it is probably a reflection of declining salt fish prices on the international market which in turn greatly reduced fishermen's incomes.

35 These ceilings for determining the amount of compensation were challenged in the courts in 1930; the County Court found in a fisherman's favour, but the Supreme Court of Nova Scotia overturned the ruling and found for the company and the lower rate of compensation. Maritime Fish Company vs Cohoon, *Dominion Law Reports*, 1 (1930), pp. 809-13.

36 Workmen's Compensation Board of Nova Scotia *Annual Reports* (Halifax, 1917-1925).

severely depleted the funds of the Board for the sub-class.[37] In January 1927, therefore, the Workmen's Compensation Board announced sharply increased insurance rates for the fishing industry. The rate announced was 10 per cent or $10 for every $100 of wages paid, twice what it had been the previous year.[38]

The vessel owners and the captains reacted swiftly. Within two weeks of the announcement by the Workmen's Compensation Board, the vessel owners organized meetings with the provincial government. They argued that, since it was not compulsory for them to participate under the Workmen's Compensation Act, they would stop doing so and threatened to tie the vessels to the wharves in Lunenburg and leave them there until the Workmen's Compensation Board lowered its rates.[39] In the face of this opposition the government gave in and guaranteed that the compensation rate for 1927 would remain at five per cent, still one of the highest for any industry.

Although it had given way to the pressure from the vessel owners on rates, the provincial government decided to appoint a Royal Commission on 29 June 1927, to investigate the Workmen's Compensation Act as it applied to offshore fishermen and lumbermen.[40] This investigation was underway when the disaster of August 1927 occurred. Despite the scale of this disaster, the Commission on fishermen's compensation remained out of the public eye until 12-13 October 1927 when it convened a single hearing in Lunenburg. The chairman of the Commission was Carl D. Dennis, an accountant from Amherst, who appears to have had no previous experience in the fishing industry and no prior experience with the Workmen's Compensation Act. According to his report, several groups appeared before the Commission, including a group representing vessel owners and captains from Lunenburg, but no representations were made on behalf of the crews of the Lunenburg schooner fleet. No ordinary crew member of any offshore vessel appeared before the commission to give testimony. In his report Dennis remarked on this anomaly, but he put it down to a lack of interest on the part of the crew members.[41]

The vessel owners and captains, plagued by uncertain prices and the loss of six vessels and 138 men in the two big storms, told Dennis at the Lunenburg hearing that if they were not removed from the Workmen's Compensation Act they would close down the industry in Lunenburg and go out of business, as they could not

37 Workmen's Compensation Board of Nova Scotia, *Annual Report* (Halifax, 1926), p. 8.

38 *Progress-Enterprise*, 26 January 1927.

39 It is questionable whether the owners could challenge the authority of the Workmen's Compensation Act of Nova Scotia, particularly Section 3, and Section 8(3), to determine if participation was compulsory. *Progress-Enterprise*, 9 February 1927.

40 Carl D. Dennis, *Royal Commission on Ratings of the Lunenburg Fishing Fleet and the Lumber Industry as Applied by the Workmen's Compensation Board* (Halifax, 1927).

41 Dennis, *Royal Commission on Lunenburg Fishing Fleet*.

afford to pay the rates set by the Board.[42] Dennis sympathized with the vessel owners and captains. Although he recognized that fishing, as practiced aboard the schooners from Lunenburg, was a dangerous occupation, his recommendations indicated his basic ignorance of the underlying concepts of worker's compensation by pointing to a lack of willingness on the part of the fishermen to pay some of the cost and querying why employers paid the full rate. He emphasized that other maritime countries had not included fishermen under worker's compensation, but there is no evidence which countries were examined or what consultations, if any, were held with individuals in other countries. He completely ignored questions of safety and accident prevention, two of the pillars in the philosophy behind the thinking of the Workmen's Compensation Act. From the newspaper accounts of the Commission hearings, it seems apparent that the Nova Scotia Accident Prevention Association (the group charged with developing health and safety policy for the province) never made any submissions on possible steps to improve health and safety on fishing vessels, and there is no reason to believe that the Royal Commission ever attempted to solicit a submission from the association. No one raised the issue of placing proper fire-fighting or life saving equipment on board the vessels.

With such a cursory and one-sided investigation, the findings were predictable. When the report was released in December 1927, it recommended that the fishing industry be relieved of the deficit run up by the fishing sub-class and the high rates the accident record would require under Part I of the Act. Dennis recommended that the Workmen's Compensation Board set a rate of 11 per cent of wages paid for the fishing sub-class, and noted that Lloyd's of London would offer a scheme at this rate.[43] He assumed that over a period of eight or nine years of low accident rates the deficit in the fishing sub-class would be eliminated, and the rate would be permitted to drop. In reaching this conclusion, Dennis accepted the evidence of the Lunenburg captains and vessel owners, who had stated in their brief to the commission that the disasters of 1926 and 1927 were unusual, and had not occurred in the 40 years previous. In fact, while the "natural" disasters themselves were unusual, because of the considerable loss of life in a very short time period, the records of the Workmen's Compensation Board show that the incidence of injury and loss of life in the fishing industry had been high even before these disasters.[44]

In January 1928, the Workmen's Compensation Board announced the insurance

---

42 *Herald*, 20 January 1928.

43 Dennis, *Royal Commission on Lunenburg Fishing Fleet*.

44 Between 1920 and 1925 there were 162 injuries and 54 deaths in the Nova Scotia offshore fishery as recorded by the Workmen's Compensation Board. The rate set by the Compensation Board for this period was five per cent ($5 for every $100 of wages). This was a high rate for worker's compensation in any occupation.

rate proposed for the fishing sub-class for that year. True to its philosophy of setting rates that reflected the level of risk to the worker in the industry, the Board determined the necessary rate to be $20 per $100 of wages paid, or 20 per cent. The recommendation of the Board was much higher than Dennis' because the rate by the Board reflected what the safety record of the fishing industry had been and what premiums the industry needed to pay to get the kind of insurance coverage provided by the Board. According to the model of worker's compensation adopted by other industries such an increase should supply the economic incentive for the industry to provide a safer workplace.

The Lunenburg captains and owners reacted as they had a year earlier and in their submission to the Dennis Commission. They stated that the rates were too high to afford, and threatened once again to leave their vessels tied to the wharves. Given the importance of the fishing industry to the economy of Lunenburg County, the captains and the owners could count on the support of local politicians, who were closely connected with the industry. The vessel owners' lobbying group included the provincial Member of the Legislative Assembly for the riding, W.H. Smith, and the federal Member of Parliament, W.G. Ernst.[45] The government responded quickly. After meeting with the captains and the owners, on 30 January 1928 the provincial government agreed to a scheme apparently recommended by the vessel owners under which compensation for fishermen would be provided by a private insurance company. In a letter from Premier E.N. Rhodes to M.M. Gardner of Lunenburg, who represented the captains and vessel owners, the provincial government outlined the steps it was prepared to take. The government would enact a law removing the fishing industry from the operation of Part I of the Workmen's Compensation Act, but making compulsory the purchase of insurance up to a maximum liability of $50,000 or $60,000 per vessel. The rate for vessel owners would remain fixed at 5 per cent, and the government would pay any additional amount necessary to purchase insurance. In addition, the vessel owners were to be released from the obligation to repay the deficit already built up with the Compensation Board.[46] These recommendations were passed into law in March 1928. Although still covered by the Workmen's Compensation Act, offshore fishermen were now placed under a new section of the Act, Part III, which provided that instead of the Workmen's Compensation Board setting the rates, collecting the premiums, and paying the claims, a private insurance company would assume these duties.[47] No other group of workers in Nova Scotia was subjected to such treatment.

---

45 *Herald*, 20 January 1928.

46 *Herald*, 30 January 1928.

47 Workmen's Compensation Act, Part III, Sections 91-120, *Statutes of Nova Scotia* (Halifax, 1928), ch. 42, pp. 182-92.

This decision placed fishermen in a position where they were outside whatever public scrutiny the Workmen's Compensation Board could provide, and yet were denied the opportunity to sue the vessel owners through the courts for unsafe conditions. Under the new plan fishermen were no longer eligible for burial expenses, medical aid, artificial prosthesis, or the right to rehabilitation.[48] These now became the responsibility of the fisherman or his family. If a fisherman wanted this coverage he could pay for it himself through the Sick Mariners' Fund, a medical insurance plan for mariners.[49] Even more clearly than previously, under the private compensation scheme coverage was limited to those fishermen and their immediate families who were resident in Nova Scotia.[50] Fishermen from Newfoundland who came to Nova Scotia to work on the offshore fleet but whose families remained at home were excluded. Although a fisherman or his family had the right to appeal decisions concerning eligibility or the amount of an award, the system was stacked against them. County Court Judges heard such cases and acted as arbitrators.[51] A fisherman wishing to appeal an award faced the daunting choice of hiring an expensive lawyer or presenting the case himself. A financially insecure fisherman in an isolated fishing village might well find it difficult to obtain access to a lawyer and even if he did, his chances of affording such legal aid were slim.

In general, inadequate as compensation had been for the fishermen under the Workmen's Compensation Board, their coverage and the difficulty of getting an impartial hearing for claims was worse under the private scheme. Vessel owners or managing owners had a direct interest in keeping the rates low and their expenses down; reducing awards meant reducing costs. Fishermen who attempted to challenge the decisions of the insurance company faced the possibility of blacklisting. The interests of the vessel owners took precedence over any interests that might be expressed on behalf of the fishermen within this private structure. Thus, privatization of the insurance scheme relieved the vessel owners from any heavy costs resulting from death or injury to fishermen. Moreover, additional

48 Terms and Conditions of 1928 Private Insurance Policy from William Currie Agencies Ltd., F. E. Zwicker Papers, Section (H), MS 4, 37, File 319, Dalhousie University Archives.

49 A holdover from the days prior to Confederation, the Sick Mariners Fund was initially a medical aid plan for all injured seamen. Administered after Confederation by the Department of Marine and Fisheries, after 1945 it was transferred to the Department of National Health and Welfare.

50 Terms and Conditions of 1928 Private Insurance Policy from William Currie Agencies Ltd., F.E. Zwicker Papers, Section H, MS 4, 37, File 319, Dalhousie University Archives.

51 "Maritime Fish Corporation vs Cohoon" in *The Labour Gazette* (April 1930), pp. 475-6. The case of Maritime Fish Corporation vs Cohoon best exemplifies how the system worked. Cohoon appealed a decision on worker's compensation to the County Court Judge in Antigonish. The Judge found in his favour. The Maritime Fish Corporation appealed the decision to the Supreme Court of Nova Scotia and had the County Court Judge's decision reversed.

subsidies were provided by the government to the vessel owners with this change. The debt that had been incurred by the fishing industry to the Workmen's Compensation Board as a result of claims exceeding premiums over the previous seven years, amounting to $357,680, was written off. The provincial government further subsidized the Lunenburg fleet by a direct payment of $13,690 from the Provincial Treasury in1928 to William Currie Agencies Limited of Halifax, a private insurance company.[52] This subsidy was geared specifically to the 74 vessels of the Lunenburg fleet — no other vessels involved in the offshore fishery in Nova Scotia, such as the side trawlers or the schooners from ports outside of Lunenburg, were included.[53] Although a private insurance company now judged the validity of the claims, the Workmen's Compensation Board was still used to register claims, and the Board's forms were used.[54] The work completed by the Board was done without fees levied against either the employers or the private insurance companies. How this practice was justified inside the Workmen's Compensation Board is not clear, but it constituted another form of government subsidization of the private insurance plan.[55]

The *Halifax Herald*, in an editorial on 30 January 1928, cited the decision taken by the Provincial Government to remove fishermen from Part I of the Workmen's Compensation Act as "Solving a Problem".[56] Although this editorial was written in the aftermath of the greatest single disaster to occur in the history of the offshore fishing industry in Nova Scotia, it did not see that the problem was to make the vessels safer, but emphasized the need to keep the fleet fishing. There is no record of any formal inquiry into health and safety conditions on the vessels. Radios for communication with the land were placed aboard the schooners after this disaster but this was technology that had been available and in use in the fishing industry for the previous 15 years.[57] Instead of examining the causes for

---

52 The private insurance plan operated through large insurance companies known as Protection and Indemnity Associations ("P" and "I" Clubs) in Britain, associated with Lloyds of London, and initially represented in Nova Scotia by William Currie Ltd. of Halifax. After many complaints of this company's inefficiency the Lunenburg vessel owners replaced it in 1932 with the Lunenburg Fishermen's Mutual Relief Association, organized and run by the owners themselves. Correspondence between Zwicker and William Currie Agencies, F.E. Zwicker Papers, Section (H), MS 4, 37, File 357, 376, Dalhousie University Archives.

53 *Public Accounts of Nova Scotia 1927-1928*, pp. x-xi, Legislative Library, Province House, Halifax, Nova Scotia.

54 Correspondence from Workmen's Compensation Board to E.H. Armstrong, 13 September 1929, E.H. Armstrong Papers, MG 2, vol. 7, F2/2094, PANS.

55 Correspondence from Workmen's Compensation Board to E.H. Armstrong, September/ October 1929, E.H. Armstrong Papers, MG 2, vol.7, F2/ 2094, 2108, 2111, 2113, PANS. Workmen's Compensation Board form with the name of William Currie's Agency typed in on the form, F.E. Zwicker Papers, Section (H) MS 4, 37, File 319, Dalhousie University Archives.

56 *Halifax Herald* editorial, 30 January 1928, E.N. Rhodes Papers, MG 2, vol. 635, No. 32006, PANS.

57 One of the causes for the Newfoundland sealing disaster of 1914 is attributed to the failure of all

the disaster, the provincial government and the Lunenburg vessel owners developed rationalizations which not only explained away its occurrence but also relieved the fishing industry of any burden of responsibility.

The Nova Scotia government, in its privatization of compensation and neglect of safety in the fishing industry seems to have hoped responsibility for safety measures in the fishery would be assumed by the federal government. In the 1928 Speech from the Throne the provincial government stated that "it is their expectation that the federal government will assume the full burden of their responsibility which arises out of its jurisdiction over and control of the fisheries".[58] This optimism arose out of the appointment of the 1927 MacLean Royal Commission by the federal government to investigate problems in the East Coast fisheries.[59] Although the MacLean Commission held meetings all over the Maritimes, it was mainly concerned with the inshore fishery and heard testimony from only offshore fishing captains; no crew member from any offshore vessel gave testimony before the Commission. But since the Commission was conducting its hearings at the same time as the controversy over the rates for worker's compensation for the fishing sub-class, both the vessel owners and captains from Lunenburg and the provincial government made representations. However, when the MacLean report was released in 1928, it stated that the question of federal jurisdiction for workers' compensation for fishermen was outside its mandate. The hope of the provincial government that the federal government would take the problems of both safety and an adequate compensation system for fishermen off its hands was never to be realized. In fact, neither the federal nor provincial government were prepared to take responsibility for ensuring reasonable compensation or safety standards for fishermen. Privatization moved the issue away from public attention and provided both governments with a method of evading their responsibilities. Fishermen were to remain in this situation for another 43 years,until 1971, when as a result of a commission of enquiry and the local organizing efforts of British Columbia's United Fishermen and Allied Workers Union, they were once again placed under Part I of the Workmen's Compensation Act.

In part the Nova Scotia government's attitude indicates how much the state was willing to do for private interests, particularly the Lunenburg fish companies who could mount a strong political lobby. Yet one must also consider the generally depressed economy of Nova Scotia, the rapid decline of manufacturing in the province after World War I, and the subsequent high rates of unemployment, poverty, and outmigration. Between 1919 and 1926 there was a consider-

sealing vessels to carry wireless radios. See Cassie Brown, *Death on the Ice* (New York, 1972).

58 Parts 10 and 11 of the text of the Speech from the Throne of the Third Session of the 38th General Assembly, Province of Nova Scotia, E.N. Rhodes Papers, vol. 625, no. 16, PANS.

59 *Herald*, 14 October 1927.

able loss of jobs in the province, as industries shut down or relocated elsewhere.[60] In Cape Breton, the determination of the British Empire Steel and Coal Corporation (BESCO) to cut wages had resulted in numerous strikes in the coal mines. Given the precarious state of coal mining, an industry on which the provincial government relied heavily for revenue, a crisis in another industry was something the province could not afford at this point.[61]

Moreover, the fishing economy of Nova Scotia was in decline after 1920. Ruth Fulton Grant in *The Canadian Atlantic Fishery* points out that the price for a quintal (112lbs.) of dry salt cod declined from a high of $10.30 in the period 1916-1920 to a low of $3.50 a quintal in 1932.[62] Internationally there was a decline in the price of salt fish, which in turn led to fierce competition in the international market. Countries such as Iceland and Norway, which had socialist governments and which had introduced economic planning into their fisheries, were able to supply consistently high quality products drawing top dollar on the market. Nova Scotia fish merchants rejected any such "socialistic" approach and continued to apply 19th century free-enterprise methods, which consisted mainly of undercutting each other on the international market. To maintain profit margins, the lower prices the merchants received were compensated for by the lowered amount they gave to the primary producers, the fishermen.[63] Since these merchants were almost always the owners of the offshore fishing vessels, they had little incentive to improve the technology or the safety conditions on these vessels. As long as they could, they clung to the old ways, and the costs of the fishery were borne by the ordinary fishermen. Because their power in the fishing communities met few challenges, these merchants and schooner owners were not forced to find ways of rationalizing the industry or increasing efficiency.

Offshore fishermen lacked the power to influence these decisions. They were hired and fired by either the owner of the vessel or the captain, who acted on the owner's behalf. Each fisherman relied on patronage to ensure gaining "a sight" (a job) on a vessel;[64] thus fishermen as individuals were very much under the economic control of their employers. This was true of workers in most industries, but the degree of dependency of the fishermen was in many respects greater than other workers. The "truck" system still functioned in the inshore industry and many of the components of the social relations of production which existed there prevailed in the offshore industry as well. The economy of

---

60 Ernest Forbes, *The Maritime Rights Movement, 1919-1927* (Montreal and Kingston, 1979), pp. 54-72.

61 David Frank, "Class Conflict in the Coal Industry", in Gregory S. Kealey and Peter Warrian, eds., *Essays in Working Class History* (Toronto 1976), pp. 161-84.

62 Ruth Fulton Grant, *The Canadian Atlantic Fishery* (Toronto, 1934), p.76.

63 *Ibid.*, pp.31-4, 75-7.

64 Wallace, *Roving Fisherman*, p.11.

the inshore industry was characterized by a specific form of unequal exchange between the fish buyer and the fisherman. Credit, at prices set by the merchant, was advanced to maintain the fisherman and his family over the winter. In return the fisherman had to sell the merchant all of his fish at a price also determined by the merchant. The resulting economic relationship allowed the fish merchant to wield far more power than that wielded by capitalists in other buyer-seller relationships.[65] The truck system as it functioned in the offshore fishery similarly entailed strong relations of dependency of the fisherman on the vessel owner. The fish company or vessel owner made credit arrangements with general merchants in the outports to supply the family with supplies while the vessel outfitted for the fishing voyage. After the voyage the fishermen still depended on the merchants' credit over the time between the landing of the fish and its sale in the West Indies or other markets. With a combination of low prices and poor catches, it was conceivable that after a voyage of two or three months a fisherman could wind up making nothing after repaying the merchant. Yet few if any fishermen had any formal education. Fishing was the only employment they knew and in the depressed economic conditions of the 1920s and 1930s, the labour market did not offer much opportunity for better employment.[66] The offshore fishermen in these single-industry communities with the skipper of the vessel or the owner on a strictly one-to-one basis with the captain or the owner always holding the upper hand.[67]

Paternalism, deference, and the lack of commonality nurtured by this system had much to do with the lack of the establishment of any union. At sea the captain ruled supreme and to question or challenge his word was considered mutiny. Fishermen were at sea for weeks at a time, isolated from both their families and fishermen on other vessels. When they arrived in port, they returned home to their families frequently in an outport some distance away from the home port of the vessel. Many of the crew members were from Newfoundland, and at the end of a voyage or several voyages, would return home, sometimes for months. This lack of commonality of residence acted to prevent any common bonds being formed by fishermen on different vessels, and further hindered any attempts to unionize.[68]

65 Unpublished "Background Testimony" to the *Royal Commission Investigating the Fisheries of the Maritimes and the Magdalen Islands*, vol. 8, pp. 2848-9, 2864 in MG 6, vol. 14, PANS. R. Ommer, "All the Fish of the Post", *Acadiensis*, X, 2 (Spring 1981), pp. 107-23; Gary Hughes, *Two Islands: Lameque and Miscou, and their State of Bondage* (Saint John, 1979).

66 Most fishermen who had the chance left for more lucrative, though illegal, employment in the rum running business, in which one could make more money in one month than one could make in a whole year fishing. Personal Interview with Loraine Weagle, dory fisherman and engineer on a rumrunner, Dayspring, Lunenburg County, July 1987.

67 Gene Barrett, "Capitalism and the Fishery of Atlantic Canada", unpublished paper, Saint Mary's University, 1986, pp.33-7.

68 Attempts to unionize fishermen date back to 1905 when the American Federation of Labour

There is a strong contrast between the government reaction to the 1926 and 1927 "August Gales" and the aftermath to disasters in the Nova Scotia coal mines, which were invariably followed by official inquiries and eventually by improvements in safety conditions in the mines and in the compensation available for miners injured or killed on the job. After the August gales of 1926-1927, radios were provided for communications and engines for greater stability, but these changes were entirely voluntary on the part of the fishing vessel owners and captains. For example, there was no government regulation that if a vessel had a radio on board, it had to be working, or even that there had to be someone on board who knew how to use it.

The difference between the mining and fishing industries was surely the existence of a powerful miners' trade union movement that could bring considerable pressure on the government and demand improvements. Without being forced to act by a strong union defending fishermen's interests, the government, like the fish companies, was unwilling to do anything about the backwardness, inefficiency and irrationality in the Nova Scotia fishing industry — the causes of its weakness in the world market. It preferred to preserve the existing conditions in the industry, at the cost of the fishermen of the province. This cost, over many years, not only included very poor remuneration for back-breaking and dangerous work, but also inadequate compensation for death or injury and deplorable safety conditions. It is a sad commentary that even a disaster like the August gales failed to change this reality.

made forays among inshore fishermen in the province. See Robert H. Babcock, *Gompers in Canada* (Toronto, 1974), p.120 and Gene L. Barrett, "Nova Scotia Fishermen's Unions" in Robert Brym and James Sacouman, eds. *Underdevelopment and Social Movements in Atlantic Canada* (Toronto, 1979), pp. 127-60.

M. EARLE AND H. GAMBERG

The United Mine Workers
and the Coming of the CCF to
Cape Breton*

WHEN THE DISTRICT 26 CONVENTION OF the United Mine Workers of America (UMW) in August 1938 voted to affiliate with the Cooperative Commonwealth Federation (CCF), the immediate reaction of the national CCF leadership was one of surprise and suspicion. Surprise because the CCF had almost no organization in Nova Scotia and it had received no advance information concerning this decision.[1] Suspicion because, given the history of Communist Party (CP) influence among the miners, there was some fear that the affiliation might be a CP ploy to infiltrate the CCF. District 26's decision, however, was not the result of a Communist Party scheme, although no opposition was put forward by the party. The CP organization in Cape Breton was weaker than it had been in earlier years, and the late 1930s was a period of relative truce in the long battle between left and right in Cape Breton labour politics and in the internal politics of the UMW. Affiliation with the CCF was supported almost unanimously at the convention, and enthusiastically endorsed by both left and right in the mining communities, who joined in a united front to secure labour representation in federal and provincial legislatures so that the workers might have a voice in the framing of laws and the actions of government. This decision marked a turning point in the direction of labour politics in the Cape Breton area and an important stage in the decline of Communist Party influence in the miners' union. The UMW affiliation led to the election of a CCF federal Member of Parliament and several provincial M.L.A.s, the earliest successes the party had in eastern Canada, and among the few it ever achieved in this region of the country.

The U.M.W.'s affiliation was the first union affiliation to the CCF, and there were few union organizations in Canada who could have provided as much assistance in a locality as the UMW could in Cape Breton. Many later affiliations of unions to the CCF and the New Democratic Party (NDP) have been disappointing in their political results. These affiliations were arranged with union leaders, who could not deliver the votes of the union membership at election time. The District 26 affiliation arose from a rank-and-file initiative, and signalled a mass adherence to the CCF. Therefore the party got enthusiastic election workers and

* Research for this article was assisted by a grant from the Social Sciences and Humanities Research Council of Canada, for which the authors wish to express their gratitude.
1   David Lewis, *The Good Fight* (Toronto, 1981), p. 153.

votes from the union's rank and file in the Cape Breton constituencies, as well as substantial support in money and organization from the District 26 union bureaucracy. Moreover, the affiliation of one of the most powerful unions in Canada greatly strengthened the CCF's influence in the national labour movement.[2] But the affiliation also had an important impact upon the union itself, on inner union politics, the ideology and leadership of the union and the policies of the union movement. Just as the union greatly influenced electoral politics, affiliation with a labour oriented political party interacted with and influenced the nature of the union movement in Cape Breton.

Most political parties of the left have sought connections with trade unions, but there have been differing views on what form the relationship between a union and the party should take. One position is that a trade union is exclusively an organization which regularly attempts to improve the wages and working conditions of members of the union and sometimes supports the economic struggles of other workers, and union efforts to influence government actions or laws should be limited to issues concerning the economic position of the workers or trade union rights. The more political needs of labour ought to be met by the actions of political parties in sympathy with labour's needs, or better yet, a party specifically representing labour's cause. This was the position held by the leadership of the CCF, although not shared by all its grass-roots activists. The party's central focus was always on seeking political power through elections in order to carry out constitutionally acceptable reforms, and union affiliations were sought in order to obtain the votes of the union members, and financial and organizational support for electoral politics. But direct political activity in any other forms by the workers was neither desired nor approved by the CCF leaders, even though they were sometimes obliged to support such activities when they occurred.

At the other extreme is a position which regards a close integration of trade union activity with the party's political program as a necessary and desirable goal, while recognizing that the union and the party must be distinct organizations and that daily demands result in different emphases in policy. Underscoring this theoretical position is a model of society which sees class conflict as permanent and exacerbating, and the only resolution to the problem as total class transformation. Economic struggles of labour are therefore conceived in political terms and, although bread and butter issues are not eschewed by this outlook as somehow trivial or insignificant, the victory or defeat in these issues is interpreted in

---

2   This was particularly true after the formation in 1940 of the Canadian Congress of Labour. In 1942, for example, Clarie Gillis, M.P. from Cape Breton and a UMW member, toured union locals in Ontario seeking affiliations to the CCF. Gad Horowitz, *Canadian Labour in Politics* (Toronto, 1968), pp. 72-3.

terms of how well workers have fared in a process (albeit long) heading to potential accession to political power by the working class. This was the position generally, though not always consistently, upheld by the Communist Party of Canada. Any material gains won for workers by unions under capitalism could only be partial and temporary and the revolutionary transformation required more of workers than their votes. Mass political action would be necessary, and this meant that workers must develop a revolutionary political consciousness. The role of the Communist Party in unions, therefore, was to lead workers in struggles that were primarily economic, to be sure, but also to endeavour in these struggles to educate the workers to the nature of the class conflict and the necessity for proletarian class power.

In North America after the Second World War a form of narrowly economic "business unionism" assumed an almost unquestioned dominance in national labour movements, although it was unlike the earlier "pure and simple" unionism of Samuel Gompers in that it did have fixed alliances with specific political parties, the Democratic Party in the United States and the CCF in Canada.[3] It is often implied that some inevitable social and historical law was at work here, and that modern industrial society invariably develops in a bureaucratic direction in which economic and political institutions, whether of capital or labour, become separate in form and function. The integration of trade unions as institutions playing a specifically defined and limited role within a stable capitalism is regarded as an inexorable result of the industrial process.[4] Yet in the crisis ridden context of the 1930s it was far from clear that the radicals in the labour movement would be defeated. Powerful as were the tendancies and pressures leading unions towards bureaucracy and accomodation with capitalism, their victory was not certain.

The dramatic confrontations of Cape Breton miners and the giant British Empire Steel and Coal Corporation (Besco) in the early 1920s are well known, as is the solidarity that existed within the mining communities during the big strikes against the company's wage cuts.[5] But within the miners' union there was an

3   See Gad Horowitz, *Canadian Labour in Politics* (Toronto, 1968).

4   Still widely influential on this matter is the study originally published in 1915 by Robert Michels, *Political Parties. A Sociological Study of the Oligarchical Tendancies of Modern Democracy* (New York, 1962).

5   On the miners' struggles in the 1920s see: David Frank, "The Cape Breton Coal Miners 1917-1926", Ph.D. thesis, Dalhousie University, 1979; "The Cape Breton Coal Industry and the Rise and Fall of the British Empire Steel Corporation", *Acadiensis*, VII, 1 (Autumn 1977), pp. 3-34; "Class Conflict in the Coal Industry; Cape Breton, 1922", in G.S. Kealey and Peter Warrian, eds., *Essays in Canadian Working Class History* (Toronto, 1976), pp.161-84; Donald MacGillivray, "Military Aid to the Civil Power: The Cape Breton Experience in the 1920s", *Acadiensis*, III, 2 (Spring 1974), pp. 45-64; as well as popular histories: Paul MacEwan, *Miners and Steelworkers* (Toronto, 1976); John Mellor, *The Company Store* (Toronto, 1983).

almost perpetual state of contention between left and right for leadership within the locals and the whole of the district. The left was composed of miners who were militant on union issues and who were often also political radicals, and an influential handful were Communist Party members. The right were moderates who were loyal to the American head office of the UMW and the business unionist principles of International President John L. Lewis. As has often been noted in the history of trade unions, there was a strong tendancy for the elected officers of the district, even those elected as candidates of the left, to develop bureaucratic and right wing outlooks in office. Two noted examples were district presidents John W. MacLeod, elected in 1924, and Freeman Jenkins, elected in 1942; both won office as candidates of the left, and both came to be regarded as extreme right wingers while in office. Alex A. (Sandy) MacKay, the long time district secretary-treasurer and stalwart of the right, was actually a Communist Party member when elected in 1924.

The undoubted leader of the left for many years was J. B. McLachlan, who was deposed from office by John L. Lewis in 1923, and imprisoned for sedition that same year. Because of this he was seen by many as an heroic martyr, as a man who was prepared to suffer for his principles. McLachlan was well known to be a communist, and while he was in office as secretary-treasurer District 26 voted to affiliate with the Red International of Labour Unions (RILU). McLachlan constantly, in his rhetoric, presented the miners' battles with the coal company as part of an irreconcilable class struggle. He called for "100 percent strikes", strikes in which essential maintenance men were withdrawn, raising the threat of flooding and irreversible damage to the mines, and in 1923 he led the miners out on a strike in solidarity with the steel workers in Sydney, demanding the withdrawal of the military from the area. The right wing among the local miners, and the UMW International President John L. Lewis, opposed all of these actions, and during the 1923 sympathy strike Lewis moved, deposing McLachlan and all the rest of the district officers and appointing Silby Barret provisional president of District 26. The sympathy strike violated the UMW constitution and general policy, Lewis claimed, since it engaged the union in a political strike in defiance of governmental authority, and breached a signed contract with the company.[6] The issue was not that Lewis stood for "bread and butter" unionism while McLachlan had wider political motivations. Given the intransigence of the Besco corporation, the employer of both the miners and the steel workers, and the support given Besco by the state, militant and even radical union action was

---

6   John L. Lewis had used an almost identical issue to expel an important rival from the UMW in 1921. This was Alex Howat, the fiery leader of the miners in Kansas, who was deposed for breaking a contract and defying state law, and who also, like McLachlan, was briefly imprisoned. Melvyn Dubofsky and Warren Van Tine, *John L. Lewis, A Biography* (New York, 1977), pp. 115-8.

necessary to hold the line on "bread and butter" issues. Lewis was prepared to neglect the immediate material interests of the union membership in order to uphold the principle that the UMW was a law abiding organization, invariably faithful to its contracts. He was also willing to accept the risk of this or other districts leaving the UMW, rather than weaken his control over the union.

In the early 1920s the militant unionism of J. B. McLachlan certainly had the support of the majority of the miners in Cape Breton, and in the years that followed there was always a strong constituency for political radicalism in the mining towns, particularly the largest of these towns, Glace Bay. But the militancy of the miners and the organizational strength of the Communist Party in the area declined in the late 1920s following the big strike of 1925, when, despite their solidarity, the miners failed to avert substantial cuts to their wages. Bureaucratic and moderate leaders were able to hold the leading positions in the district through these years, although a radical oppositional force always existed in the union, contending for office and influence.

In electoral politics the right wing union leaders tended either to support one or the other of the mainstream parties, or to be moderate labourite reformers. There existed no organized social-democratic party to command their allegiance. In the 1920s local Labour clubs and Independent Labour Party (ILP) branches appear to have been activated only at the time of elections, and then generally to have made a broad labourite appeal calling on workers of all factions to unite behind a labour candidate. The attractiveness of this appeal to the right wing leaders of the UMW was no doubt much less when the candidate put forward was McLachlan or another radical.

In the provincial election of 1920 Farmer-Labour candidates swept the four seats in Cape Breton county, winning 11 seats throughout the province.[7] D. W. Morrison, the mayor of Glace Bay and later the long term right wing president of District 26, was among those elected, and served one term in the provincial legislature. Thereafter, until the victories of the CCF in 1939-1940, no labour candidates were elected, although J. B. McLachlan in his frequent electoral campaigns always made a respectable showing. Until 1935, when McLachlan ran openly as a Communist candidate, the Communist Party and McLachlan almost always attempted to run a united front election campaign, but they could never win the support of the right in the union. From the early 1920s until 1936, however, the Communist Party remained the strongest continually organized force in labour politics in the area, even though the party's numerical strength and the extent of its influence waxed and waned, and it could never succeed in elections or in displacing the right wing leaders of the union.

In the early 1930s the Depression conditions in the mining communities and the lack of effective resistance by the UMW officers to the company's wage cuts

---

7   MacEwan, *Miners and Steelworkers*, pp. 70-1.

led to a widespread communist-led revolt against the international union, and to the formation of the Amalgamated Mine Workers of Nova Scotia (AMW). This breakaway union had the allegiance of a majority of the miners, but with the support of the company and the government the UMW was able to retain a substantial minority of the miners as members. During the early Depression years the Communist Party was in its most radical phase, striving through the Workers Unity League (WUL) to win workers throughout Canada to "revolutionary unionism", and strongly denouncing right wing labour leaders and social-democratic politicians as traitors to the working class.[8]

In 1933, therefore, when the newly formed CCF made its first efforts to win adherents in Cape Breton, Communist Party influence in the area was at a high level, the miners' union movement was split between the UMW and the AMW, and the communist condemnation of the reformist policies of the new party was at its most extreme. The CCF was formally established, with a provisional leadership and program, at the Calgary conference in August 1932. In November two labour Members of Parliament from the West, Angus MacInnis and E.C. Garland, spoke at a meeting in Glace Bay promoting the new party. They were severely heckled by a group of local communists and the meeting ended in a shouting match between MacInnis and J.B. McLachlan.[9] However, in February 1933 a Glace Bay Labour Club was formed and voted to affiliate to the CCF.[10] This was a small organization dominated by those close to the rump UMW district officers; Silby Barret was its president, and "Sandy" MacKay, District 26 secretary-treasurer, was on its executive board. A letter was written to CCF leader J. S. Woodsworth informing him of the new CCF club in Glace Bay and inviting him to come and speak in the area.[11]

This response to the CCF from the right wing leaders of the divided union movement was surely motivated by their anxiety to find a moderate political force to counter the Communist Party in local labour politics. J. B. McLachlan, writing in his weekly newspaper, the *Nova Scotia Miner*, certainly thought so. He denounced the CCF, claiming its affiliated United Farmers government in Alberta was worse in its attacks on workers than were the Grits or Tories. He then assured "CCF High Priest Woodsworth" that the "gang in Glace Bay" were suitable material for the new party:

8   For accounts of the changes in Communist Party policies see Ivan Avacumavic, *The Communist Party in Canada* (Toronto, 1975); Ian Angus, *Canadian Bolsheviks* (Montreal, 1981); William Rodney, *Soldiers of the International* (Toronto, 1968); and Norman Penner, *Canadian Communism* (Toronto, 1988).

9   "Visiting Labor M.P. is Badly Heckled at Meeting Here", *Glace Bay Gazette*, 24 November 1932.

10   *Glace Bay Gazette*, 25 February 1933.

11   J. H. Jamieson to J. S. Woodsworth, 23 February 1933, CCF Papers, MG28 IV1, Vol. 26, Public Archives of Canada [PAC].

They are as fine a bunch as ever diddled a cushy job out of the workers, or usurped their funds, or burned workers' papers, or jailed their leaders, or any of the other distinguishing features of good C.C.F. leaders. In building up the bosses' third party in Canada they ought to appear, if not useful, at least ornamental. They have considerable practice in swindling the working class and can belly crawl to the master better than most.[12]

In June 1933, when Woodsworth came to Glace Bay as part of a tour of Eastern Canada, he had a large and successful meeting, but he faced verbal attacks from McLachlan and other radicals.[13] One Glace Bay miner who was 14 years old at the time later remembered being coached before the meeting to ask Woodsworth if the CCF would be similar in policy to the British Labour Party. When Woodsworth agreed that it would be, McLachlan and others spoke up denouncing British Labour Prime Minister Ramsay MacDonald for selling out the working class.[14]

Shortly after Woodsworth's visit a CCF candidate came forward in Glace Bay for the provincial election held that year.[15] Donald O. "Dawn" Fraser, better remembered as a labour poet than as a politician, did badly in the contest, getting 297 votes compared to the 1734 given J. B. McLachlan, who ran as a "United Front" candidate.[16] Three other labour candidates ran in the Cape Breton area. A miner named John MacDonald campaigned in Sydney Mines under the United Front banner.[17] In New Waterford Tom Ling, the local leader of the AMW, ran as an ILP candidate.[18] In Sydney, steelworker Dan MacKay was nominated as an ILP candidate, but after Woodsworth's visit adopted the CCF platform and name.[19] None of these candidates did as well as McLachlan.[20]

---

12 *Nova Scotia Miner*, 25 February 1933.
13 *Glace Bay Gazette*, 15 June 1933.
14 Interview with Nelson Beaton, Glace Bay, 12 April 1986.
15 This was the election in which the Liberals under Angus L. MacDonald swept to power, taking 22 seats out of 30. *Glace Bay Gazette*, 23 August 1933.
16 The full Glace Bay results were Currie (Liberal) — 3626, Cameron (Conservative) — 3622, McLachlan — 1734, Fraser—297. *Glace Bay Gazette*, 30 August 1933. These are corrected results after a recount requested by McLachlan, who hoped to save his deposit. *Glace Bay Gazette*, 24 August 1933.
17 A third communist or United Front candidate in the province was Joe Wallace in Halifax. *Halifax Herald*, 29 July 1933.
18 Ling defeated Clarie Gillis of Glace Bay, later to become the CCF M.P. for the nomination. *Glace Bay Gazette*, 6 June 1933.
19 *United Steelworker*, 29 April, 15 July 1933.
20 Ling got 587 votes, MacDonald 586, and MacKay 1451. MacEwan, *Miners and Steelworkers*, p. 174.

Ling and MacKay, left-wingers who were not communists and who later were to join the CCF, spoke in support of McLachlan, and opposed Dawn Fraser, an official CCF nominee.[21] M. A. MacKenzie, editor of the left wing paper *United Steelworker* in Sydney, gave some support to the CCF as a national party, but supported McLachlan, as well as MacKay and Ling, locally.[22] At this point the communists were the most influential force in local labour politics. Almost all labour men in the area who were militant in union activities backed the communist-led AMW against the UMW and were prepared to co-operate with the party in political activities.[23]

Dawn Fraser, however, attacked McLachlan and the Communist Party, and was denounced in return.[24] Although Fraser had been nominated by the Glace Bay CCF club, none of the well known UMW leaders seem to have been active in supporting his ineffectual campaign. He also adopted the rather poor tactic of bringing religion openly into the political discussion, and wrote letters to the newspaper arguing that CCF policy exactly fitted Papal encyclicals on labour and other Christian teachings, which was denied by a number of angry reponses, quoting Quebec bishops.[25] In fact, the authorities of the Roman Catholic Church in Canada had come out at this time with statements opposing all forms of socialism, including the CCF, and Fraser only succeeded in drawing attention to this fact.[26] However, he was right in discerning that the Church in the Cape Breton area was moving in a direction that would in the long run help the CCF politically. In an effort to combat the communist influence locally in these desperate early years of the Depression, many of the clergy and other Catholic spokesmen were keen to publicise those Catholic social teachings that were critical of the failings of capitalism. Along with denunciations of the communists as atheists and promoters of violence, frequent explanations were given of the Papal encyclicals *Rerum Novarum* and *Quadragesimo Anno*, as providing Christian answers to the sufferings of the working class.[27]

---

21 Both Ling and MacKay spoke at meetings in support of McLachlan. *Glace Bay Gazette*, 21 August 1933.

22 *United Steelworker*, 20 May, 19 August 1933. This Sydney paper was soon to be renamed the *Steelworker*, and later became the *Steelworker and Miner*.

23 For example, Forman Waye of Sydney, former Labour M.L.A. and later to become a CCFer, spoke in support of McLachlan's campaign. *Glace Bay Gazette*, 21 August 1933.

24 *Glace Bay Gazette*, 9 August 1933.

25 *Glace Bay Gazette*, 21 April 1933; 9 May 1933; 15 May 1933.

26 Gregory Baum, *Catholics and Canadian Socialism* (Toronto 1980).

27 For example the Knights of Columbus sponsored a series of radio broadcasts in 1934 by Rev. Dr. T. O'R. Boyle on these encyclicals. *Glace Bay Gazette*, 9 March 1934. Another indefatigable Catholic anti-communist propagandist was Fergus Byrne, "Labour Editor" of the *New Waterford Times*, whose articles were often reprinted in the *Glace Bay Gazette*. See, for example, "Orderly Reform of Chaos", *Glace Bay Gazette*, 9 January 1933.

The most important form of Catholic social action in the area was the Antigonish Co-operative Movement led by priests from the St. Francis Xavier University Extension Department, in particular Dr. Moses Coady and Fr. Jimmy Tompkins. This movement had begun with work promoting producer co-operatives among fishermen in eastern Nova Scotia, and expanded into industrial Cape Breton in August 1932 when an office was opened in Glace Bay to develop a programme of adult education and the building of credit unions and consumer co-operatives.[28] Alex S. MacIntyre, an ex-communist and the UMW vice-president in the deposed 1923 executive, became the movement's chief organizer in Cape Breton. The central motivation for the Antigonish Movement's concentration on Cape Breton at this time was the wish to defeat communist influence among the miners and other workers.[29] However, its co-operative message, while directly contradicting communist ideas of class struggle and opposing all violence and illegality, was based on a radical sounding critique of capitalism. The evils of capitalism could be overcome when the workers became "masters of their own destiny" through their power as consumers.[30] In opposing communism, therefore, this movement did not promote ideas of a directly conservative or reactionary nature. Instead it put forward a "middle way," the co-operative path to the peaceful transformation of society.

The Antigonish Movement always claimed it was strictly neutral in politics or union affairs, and it never endorsed the CCF. In the early years it could not have done so without defying the hierarchical authorities. But a movement of this type, having the sanction of the Church, did gradually prepare the minds of local Catholic voters, some of whom would never have supported communist or radical labour candidates, to regard the social reformism of the CCF as within the range of acceptable politics. The CCF, for example, was to win the majority of votes in the strongly Catholic New Waterford area in the early war years, a district in which the communists always had relatively few supporters,[31] and many individuals directly involved with the co-operative movement were eventually to become active CCFers.

This religious factor did not help the CCF in its early years, however, and following the 1933 election no CCF organization appears to have survived in the

28 *Glace Bay Gazette*, 19 August 1932.

29 In Sydney in early 1932, at the annual Catholic Rural and Industrial Life Conference, sponsored by the Archdiocese of Antigonish, Alex S. MacIntyre gave an influential speech on the alarming spread of communism among the workers and the Church's weak response. Gregory Baum, "Social Catholicism in Nova Scotia" in Peter Slater, ed., *Religion and Culture in Canada* (Waterloo, 1977).

30 See M.M.Coady, *Masters of Their Own Destiny* (New York, 1939).

31 McLachlan only got 403 votes in New Waterford in 1935; Hartigan (Liberal) got 2836, MacDonald (Conservative) got 634, and D.W. Morrison (Reconstruction) got 674. *Glace Bay Gazette*, 15 October 1935.

Cape Breton area.[32] In the federal election of 1935 Cape Breton South constituency had a four party race, but no CCF candidate. Aside from the Liberal and Conservative candidates, McLachlan ran explicitly as a Communist Party candidate, while D.W. Morrison, the UMW district president, ran for the Reconstruction Party with the support of most of the right-wing in the union movement. Both Dawn Fraser, the former CCF candidate, and Clarie Gillis, who was to win for the CCF in 1940, spoke for Morrison and Reconstruction.[33] In the full constituency, which included Sydney and New Waterford as well as Glace Bay, McLachlan's third place result was better than any labour candidate had achieved since his campaign in 1921. In Glace Bay he did particularly well, coming a close second.[34]

The bureaucratic leadership of the UMW could find little comfort in these election results. In 1933 and in 1935 they had adopted the CCF and the Reconstruction Party in succession, attempting with little success to find a political vehicle which would win the large number of miners who were dissatisfied with the mainstream political parties away from the dangerous ideology of communism. The following of McLachlan and the CP was never large enough to win elections; but it was nonetheless substantial, particularly in Glace Bay, the largest of the mining towns. Militancy on union issues and a drive for rank-and-file democracy in the union movement were given leadership by the communists, and though the coal company and the government upheld the UMW as the recognized union, a majority of the miners of Cape Breton still gave their support to the communist-led AMW.

In 1935, events far from Cape Breton helped to change this situation. Internationally the communist movement, following the rise of the Nazis to power in Germany, adopted the policy of the "Popular Front Against Fascism and War". For the Canadian party this policy meant seeking united action with the CCF, disbanding the WUL and pressing for the unity of the Canadian union movement.[35] In the United States the Committee for Industrial Organization

32 See J.J. Holmes, Sydney, N.S., to J.S. Woodsworth, 7 February 1934, CCF Papers, MG28 IV1, Vol. 26, PAC.

33 *Glace Bay Gazette*, 19 August, 5 October 1933.

34 The results were: Hartigan (Liberal) 10,409; MacDonald (Conservative) 7,335; McLachlan (Communist) 5,365; Morrison (Reconstruction) 5,008. In Glace Bay McLachlan had 28.1 per cent of the vote, while Hartigan received 29.6 per cent. *Glace Bay Gazette*, 15 October 1935. William White, "Left Wing Politics and Community: A Study of Glace Bay 1930-1940", M.A. thesis, Dalhousie University, 1978, pp.183-4, breaks down the vote showing that McLachlan had substantial majorities in working-class wards in Glace Bay.

35 For the CP's policy on unity, both nationally and in Cape Breton, see *Towards a Canadian Peoples Front. Reports and Speeches at the Ninth Plenum of the Central Committee, Communist Party of Canada* (Toronto, 1935).

(CIO) was formed under the leadership of UMW International President John L. Lewis, and Lewis and the UMW acquired a much more progressive and militant reputation and showed a new willingness to permit communists to work within the CIO. By late 1935 the Central Committee of the Canadian CP was strongly urging the return of the AMW miners to the UMW.[36] This pressure and the miners' desire for unity in confrontations with the coal company led to the reunification in early 1936.[37] It seemed a necessary move, since it was apparent that the AMW would never succeed in driving the UMW out of the district. Yet it required the militant miners and the local communists to give up many of their aims for local autonomy and rank-and-file democracy, and to accept, at least outwardly, a good deal of the business unionist principles that the UMW upheld. In fact, communist organizers almost everywhere in North America led shop floor struggles for the new industrial unions of the CIO, and soon communists were to have their greatest influence in the union movement, if this is measured by the number of leading positions in large unions held by Party members. A few major union leaders, most notably John L. Lewis, were now willing to work with communists, at the same time as the communists themselves moved somewhat nearer to the position of the separation of politics from union work, of less emphasis on the class struggle.

The communists justified this change in policy as a necessary reaction to the overwhelming threat of fascism and war, which required unity with social-democrats like CCFers whom they had previously condemned as agents of capitalism. Within the trade unions communists were never again able or willing to argue openly for the integration of class struggle politics with the economic struggle, and Party members often felt forced to conceal or downplay their politics, to become much more conventional union leaders, even to accept with gratitude the defence that they were "good" unionists "in spite of" their CP affiliation.[38] While this new policy may have at least temporarily given the CP

---

36 *Ibid.*, pp. 65, 152-3.

37 *Glace Bay Gazette*, 30 March, 1 April 1936. The miners in Sydney Mines refused to return to the UMW until 1938.

38 The one brief period in which Communists again injected more of the general class struggle into their union work was the during the Second World War before the Soviet Union was invaded by Germany. The changing trade union policies of the Canadian Party are covered briefly in Avacumavic, *The Communist Party in Canada*; and Angus, *Canadian Bolsheviks*. A useful account of the practices of Communists in the leadership of a Canadian union is given in Douglas Neil Caldwell, "The United Electrical, Radio and Machine Workers, District Five, Canada, 1937 to 1956", M.A. thesis, University of Western Ontario, 1979. Accounts of the policies of the America CP are given in Roger Keeran, *The Communist Party and the Auto Workers* (Bloomington, 1980); Bert Cochrane, *Labor and Communism* (Princeton, 1977); James R. Prickett, "Communists and the Communist Issue in the American Labor Movement, 1920-1950", Ph.D. thesis, University of California, Los Angeles, 1975.

greater scope for activities in many places, it led to a serious disruption of its organization and a permanent weakening of its influence in Cape Breton. The rightward move of the party was too much for J.B. McLachlan, particularly with his bitter personal hatred of John L. Lewis and the UMW. He resigned from the Communist Party in 1936, and other local communists followed him. Although McLachlan was in poor health up to his death in 1937, and unable to play a major role in local politics, the CP was never to recover the influence it had held before his resignation. The influence the party did retain in those years was not openly displayed as it had been in the days of the AMW and the Communist candidacy of McLachlan. The United Front policy required party members to seek unity with other forces in the union movement and in labour politics.[39]

From 1936 until CP policy changed in 1939 with the beginning of the war and the Soviet-German Non-Aggression Pact, there was what can be termed a working unity in the Cape Breton labour movement. UMW district officers Morrison, MacKay and Barrett retained their bureaucratic power, but adopted a more militant posture following the lead of their autocratic boss John L. Lewis, president of the CIO as well as the UMW in those years.[40] Silby Barrett was appointed the Steel Workers Organizing Campaign (SWOC) head for Canada by Lewis, and brought the prestige of the UMW and CIO to meetings and rallies of the steelworkers in Sydney for which the shop floor organizing work was done by local communists and militants, notably George MacEachern.[41] The Sydney SWOC committee and the UMW executive also worked together to pressure the Nova

39 The interpretation of McLachlan's resignation from the CP presented here, and indeed the interpretaton of all the events leading to the dominance of the CCF in industrial Cape Breton, differs sharply from the explanation given in most published accounts of politics in Cape Breton in this period. Such writers as White, "Left Wing Politics and Community"; Mellor, *The Company Store*; Terrance D. MacLean, "The Co-operative Commonwealth Federation in Nova Scotia 1938-56", in R.J. Morgan, ed., *More Essays in Cape Breton History* (Windsor, 1977); and Gerry Harrop, *Clarie* (Windsor 1987); all follow Paul MacEwan, *Miners and Steelworkers* very closely on these matters. MacEwan's general argument is as follows: there was never a wide communist influence in Cape Breton, merely a great personal following for J.B. McLachlan; McLachlan brought his followers around to support of the CCF before his death; communist influence thereafter was restricted to a tiny handful of malcontents who fruitlessly opposed the Glace Bay Labour Party and the coming of the CCF; Clarie Gllis and the CCF were fully in the grand tradition of McLachlan and Cape Breton militancy. On all of these points this essay disputes both MacEwan's data and his interpretation.

40 One example of the increased militancy of the UMW district organization was the struggle to organize the miners in Minto, New Brunswick. The strike in 1937-38 was defeated, but the groundwork was laid for the successful unionization of Minto in 1941. See Allan Seager, "Minto, New Brunswick: A Study in Class Relations Between the Wars", *Labour/Le Travailleur*, 5 (Spring 1980), pp. 81-132.

41 George MacEachern's account of the organizing of the steel plant is given in D. Frank and D. MacGillivray, eds., *George MacEachern: An Autobiography* (Sydney, 1987), pp. 61-92.

Scotia government to pass the 1937 Trade Union Act, which helped to bring the union to the Sydney steel plant.

The unity between left and right seems to have been most effective in 1937. Immediately after the passage of the Trade Union Act, the Liberal government called a provincial election. A Labour Party was formed in Glace Bay, and, less than a month before the election, nominated a United Church minister, William Mercer, to contest the seat. James Madden and Fred Brodie, both active communists at this time, were active on Mercer's election committee, as were many other radicals, such as John Alex. MacDonald, former AMW president. This was a real "United Front" campaign, since UMW right-wingers like Silby Barrett were also involved, as were future CCF M.P. Clarie Gillis and M.L.A. D.N. Brodie, along with CP organizer William Findlay.[42] Funds were donated to the campaign by various UMW locals.[43] The Liberal candidate, L. D. Currie, was elected, but Mercer came second, well ahead of the third place Conservative.[44]

Such a result, after a very brief campaign, encouraged the idea that a labour candidate supported by left and right could win. This no doubt made the miners more receptive to the concept of turning to the CCF, although the unity of local militants with the union leaders was soon under strain. Little advance was made in wage settlements for the miners; and the new steelworkers' union could achieve no satisfactory contract with the company for its first few years, while restrained from strike action by the lack of support from the U.S. leadership [45] Local communists, however, clung to the unity policy, refused to openly criticize union leaders, and even defended them from the criticism of militants.[46] The frustrations built up in this period were to lead to an explosion of wildcat strike action in the early war years. They also presumably helped to enhance a desire for political representation in the provincial and federal legislatures that led the miners and the steelworkers to support the CCF enthusiastically.

---

42 *Glace Bay Gazette*, 31 May, 12 June 1937. Paul MacEwan, in his account of the Glace Bay Labour Party, claims "The new party was greeted with enthusiasm ... by all the local opponents of the Grits and the Tories — except the Communists". MacEwan, *Miners and Steelworkers*, p. 189. The newspaper accounts make clear that the communists were among Mercer's most active supporters, as at the culminating meeting of the campaign, when the principal speakers were Mercer, William Findlay the CP organizer, Clarie Gillis, and Silby Barrett. *Glace Bay Gazette*, 25, 26 June 1937.

43 *Glace Bay Gazette*, 11 June 1937.

44 The official returns were Currie (Liberal) 4172, Kerr (Conservative) 2832, Mercer (Labour) 3396. *Glace Bay Gazette*, 7 July 1937.

45 Sydney's independent radical weekly, the *Steelworker*, sharply criticized the steel union executive, including its communist members, during this period. *Steelworker*, 30 July 1938.

46 See, for example, letter from William Findlay, Communist Party organizer, defending the UMW District Executive from various criticisms. *Steelworker*, 11 December 1937.

In 1938 the miners of Glace Bay became extremely concerned about the threat of mechanization in the mines. A new mine was opened through a shaft sunk from the No. 2 mine on the Phalen seam to connect with the parallel Harbour seam. In the new mine the Dominion Coal Company, with the permission of the Nova Scotia government, the regulating authority, planned to install electric cutting machines and electrically operated loading machinery.[47] The militant miners of the Phalen local feared that this was the beginning of the mechanization of all the mines, leading to a massive loss of jobs.[48] The miners refused to operate the new machinery, and the company shut down the new mine, locking out 85 men, who were then supported for months by a levy of 25 cents on all the Glace Bay sub-district miners.[49] At the UMW convention in August 1938 this issue was the hottest item on the agenda. The official policy of the UMW, as expressed in a letter from John L. Lewis and by International Secretary-Treasurer Thomas Kennedy in his speech at the District 26 convention, was that the UMW could not oppose progress in the form of mechanization of mines.[50] The Nova Scotia Minister of Mines and Labour, Michael Dwyer, also spoke at the convention urging the miners to accept the necessity of mechanization.[51] The degree of anger of the miner delegates on this issue, however, forced the district officers to oppose the scheme, not in principle, but as unsafe in the mine concerned and badly timed, given the widespread unemployment.[52] The delegates voted a levy of 10 cents per month on all District 26 miners to support the locked out men, and passed a resolution calling on the government to ban new electrical machinery at the coal face.[53] The miners' resistance was to win a long delay in the extensive mechanization of the mines; the company was forced to shelve plans until after the war.

The Liberal government's role in supporting the company's plans for mechanization helped to convince the miners of the urgency of electing labour representatives to political office. Various resolutions calling for the UMW to support a "Farmer-Labour" party had been sent in to the convention, from the Glace Bay Labour Party and others. James Ling of No. 12 Local in New Waterford put

---

47   *Glace Bay Gazette*, 9 January 1938.

48   This was what eventually happened following the 1947 strike. Mechanization and rationalization reduced the number of men employed in the mines from between 12,000 and 13,000 to approximately 3,500 within a few years.

49   *Glace Bay Gazette*, 9, 10, 13, 24 June 1938.

50   *Glace Bay Gazette*, 16 April, 13 August 1938.

51   *Glace Bay Gazette*, 20 August 1938.

52   See report of speeches by D.W. Morrison and Silby Barrett on this issue, *Glace Bay Gazette*, 12 August 1938.

53   *Glace Bay Gazette*, 17 August 1938.

forward a resolution calling for affiliation of the UMW with the CCF, arguing that a national party was needed to unite labour representatives in Ottawa. On the recommendation of Clarie Gillis, a special convention sitting was called to consider these proposals, to which delegations of the steelworkers, fishermen, co-operatives and others were invited.[54]

At this sitting, on 15 August 1938, the resolution to affiliate with the CCF was adopted almost unanimously.[55] Only Robert Stewart, former secretary of the AMW, soon to be elected Glace Bay Board Member on the UMW District Executive, voted against the resolution. His was not a Communist Party vote against the affiliation, as has been claimed.[56] Stewart had left the party with McLachlan in 1936 and, although he later rejoined, was not a party member at this time. Communists were present at the convention, and not without influence, as is evident from the resolutions passed in support of the Republican government in Spain.[57] Yet the CP members present did not oppose the CCF affiliation. Militants and the district officers, frequently opposed on issues, all spoke in favour of the resolution, and the decision was hailed throughout the Cape Breton mining districts and by labour spokesmen in Sydney. The radical Sydney weekly, the *Steelworker*, editorialized:

> There is a lot of ominous knee shaking in the ranks of the paid political agents of monopoly capitalism as a result of the unequivocal decision of the UMW Convention at Truro to affiliate with the CCF in order to take their rightful place in the political field to defend the rights of labor — both industrial workers and farmers — at the next election.[58]

The wording of the UMW resolution to affiliate with the CCF does not support the view that the miners themselves understood they were thus moving towards more moderate politics. It referred to "a class struggle, between those who possess but do not produce, and those who produce but do not possess", and declared that "The working class must organize...for the purpose of acquiring the power of government, in order that this power may be converted from an instrument of oppression into an instrument for the overthrow of special privilege for the owning class". A convention should be held of all "organizations and groups who were sincerely interested in the bettering of conditions for the working class...for consolidating the different groups into one United Front

---

54 *Glace Bay Gazette*, 11 August 1938.
55 *Glace Bay Gazette*, 16 August 1938.
56 See White, "Left Wing Politics", p. 127.
57 *Glace Bay Gazette*, 23 August 1938. Communists were not alone in supporting the struggle against Franco, but were usually the initiators of solidarity action on this issue.
58 *Steelworker*, 20 August 1938.

for Political Action". [59] This language reflects more the history of the communist influence on the miners than any speeches of CCF leaders like Woodsworth.

But the enthusiasm for the CCF did reveal a changed situation in local labour politics mainly due to the alteration of CP policy in 1936. Support for the CCF, in 1938, from local militants and radicals who had often taken their lead from the communists was not surprising when the reaction of the CP itself is considered. Responding to the UMW affiliation with the CCF, CP national leader Tim Buck, in a Toronto speech, said:

> The historic decision of the Nova Scotia miners is evidence of the fact that tens of thousands of trade unionists all over the country want independent working class political action. They want to unite their forces to defeat reaction on the parliamentary field. .... United action between the Communist Party and the CCF remains one of the vital needs of the labor movement. [60]

John C. Mortimer, an important spokesperson for the CP in Nova Scotia, wrote welcoming the affiliation and claiming his main criticism of the CCF's leaders was their resistance to unity. "I'm expecting the UMW to infuse new blood into Woodsworth's party...to make itself felt, not merely by strengthening the movement for a united front, but by throwing the CCF more completely into the day to day struggles of the working class and all the common folk". [61] The CP was very likely more uneasy about the affiliation than these statements would indicate, but the unity policy left the party no choice but to support the UMW decision at this time. There is also more than a hint in Mortimer's reference to "new blood" that the CP hoped that they could influence the CCF or even get members involved in it locally through the UMW.

However, there is no evidence that the CP had planned the affiliation as a means of infiltrating the CCF, as CCF National Secretary David Lewis at first feared. [62] The leadership of the CCF were determined to prevent any such communist involvement. Lewis, as soon as he heard of the UMW affiliation, wired D.W. Morrison "to greet" the decision, but asked "whether decision supported by rank and file and whether move sponsored by communists or other people". [63] Early in September Lewis met the UMW officers at the TLC convention held in Niagara Falls, and was reassured that the communists were not behind

---

59   Resolution quoted in Stephen MacPherson to D. Lewis, n.d., CCF Papers, MG28 IV1, Vol. 27, PAC.

60   Tim Buck, "Reaction is Advancing — What Must Be Done", *Daily Clarion*, 23 August 1938.

61   *Steelworker*, 27 August 1938.

62   Lewis, *The Good Fight*, p. 153.

63   Telegram, D. Lewis to D.W. Morrison, CCF Papers, MG28 IV1, Vol. 195, PAC.

the affiliation.[64] However, there remained organizational problems and still considerable worry about communist infiltration. The CCF had never previously had the direct affiliation of a union, and the constitution had no provisions that covered this development. In particular, what was to prevent communists being chosen by union locals to represent them in CCF bodies? The miners might well be swayed by the CP united front line. Indeed, the UMW resolution had explicitly called for "one United Front for Political Action", although there was no specific mention of the Communist Party.[65]

To assist in setting up the CCF organization in Nova Scotia, and to ensure that communists were excluded, Lewis and Angus MacInnis, Vancouver M.P. and Woodsworth's son-in-law, made an organizing trip to the area in October. Their visit was highly successful, with many well attended meetings in the mining towns.[66] CCF clubs were set up in the various towns, all with constitutions expressly excluding anyone who was a "member or active supporter of any other political party".[67] Over the protests of its communist members, the Glace Bay Labour Party was disbanded and reformed into a CCF club excluding them.[68] Lewis also quickly put together a set of national by-laws regarding union affiliations that similarly excluded communists for eligibility as union delegates to CCF conventions.[69] Lewis's concern to prevent the election of communist delegates was still evident several months later when the first Nova Scotia provincial convention was being organized. He suggested the UMW be represented by a block delegation appointed by the district executive rather then elected by the locals, on the grounds that this would be "more democratic".[70] The executive decided that this procedure would not be acceptable to the miners, and arranged that the locals elect delegates but that all delegates must be members of a CCF club.[71] A few communists were in fact elected as delegates to the early CCF

---

64 David Lewis and Angus MacInnis, "Report of Organizing Tour Through Nova Scotia and New Brunswick", n.d., John L. MacKinnon Papers, MG 19-11, Beaton Institute, Sydney.

65 Resolution given in Stephen MacPherson to D. Lewis, n.d., CCF Papers, MG28 IV1, Vol. 27, PAC.

66 *Glace Bay Gazette*, 10, 11, 14, 15, 17 October 1938.

67 Glace Bay Central CCF Club Constitution, John L. MacKinnon Papers, MG 19-11, Beaton Institute.

68 *Glace Bay Gazette*, 17 October 1938.

69 Lewis wrote in his report: "It was clearly impossible to consult the members of the National Council [of the CCF] as to these provisions without delaying the affiliation for two or three months, a delay which could have proved fatal. The delegation [Lewis and MacInnis], therefore, took the responsibility of presenting them to the UMW on behalf of the National Council in the conviction that they are in complete accord with CCF policy". Lewis and MacInnis, "Report of Organizing Tour".

70 D. Lewis to D.W. Morrison, 22 April 1939, CCF Papers, MG28 IV1, Vol. 28, PAC.

71 A.A. MacKay to D. Lewis, 29 April 1939, *ibid.*

conventions, but they were turned away at the door.[72] With these prompt and astute moves, and with the co-operation of the UMW executive, David Lewis was able to see that an active and effective CCF organization was set up in Cape Breton, and the local communists were excluded from all participation, although they continued to appeal for unity and pledged support to CCF candidates in elections.[73]

Political enthusiasm for the CCF continued to grow in the area through 1939, with visits from prominent CCF leaders. In February Harold Winch, prominent in the party in British Columbia, spoke to several meetings in Glace Bay; and David Lewis and party leader J.S. Woodsworth attended the first provincial convention of the Nova Scotia CCF, held in Sydney in May.[74] In August a convention was held to nominate a candidate to contest Cape Breton in the next federal election, and when Rev. William Mercer declined, Clarie Gillis was chosen.[75] Before the federal campaign began, however, the CCF scored its first Cape Breton electoral victory.

The Minister of Mines and Labour in the provincial cabinet, Michael Dwyer, had resigned in order to become president of Nova Scotia Steel and Coal Company, a Dosco subsidiary. In the December 1939 by-election called to fill his New Waterford seat, CCF candidate Douglas MacDonald, the UMW District Board Member for the New Waterford sub-district, was victorious.[76] MacDonald's success was a remarkable sign of the political transformation that had taken place in the strongly Catholic New Waterford area, where union militancy and political radicalism had traditionally received less support than in Glace Bay. In the 1933 election, for example, Labour candidate Tom Ling had received only a small vote.[77] In the federal campaign in 1935 J.B. McLachlan also did badly in the New Waterford voting.[78] In 1937 no Labour candidate made the effort to win the provincial seat, and it appears that even the CCF leadership thought Douglas MacDonald had very little chance in the 1939 by-election.[79]

72   H.I.S. Borgford to D. Lewis, 17 August 1939, *ibid.*, Vol. 27.

73   Statement and letter, William Findlay to H.I.S. Borgford, 5 June 1939, *ibid.*

74   *Glace Bay Gazette*, 20 February, 26 May 1939.

75   *Ibid.*, 7 August 1939.

76   *Sydney Post-Record*, 6 December 1939.

77   Ling received 587 votes, while the Conservative candidate got 2969 and the Liberal, Michael Dwyer, got 3263. *Glace Bay Gazette*, 23 August 1933.

78   The New Waterford results were: D.J. Hartigan (Liberal)- 2836; Finlay MacDonald (Conservative) — 634; J.B. McLachlan (Communist) — 403; D.W. Morrison (Reconstruction) — 674. *Glace Bay Gazette*, 15 October 1935. These results are not easy to interpret. Hartigan was a hometown candidate; the Conservative, MacDonald, did very badly; and it is questionable whether Morrison's vote hurt MacDonald's or McLachlan's result.

79   MacEwan, *Miners and Steelworkers*, p. 203.

The Conservatives did not put up a candidate, but the CCF was helped by a split in the Liberal ranks, a candidate who failed to get the Liberal nomination running as an "Independent Liberal".[80] The official Liberal campaign was directed mainly against the CCF, and relied heavily on red scare tactics. Presumably it was believed this would work well in the New Waterford area, particularly in wartime. Liberal advertisements claimed the CCF was rapidly coming under the control of the Communist Party and asked how "any Christian" could vote CCF "after the wanton invasion of peaceful little Finland by the brutal hordes of Communist Russia". "It is an undisputed fact that several avowed Communists are now actively engaged, on public platforms and otherwise, in support of the CCF candidate in this election".[81] The voters, however, seem not to have been swayed by this red-baiting campaign. MacDonald received 3093 votes, the official Liberal 2614, and the Independent 1204.[82]

In the federal election on March 1940, Clarie Gillis was elected M.P. for Cape Breton South by a narrow margin.[83] In this campaign Gillis's opponents did not use the anti-communist rhetoric which had failed in the New Waterford by-election. The Liberals relied on the appeal to keep an experienced government in office that was to win Mackenzie King a national majority in this wartime election.[84] The CCF campaign in Cape Breton was socialistic with patriotic overtones, Gillis claiming that both Liberals and Conservatives "serve capitalism to the disadvantage of the workers", and there was a strong likehood of war profiteering.[85] But the CCF was also determined "to bring the war to a successful conclusion", stated party leader M. J. Coldwell in his speech in support of Gillis.[86] Clarie Gillis was a veteran of the First World War, and had long been a prominent leader of the Canadian Legion in the area.[87] Gillis was a miner who had, up to

80 *Glace Bay Gazette*, 4 December 1939. The official Liberal was J.L. MacKinnon, and the Independent was Francis Stephenson.

81 *Glace Bay Gazette*, 4 December 1939.

82 *Glace Bay Gazette*, 6 December 1939.

83 *Glace Bay Gazette*, 27 March 1940. Gillis was to hold the seat until 1957.

84 See Liberal advertisement, "King and Hartigan are vital for victory", *Glace Bay Gazette*, 18 March 1940.

85 *Glace Bay Gazette*, 12 March 1940.

86 *Glace Bay Gazette*, 11 March 1940. The crisis the CCF faced nationally at the beginning of the war when Woodsworth clung to his pacifist principles had little impact in Cape Breton, where the miners reacted with strong patriotic reflexes to the war. For example, the Secretary of the Glace Bay CCF, John MacDonld, enlisted immediately on the outbreak of war. *Glace Bay Gazette*, 11 September 1939. By contrast, Rev. H.I.S. Borgford, the Nova Scotia Provincial Secretary of the CCF, from Halifax, considered resigning because of the stand the CCF National Council took in support of the war effort. See H.I.S. Borgford to D. Lewis, 17 October 1939, CCF Papers, MG28 IV1, Vol. 27, PAC.

87 *Glace Bay Gazette*, 7 November 1932, 20 March 1933, 19 August 1935.

this time, gained a reputation as a somewhat militant critic of the policies of the union executive, but at the same time showed himself to be an opponent of the more extreme radicalism of the CP.[88] In Glace Bay he received a majority of more than 2000 over the incumbent Liberal, Dr. D. J. Hartigan; and he was able to reduce Hartigan's majority in Sydney to 444, and in New Waterford, Hartigan's home town, to only 300.[89] The final result, after the soldiers' vote was included, was: Gillis (CCF) — 11582; Hartigan (Lib) — 11364; Nunn (Cons) — 9719.[90]

The CCF was able to dominate electoral politics in industrial Cape Breton for years to follow. In the 1941 provincial election CCF candidates won in Sydney, New Waterford and Glace Bay.[91] It is always difficult, if not impossible, to determine precisely the motivations behind the voting patterns of large numbers of people. Yet it seems very probable that these early successes of the CCF in Cape Breton were based mainly on the enthusiastic support of the miners and steelworkers aiming through their votes to help bring about a socialist transformation of society. The CCF could appeal to the radical workers who had supported the communists, and it could also draw in voters ideologically influenced by the Antigonish Movement who would never have voted communist. The CCF in the war years still upheld the Regina Manifesto as its basic political creed, with its call for the eradication of capitalism, "the cancer which is eating at the heart of our society".[92] As the CCF policies became more moderate, the fervour of this working class support in Cape Breton probabably grew less, but for working-class voters the CCF no doubt remained preferable to the Liberals and Conservatives, and the less radical the party appeared, the more it came to attract middle class votes in the Cape Breton area. In provincial elections, the CCF held two of the Cape Breton seats until 1956, and one lasted to 1963.[93] Clarie Gillis increased his majority in the 1945 election, while the CCF national upsurge

---

88 He had, for example, been for a brief time the vice-president of the breakaway AMW, but had never supported McLachlan in election campaigns.

89 *Glace Bay Gazette*, 27 March 1940.

90 *Glace Bay Gazette*, 3 April 1940.

91 Donald MacDonald was elected in Sydney, Douglas MacDonald re-elected in New Waterford, and D.N. Brodie in Glace Bay won a straight contest against L. D. Currie, the Minister of Mines and Labour, by 6191 to 4049, the largest majority in the province. MacEwan, *Miners and Steelworkers*, p. 243.

92 Regina Manifesto, reproduced in M. Cross, *The Decline and Fall of a Good Idea* (Toronto, 1974), p. 23.

93 In the 1945 election, Donald MacDonald was defeated in CB South (Sydney), but Michael MacDonald won CB Center (New Waterford) and Russell Cunningham won CB East (Glace Bay). Both held these seats, with declining majorities, in 1949, and were re-elected in 1953. In 1956 and 1960 only Michael MacDonald in New Waterford was elected for the CCF. He was defeated, running for the new NDP, in 1963.

continued, and held it in 1949, when the CCF lost seats elsewhere.[94] Gillis, in particular, seemed able to attract a wider vote, including many middle class voters. He was on the left of the CCF in Parliament when first elected, but had moved sharply to the right by the post-war period, when he became noted for the virulence of his anti-communism.[95] He probably also gained support locally for his outspoken stands on Maritime rights issues. In 1953 Gillis won his most resounding victory, getting an absolute majority of all the votes cast. He was defeated in 1957, and failed to win re-election in 1958.[96] Clarie Gillis thus remained a successful politician over many years, but the tone of his campaigns in the post-war years was very much less radical than at the time he was first elected. It is therefore apparent that if the working-class electorate in Cape Breton retained much socialist fervour after the war this could find little expression through voting for Clarie Gillis and the CCF.

The Communist Party, when it ran candidates against the CCF at the end of the war, was never able to gain more than a negligible vote.[97] The decision at the 1938 UMW convention, whether the delegates understood this fact or not, had ended any hope of the CP being again a significant independent force in elections, although the communists retained a considerable influence in the local unions of the UMW and among the Sydney steelworkers so long as traditions of union militancy and radicalism, of the class struggle, remained strong. In the 1941 slowdown strike of the miners, the election of a left-wing UMW executive in 1942, and many other labour battles, rank-and-file militancy came to the fore, and local communists were active in the leadership.

Many CCF supporters also demonstrated strong union militancy; but the influence of the CCF leadership was constantly aimed at promoting moderation in union affairs, and an acceptance of the bureaucratic rule of union officials and a purely economic and strictly law abiding definition of what constituted acceptable union activities. The CCF leaders, allied with the international and national leaders of the miners' and steelworkers' unions and with the right-wing of the local unions, were eventually able to purge communist leadership from Cape Breton unions, as they did throughout most of the Canadian union movement. Two landmark final episodes in Cape Breton were the CCF-led

---

94   The CCF percentage of the provincial vote fell from 14 per cent in 1945 to 9.5 per cent in 1949, and nationally, its seats in Parliament fell from 31 to 13. MacEwan, *Miners and Steelworkers*, pp. 249, 278-9.

95   An example of Gillis's public stance of extreme anti-communism was given when he publicized a tavern brawl he supposedly had with a "red" in Ottawa in 1950. *Steelworker and Miner*, 22 April 1950.

96   MacEwan, *Miners and Steelworkers*, pp. 291, 306-8.

97   In 1945 Jim Madden, running for the Labour Progressive Party, got only 854 votes. *Sydney Post-Record*, 12 June 1945.

Sydney steelworkers breaking the Canadian Seamen's Union picket line in 1949, and the bureaucratic red-baiting activities of UMW District President Freeman Jenkins in 1950.[98] As elsewhere in this period, the methods used to smash radical influence did much to undermine democracy in the local unions, and the process also involved centralization of power by the national and international head offices of the unions. Local union bosses such as Ed Corbett, president of the Sydney Steelworkers, and Freeman Jenkins, president of District 26, were under pressure from both the CCF and their union headquarters to clean out communists in the leadership of the locals. The anti-communist role played in unions by the national CCF and by such figures as Charles Millard, Canadian Director of the Steelworkers Union and prominent in the Ontario CCF, is well known. It is, of course, difficult to establish exactly the behind-the-scene role played by CCF national leaders and the top union officials in specific local events. For example, George MacEachern claims Ed Corbett's reversal of policy on the Seamen's strike came after a visit to meet with Steelworkers Union leaders in Ottawa from which he returned in "a terrible nervous state".[99] Similarly, Jenkin's anti-communist coup in the UMW in 1950 was rumoured to be master-minded by Clarie Gillis.[100] Such stories do not provide hard evidence, but are plausible given the prominent role played in those years by CCFers in the central leadership of the union movement in purging communists and CP-led unions throughout Canada.[101]

The CCF as a national party, all commentators agree, had generally much more radical sounding rhetoric and stated purposes in its early years than it did later, particularly after the war.[102] In much that has been written on the CCF the explanation provided for this rightward transformation is that the broadly based CCF "movement" of pre-war years became subordinated to the CCF "party" and its leaders, concerned exclusively with the attaining of political power through elections.[103] In order to have a wider appeal to voters, the CCF moderated its policies and suppressed or purged its radicals. Radicalism, it is added, came mainly from the CCF clubs, filled with socialist intellectuals, and

---

98 For brief accounts of these events, see MacEwan, *Miners and Steelworkers*, pp. 275-6 and 281-4.

99 Frank and MacGillivray, eds., *George MacEachern*, p.135.

100 Interview with John Roach, Stellarton, July 1984.

101 See Irving Abella, *Nationalism, Communism and Canadian Labour* (Toronto, 1973).

102 See Cross, *The Decline and Fall of a Good Idea*, for documentary evidence of the CCF's move to the right.

103 The movement to party thesis is presented in full force in Leo Zakuta, *A Protest Movement Becalmed: A Study of Change in the CCF* (Toronto, 1964); but similar ideas are expressed in Walter D. Young, *The Anatomy of a Party: the National CCF* (Toronto, 1969).

the alliance of CCF party leaders with union leaders aided this process of moderating the CCF's image and outlook.

In the miners' and steelworkers' unions in Cape Breton, it was more a matter of the CCF helping ensure the victory of the right wing. If the unions became a right wing influence on the CCF and the later NDP, CCF influence had helped to create a union movement that would play this role.[104] Overall, it is difficult to apply the 'movement to party' thesis to the CCF in Cape Breton, where radicalism was not introduced to the miners by CCF movement intellectuals, but was widespread among union members before the CCF came on the scene. The CCF in Nova Scotia faced the insoluble problem that while socialist rhetoric could win elections in industrial Cape Breton, it had no power to draw votes throughout the remainder of the province. Unlike the farmers of the West, people in the rural areas of the Maritimes never responded to the CCF appeal. The efforts to moderate the party's platform in the post-war years did nothing to improve its electoral performance in other parts of Nova Scotia, and, if anything, gradually undermined its support in Cape Breton. The miners had called in the CCF as a vehicle for seeking political power through elections to supplement their militant union activity, as well as to move towards the more distant and vague political aim of a socialist society. The party leaders, to appeal to a broader electorate, moderated the party platform and sought to prove themselves as anti-communist as anyone in the Cold War era. They also acted to moderate union activity, restrict it to purely economic matters, and allied themselves with the bureaucrats and business unionists in the union movement. In Cape Breton it was not a matter of a broad movement becoming a narrow party, but of what type of party this was from its beginning. It may have moved to the 'right', but its national leaders were never very 'left' at any time. As one recent commentator on the 'movement to party' thesis on CCF history has pointed out, all political parties need not be defined as organizations subordinating all else to striving for electoral victories.[105] Communist parties, in some periods, provide one example of parties emphasizing, more highly than elections, general social change and the creation of 'revolutionary class consciousness' through union struggles and other mass activity. To show that the CCF always concentrated on elections

---

104 This is probably true in other centres of local militant industrial unionism. For example, in 1948 Bob Carlin of the Mine, Mill and Smelter Workers in Sudbury was purged from the CCF for "appeasing" communists in his union, although he had won the Sudbury seat in the provincial legislature for the CCF in 1943 and 1945. Abella, *Nationalism, Communism, and Canadian Labour*, pp.100-1.

105 Alan Whitehorn, "An Analysis of the Historiography of the CCF-NDP: The Protest Movement Becalmed Tradition", in J. William Brennan, ed., *'Building the Co-operative Commonwealth' Essays on the Democratic Socialist Tradition in Canada* (Regina, 1985).

almost exclusively is to characterize it as basically a liberal-reformist party with very little socialism or radicalism in its essential nature.

It certainly cannot be asserted that CCF political ascendancy was entirely responsible for the lessening of the militancy of the workers of industrial Cape Breton. The industries of the area, the mines and the steel plant, were in drastic decline in the years that followed the war. The 1946 strike of the steelworkers and the 1947 coal strike were the last large scale militant actions the workers of the area could mount for many years. While much of Canada entered into the economic boom of the 1950s, economic stagnation and declining employment was the lot of industrial Cape Breton. These were not conditions that were propitious for militant unionism. Nevertheless, the long history of union battles in Cape Breton might raise an expectation that the miners, in particular, would not accept with quiet resignation the rationalization of their industry and the loss of so many jobs in the early 1950s. But leadership is important, sometimes even decisive, in the development of political and social movements, and in Cape Breton there was no longer leadership able to give radical form to the discontent of the miners. The communists had been defeated and the political leadership of the CCF pressed for moderation and co-operation with the company in increasing productivity, not militancy. In its published manifesto during the 1953 election campaign the CCF called for "Labour policies to promote understanding and teamwork between employer and employees in a *program for greatly increased production* [emphasis in original], making it possible for the employees to share in the increased wealth produced".[106]

Thus by the 1950s the class struggle unionism that Cape Breton had seen in earlier years was only a memory, and the political leadership of the CCF had helped to undermine radicalism and union militancy in the area. The acceptance of the political leadership of the CCF in 1938 can be seen as an indication that political radicalism was already in decline among the workers of Cape Breton. This is certainly partly true. The radical leadership many had followed, the CP, had itself adopted much less radical policies; and the ideological opposition to radicalism represented by the Antigonish Movement most probably had considerable effect. But many of the class conscious miners who welcomed the CCF to Cape Breton in 1938 and 1939 had far more radical aims than did the leadership of the party they supported. In both the union movement and the general political field the CCF, as an organization, was a force for moderation, for a lessening of class struggle, in Cape Breton.

106 CCF Manifesto Nova Scotia Election 1953, CCF Papers, MG28 IV1, Vol. 28, PAC.

MICHAEL EARLE

"Down with Hitler and Silby Barrett": The Cape Breton Miners' Slowdown Strike of 1941

THROUGH THE SUMMER OF 1941 THE virulently anti-union Toronto *Globe and Mail* published a series of editorials fulminating against the slowdown strike being conducted by the coal miners of Cape Breton. In July the paper denounced "the sheer pusillanimity" of federal Minister of Labour Norman McLarty in dealing with this "crystal clear case of deliberate sabotage of the national war effort" and by the end of August the editor was exhorting the government to "send in the troops now and end the grotesque and indefensible situation at the Cape Breton coal mines".[1] The slowdown began on 11 May and was called off on 28 September 1941, after something over 90 working days, during which the approximately 7,500 Glace Bay and New Waterford miners produced about two thirds normal output.[2] The 1500 miners of Sydney Mines took part in the slowdown for only one month, or about 20 working days. By a quick estimate, if the slowdown was regarded as a full strike involving only one third of the men, the working days lost would be approximately 235,000. For the five month period of May to September 1941 Nova Scotia's total coal production was over 600,000 tons less than for the corresponding months in 1940.[3] Although this was one of the most costly labour disputes that occurred in Canada during the Second World War it has received little attention in what has been written on the labour history of this period.[4] Most historians have concentrated on the important trend of the time, the eventually successful struggle for unionization of the workers in heavy industry and the consequent transformation of the Canadian labour relations system. Since strikes for union recognition have been regarded as the most important industrial disputes of the time, the significance of the coal slowdown, an action of workers who had long been unionized and a rebellion against established union authorities, has not been recognized. But a close examination of this dispute provides a revealing perspective on the nature of the union movement and on the transformation of labour relations that took place during the war.

In Nova Scotia the miners of District 26, United Mine Workers of America

---

1 *Globe and Mail*, 24 July, 29 August 1941.

2 Ninety days is an underestimate, based on a five day week. Some of the mines worked six days per week. See *Glace Bay Gazette*, 2 May 1941.

3 Dominion Bureau of Statistics, *Coal Statistics for Canada* (Ottawa, 1942), Table 45, p. 39.

4 The only published account of the slowdown is in Paul MacEwan, *Miners and Steelworkers* (Toronto 1976), pp. 225-38.

(UMW) possessed what many workers in Ontario and Quebec were struggling to acquire: a well established union organization and collective bargaining rights, protected by law. Yet this did not lead to a contented workforce and stable industrial relations. On the contrary, the miners would appear to be the most dissatisfied group of workers in Canada at this time, prepared to defy the provincial and federal governments and the leadership of their union. There were, of course, specific local conditions that led to militancy in Cape Breton, but the rebellion against union authorities was motivated by the same impulse which led other workers to struggle for the establishment of a union. Coal miners in Cape Breton, like steel workers in Hamilton or metal miners in northern Ontario, wanted better wages and working conditions. They also wanted something less easily defined: much greater control over their work process and over their lives, democracy at the workplace. What the history of the miners' union in this period reveals most clearly is that from the beginning of large scale industrial unionism in Canada there was a divergence of aims between the most active and militant workers and the leadership of the unions.

As the writings of such historians as Irving Abella and L. S. MacDowell have shown, the upsurge of industrial unionism was powered mainly by the efforts of large numbers of rank-and-file Canadian workers to achieve union rights.[5] Formal leadership in the fight for collective bargaining rights was provided by Canadian sections of the Committee for Industrial Organization (CIO), which after 1940 formed part of the Canadian Congress of Labour (CCL). The new unionism had to overcome determined resistance from industrialists, and the reluctance of the Mackenzie King Liberal government to assist unionization by passing legislation comparable to the American Wagner Act. It was the rising tide of strikes in 1943 and the growing shift of workers' votes to the Cooperative Commonwealth Federation (CCF) that eventually pressured the federal government in early 1944 to enact P.C.1003 which granted enforceable trade union rights to workers. But compulsory conciliation before a strike could begin was incorporated in the new law, as in the Industrial Disputes Investigation Act, and work stoppages were made illegal during the length of a contract. As MacDowell points out: "The government's primary concern had been, and continued to be, the elimination of industrial conflict, and the concessions to labour contained in the new legislation were primarily designed to accomplish that purpose".[6]

---

5   Irving Abella, *Nationalism, Communism, and Canadian Labour* (Toronto, 1973); Laurel Sefton MacDowell, *'Remember Kirkland Lake'* (Toronto, 1983) and "The Formation of the Canadian Industrial Relations System During World War Two", *Labour/Le Travailleur*, 3 (1978), pp. 175-96.

6   MacDowell, "The Formation of the Canadian Industrial Relations System", p. 194. See also Jeremy Webber, "The Malaise of Compulsory Conciliation: Strike Prevention in Canada during World War II", in Bryan Palmer, ed., *The Character of Class Struggle* (Toronto, 1986).

What MacDowell's account does not make clear is the degree to which such controls over workers were acceptable to the right-wing leaders of the union movement and their mentors in the national leadership of the CCF. Although the top leadership of the CCL, men such as Aaron Mosher, Charles Millard or Silby Barrett, found some of the legal constraints on unions irksome, they were fully prepared to accept, indeed consciously welcomed, a legal system designed for controlling the spontaneous militancy of workers. These men were business unionists who accepted the permanence of the capitalist system, and saw a common interest between capital and labour in productivity and prosperity. They were at times capable of a degree of militancy in pursuing wage concessions and, above all, union recognition and union security, but they believed that union officials must exert discipline over the workers in order to preserve the terms of contracts and repress direct action by the rank and file. Their conception of democracy was satisfied by formal elections in the unions which served to legitimize the power of bureaucrats. The system of labour relations that attained a mature form in Canada during the Second World War offered workers the concession of collective bargaining rights, but only within a structure of strong legal pressures designed to force all union activity into this bureaucratic, business unionist mold. This system helped to enshrine the power of union leaders, and from the beginning of the war the top CIO and CCL leadership held out the promise to government and industry of labour peace in return for union recognition. Even big business, if guided by enlightened self interest, it was argued, should see that more stable and peaceful labour-management relations, and hence higher and uninterrupted production, would result from recognizing unions and engaging in orderly collective bargaining. Responsible union leaders would then be able to control the militancy of workers, and both workers and business would thereby prosper.[7]

Consistent support for these principles of "responsible" business unionism in the new industrial unions came from the national leaders of the CCF. Almost all members of the CCL executive were CCF supporters, and there was a close alliance between the top leaderships of the CCL and the CCF. But this alliance was not without frictions, since some union leaders were more reluctant than others to involve the unions closely with CCF electoral ambitions. The CCF alliance with union bureaucrats was most evident at the top; at the local level individual CCFers not infrequently were strong leftists and militants. The left forces in the unions were generally led by Communist Party members, although this left wing ranged from relatively apolitical union militants to political radicals. Changes of policy placed the Communist Party sometimes to the right

---

7 Ideologically such concepts of the role of unions owed much to right wing social democracy. One of the most explicit and influential expressions of this viewpoint in the CIO of the time can be seen in a book written by two American Socialist functionaries of the SWOC. Clinton S. Golden and Harold J. Ruttenberg, *The Dynamics of Industrial Democracy* (New York, 1942).

and sometimes the left of the militants who usually followed its lead. As with the CCF, a distinction has to be made between rank and file Communists and the Party leaders; many supporters were militant trade unionists first and followers of the political ideology second. Most often, at the shop floor level, Communists were recruited from the most militant workers and continued, whatever the Party line of the time, to function mainly as leaders of local militancy and demands for union democracy.

Rarely has the divergence between the militancy of the rank and file and the conservative business unionism of union officers emerged so clearly as in Cape Breton in the early years of the war. At this time the UMW was still the largest industrial union in Canada, and the most powerful union in the CIO/CCL which was leading the fight for the new unions in heavy industry. Canadian industrialists and politicians who hated and feared the CIO, and resisted as strongly as they could the establishment of industrial unions, regarded the UMW as the archetype of these unions and a leading force behind auto workers, steel workers, metal miners and other workers seeking union organization. Government authorities whom union leaders hoped to influence also had only the UMW to consider as an example of a long established industrial union in heavy industry.

In the United States the UMW had been the greatest organized force behind the CIO, providing the top leadership and much of the funding that combined with the often Communist-led but largely spontaneous upsurge of worker militancy to create the new industrial unions. John L. Lewis, the UMW International President, had at this time a degree of public fame and notoriety throughout North America that has probably never been approached by any other union leader. When he resigned the presidency of the CIO in 1940, the position was taken by his lieutenant Philip Murray, UMW Vice-President and Director of the Steel Workers Organizing Campaign (SWOC).[8] The UMW also served as the organizational model on which the new industrial unions were built, particularly those organized more from the top down, like the SWOC. To a lesser extent, this was also true in Canada. In Nova Scotia the UMW's largest Canadian section, District 26, played a crucial role in some of the CIO's earliest Canadian successes, such as the organization of the first SWOC locals in Canada, at the Sydney and Trenton steel plants. It also successfully lobbied the provincial government to pass the 1937 Trade Union Act, the first law in Canada that, however weakly it was to be enforced, expressly declared a positive right of workers to organize trade unions. Perhaps of more importance to the early CIO, the Nova Scotia law forced companies to provide the automatic check-off of

8   See Melvyn Dubofsky and Warren Van Tine, *John L. Lewis A Biography* (New York, 1977) and Nelson N. Lichtenstein, "Industrial Unionism Under the No-Strike Pledge: A Study of the CIO During the Second World War", Ph.D. thesis, University of California at Berkeley, 1974.

union dues, as had been done for the UMW for many years.[9] The Nova Scotia miners' union had also advanced further on the road of direct involvement in electoral politics than any other section of Canadian organized labour. In 1938 District 26 had made the first union affiliation to the CCF, and it was able to help elect a CCF Member of Parliament, Clarie Gillis, in 1940. In many respects, therefore, the UMW in District 26 at the beginning of the war had achieved the position that the new union movement sought elsewhere in Canada. It was a well established industrial union, protected by law, with very considerable local political and economic power.

UMW officers were prominent in the national labour leadership. Up to 1939, when the CIO unions were expelled from the Trades and Labour Congress (TLC), District 26 President D. W. Morrison had been TLC vice-president. Silby Barrett, the International Board Member for District 26, had been appointed by John L. Lewis to head the SWOC and CIO organizing drives in Canada. These men, and other appointed union leaders such as Charles Millard of the SWOC, were disturbed by the fact that a large proportion of the active organizers in the emerging CIO unions were Communists or militants prepared to work closely with the Communist Party. This fear provided much of the motivation for the 1940 merger of the Canadian CIO unions with Aaron Mosher's All Canadian Congress of Labour to form the CCL, which ensured that older and conservatively led unions would be in the majority. Two of the six man CCL executive were from the UMW, Silby Barrett of District 26 and Pat Conroy of District 18, who was to become CCL Secretary-Treasurer.

But the conservatism of the officers of UMW District 26 had only a limited and insecure base among the union members. Over a very long period this leadership had been strongly opposed by militant and politically radical groups among the miners. The fact that this union organization was one of the oldest in Canada meant that its right wing were well steeped in the principles of conservative union philosophy, but the miners of Cape Breton had lived and breathed unionism and class struggle for several generations, and still burned with a sense of their exploitation by corporation bosses and repression by state authorities.[10] It was to be the endeavour of the officers to prove their

---

9   While the SWOC members in Nova Scotia received little advance in pay or conditions until the war years, their dues regularly flowed into SWOC organizing in Canada and the United States in a period when few other locals had the guaranteed check-off. See Abella, *Nationalism, Communism, and Canadian Labour*, p. 55.

10 See David Frank, "The Cape Breton Coal Miners 1917-1926", Ph.D. thesis, Dalhousie University, 1979 and "The Cape Breton Coal Industry and the Rise and Fall of the British Empire Steel Corporation", *Acadiensis*, VII, 1 (Autumn 1977), pp. 3-34; "Class Conflict in the Coal Industry; Cape Breton, 1922", in G.S. Kealey and Peter Warrian, eds., *Essays in Canadian Working Class History* (Toronto, 1976); Donald MacGillivray, "Military Aid to the Civil Power: The Cape Breton Experience in the 1920s", *Acadiensis*, III, 2 (Spring 1974), pp. 45-64; as well as popular histories: MacEwan, *Miners and Steelworkers* ; John Mellor, *The Company Store* (Toronto, 1983).

responsibility and moderation to government by repressing militancy that precipitated the rebellion of the miners and the 1941 slowdown strike.

The leadership of District 26 had long cooperated with the government of Nova Scotia, seeking to influence laws and regulations effecting the miners. One issue on which the miners, the union, the corporation and provincial politicians had long been united was that of lobbying federal authorities to maintain or increase the subventions paid on Nova Scotia coal delivered to central Canada, enabling the less efficient Maritime coal industry to compete with cheaper imports of American coal. The union could also point to the UMW policy, enshrined in its constitution, of always honouring contracts, a policy which had frequently brought the officers into alliance with the company and government. In the early 1930s the UMW had seemed very much a lesser evil to these authorities than the Communist-led militants of the Amalgamated Mine Workers of Nova Scotia (AMW), the breakaway union that a majority of Cape Breton miners supported. Although in 1936 the "united front" policy of the Communists and the reunification of AMW miners with the UMW had helped to bring the right and left temporarily together in Cape Breton, by 1939 left and right were again moving apart, and the District officers were anxious to display their moderation to government.

The District 26 officers scored one great success by following this policy in the early war years, the organization of the miners in Minto, New Brunswick. At Minto a major UMW strike in 1937-1938 had failed to win union recognition, and a conciliation board had recommended against the UMW.[11] In July 1941, however, the UMW finally forced the Minto Coal Company, the largest coal company in the area, to sign a contract.[12] That same month the report of a commissioner appointed by the federal government to study the lack of coal productivity in Minto was sent to the Minister of Labour, Norman McLarty. The commissioner, Justice M. B. Archibald of the Nova Scotia Supreme Court, recommended as a first priority that:

> The organization of the miners throughout the entire area should be continued and made as complete as possible, and in this organization the employees should have the encouragement of the operators. I am satisfied that the miners if permitted to organize and enjoy the benefits of collective bargaining and agreements with respect to working conditions would co-operate with the operators in producing the maximum amount of coal that is possible under present conditions.[13]

11 See Allan Seager, "Minto New Brunswick: A Study in Class Relations Between the Wars", *Labour/Le Travailleur*, 5 (1980), pp. 81-132.

12 *Glace Bay Gazette*, 14 July 1941.

13 "Report of Commissioner on Inquiry into Causes of Lack of Capacity Coal Production in Minto-Chipman District, N.B.", *Labour Gazette*, 41 (September 1941), pp. 1073-84.

This reasoning is exactly what Silby Barrett and other UMW leaders wanted to impress upon the authorities. However, in the long organized Cape Breton sub-districts of the union, the policy of war-time cooperation with the government and careful avoidance of strikes came into direct conflict with the long frustrated aim of the coal miners to recover the wage reductions imposed on them during the 1920s and the early years of the depression. Not until 1943 did the wages of coal miners across Canada equal 1921 levels, and the wage rates in Nova Scotia remained substantially below those of miners in Alberta and British Columbia.[14] Although almost all of the UMW miners of Nova Scotia worked for subsidiary companies of Dominion Steel and Coal Corporation (Dosco), the miners of Dosco's subsidiaries in Sydney Mines and Pictou County, Nova Scotia Steel and Coal (Scotia) and Acadia Mines, had lower wage rates than did the Dominion Coal Company (Domco) miners in Glace Bay, New Waterford and Springhill. This inequity dated from the early 1930s, when Dosco had allowed Scotia and Acadia to go into receivership, and additional wage cuts had been forced upon the miners. When Dosco took over these companies again in 1938, it refused to agree to corporation wide contracts or equal wage rates for its miners throughout the province.

A sense of the inevitability of mine closures and mass layoffs when mechanization of the mines became a reality added to the militancy of coal miners. In 1938 an attempt by Dosco to introduce electrical cutting and loading machinery in a new mine at Glace Bay was defeated by the refusal of the miners to work the mechanized mine. After a strike that turned into a lengthy lockout involving 89 men, the company finally removed the machinery in early 1939, but corporation statements claimed that the Nova Scotia mines could never compete profitably with American coal production until they attained the same level of mechanization. The miners understood this threat to mean mass layoffs in the mines in the near future.[15] And, like workers throughout North America during the war, the miners had a foreboding that the Depression would return at the war's end, and hence there was pressure to achieve good wage settlements while the war economy boomed.

For the leaders of District 26 to have had any realistic hope of suppressing the militant actions of the miners, some substantial concessions would have had to be made by Dosco, but the corporation was prepared to make no concessions it could avoid. Dosco advertised itself as "Canada's Largest Industry" with products that were "more nearly 100% Canadian than any similar products available anywhere", and the "Only Producer of Steel and Steel Products in

---

14 *Labour Gazette*, "Wage Rates and Hours of Labour in Canada, 1944", Supplement, October 1946, Table II, p. 9;
"Numbers and Earnings of Coal Miners in Canada, 1921-1938", Appendix C, Supplement, March 1940, p. 131.

15 *Glace Bay Gazette*, 23 January 1939.

Canada Wholly Self-Sustained Within the Empire",[16] but its war-time pride in being Canadian did not lead to generosity to its workers. In its Sydney and Trenton steel plants, at its Peck Rolling Mills at Montreal, and at its Halifax Shipyards, as well as in its Domco mines, Dosco was the adversary of the workers in important war-time strikes. It tenaciously resisted the establishment of unions in its unorganized subsidiaries and fought against any wage increases where it faced organized workers. In its mines, Dosco appears to have been determined to hold on to any short term profits it could make while the expanded wartime coal market lasted.

This intransigent attitude prompted a sustained militancy on the part of the miners. For Canadian labour in general the 1938-1940 period was one of few industrial disputes,[17] but in Nova Scotia strikes increased, amounting to nearly half of all the Canadian strike activity throughout 1939 and 1940.[18] Although a few of these strikes involved the newly organized steel workers in Sydney and Trenton, and the fish plant workers at Lockeport, locked out by their employers in 1939, the great majority were "outlaw" or "illegal" strikes of the miners. The *Labour Gazette* listed 39 miners' strikes in Nova Scotia in 1939 and 55 in 1940.[19]

These were all short stoppages at individual mines, spontaneous actions by the miners or called by meetings of the union local. All were referred to as

16 *Globe and Mail*, 14 July 1941.

17 Stuart Jamieson, *Times of Trouble: Labour Unrest and Industrial Conflict in Canada, 1900 — 66* (Ottawa, 1976), pp. 277-8. Jamieson points out that the war years were the first time for decades that the pattern of labour strife in Canada diverged from that in the United States, and argues that this was a "delayed response", as the great wave of industrial unionization that occurred in the United States in the late 1930s came to Canada in the middle years of the war. Jamieson notes that the number and duration of industrial disputes was high in 1937, fell to a low level through the 1938-1940 period, gradually mounted again in 1941 and 1942, and reached a peak in 1943. This is confirmed by other sources such as Douglas Cruikshank and Gregory S. Kealey, "Strikes in Canada, 1891-1950", *Labour/Le Travail*, 20 (1987), pp. 85-145.

18 Nova Scotia had 36.1 per cent of all strikes in Canada in 1939, 71.9 per cent of the workers involved in strikes and 43.4 per cent of the time lost through strikes. *Labour Gazette*, 40 (February 1940), Table V, "Strikes and Lockouts in Canada in 1939 by Province". In 1940 Nova Scotia had 42 per cent of strikes, 51.3 per cent of the workers involved, and 24.9 per cent of time lost through strikes across the country. *Labour Gazette*, 41 (February 1941), Table V, "Strikes and Lockouts in Canada in 1940 by Province". Cruikshank and Kealey, "Strikes in Canada", pp. 136-8, estimate strikes in the national coal industry at 46 in 1937, 26 in 1938, 53 in 1939, and 66 in 1940, and show Nova Scotia provincial totals as 50 strikes in 1937, 31 in 1938, 49 in 1939, and 79 in 1940, while also showing that Alberta and British Columbia, the other areas of extensive coal mining, had few strikes during 1939 and 1940.

19 *Labour Gazette* 39, p. xiii; *Labour Gazette*, 40, p. xiii. During 1940 government authorities frequently complained of a total of 211 illegal miners' strikes in District 26 in the two and one half years preceding November 1939. It is not clear how this figure was derived. It was advanced in Judge McArthur's report and then constantly repeated in the rhetoric of politicians attacking illegal strikes.

"illegal" strikes for several reasons: none complied with the legal strike requirements in the Industrial Disputes Investigation Act; the strikes were not authorized by the UMW executive and contravened the well proclaimed UMW policy of abiding faithfully by the terms of its contracts; and the UMW contracts with Dosco subsidiaries all contained clauses outlawing any work stoppage for any grievance during the life of the contract. When, as was frequently the case, long negotiations for a new contract took place after the end of a contract period, the UMW officials invariably agreed that the miners would work under the terms of the old contract in the interim. Domco and the other Dosco companies consistently refused any direct negotiations of grievances with miners on "illegal" stoppages of work. From 1938, the UMW and Domco had agreed to submit grievances that could not be resolved between local union mine committees and management to a single "Umpire", whose decision would be binding. The man whom the company and union officials had agreed upon to serve as Umpire was John W. MacLeod, a former District 26 president and then company official for many years. Neither the umpire system nor the decisions handed down by MacLeod were satisfactory to the rank-and-file miners, and by 1939 grievances were leading to strikes.

The varied grievances involved in these strikes seemed to contemporary authorities to show no pattern other than a militant predisposition of the miners to stop work on any provocation. In May and June 1939 Springhill and No.11 Glace Bay miners both struck in solidarity with men dismissed by the company after serving jail sentences for liquor offenses. Miners at Florence struck on a grievance concerning rates for working a new system; at Sydney Mines' Princess mine a dispute concerned the demand of a few men for contract rates rather than daily pay; at No 16 in New Waterford the walkout concerned the rate for some longwall men; at 1B mine in Dominion a stoppage of several days occurred over the sale of a company house. The men of No.12 at New Waterford struck over the dismissal of a miner who had a fist fight with a company official, and the strike ended only when the official was charged with assault. A similar issue at the Albion Mine in Stellarton, the dismissal of a man for "inefficiency", brought all four Pictou County mines to a standstill, and the Stellarton miners even threatened to bring out the maintenance and pump men.[20]

These strikes indicate the widespread dissatisfaction of the miners with company policies and with the established grievance procedures. Most grievances involved a direct struggle between the miners and company officials for control of the work process in the pits. But while issues of control were the direct cause of most of these "illegal" strikes, they would have undoubtedly been much less frequent had the miners felt they were receiving fair or adequate wages from the hated Dosco corporation. Underlying all this wildcat strike activity was the

20 *Glace Bay Gazette*, 9 May, 3 June 1939; 24 May, 8, 11, 18 July 1939; 28, 31 July 1939; 27 July, 2 August 1939.

frustration of the men at the failure of union efforts to increase substantially the basic wage rates, or even to reach the wage level that existed before the wage cuts the miners had been forced to accept in 1932.[21] In the 1937 contract there was a six per cent increase for the contract miners and most of the daily paid (datal) men, leaving wages still below the 1931 rates. The Domco miners, in a pit head referendum, voted by a narrow margin to accept this two year contract, although there was considerable opposition to it led by the former AMW leadership. The Glace Bay miners voted heavily against the contract, but it was carried by the votes of the miners of New Waterford and Springhill.[22] It was under this unsatisfactory 1937 contract, which formally ended on 1 February 1939, that the miners were still working in 1939 and most of 1940. In the view of the militant miners the officers were taking a weak line in negotiations with the company. In August 1939, just as war was breaking out in Europe, a contract including no wage increases was voted down by the miners.[23] No strike action was proposed by the union executive, which declared it would re-enter negotiations with the company. The anger of the militants was shown by a two day general strike at most of the mines in both Glace Bay and New Waterford, purportedly in solidarity with strikes on local grievances going on at Caledonia mine and No.11. The district executive as well as the company denounced this "outlaw" strike. The miners returned to work on the promise from the union and the provincial government authorities of a general inquiry into grievance procedures; but as the Glace Bay and New Waterford men resumed work, the miners at Florence mine came out on strike on a local grievance.[24]

Early in September the UMW officers of both Canadian mining areas, District 26 and District 18, met with the federal Minister of Labour and promised full co-operation in the war effort.[25] However, the beginning of the war

---

21 These wage reductions and the inability of the UMW to defeat them had played an important part in bringing about the creation of the rival AMW in 1932. See Michael Earle, "The Rise and Fall of a 'Red' Union: The Amalgamated Mine Workers of Nova Scotia — 1932-1936", M.A. thesis, Dalhousie University, 1984.

22 *Glace Bay Gazette,* 8 March, 1, 3 April 1937. Glace Bay sub-district voted 1973 for, 2891 against; New Waterford 1472 for, 551 against; and Springhill 941 for, 213 against. The total was 4386 for, 3655 against. The miners of Pictou and Sydney mines, as well as other UMW men who did not work for Domco, did not have a vote on this referendum. This was the usual breakdown of miners' votes throughout the 1930s and early 1940s. Glace Bay invariably had a majority against accepting contracts and for left wing candidates in union elections, while New Waterford and Springhill usually took less militant positions. A very significant change in the 1939-1941 period was to be the adoption of a more militant line by the New Waterford men.

23 *Sydney Post-Record,* 23 August 1939; *Glace Bay Gazette,* 23 August 1939. The vote was 3781 votes against, 2805 for acceptance, the heavy Glace Bay vote this time swamping smaller majorities for acceptance in New Waterford and Springhill.

24 *Glace Bay Gazette,* 24, 28, 29, 30, 31 August 1939.

25 *Glace Bay Gazette,* 15 September 1939.

added a cause for additional work stoppages because of the refusal of the miners to go into the pits with "enemy aliens". These stoppages had little direct connection with the miners' militancy on other issues,[26] but they did add to the number of strikes, which quickly became a matter of concern to provincial and federal governments. After a strike at Sydney Mines in October 1939, the new provincial Minister of Mines and Labour, L.D. Currie, established a formal inquiry, conducted by Judge Neil R. McArthur.[27] In his report McArthur deplored the frequent illegal strikes in the mines, which he declared were brought about by small groups of men who "regard with no sense of responsibility the resultant loss of earnings occasioned to their fellow workmen". Praising the UMW district and international organization, he pointed out that "the advocacy of illegal strikes and tie-ups is contrary to the established policy of the union":

"Pit action," as it is sometimes called, and collective bargaining through the avenue of negotiation, cannot both survive side by side. One is an orderly system, the other in the end destructive. One demands that Labour function through the voice of its elected officers and Local Unions, the other ignores and disregards constituted authority.... I urge, in the interests of the Union and its membership, a one hundred per cent loyalty to your elected officers while they hold office. It is their duty and responsibility, not only to promote the interests and protect the rights of the membership generally, but also to safeguard the constitution, principles and established policies of the Union. This responsibility may, and at times does, involve the distasteful task of using drastic measures in order to keep the "family home" in order. Nevertheless, when conditions require it, this duty and responsibility should be fearlessly faced.[28]

26 It is perhaps relevant that 1B mine, which was most disrupted by the miners' refusal to work with the local Italians, was to be the weakest Glace Bay local in terms of the miners' support for the slowdown in 1941.

27 Currie, the M.L.A. for Glace Bay, had become Minister of Mines and Labour early in 1939 (*Glace Bay Gazette*, 7 February 1939), replacing Michael Dwyer, who had resigned to become President of Dosco's subsidiary Nova Scotia Steel and Coal Company when it came out of receivership. At this time the two Sydney Mines pits of this company, previously popularly referred to as "Scotia" mines, were renamed the "Old Sydney" pits. For simplicity the name "Scotia" is used throughout this article.

28 *Glace Bay Gazette*, 27 November 1939, gives a summary of the report. Lengthy passages were quoted in "Report of Board in Dispute between the Acadia Coal Company, Limited, and its Employees" and "Report of Board in Dispute between the Old Sydney Collieries, Limited, and its Employees," *Labour Gazette*, 40(August 1940), pp. 768-78. Similar remarks to MacArthur's were made by Judge J.K. Crowell in an inquiry into a strike at Springhill. *Glace Bay Gazette*, 21 November 1939.

The McArthur report was referred to favorably in all the conciliation proceedings in the Nova Scotian coal industry in the following year, for the union officers remained anxious to display their co-operative attitude to the government. In December the UMW executive circulated a letter to all locals warning against "petty strikes" and threatening union disciplinary action against violations of contracts and the UMW constitution, and the principal message in President D.W. Morrison's annual New Year message was that the UMW was now on a "wartime responsibility basis", pledged to avoid disruptions of war production as a patriotic duty.[29] By this point the Domco miners had been working for almost a year under the expired 1937 contract, and early in January a four party conference took place in Glace Bay between representatives of the UMW, Domco, and the provincial and federal Labour Departments. The result was a joint application by the UMW and Domco for a federal conciliation board.[30] When some UMW locals passed resolutions of no confidence in the district executive and opposed the conciliation board, President Morrison responded that particularly in wartime it was necessary to follow legal procedures, that the executive had rejected a company proposal for binding arbitration, and that the UMW would have an excellent representative on the board, Professor F.R. Scott of Montreal, well recommended by the CCF. Morrison further stated that at the recent International UMW convention he had discussed the situation with President John L. Lewis, who was very critical of the illegal strikes. Lewis had "said that the UMW was a business concern and had to carry out its operations and contracts on business lines".[31]

The conciliation board was chaired by Justice C.P. McTague of the Ontario Supreme Court, who was appointed by the federal government to head most of the important conciliation proceedings during the early war years. The Domco representative was businessman Ralph Bell of Halifax, while Frank Scott represented the UMW. The UMW argued for a 15 per cent rate increase on the grounds of the increasing cost of living in wartime, while Domco maintained it was financially unable to pay any additional wages.[32] The report of the board, released in late March, was unanimous. It recommended minor pay increases ranging from three to 19 cents a day, retroactive to February 1939, for the lowest

---

29 *Glace Bay Gazette*, 22, 30 December 1939.

30 *Glace Bay Gazette*, 5, 23 January 1940.

31 *Glace Bay Gazette*, 5, 7 February 1940. Lewis was, in his leadership of the American UMW, entering perhaps his most militant period, when he broke with Roosevelt and the Democratic administration and the CIO leaders who continued full co-operation with the government, and led massive strikes that forced the equalization of the rates paid miners in the Southern and Northern coalfields and the union organization of the "captive" coal mines owned by the steel corporations. His policies with regard to District 26, however, were very different, since he constantly supported moderation throughout this period.

32 *Glace Bay Gazette*, 20, 21, 22, 23, 24, 26, 27 February 1940.

paid datal men, and nothing for the contract miners except for a few of the longwall men at Springhill. It also recommended that the company write off any arrears of rent and coal payments owed by miners as of February 1940 and the report called for a tribunal to be set up in advance to arbitrate if a new contract was not negotiated by 15 January 1941. The report also criticized the custom of referring wage contracts to a referendum of the miners:

> Such procedure is no longer effective in the same Union in the United States. It definitely imposes an almost unbearable burden on the Executive. The referendum frequently is not a genuine expression on the merits of the contract but tends to be one of want of confidence in the union executives who have negotiated it. We do not put our views in the form of any recommendation but merely throw out the suggestion that it is in the interests of the Union as a whole that these matters should be considered and within the Union itself rectified in the interests of efficiency and strength.[33]

Since it seemed unlikely the miners would accept this poor offer, UMW President Morrison issued a statement that negotiations would be conducted with Scotia and Acadia coal companies seeking a uniform rate for all miners, and a referendum on the Domco recommendations would be delayed until the miners of Pictou County and Sydney Mines could vote at the same time. These negotiations led to another conciliation board, chaired by Justice W.H. Harrison, which recommended no wage increases.[34] Soon after this report the UMW executive announced that since the district convention was to be held at the end of August, the various conciliation boards' recommendations could be discussed then.[35]

During these lengthy negotiations and conciliation proceedings the frustration of the miners had grown, as was evident from the support given to mass meetings called by left-wingers in Glace Bay.[36] None of the executive officers was present at these meetings, and prominent on the platform were men who had

33 "Report of Board in Dispute between the Dominion Coal Company, Limited, and its Employees," *Labour Gazette*, 40 (August 1940), pp. 321-3.

34 *Glace Bay Gazette*, 9 April, 30 July 1940. In separate reports on the two companies, Scotia and Acadia, the majority recommended no rate increases, accepting the employer's claim that it could afford no higher wages and that productivity at these mines was lower than the Domco mines. The UMW's representative, District 26 Vice-President P.G. Muise, in a minority opinion called for equal pay with the rates offered Domco miners by the McTague board. "Report of Board in Dispute between the Acadia Coal Company, Limited, and its Employees" and "Report of Board in Dispute between the Old Sydney Collieries, Limited, and its Employees", *Labour Gazette*, 40 (August 1940), pp. 768-78.

35 *Glace Bay Gazette*, 6 August 1940.

36 *Glace Bay Gazette*, 27 May, 24 June 1940.

been, and perhaps still were, members or sympathizers of the Communist Party.[37]

At the same time government pressure on the officers to control the wildcat strikes continued. Labour Minister Currie said in the Legislature that the public would soon demand government intervention: "Every time we pick up a newspaper we find there's a new strike. Until laboring men agree to live up to contracts, I am sure that we cannot get new industries into this province". In response, CCF M.L.A. Douglas MacDonald, speaking as a member of the UMW District Board, said that the Board would do "anything we can" to help the Labour Department.[38] The concern of the federal government was emphasized by the appearance of Labour Minister Norman McLarty at the District 26 convention in Truro at the end of August 1940. In an interview in Halifax, McLarty said he had come to Nova Scotia to look into the disputes in the coal fields, a situation that was "not healthy in wartime". In his speech to the delegates at the convention, he pointed out that there were "more sporadic strikes in Nova Scotia than in all the rest of Canada.... It is true that the most labour strife is centred in a province where Canadian Labour has its widest privileges". He also argued that "some action must be taken to remove this canker. I am advised that these strikes are without the approval of your union and without disciplinary action from your union.... maintain the dignity and integrity of your union and see that these ill considered, irresponsible strikes are eliminated".[39] Provincial Minister Currie also warned the convention:

> [The strikes] do you men more harm than the operators. It has been argued that the companies are largely responsible, but remember, gentlemen, that two wrongs do not make a right.... To a large extent I have every reason to believe your claims that the operators do not want your unions are correct, but as long as there is a trade union act in this province they will not be allowed to break your organization... [It is] the duty of the executive to discipline the men. The time has come to impose self regulation. It may be that some punitive law will have to be imposed, but so far I have refused to allow anything like that.... [The Nova Scotia Trade Union Act] is very imperfect, but it is pioneering the way.[40]

---

37 It does not appear that much in the form of direct Communist Party organization was maintained in Cape Breton in this period of illegality, though there is evidence that some literature was distributed. *Glace Bay Gazette*, 4 June 1940, reports a Canadian Legion meeting denouncing the spread of "Communistic literature". No internments of local Communists are recorded, although there was a certain amount of RCMP investigation and harrassment. (*Steelworker and Miner*, 20 March, 6 April, 16 November 1940.)

38 *Glace Bay Gazette*, 12 April 1940.

39 *Halifax Herald*, 28 August 1940; *Glace Bay Gazette*, 29 August 1940.

40 *Glace Bay Gazette*, 29 August 1940. Presumably it was this concern with wildcat strikes that led

The principal message of both ministers was directed at the officers: government support for unions was conditional on the leaders showing that they were prepared to discipline and control the workers.

This message impressed the officers much more than it intimidated the rank-and-file delegates. A stormy debate followed the speeches and McLarty was "engulfed in a flood of complaints" against the policies of Domco. One delegate said: "They have put us in a bad position in the eyes of the people. The statement that there is no more loyal body of men than the miners of Nova Scotia is true, but we refuse to have our patriotism exploited for the profit of the Dominion Coal Company". Although no delegate openly defended the principle of wildcat strikes, many argued that the specific strikes that had occurred were the fault of Dosco, not the workers. The executive was eventually able to get a clause opposing illegal strikes included in a vote of thanks to the speakers, but the mood of the miners was clearly far from conciliatory.[41]

When the convention was addressed by CCF leader M.J. Coldwell, CCF National Secretary David Lewis, and M.P. Clarie Gillis the delegates were more warmly welcoming. All three speakers argued that the war should lead to a new order in Canada, that it could best be fought by developing social and economic justice at home, and that labour should be given a place in government as had been done in wartime Britain. Gillis was the only one of the CCF speakers who dealt directly with the situation of the miners, and he attempted to dress up his basic support for the position of the UMW executive in militant language:

> I am not in favour of these petty strikes. When we fight it should be a good fight.... Dosco owns some twenty-three subsidiary companies across Canada. They control the industry, yet we are tackling our problems in sections.... They will close up all the openings in Nova Scotia and they won't open new ones unless they are mechanized. They will reduce the number of employed and increase their own profits.... The Corporation can use the profits of one branch to establish another and come to the workers with empty pockets.... Conciliation boards are appointed by the government in the interest of the operators. We must go into the financial structure of the corporation, but not by a conciliation board.

the Nova Scotia Legislature, early in 1941, to pass an act empowering the Minister of Labour to appoint conciliators "whenever in his opinion the interests of industrial peace may require it to be done". *An Act Respecting the Appointment of Commissioners of Conciliation*, Statutes of Nova Scotia, 1941. This act was never used, no doubt because of the extensive involvement of federal authorities in labour relations throughout the remainder of the war.

41 *Glace Bay Gazette*, 29 August 1940. The delegates' unhappiness with the existing grievance system was made clear by the resolution passed that in a new contract the UMW would no longer agree to pay its share of the umpire's salary. *Glace Bay Gazette*, 6 September 1940.

However, Gillis added,

> the cause of the petty strikes in mines in this province was more deep rooted than any discontent among the men. Industry had advanced money to the American Federation of Labor in the effort to eliminate the Committee for Industrial Organization. The petty strike was used as a weapon to discredit and wreck the CIO.... This movement had extended to Canada and the same effort was being made against the UMW, a CIO affiliate. We should attempt a closer examination of our problems in each difficulty, closer co-operation with our executive and stricter adherence to our constitution.... The movement to wreck the unions had succeeded to a considerable extent and chaos exists in every local.... our organization is in danger.[42]

The response of the miners to Gillis's ludicrous suggestion that their local strikes were the result of a plot laid by big business and the AFL was not recorded, but overall he and the other CCF speakers were well received and the convention passed a resolution praising Gillis for the "able and consistent manner in which he has represented his constituency and the workers of Nova Scotia" in Parliament.[43]

When the contract dispute and the McTague recommendations were discussed, however, one delegate asked why there had been no minority report from Frank Scott, and said: "I, for one, don't believe Scott is the honestest man in Canada". The explanation from Secretary-Treasurer MacKay, that Scott had wanted to oppose the board's findings but could find no way to disprove the company's claims about its financial situation, was not well received by the delegates.[44]

The convention would not accept the McTague recommendations, and some of the more militant even called for a general strike to restore the 1921 wage rates. Delegates also refused to agree that the recommendations were sufficiently acceptable to be put to the men in a referendum, and there were strong demands that the rates for the Scotia and Acadia miners be raised to equality with the Domco men. The convention eventually instructed the executive to

---

42 *Glace Bay Gazette*, 30 August 1940.

43 *Glace Bay Gazette*, 4 September 1940. Clarie Gillis was in his most left phase in this early stage of his career as M.P. For example, he was the only CCF Member who supported Mrs. Dorise Neilsen's amendment to the bill introducing Unemployment Insurance that workers on strike should be eligible for benefits. (*Glace Bay Gazette*, 27 July, 1 August 1940.)

44 *Glace Bay Gazette*, 31 August 1940. This question of Scott was particularly embarrassing to the CCF leaders and the UMW officers in their attempts at this convention to get agreement on the employment of a full-time research director, since it seems that the man they had in mind for the job was another CCF intellectual from Montreal, Eugene Forsey.

enter new negotiations demanding increases. If a better offer was not received by 30 October, the International was to be approached for assistance and a strike ballot was to be sent out.[45]

President Morrison and the rest of the executive made no effort to conceal the fact that they were for acceptance of the McTague recommendations. "The fight we have on our hands is not to organize a strike but to prevent one", said Vice-President Muise. Morrison wound up the convention by appealing to the men to "bend our every effort to assist Canada's war effort", and by arguing for putting the McTague recommendations to a referendum: "Is it fair that 72 men here should tie the hands of 12,000? It is not, and I will not be a party to it".[46]

The week following the UMW convention, the executive officers along with Clarie Gillis and David Lewis of the CCF were active participants at the founding convention of the CCL, having managed to get the District 26 delegates to endorse the merger with the CCL. As anticipated, the conservative slate, including Silby Barrett, was easily able to defeat the left wing in the election of the CCL executive. Barrett and the other right wing officers of District 26 had a much narrower victory in the district elections in October. All managed to win re-election, but the voting in Glace Bay sub-district and Pictou County was heavily against President D. W. Morrison and International Board Member Barrett, and their margin in New Waterford was slim. Barrett in particular was very nearly defeated by left-winger John Alex MacDonald, who led in the election until the votes of the peripheral regions of the district came in. Close as the election was, the domination of the right on the District Board was strengthened. The radical Bob Stewart, former AMW Secretary-Treasurer and the Board Member for Glace Bay since 1938, was defeated by 25 votes in a five man contest by John Morrison of the large Phalen local.[47] Several factors explain why right wing officers held District power even though the left was more influential among miners in the largest sub-district, Glace Bay: the "favorite son" bias of the miners, who tended to vote for a man from their own local or sub-district; the large number of candidates splitting up the vote, election to paid union office being one of the only avenues of social mobility open to ambitious miners; and the fact that incumbent officers were usually the only candidates known to miners in locals far from the centre, so that the incumbent could almost invariably count on the votes of men in the Joggins mines, in Inverness, or in Minto, New Brunswick.

With their tenure in office established for another two years, the executive officers held a referendum on the recommendations of the McTague and Harrison Conciliation Boards, disregarding the protests of union locals against

45 *Glace Bay Gazette*, 6, 7 September 1940.
46 *Ibid.*
47 *Glace Bay Gazette*, 14 September, 9, 10, 16 October 1940.

this flaunting of the decision of the convention. The executive argued for acceptance of the awards since the contracts would only be applicable for a few months, until the end of January 1941, and they did offer some miners small increases retroactive to February 1939 and the remission of coal and housing debts. In the pithead vote of Domco miners on the McTague recommendations the contract was accepted by a vote of 3614 to 2775. As usual, the Glace Bay men voted against acceptance, but the New Waterford and Springhill votes provided the margin for agreement. The Pictou County and Sydney Mines miners totally refused to cast any votes in their referenda on the Harrison reports, and demanded the recall of the officers for holding the referenda in contravention of the convention decision.[48]

Because "illegal" strikes had continued since the convention, the federal government called a meeting in early December at Ottawa attended by the District 26 officers, Thomas Kennedy, the International Secretary-Treasurer of the UMW, Nova Scotia Labour Minister L. D. Currie, and federal Minister McLarty. They decided to hold an enlarged conference at Halifax on 12 December which top Dosco officials would be asked to attend.[49] A few weeks previously District 26 leaders had attended the CIO convention at Atlantic City, and the presence of Kennedy at Ottawa and later at the Halifax meeting indicates a new level of intervention by the International.

On 8 December the 200 UMW workers at the International Pier in Sydney went on strike. These were not miners, but the men who loaded the ships with coal at the Pier. Their work had greatly increased since the war began, "bunkering" ships for the Atlantic convoys, but their wages had gone down because of a new system of payment. Dosco officials immediately blew up the importance of this strike by stopping operations at three Glace Bay mines on the grounds that there was nowhere to send the coal produced with the Pier closed down.[50] Immediately after the strike began the District officers revoked the UMW charter of the Pier local. Although the men returned to work after a strike of only three days, the charter remained suspended pending an investigation by the International Board.[51] The charter was returned by the International, but the local's eight officers were expelled from the union, and blacklisted by the company. Among those blacklisted was the articulate young President of the local, Donald MacDonald, who ten months later was elected CCF M.L.A. for Sydney. It is difficult to think of MacDonald, who was to become President of the Canadian Labour Congress, as an extreme union militant, and he later claimed he had been opposed to the strike.[52] However, the district leaders, going

48 *Glace Bay Gazette*, 8, 20, 22 November 1940.

49 *Glace Bay Gazette*, 4 December 1940.

50 *Glace Bay Gazette*, 10 December 1940.

51 *Halifax Herald*, 11 December 1940; *Glace Bay Gazette*, 11 December 1940.

52 *Glace Bay Gazette*, 13 January 1941.

into the conference on 12 December, may have felt that these Pier workers, isolated from the bulk of the miners, were a relatively safe group to choose for exemplary victims of the toughened discipline against wildcat strikes.[53]

The Halifax conference was chaired by provincial Minister L.D. Currie, and was attended by the District 26 Board, International UMW Secretary-Treasurer Kennedy, Dosco President Arthur Cross of Montreal, Dosco Vice-President and General Manager H.J.Kelley, Nova Scotia Steel and Coal President Michael Dwyer, and numerous provincial and federal Labour Department officials. Federal Minister McLarty was not present, but was represented by Dr. Bryce Stewart, the Deputy Minister of Labour, and M.S. Campbell, Chief Conciliation Officer. Also representing the federal government was J. McGregor Stewart, Dominion Coal Administrator. This well publicized meeting was clearly intended to take some decisive steps to end strikes in the coal fields. The principal result, presented as an important breakthrough in labour-management relations by both the *Labour Gazette* and the *UMW Journal*, was the establishment of a tribunal for final and binding settlement of grievances in the mines, named the "Joint Board of Adjustment", with one representative from management, one from the union, and a jointly agreed upon chairman.[54] J.W. MacLeod, who had been the "Umpire" under the preceding grievance system, became the chairman, and Secretary-Treasurer MacKay the UMW representative, but there is no evidence suggesting that this board had better success in curbing walkouts than did the single "Umpire" it replaced.[55]

The Halifax conference agreed with the recommendation of the McTague Board that, should the company and union fail to reach agreement in negotiations by 15 January 1941, a tribunal consisting of the same men, Judge

53 This threat of ejection from the union by removal of locals' charters was not to prove a very potent weapon, however. The UMW always faced the possibility that the miners would be driven to attempt a break with the International as in the AMW years. Early in the new year, when Stellarton and Sydney Mines pits each went on strike, a wire from John L. Lewis threatening charter revocation was used to get the Stellarton men back to work. There were no blacklistings, however, and no record of even the threat of removal of their charter against the Sydney Mines men. *Glace Bay Gazette*, 3, 6, 7, 8, 10 February 1941. The UMW officers may have been hesitant to use the threat of charter revocation against the Sydney Mines men in case the bluff would be immediately called, since these miners had stayed with the AMW for several years after the rest of the miners had returned to the UMW.

54 *Halifax Herald*, 13 December 1940; *Glace Bay Gazette*, 17 December 1940; *Labour Gazette*, 40 (December 1940), p. 1239; *UMW Journal*, January 1941. A revealing aspect of this agreement is that although Dosco persisted in the pretence that its various coal subsidiaries were quite separate, and must conduct negotiations independently, it agreed that the management appointee to this binding grievance board for all companies should be "from the management of one of the companies". If the company and union could not agree on a chairman, he was to be appointed by the federal Minister of Labour.

55 The attitude of the radicals is indicated from the name "Disjointed Board of Maladjustment" immediately given to the board by the *Steelworker and Miner*, 4 January 1940.

McTague, Ralph Bell and Frank Scott, should "settle the terms of a new contract". With unconscious irony the *Labour Gazette* report stated that it was a "fine tribute" to the work of the conciliation board that the same personnel for the tribunal should now be agreed upon by all parties.[56]

The government's wartime wage policy for all Canada was made clear the next week, when P.C.7440 was issued on 16 December. Wage settlements were to be tied to a "fair and reasonable" standard, the rates payable in the period 1926-1929. However, for each five per cent rise in the cost of living index a five per cent wartime bonus could be permitted. Justice McTague was appointed "Conciliation Advisor" to the Minister of Labour, with the specific responsibility of reviewing all conciliation findings to ensure they complied with the order.[57] Predictably, the UMW and Domco negotiations failed, and on 15 January 1941 notice was given that the services of the McTague Tribunal would be required. The tribunal did not meet until 28 February, when the company again claimed it was financially unable to pay any general increase, while the UMW disputed this and argued that miners' wages in the 1926-29 period had been abnormally depressed, and that the cost of living was now unusually high in the area. The tribunal disregarded the union's pleas and accepted the company's claim that it could not afford a large pay hike. When the award, again unanimous, was made public on 13 March, small pay raises were included for the Scotia and Acadia men, for shippers at the Sydney Pier, and for the mechanics working in the mines, but no basic rate increase for most of the men. Although it was found that due to a rise in cost of living of 7.2 per cent, they were entitled to a 30 cent bonus per shift, the "finances of the companies and general condition of the industry ... do not ... warrant the full payment of this amount now". Instead, a 15 cent per shift war bonus was recommended, with an additional 15 cents to be added when it was judged appropriate. The tribunal stipulated that the increases and bonus would be retroactive to 1 February only if the union accepted the contract within 30 days.[58]

It was extremely improbable that the miners would vote to accept this contract, since the "outlaw" strikes had continued through early 1941 and sub-district conventions had been held, with representation from Glace Bay, Sydney Mines, and New Waterford locals, that showed the increasing influence of the left. At these meetings the delegates had fruitlessly pursued the idea of a recall of executive officers, registered their opposition to the provisions of P.C.7440, and threatened a general strike over the delay in getting a reasonable contract. After the McTague report was published not even the *Glace Bay*

---

56 *Labour Gazette*, 40 (December 1940), p. 1240.

57 *Labour Gazette*, 41 (January 1941), pp. 22-4.

58 *Labour Gazette*, 41 (March 1941), pp. 231-36; *Glace Bay Gazette*, 15 January, 28 February, 1, 14 March 1941.

Gazette thought that the miners would agree to its terms. Rumours circulated that the executive might sign without a referendum, and resolutions were passed in several locals against any such action. However, at a board meeting on the eve of the Easter weekend, just before the 13 April deadline for signing the contract, the District Executive Board decided to accept the contract without a referendum, by a vote of five to three. This decision was revealed almost immediately by one of the minority, New Waterford Board Member and CCF M.L.A. Douglas MacDonald.[59]

The indignation of the miners was at once made apparent. Miners at the Florence pit were already on strike on a local grievance, and they were joined in a general walkout of the men in all the mines in Glace Bay, New Waterford and Sydney Mines sub-districts. A statement supporting the miners' strike "to restore democracy" was issued by SWOC Local 1064 in Sydney. The strike call was sent out by a "tri-sub-district convention" attended by delegates from locals in the Glace Bay, New Waterford and Sydney Mines sub-districts.[60] This body and its "policy committee" were to guide the actions of the miners throughout the slowdown. Prominent in its leadership were the well known militants and radicals of the district, almost all old AMW men. Some, like John Alex MacDonald and Bob Stewart, were members or former members of the Communist Party.[61] Others, such as Tom Ling of New Waterford and Angus McIntyre of Glace Bay, were from the left wing of the local CCF.[62]

The executive officers, faced with this rising storm, argued that the only choices were to sign the contract or carry out a disastrous strike. There was no time for a referendum, given the 30 day deadline the tribunal had set; and they were advised by Professor Scott and the UMW International Board that it would be advisable to sign at once. The executive pointed out that while a referendum "is looked upon by some as a great democratic and sacred principal [sic], it is also true that our last district convention decided that no referendum

---

59 *Glace Bay Gazette*, 13, 15, 24 January, 10, 17, 25 February, 17, 29, 31 March, 12 April 1941. See also MacEwan, *Miners and Steelworkers*, p. 230.

60 *Glace Bay Gazette*, 9, 10, 12, 14, 15, 16, 17 April 1941; *Sydney Post-Record*, 16 April 1941.

61 Stewart had left the Party in 1936, following J.B. McLachlan out in protest at the right turn of the time and the disbandment of the A.M.W. He does not appear to have rejoined the Party at this period, although he was a member or a very active supporter in the post war years. MacDonald may well still have considered himself a Party member at this time, and his stand in 1940-1941 seems to have adhered closely to party positions.

62 The Ling brothers had put forward the resolution at the 1938 convention for District 26 affiliation with the CCF. McIntyre had been the first secretary of the Cape Breton Regional CCF Council, and was one of the men Clarie Gillis defeated in the contest for nomination as party candidate for C.B.South. He then resigned as secretary and possibly from the beginning his leftism led to some uneasiness concerning him on the part of the leadership. See H.I.S. Borgford to D. Lewis, 17 August 1939; Lewis to Borgford, 24 August 1939, CCF Papers, MG 28 IV I, Vol. 27, Public Archives of Canada [PAC].

vote would be held at that time, notwithstanding the fact that the executive officers had recommended that a referendum vote might be taken". A telegram sent to all District 26 locals by the top International officers, John L. Lewis, Philip Murray and Thomas Kennedy, called on the men to end the strike. Within a few days the Springhill local voted to endorse the district officers' actions.[63] Despite these endorsements, the district officers had permanently lost any substantial support from Cape Breton miners, even among the moderates. Only a small minority of right wing miners would henceforth speak in their favour, although the *Glace Bay Gazette* attempted to bolster up the confidence of the right wing by printing letters backing the officers. Reflecting radical opinion, the *Steelworker and Miner* declared that D.W. Morrison had joined the ranks of the world's great betrayers like "Judas, Benedict Arnold, Laval and Quissling [sic]".[64]

The strike was ended after four days by a tri-sub-district convention decision, and a petition to the International Board was circulated, asking for the removal of President Morrison and Secretary-Treasurer MacKay from office. According to a later statement by the convention committee, this petition was signed by 5845 miners within a few hours.[65] The response of the International was to appoint Senator William Sneed of Pennsylvania, whom Lewis sent frequently to deal with District 26 problems, and David Stevens, UMW International Board Member for District 7, Illinois, to investigate "internal dissension" in the district. Sneed and Stevens arrived on 14 May, met with the executive on 16 May and then held hearings for two days at the Sydney Courthouse, after which they returned to the United States to report to the UMW International Board.[66] The miners were not placated by this investigation. Before the commissioners arrived, the slowdown strike had begun, at first as an apparently spontaneous movement among the miners in New Waterford and Sydney Mines. Memory of the slowdown strike conducted in 1921 under the leadership of J.B.McLachlan may have contributed to the popularity of this idea among miners. At a tri-sub-district convention held on 11 May the policy of "curtailment of production" was almost unanimously endorsed. The delegates also pledged that the locals would abide by this decision until it was rescinded by another convention.[67]

A circular letter was promptly sent out by the district executive stating this policy was contrary to the constitution of the UMW, and would not be tolerated.

63 *Glace Bay Gazette*, 17, 21 April 1941.

64 *Steelworker and Miner*, 19 April 1941.

65 *Glace Bay Gazette*, 19 April, 11 July 1941. According to the Policy Committee's "A Message to the Unions of Canada", published in the *Canadian Tribune*, 16 August 1941, 10,000 miners eventually signed the petition demanding the resignations.

66 *Sydney Post-Record*, 16, 19 May 1941; *Glace Bay Gazette*, 16, 17, 19 May 1941.

67 *Glace Bay Gazette*, 5, 8, 12 May 1941.

A full page Dosco advertisement in the *Glace Bay Gazette* appealed to wartime patriotism, quoted Winston Churchill, and declared: "We therefore join with the President and officers of District 26 of the United Mine Workers of America in requesting the immediate discontinuance of this policy of curtailment of coal production". These blandishments had little effect, nor did the first attempts by the company to coerce the miners. At the Sydney Mines collieries, when the management tried reducing the workforce after the mine output fell due to the slowdown, there was a week of strikes until the company rescinded the policy.[68]

The "curtailment policy" posed several difficulties for the company. In both the mines working the longwall system and those operating under the older "room and pillar" system, the workforce was composed of roughly half contract miners and half "datal" men. The contract miners dug the coal and loaded it in cars to be sent to the surface, and were paid for the weight they produced. The datal men transported the coal and maintained the mine, and were paid a daily wage. It was the contract miners who were formally on slowdown, and although the amount they were paid would be reduced, they still had an income much greater than any strike pay they could have received in a full tieup. So long as the mine operated, the lower paid datal men would receive their full wage per shift. Since the company's profits suffered, the natural counter to such tactics was a lockout, but the company was under pressure from their customers and the government to keep up coal production, and wished to make what profit they could from coal operations while sales were assured. Presumably Dosco also preferred that all the odium incurred for disrupting war production be directed at the miners.

Support for the slowdown remained quite solid and effective in the Glace Bay and New Waterford mines throughout the summer. In some respects this solidarity was remarkable. The penalty of public disgrace for being a strike-breaker was immense in the union conscious mining towns, but breaking solidarity was neither so clear cut or readily detected during a slowdown. The miners generally worked in pairs in isolated places in the mine, and all that was required to increase a man's income when the unpaid bills began to mount was to load a little more coal. Yet it was universally agreed, by both proponents and opponents, that the slowdown was effective in cutting production in almost all Cape Breton's Domco mines by at least one third from May until September.[69] Although the Scotia miners in Sydney Mines voted to end their slowdown in the middle of June, when they and the Acadia miners received a slight pay increase,

68 *Glace Bay Gazette*, 13, 17, 21, 22, 27, 28 May 1941.

69 Since the Reserve mine was in the process of closing down and having a new pit opened, it took no part in the slowdown with the consent of the other locals at the conventions. The one mine in which support was reported to be somewhat weak and fluctuating was 1B at Dominion. *Glace Bay Gazette*, 19 July 1941.

the sympathies of the Sydney Mines men appear to have remained with the convention, since they continued to send delegates as observers, and it retained the title "tri-sub-district convention". At both Sydney Mines and Stellarton wildcat strikes took place during the slowdown.[70]

On 6 June, by Order in Council P.C. 4016, coal mining was declared an "essential service" under the Defence of Canada Regulations. Although this amounted to no more than bringing mining into the same category as many other industries regarded as necessary to war production, the local newspapers interpreted the timing of this step as an effort to intimidate the Nova Scotia miners.[71] Later in June the district officers went to Ottawa to meet with government officials, and this meeting was followed by a renewed effort by the UMW International to bring the Cape Breton miners under control. At the beginning of July John L. Lewis placed Silby Barrett in control of District 26, with "full authority to act for the international office in all matters involving the locals".[72] Although the other district officers were not removed as the miners had demanded, Lewis seems to have thought this step could defuse the situation. However, it only succeeded in making Barrett, who for some time had not been much involved with district affairs, the main focus of the miners' resentment. Silby Barrett was certainly not helped by the historical parallel with his 1923 appointment as provisional head of the district when the left executive led by J. B. McLachlan had been deposed by John L. Lewis. Moreover, in July 1941 the *Steelworker and Miner*, with unconcealed relish, published the 1924 letter accusing Barrett of misappropriation of funds, which had led to his removal from office.[73] Barrett may have gained national prominence in the labour movement by his leading role in the Canadian CIO, but locally no union leader was more closely associated with heavy-handed bureaucracy.

Barrett met with the District Board, and then sent out a circular to the locals repeating the charge that the slowdown was unconstitutional, and demanding compliance with this stand by 15 July. The Board declared the tri-sub-district conventions "illegal and unconstitutional", on the grounds that conventions of a single sub-district only were permissable, and then only when properly convened by the Board Member. Letters were also sent to 13 individual leaders of the convention, ordering them to appear before a union tribunal on 15 July to face charges of violating the constitution. Barrett appealed to the miners to end the slowdown in the name of loyalty to the UMW and to Canada. Additionally he referred to "illegal spending" by the locals, and from this time the locals were cut

70 *Glace Bay Gazette*, 5, 9,16, 24 June, 31 July 1941.

71 *Labour Gazette*, 41 (August 1941), pp. 963-4; *Sydney Post-Record*, 7 June 1941; *Halifax Herald*, 7 June 1941; *Glace Bay Gazette*, 7 June 1941.

72 Telegram John L. Lewis to D.J. MacDonald, Chairman of the tri-sub-district committee, *Glace Bay Gazette*, 2 July 1941.

73 *Steelworker and Miner*, 12 July 1941.

off from receiving their share of the checked-off dues payments. The convention policy committee defiantly replied that the miners would end the slowdown only when the officers were removed, and the largest local, Phalen, sent a wire to Lewis demanding the removal of all the executive, not merely Morrison and MacKay. On 11 July the policy committee indicated that curtailment of production would stop only if the entire executive, including Barrett, resigned and were replaced by three provisional officers sent by the International to hold an election as speedily as possible, and if the miners received a "decent increase in wages that will allow us to live as Canadian citizens should live".[74] The committee also called for a one day strike, a demonstration and a mass meeting on 15 July, the day the 13 men were to appear before the UMW tribunal.

On 15 July all the mines in the Glace Bay and New Waterford areas were shut down. Over 5000 men marched through Glace Bay "to form what was considered the largest parade of workers in the history of this mining community". The event was very orderly, the miners of each local marching as a contingent carrying "Union Jacks and banners". The entire procession was led by two large banners reading: "WE ARE FIGHTING FOR DEMOCRACY" and "DOWN WITH HITLER AND SILBY BARRETT". The parade escorted the 13 accused men to the UMW District Office, and then proceeded to the Miners' Forum, the hockey arena, where a mass meeting was held. The 13 accused, having made their brief appearances before what they called the "kangaroo court", were greeted as heroes at the rally. Bob Stewart, John Alex MacDonald, Tom Ling, Angus McIntyre, Freeman Jenkins, and Convention Chairman Dan J. MacDonald, along with other speakers, all denied the validity of the trials, and urged the miners to continue the slowdown and not make the mistake of starting a full strike, in which the authorities could defeat them. Norman MacKenzie and George MacEachern of the Sydney steel workers' union spoke in solidarity with the miners, and the meeting unanimously passed a resolution demanding the repeal of P.C.7440.[75]

The efforts of Barrett and the UMW executive to bring the miners under control had been turned into a triumphant display of solidarity and of the ascendancy of the left in the locals and among the rank-and-file miners. A few days later a Phalen meeting passed a resolution that the local would have no further dealings with the district officers. Phalen did not, local President Freeman Jenkins assured the press, intend to break with the UMW, but it would no longer recognize this executive. Three other locals, Caledonia, No.11 and No.12 at New Waterford, sent telegrams to John L. Lewis demanding the executive's removal. Lewis wired back an ultimatum that unless these locals complied with the constitution and subordinated themselves to the district office

74 *Halifax Herald*, 10 July 1941; *Sydney Post-Record*, 10 July 1941; *Glace Bay Gazette*, 7, 8, 9, 10, 11 July 1941.

75 *Sydney Post-Record*, 16 July 1941; *Glace Bay Gazette*, 15, 16 July 1941.

before the end of a week, their UMW charters would be revoked. On the same day, 19 July, Barrett issued another press statement repeating demands that the men return to full production. On 21 July letters were sent out to the locals informing them that the 13 men who had appeared before the tribunal were suspended from UMW membership.[76]

By this time the slowdown had become a hot national news story, and editors throughout the country were demanding that the government deal promptly with this unpatriotic disruption of war production. Domco purchased space for full page spreads in newspapers and explained that the curtailment policy resulted from an inner-union quarrel, for which the company had no responsibility.[77] This pressure also affected Minister of Labour Norman McLarty, who decided to make a direct appeal to the miners' patriotism in a full page advertisement published in various newspapers and in a radio broadcast over CJCB Radio Station in Sydney, with the Minister's voice coming over the telephone lines from Ottawa. McLarty claimed that "all parties admitted the dispute concerned only the union members themselves", ignoring the fact that the men were also demanding better wages and repeal of the government's wage policy. Referring to the miners' defiance of the UMW executive he said: "Your government has declared in favour of collective bargaining but it is your responsibility to see that it works". Only one sentence came close to a threat: "This slowdown is discouraging the continuance of the government's policy of subventions to the coal mines of Nova Scotia and endangers the employment which they stimulate".[78]

The CCL executive also met with McLarty and appealed for government support for collective bargaining rights by the active enforcement of P.C.2685, which called for employers to recognize unions. The slowdown was discussed, and Mosher, Conroy, Millard and the others were quick to back their colleague Silby Barrett. The executive passed a resolution expressing the "unqualified support" of the CCL for the UMW Board's efforts to obtain "full compliance with the policies and laws of the union by certain members of the union in the Cape Breton coal fields".[79]

Neither the CCL endorsement of the executive nor McLarty's appeal weakened the stand of the miners. Delegates at the tri-sub-district convention said the Minister was mistaken if he did not understand that the wage rate was the principal issue. McLarty was then sent a request for a direct conference involving the convention, the government and the coal company. The response to John L. Lewis was even more determined. The convention sent him a

---

76 *Glace Bay Gazette*, 18, 19, 23 July 1941.

77 *Globe and Mail*, 9 July 1941; *Halifax Herald*, 9 July 1941.

78 *Glace Bay Gazette*, 22 July 1941; *Sydney Post-Record*, 22 July 1941; *Halifax Herald*, 22 July 1941.

79 *Glace Bay Gazette*, 24 July 1941.

telegram stating that if the charters of the three locals were revoked, all ten UMW locals in Glace Bay and New Waterford would secede from the union. Lewis, in fact, quietly backed down. The threatened locals were given an extension of the ultimatum, and then the matter was allowed to drop.[80]

The miners' slowdown now began to get some support from a somewhat surprising source, the representatives of small businessmen in the area. The Glace Bay Board of Trade and the Retail Merchant Association informed McLarty that the men's unfairly low wages were the root of the problem, and that the miners had good reasons to have lost confidence in their union officers.[81] The sympathetic stance of local small business towards the miners' rebellion continued through the summer, and perhaps is largely explained by the extent to which these merchants depended upon the miners as customers, and had a direct interest in higher wages being paid them. Some food retailers were by this time themselves in difficulties, having extended credit to miners.

McLarty remained impervious to this pressure, informing the the Retail Merchants' Association and the convention committee that the miners' grievances would only be considered when full production resumed. At the end of July the Minister met with UMW Secretary-Treasurer Kennedy and Barrett and they adopted two new initiatives: McLarty would visit the area himself and the UMW International would send Senator Sneed again to District 26 to take charge of union affairs. McLarty then travelled to Glace Bay where he repeated that nothing could be done for the miners until they gave up the slowdown, and urged them to co-operate with Senator Sneed. Although Sneed met with the convention committee on several occasions, and sent an optimistic wire to McLarty, he also failed to convince the miners to give way. In a last ditch effort, he warned the men in a radio broadcast that unless they resumed full production they could not "expect the protection" of the union. "Officers of local unions and membership in Cape Breton, you cannot fight your government; neither can you fight the international union of the UMW of A". If they complied, he hinted strongly, they would almost immediately get the full bonus payment under P.C.7440.[82]

In the last week in August the coal company took more decisive action, apparently acting on a plan coordinated with the UMW officers and the government. On 23 August, a Saturday, executive officers Morrison, MacKay, and Muise met with Domco officials. On the Monday company officials formally questioned miners as they arrived at the pits on their stand on curtailment. On 27 August the officials at Caledonia mine began "refusing lamps" to some of the miners, turning them away when they reported for work.

80 *Glace Bay Gazette*, 24, 29 July 1941.

81 *Glace Bay Gazette*, 25 July 1941.

82 *Sydney Post-Record*, 28 July 1941; *Glace Bay Gazette*, 28, 30 July, 1, 2, 5, 6, 7, 8, 9, 11, 15, 16, 21 August 1941.

Over the days and weeks that followed, these "lamp stoppages" went on in a planned system of escalation, first at one mine and then another. Only contract miners who supported curtailment were dismissed, 16 the first day at Caledonia, 20 the next day, and the same number on succeeding days. The same process began at No.2 on 29 August, and at No.12 New Waterford on 30 August, and later at other mines. Fruitless protests were sent to the Labour Minister and other authorities, a committee was set up to collect funds for the support of the laid off men, and there was discussion of launching a full strike. The Sydney SWOC passed a resolution that its members would strike in sympathy if the miners were forced into this action. By 3 September No.12, where 140 longwall men had been dismissed and others refused to work their places, had been completely closed down. M.L.A. Douglas MacDonald asked Minister of Justice Ernest Lapointe to take action against this "lock-out of 1100 men", in "direct violation of the industrial disputes investigation act". A similar protest was sent by the Glace Bay Army and Navy Veterans Association, who said many of those dismissed were veterans or the fathers of men serving overseas. McLarty replied that this was not a lockout; the coal company "is merely suspending men who do not give a day's work for a day's pay", and they would be immediately re-employed if they expressed willingness to abandon the slowdown.[83] The government's attitude to strikes was definitely stiffening at this time. On 17 September P.C.7307 was passed, tightening the regulations governing legal strikes and increasing the penalties for illegal strikes.[84]

At the same time the "lamp stoppages" began, the government and company authorized the payment of the additional 15 cent per shift bonus to the Springhill miners.[85] This was presumably the "carrot" to go with the "stick" of the dismissals. There was also another rather farcical attempt to use the "stick" at this time. A strike of 15 pump workers in late August had led to the closing down of the two mines at Stellarton for several days. The authorities apparently decided to make examples of these men, and two of them were actually arrested and brought to trial for "illegal" striking, although the men charged could not be proven to have been involved in the strike, and the cases were dismissed.[86]

In Cape Breton the company continued the lamp stoppages until the second week in September, when the total dismissed came to approximately 400 men, including most of the leading convention delegates. Other miners were unable to work because the number to operate a shift was insufficient, and they refused

---

83 *Halifax Herald*, 23 August 1941; *Sydney Post-Record*, 27 August, 4, 10 September, 1941; *Glace Bay Gazette*, 23, 26, 27, 28, 29, 30 August, 4, 8, 10 September 1941.

84 *Labour Gazette*, 41 (October 1941), p. 1209.

85 *Glace Bay Gazette*, 1 September 1941. A day later, the employees of the company-owned Sydney and Louisburg Railway also got the additional bonus. *Glace Bay Gazette*, 3 September 1941.

86 *Halifax Herald*, 3 September 1941; *Glace Bay Gazette*, 22 August, 3 September 1941. One man was drunk on the day in question, and the other had been sent home by his supervisor.

transfers on principle. Money was collected from working miners for the men thrown out of work, and the slowdown policy was reaffirmed by votes of convention delegates, but the pressure had begun to have an effect on the miners' earlier unbreachable solidarity. As early as 24 August Bob Stewart of Caledonia mine had proposed that the miners return to full production for a month to see what the government would do for them. This idea was overwhelmingly rejected by convention delegates, and Stewart was attacked as a traitor by the *Steelworker and Miner*, but Stewart continued to press for this plan at subsequent convention sessions.[87]

Pressure was particularly intense on the discharged miners, who had no income other than the amount that could be collected for their relief. Rumours were now prevalent that many working miners were increasing production to save their jobs, yet not contributing heavily to the fund for the men out of work. Soon after their dismissals these men had been handed discharge slips, implying their severance from the company was permanent. But the company also offered to return the lamp of any man who signed a paper promising full production, and by the middle of September a number of the men began to accept this offer. On 16 September, 84 No.12 men were reported to have accepted back their jobs on the basis of full production. On 22 September the local at No.16 voted to abandon the curtailment policy for 30 days; and at Caledonia, the mine hardest hit with dismissals, men were gradually returning to work, promising to end the slowdown.[88]

The second annual CCL Convention was held at Hamilton in early September. The Cape Breton miners understood the importance of having their position presented, and in mid-August had elected delegates. Because the locals' funds had been frozen by the officers no money was available to send these delegates, but at the end of August one delegate, John Alex MacDonald, was sent. He spoke at various union meetings in Ontario and collected money to pay for the attendance of miner delegates at the convention, and a delegation of 34 led by Angus McIntyre was rushed to Hamilton at the last moment. Arriving a day late, the delegation marched on to the convention floor greeted by a standing ovation. A large banner had been hung on the wall reading: "GREETINGS TO THE FIGHTING NOVA SCOTIA MINERS".[89] This welcome was extremely displeasing to the right wing, a displeasure openly revealed by President Aaron Mosher.[90] Mosher had earlier directly involved himself in attempts to prevent the left wing delegates coming from Cape Breton,

87 *Glace Bay Gazette*, 25 August 1941; *Steelworker and Miner*, 30 August 1941.

88 *Glace Bay Gazette*, 8, 16, 22 September 1941.

89 *Glace Bay Gazette*, 16, 19 August, 1, 8, 18 September 1941.

90 Mosher reportedly tried to damp down the applause, saying: "You can please yourselves if you want to make a rebel of this convention or carry on in the proper manner". *Glace Bay Gazette*, 10 September 1941.

in his anxiety to ensure a right majority.[91] Before the convention opened the CCL executive had passed a resolution opposing any strikes that broke existing contracts, and Mosher's opening speech, broadcast nationwide by the CBC, appealed to government to make it mandatory for employers to engage in collective bargaining, but called for labour peace in wartime. "It is more important to defeat Hitler and his gangsters than to bring the most tyrannical and reactionary employer in Canada to his knees".[92] The left appears to have had the majority of vocal floor delegates, but they were in the minority in role call votes conducted on the basis of workers represented. In the election of CCL executive board members John Alex MacDonald got 199 votes, more than any other left candidate, but the right slate was elected, with Charles Millard getting 269 votes and Silby Barrett 231. A heated struggle arose over a resolution tabled by the Sydney SWOC delegation which asked the convention to "condemn the action of the Executive in opposing the struggle of the miners for trade union democracy and a better standard of living". The convention resolutions committee, chaired by Pat Conroy, put forward an alternative resolution calling for the dismissed men to be re-employed, the slowdown to end, and urging the government to get more money for the miners. In the end the right wing resolution, defeated by a floor vote, was carried by a roll call vote of 199 to 158.[93]

Although the Cape Breton delegates were disappointed by this decision and by opposition shown to their position by prominent CCF leaders at the convention, they were heartened by the strong support they had been given by the left forces at Hamilton, which included the support of almost all the rank-and-file CIO delegates in attendance. At the tri-sub-district convention held on 17 September it was decided to carry on with the curtailment policy, even though there was no hope of official support from the CCL and it was clear the solidarity of the miners was collapsing. In fact, the miners surely felt they were defeated, for in a telegram sent to McLarty they agreed to resume full production if the government would guarantee that Domco would rehire all the dismissed men and pay the full bonus under P.C.7440. McLarty replied that the men must first begin normal working, and then their grievances could be dealt with. The delegates interpreted this reply to mean that "McLarty thought they were going back licked".[94]

---

91 Abella, *Nationalism, Communism and Canadian Labour*, p. 71.

92 *Labour Gazette* 41 (October 1941), pp. 1245-6.

93 *Canadian Congress of Labour 1941, Minutes*, pp. 98-9, 102. Abella, in his account of this convention, argues the left forces, influenced by the change of Communist policy now that the Soviet Union was in the war, "were less fractious than ever": "Most ironically, they even joined with the Congress executive in condemning District 26 of the UMW for conducting an 'illegal strike'". Abella, *Nationalism, Communism and Canadian Labour*, p. 71. This is untrue, as a reading of the convention minutes clearly shows.

94 *Steelworker and Miner*, 20 September 1941; *Glace Bay Gazette*, 18, 30 September 1941.

Although the convention held to the curtailment policy, it was now mainly concerned to extract some face saving concession from the government and union authorities. At a public meeting on 24 September it was decided to send telegrams to Prime Minister King and to John L. Lewis. King was asked to guarantee full bonus payments, and Lewis to meet with three delegates from the policy committee to hear their side of the matter. On 28 September a convention was held to consider the replies from the Prime Minister and President Lewis. Neither promised anything, but the delegates chose to interpret the wording of each as sufficiently conciliatory to permit a return to full production. There seemed little choice, since two locals, Caledonia and No.16, had already voted to return to full production, and individual miners were beginning to do so at the other mines. The convention almost unanimously voted to abandon the curtailment policy. This was a retreat "in good order", wrote the *Steelworker and Miner*, and the *Canadian Tribune* claimed the miners had scored a "moral victory".[95] Tom Ling was one of the few delegates who spoke frankly of the slowdown having been defeated, but he asked the miners not to get discouraged: "We took a bad licking in 1925 and came back in 1941 and 16 years from now the younger generation will come back driven by the same conditions".[96] The dismissed miners were taken back, and within a short time the additional bonus was paid to the Domco miners.[97] The union also reinstated the 13 suspended members, and restored the funds to the locals, and no local lost its charter. But at best these concessions were evidence that the miners surrendered in sufficiently good order to prevent the authorities from attempting any retribution against them. They can hardly be called the fruits of victory.

Given the forces arrayed against them it is difficult to imagine how the slowdown could have resulted in a victory for the miners. There was always an element of confusion over whether the main aim of the curtailment policy was the removal of undemocratic officers or concessions in wages. McLarty may have deliberately misinterpreted the miners' aims when he claimed this was purely a union matter in his July statement, but up to that point many statements had been made indicating that the dismissal of the officers would immediately lead to the resumption of full production. And on both questions the miners were throughout inhibited from pushing their struggle to its full extent. Part of the reluctance to stage a full scale strike arose from the fact that the miners realized how unpopular a wartime strike would be, and their own frequent protestations of patriotic support for the war effort were not insincere. Moreover, they were never prepared to seek a full break with the UMW.

95 *Glace Bay Gazette*, 25 September 1941; *Steelworker and Miner*, 27 September 1941; *Canadian Tribune*, 4 October 1941.

96 *Glace Bay Gazette*, 29 September 1941.

97 At the same time the government permitted the coal company to increase the price of coal twenty-two cents per ton. *Labour Gazette*, 41 (October 1941), p. 1268.

Memory of the defeat of the AMW must have had much to do with this reluctance, as well as the fact that both the Communist Party and the CCF threw the weight of their influence against an action that would split the union movement at this time.

The role of these two parties during the struggle had been quite different. The Communists had consistently and actively supported the miners. The *Canadian Tribune*, for example, published statements by the miners' policy committee and editorials with titles such as "Miners Fight for Justice".[98] *Tribune* editor A.A. MacLeod visited Glace Bay several times during the slowdown to express support for the miners, once speaking at a mass meeting in the Miners' Forum along with Communist supported M.P. Dorise Neilsen and CCFer Clarie Gillis.[99] The Communist Party's policy on union struggles began to change when the Soviet Union was invaded by Germany in June 1941, and in 1942 the Party had adopted a position strongly against any disruption of war production. But this policy change did not take place as sharply and suddenly as is frequently claimed.[100] In the summer of 1941, while calling for unification behind the war effort, the Party took the line that unity could only be achieved by increasing democracy, creating trade union rights, and removing inequalities in Canada, and that strikes were inevitable so long as employers were permitted unchecked exploitation of workers.[101] This was very similar to the line the CCF had adopted; the difference was that the Communists were willing to make statements critical of the policies and actions of important union leaders, and the CCF were not.

The miners' actions created a very difficult situation for the CCF, particularly for a local politician such as Clarie Gillis. The miners had elected Gillis to Parliament, but the District officers were themselves prominent members of the CCF, and the District Office provided the money for campaigns. It was also clear, from statements made by CCF leader M. J. Coldwell opposing the slowdown, that the central leadership of the party supported the UMW officers rather than the men.[102] Gillis compromised as best he could, attacking the coal company and criticizing the government, while avoiding any direct reference to the officers; and he came under strong radical attack for this.[103] Eventually, to his embarrassment, he had to share a platform with Mrs. Neilsen and A.A.

98 *Canadian Tribune*, 26 July, 16, 23 August 1941.

99 *Glace Bay Gazette*, 25 August 1941.

100 For example, see Abella, *Nationalism, Communism and Canadian Labour*, p. 70 and Ivan Avacumavic, *The Communist Party in Canada* (Toronto, 1976), pp. 139-66.

101 See "Labor is the Key to Victory", *Canadian Tribune*, 13 September 1941. This article specifically mentions the slowdown, fully supporting the miners in a section entitled "Dosco Stalls Coal Production".

102 *Glace Bay Gazette*, 13 August, 17 September 1941.

103 *Steelworker and Miner*, 19 May, 21 June 1941.

MacLeod at a rally in support of the slowdown; but while they gave full support to the miners' attacks on the officers, Gillis could only offer to act as a negotiator, saying "no side was wholly right and no side wholly wrong" and "someone has to act as a bumper".[104]

Communist support for the slowdown won some temporary increase of Party influence in Cape Breton, but nothing that could be consolidated. One reason for this was that many local CCFers were strong proponents of the slowdown, and M.L.A. Douglas MacDonald of New Waterford increased his popularity with the miners by his actions.[105] The CCF came out of the matter very well, in fact, despite the anger of some of their supporters at the role of CCF leaders at the Hamilton CCL convention. There was a threat of independent labour candidates being nominated in the October 1941 provincial election, which might have hurt the CCF badly.[106] This was not done, and when the election was held the CCF in Cape Breton was the beneficiary of the workers' frustration with the policies of government. Douglas MacDonald was re-elected in New Waterford, and Donald MacDonald won the seat in Sydney. In Glace Bay, Minister L.D. Currie went down to defeat by CCFer D.N. Brodie by the largest majority in any of the contests in the province.[107] The anger of the miners defeated in the slowdown had been translated into electoral triumphs for the CCF.

The miners' revenge against the union executive was taken a year later when all the District 26 officers were defeated in the district election by humiliatingly large majorities. Freeman Jenkins became President, Tom Ling Vice-President and John Alex MacDonald became International Board Member. Adam Scott, another former AMW leader from Sydney Mines, won the office of Secretary-Treasurer. The victory of the union left in this election was in the long term to prove illusory. Once in office these officers, particularly President Jenkins, gradually became as bureaucratic as had been the Morrison executive. This was a pattern that repeated itself again and again in District 26 history. Most district presidents first came in defeating an incumbent with the votes of the left, and ended by becoming identified with bureaucracy and right-wing policies.

The efforts of D.W. Morrison, Silby Barrett and the other UMW officers to

---

104 *Glace Bay Gazette*, 25 August 1941.

105 MacDonald, of course, was the District Board Member who opposed signing the contract, and revealed what the executive were doing, as well as taking a strong stand against the dismissals by the company. It seems likely that these actions did him little good with the right in his own party. After the October election, when he was joined in the Nova Scotia Legislature by two other CCFers, Douglas MacDonald was passed over and the position of CCF House Leader given to Donald MacDonald of Sydney.

106 *Glace Bay Gazette*, 30 September 1941; C. Gillis to David Lewis, CCF Papers, MG IVI, vol. 5, PAC.

107 MacEwan, *Miners and Steelworkers*, p. 242.

influence government by their moderate policies had thus led to the loss of their offices.[108] It is very difficult to assess whether they had any success in modifying the government's attitude on the value of the collective bargaining process in bringing labour peace. For the next two years the government made no attempt to force anti-union employers to engage in meaningful collective bargaining. In February 1942 Mackenzie King defended his government's inaction, contradicting its stated policy in P.C.2685, during the Kirkland Lake gold miners' strike, by the argument that he opposed government compulsion against either capital or labour. As an example of the government's refraining from action against workers, he pointed out that: "Although the first principle [of P.C.2685] states that every effort should be made to speed production by war industries, the government did not exercise compulsion on miners involved in the slowdown in Nova Scotia coal mines".[109] This limp argument shows the miners' slowdown had not influenced King to regard union organization as helpful to stable productivity. In fact, the policies pursued by the government through 1939, 1940 and 1941 with respect to the UMW had much to do with the coming of the slowdown and the disruption of production it entailed. If these policies were aimed at securing and increasing the production of coal during the war, they failed dismally. The government would certainly have achieved this end much more successfully by putting real pressure on Dosco to pay decent wage increases to its miners, providing subsidies if necessary. This would probably have been a less expensive policy than the policy that failed, since the coal company was given more and more subsidies during the war, with little increase in the production of coal. By the end of 1942 the government proclaimed a "grave emergency" in national coal production; in June 1943, by Order in Council, miners were "frozen" on their jobs and former miners forced to return to the pits; and in October 1943 P.C. 8021 expressly prohibited coal strikes for the duration of the war.[110]

All of this availed little. Canadian coal production fell steadily behind the increase in consumption during the war and the deficit was made up by heavier imports from the United States. While production increased somewhat in the West, in Nova Scotia the production of coal fell throughout the war years, after a temporary rise in 1940.[111] In Alberta a district-wide strike in 1943 was able to win increases exceeding the government's limits.[112] In Nova Scotia the repression

108 MacEwan, *Miners and Steelworkers*, pp. 237, 282-5. The defeated officers did not fare too badly: Morrison was appointed a special representative by John L. Lewis, Barrett continued to hold important CCL office, and A.A. MacKay was appointed Chairman of the Domco-UMW Joint Adjustment Board.

109 Quoted in MacDowell, *'Remember Kirkland Lake'*, p. 208.

110 *Labour Gazette*, 42 (December 1942), p. 1404; Jamieson, *Times of Trouble*, p. 290.

111 Dominion Bureau of Statistics, *Coal Statistics for Canada*, 1945, Table 42, p. 38.

112 Jamieson, *Times of Trouble*, p. 290.

and defeat of the miners' collective militancy in the early war years only led to an increase of individual behaviour expressive of the miners' extreme dissatisfaction. Absenteeism increased, and so did the shift of younger men to better paying jobs elsewhere, and productivity in the mines fell sharply. The policies of the government and the coal company, and the collaboration of UMW leaders with these policies in the early war years, were in large part responsible for this failure. In Nova Scotia the District officers in the early war years had, in effect, become agents of state policy in attempts to discipline the men and force them to accept poor settlements with the coal company, and this at a time when the wages of workers in other war industries were on the rise.

The experience of District 26 in the 1939-1941 period showed both the strength and the limitations of union bureaucracy in controlling a dissatisfied and militant work force. The miners' "illegal" strikes and the long slowdown foreshadowed the wave of wildcat strikes throughout the well established Canadian labour movement in the 1960s.[113] As the new industrial unionism came to central Canada, the theoreticians of business unionism spoke of introducing democracy to the workplace. Unquestionably unionization led to advances for the workers in wages and conditions, and in some freedom from arbitrary treatment by management. But, as the struggle within the UMW revealed, the concept of union democracy held by many of the leaders of the labour movement was limited mainly to forms legitimizing the authority of union bureaucrats. Indeed, much of the intervention of state regulation in industrial relations was directly aimed at ensuring only unionism of this type could legally exist. The system of labour relations and the trade union movement that emerged achieved much for Canadian workers, but they could never satisfy workers' aspirations for more control over the labour process, bringing at best a badly flawed democracy to the workplace.

113 See *ibid.*, pp. 401-3.

JAY WHITE

Pulling Teeth: Striking for the Check-Off in the Halifax Shipyards, 1944*

IN 1937 NOVA SCOTIA CREATED A legislative precedent in the field of Canadian labour relations. For the first time a provincial Trade Union Act gave organized workers the right to have union dues automatically deducted from their paycheques, a procedure known as the check-off.[1] Yet many employers continued actively to oppose principles of union security. In 1944, Halifax Shipyards Limited, a shipbuilding subsidiary of the Montreal-based Dominion Coal and Steel Company, challenged the legality of the check-off, triggering a month-long walkout of 3,000 workers at yards in Halifax and Dartmouth. During the strike, an embattled Local No. 1, Industrial Union of Marine and Shipbuilding Workers of Canada (Canadian Congress of Labour), overcame worker apathy and federal government indifference to win a Nova Scotia Supreme Court decision upholding its claim to the check-off. Until this landmark ruling in early 1945, union security in Nova Scotia as stipulated in the Trade Union Act remained a hollow promise.

Case studies of labour disputes from this period are surprisingly rare given the high frequency and vehemence of wartime strikes.[2] Although Laurel Sefton MacDowell's study of the 1941-2 Kirkland Lake gold miners' strike shows how utterly ruthless business and government could be in resisting union recognition, those affected at Kirkland Lake represented a small group of workers in one of the few economic sectors that actually curtailed its wartime operations.[3] Most

* The author wishes to thank John C. Weaver, Michael Earle and the editor of *Acadiensis* for comments on earlier versions of this paper. Helpful research assistance was given by Peter DeLottinville, Professor Gary Chaison, Dr. Phyllis Clarke, and the Public Archives of Nova Scotia. A doctoral fellowship from Canada Mortgage and Housing Corporation and a travel grant from McMaster University supported the preparation of this paper, and are gratefully acknowledged.

1   Desmond Morton with Terry Copp, *Working People: An Illustrated History of the Canadian Labour Movement* (Ottawa, 1984), p. 162.

2   Jeremy Webber, "The Malaise of Compulsory Conciliation: Strike Prevention in Canada during World War II", in Bryan D. Palmer, ed., *The Character of Class Struggle: Essays in Canadian Working-Class History, 1850-1985* (Toronto, 1986) offers a useful (though selective) overview of several key wartime strikes.

3   Laurel Sefton MacDowell, *'Remember Kirkland Lake': The history and effects of the Kirkland Lake gold miners' strike, 1941-42* (Toronto, 1983). See also Laurel Sefton MacDowell, "The Formation of the Canadian Industrial Relations System During World War Two", *Labour/Le Travailleur*, 3 (1978), pp. 175-96. David Moulton's examination of the 1945 Ford Windsor

Canadian workers during the Second World War were engaged in manufacturing in war-related industries, and at the height of the boom, shipbuilding was Canada's largest manufacturing employer, with a labour force of over 75,000.[4] While the country was busy building arms, union organizations sought to shore up their constituencies after 20 years of decline. The imposition of wage controls in 1941 politicized the collective bargaining process, since unions were now caught between satisfying government regulations and serving their own interests.[5] Signing up new members became more difficult with the removal of wages from contract negotiations. Gradually, government legislation winnowed out other issues as well, subjecting most disputes to lengthy investigation by third-party boards in the hopes that the process would effect a solution by simply wearing the two sides down.[6] But the issue of union security did not lend itself to "compulsory compromise" because there was so little room for mediation: a demand for the closed shop might be reduced to maintenance of membership,[7] or the check-off provision made voluntary instead of mandatory, but the range of options was unusually narrow.

It seems anomalous that although both the right and left wings of organized labour were outwardly supportive of the war effort after 1941 and took a "no-strike" pledge, two years later there were more work stoppages in Canada than ever before. The labour unrest stemmed partly from dissatisfaction with government wartime legislation that, while declaring support for essential union objectives like recognition and security, offered little protection from corporate countermeasures. Canada had no equivalent to the Wagner Act until 1944 and, except for isolated pockets of prewar activity in the auto, steel and a few resource industries, widespread organizing drives across a broad spectrum of manufacturing enterprises took hold under a regime of reluctant state control.[8] Just when

---

strike in Irving Abella, ed. *On Strike: Six Key Labour Struggles in Canada* (Toronto, 1974) barely qualifies as a wartime dispute; it began on 12 September 1945. For a first-hand account of wartime labour troubles at Ford Windsor, see the interview with George Burt in Gloria Montero, *We Stood Together* (Toronto, 1979).

4   Douglas Cruikshank, "Dominion Wartime Labour Policy and the Politics of Unionism: The Experience of the Canadian Congress of Labour's Eastern Canadian Shipyards Unions, 1939-45", M.A. thesis, Dalhousie University, 1984, pp. 34-5.

5   *Ibid.*, p. 66.

6   See Webber, "Compulsory Conciliation", pp. 158-9.

7   A maintenance of membership clause usually stipulated that workers who belonged to the union when the contract was signed, or who later joined the union, must remain members for the life of the agreement. See Queen's University, Department of Industrial Relations, *Union Security Plans: Maintenance of Membership and the Check-off*, Studies in Industrial Relations Bulletin No. 10 (Kingston, 1945), p. 4.

8   The U.S. National Labour Relations (Wagner) Act (1935) protected unions from discrimination by employers and legitimized the collective bargaining process. See Morton, *Working People*,

industrial unionists needed some leeway to outmanoeuvre the obstructionist tactics of hostile employers, the government installed complicated guidelines aimed at defusing confrontations between capital and labour. The result was a period of intense frustration and dissension within the labour movement, since opinions differed sharply regarding the degree to which organized labour should abide by wartime labour policy. One of the most fractious organizations was the Canadian Congress of Labour, an unlikely amalgam of Communists, CIO unionists and old-fashioned CCFers.[9]

The CCL organized thousands of workers in wartime shipbuilding and aircraft production, and encouraged these new unions to seek security clauses in their contracts. Intent on including all production workers, industrial unions affiliated with the CCL faced stiff competition from craft unions, which had heretofore been predisposed towards exclusivity. Craft unions affiliated with the Trades and Labor Congress, the Canadian arm of the American Federation of Labour, were forced to compromise some of their principles in order to meet competition from the CCL, but they remained committed to preserving the unique identity of craft unions.[10] In the Halifax Shipyards, TLC unions challenged the dominant status of the IUMSWC by maintaining a tenacious foothold in a few skilled trades, notably machinists and welders. The TLC also enjoyed considerable success at the government-run Naval Dockyard next door. For a while, an uneasy truce prevailed between the IUMSWC, which held sole bargaining rights in the shipyards, and the AFL-TLC, but with fewer contracts and the end of the war in sight, Local No. 1 began to feel even more vulnerable as AFL organizers continued to hover in and around the yards.[11]

An even greater threat emerged from within the left wing of Maritime shipyard labour. Disillusionment with the CCL for failing to eliminate wage differentials between East and West Coast yards and to establish a national shipbuilding federation spawned a movement in mid-1943 to create an independent Maritime

---

pp. 153-4. See also J. Joseph Huthmacher, *Senator Robert F. Wagner and the Rise of Urban Liberalism* (New York, 1968), pp. 190-1, 232-3, 330. On pre-Second World War industrial unionism in Canada, see Bryan D. Palmer, *Working-Class Experience: The Rise and Reconstitution of Canadian Labour, 1800-1980* (Toronto, 1983), pp. 215-21.

9   Morton, *Working People*, pp. 202-12; MacDowell, *'Remember Kirkland Lake'*, pp. 9-11.

10   Two prominent examples were the International Association of Machinists and the International Brotherhood of Electrical Workers. *Ibid.*, p. 170.

11   See, for example, Pat Conroy to Gerald McIsaac, 21 July 1942, warning him about creating too much publicity with ongoing negotiations: "it is possible that the Company will try to invite some of these Craft Unions [Machinists and Boilermakers] into the yards for the purpose of splitting your membership", MG28 I 103, vol. 64, file 14, Canadian Labour Congress [CLC] papers, National Archives [NA]. In the same file, see also a report on the Halifax Shipyards submitted to Conroy by Elroy Robson, 7 December 1942 which discusses the unsuccessful attempt of the above unions to challenge the exclusive bargaining rights of the IUMSWC.

Marine Workers' Federation.[12] In Saint John, a renegade labour leader, J.K. Bell, spearheaded the ginger group by forming the Eastern Marine Workers Council.[13] At first, Local No. 1 rebuffed overtures from Bell's organization, stating that "we are fully cognizant of the present lack of unity in the Shipbuilding Industry in the Maritimes, but...[t]he confusion which exists...is the responsibility of others than ourselves".[14] However, as the end of the war loomed closer and faith in the CCL faded, support grew among many shipyard workers in Halifax — including the president of Local No. 1, James O'Connell — for leaving the CCL fold.[15]

The lone Congress organizer in Nova Scotia, H.A. "Pat" Shea, struggled to protect the CCL's flagship local from these circling sharks. For nearly two years Shea had lobbied for the check-off in the Halifax Shipyards without much success; by September 1943 he had ruled out the possibility that Local No. 1 could win the check-off on its own, believing that the "matter will have to be fought out in the Courts".[16] But a court case might take months to complete. When the workers in three out of four shipyards endorsed the check-off, Shea made plans for taking a strike vote. A series of wartime amendments to the Industrial Disputes Investigation Act (IDIA) added a long list of prerequisites before any legal strike could take place in an essential war industry.[17] This presented another difficulty: the timing of strike action lay beyond the control of Shea or the union. Through the winter and spring of 1943-4, the government methodically laid out the ground rules; meanwhile, skepticism grew within the IUMSWC executive, HSL management prepared for the long-expected walkout and, finally, shipping operations in Halifax sank into an off-season lull. Worse still, the CCL itself lost interest in the Halifax shipyards, believing that Local No. 1 was "merely using the Congress and the service of its representatives to get the check-off". CCL national secretary-treasurer Pat Conroy advised Shea to "spend more time in outside organization".[18] But the latter refused to abandon

12 On the MMWF, see "Interview with Donald MacDonald", MG28 I 269, vol. 1, file 6, pp. 49-51, University of New Brunswick School of Administration, NA. The assistance of Professor Gary Chaison of Clark University, Worcester, MA for facilitating access to the above is greatly appreciated.

13 See Conroy to Shea, 31 May 1944, Shea to Conroy, 3 June 1944, H.A. "Pat" Shea Correspondence, Pt. 2, and Conroy to Shea, 20 July 1944, Shea Correspondence, Pt. 1, MG28 I 103, vol. 163, CLC, NA.

14 Moir to Dobbin, 25 August 1943, MG28 I 103, vol. 64, file 11, CLC, NA.

15 See for example Shea to Conroy, 13 May 1944, MG28 I 103, vol. 163, CLC, NA.

16 Shea to Conroy, 11 September 1943, *ibid.*

17 See Webber, *Compulsory Conciliation*, pp. 141-3 for a brief summary of wartime IDIA enhancements.

18 Conroy to Shea, 16 May 1944, *ibid.*

hope, particularly after a Board of Conciliation recommended in April 1944 that the union claim to the check-off be granted.[19] Though the Board had no authority to order Halifax Shipyards Limited to change its policy, this public sanction naturally strengthened the union position. Now, Shea reasoned, if the union could be dragged into a showdown with HSL, and the federal government followed the direction of its own Board, perhaps there was some hope of victory. The strategy was based on two assumptions: that Ottawa would not tolerate a protracted shutdown of the largest shipbuilding and repair facility on the East Coast and that in a dispute between an arrogant, powerful corporation on one side and a recognized union backed by a government-appointed Board of Conciliation on the other, the latter would receive favourable consideration. Shea was wrong on both counts.

Of course, Pat Shea realized that forcing the government's hand entailed a certain amount of risk. State control of "national" industries during the Second World War often appeared to be acting less in a neutral capacity than in a collaborative role with business. Douglas Cruikshank and Greg Kealey have noted that the 1941-43 "strike wave", characterized by a high proportion of third-party settlements, also included "an unusually large number of workers' losses".[20] Many wartime labour unions simply did not have the rank and file cohesion or financial resources necessary to outlast stronger opponents. In addition, wartime regulations enervated traditional work patterns in heavy industry by means of "skill dilution"; complicated jobs were broken down into more simplified tasks, each with its own wage. The result was a segmented labour force divided by hierarchical pay scales. Occupational classifications for shipyard workers were truly byzantine. A wage schedule drawn up for a National War Labour Board hearing in May 1944 listed no less than 92 occupations; most of these in turn were divided into journeymen, apprentices, "mechanics", "helpers" and "improvers" — intermediary positions attainable after certain periods of employment.[21] Tradesmen, such as machinists, welders, electricians, and carpenters, tolerated skill dilution because jobs were abundant, and experienced workers continued to receive the highest wages.[22] On the shop floor, the

19 "IUMSW of C Local No. 1 and Halifax Shipyards re: Jurisdictional Dispute", Correspondence 1944-45, MG30 A 94, vol. 42, file 3123, J.L. Cohen papers, NA. Dr. Phyllis Clarke of Toronto kindly permitted access to the Cohen papers.

20 Douglas Cruikshank and Gregory S. Kealey, "Strikes in Canada, 1891-1950", *Labour/Le Travail*, 20 (Fall 1987), p. 118.

21 National War Labour Board, "Application of Industrial Union of Marine and Shipbuilding Workers of Canada, Locals Nos. 1 and 13...for a general increase in wages", Proceedings of Public Hearing, Ottawa, 30 January 1947, RG36 Series 4, vol. 133, file 3N-715, pp. 37-43, NA.

22 In April 1941, for example, rates of pay sought by four departments in the shipyards — machinists, pipe-fitters, blacksmiths, and electricians — were 85 cents per hour for mechanics, 75 cents for

job of administering to such a diverse work force was complicated and tedious. Union officials claimed that the check-off would give them more time to settle grievances and promote industrial harmony, an argument that seemed increasingly appropriate by the end of 1943, when industrial harmony was a commodity in short supply.

The disruptions in the wartime economy finally stirred the federal government to action. Responding to the unprecedented wave of strikes which had just swept the country, Ottawa introduced emergency legislation to facilitate collective bargaining procedures in Canadian industry.[23] The Wartime Labour Relations Regulations (P.C. 1003, February 1944) placed additional onus on labour organizations to build loyal, dues-paying constituencies in order to establish their right to sit at the bargaining table.[24] As part of its mandate, P.C. 1003 authorized the establishment of Regional War Labour Relations Boards to mediate labour disputes. Of 39 major strikes over union security between October 1944 and April 1945, 15 WLRB rulings recommended the check-off alone, while eight others included it in more comprehensive settlements. In only seven cases was the union request denied.[25] Other figures, however, suggest stronger resistance to the principle of union security. Of approximately 200 strikes in Canada during 1944, "union questions" were the cause in only 34 cases, but these relatively few stoppages accounted for 70 per cent of the time loss for the year, and nearly one quarter were unsuccessful.[26] Two strikes overshadowed all others: a massive shutdown at the Ford Windsor auto plant involving 13,000

improvers and 55 cents for helpers. Board of Conciliation Proceedings (Pt. 1) 1941-42, IUMSW of C Local 1, CCL, MG28 I 103, vol. 64, file 13, NA.

23 For an overview of wartime labour, including events leading up to the Wartime Labour Relations Order, (P.C. 1003, February 1944) see chs. 16 and 17 of Morton's *Working People*. On P.C. 1003, see H.D. Woods and Sylvia Ostry, *Labour Policy and Labour Economics in Canada* (Toronto, 1979), pp. 81, 261; Daniel Coates, *Organized Labor and Politics in Canada: The Development of a National Labor Code* (University Microfilms: Ann Arbor, 1973), esp. ch. 7, pp. 167-205; Stuart M. Jamieson, *Times of Trouble: Labour Unrest and Industrial Conflict in Canada, 1900-1966* (Ottawa, 1968), p. 294; Harry W. Arthurs, *Labour Disputes in Essential Industries* (Ottawa 1968), pp. 48-50; Wayne Roberts and John Bullen, "A Heritage of Hope and Struggle: Workers, Unions, and Politics in Canada, 1930-1982", in Michael S. Cross and Gregory S. Kealey, eds., *Modern Canada, 1930-1980's* (Toronto, 1984), p. 117; MacDowell, *'Remember Kirkland Lake'*, p. 236; A.W.R. Carrothers, E.E. Palmer and W.B. Rayner, *Collective Bargaining Law in Canada* (2nd ed., Toronto, 1986), p. 50. Useful information may also be found in the *Report of the Department of Labour for ... 1945* (Ottawa, 1945), esp. "Report of the Deputy Minister of Labour", p. 11 and chs. IV, V.

24 Cruikshank, "Politics of Unionism", pp. 144-5.

25 Queen's University, *Union Security Plans*, pp. 41ff. One quarter of the Board rulings declined to make any recommendations regarding union security.

26 *Labour Gazette*, 45 (March 1945), p. 387.

workers, and the walkout of 3,000 shipyard workers in Halifax. Thus winning acceptance of the check-off as an integral component of union security was one of the toughest challenges faced by labour during the Second World War.[27]

Because the demands of the wartime economy shifted workers both geographically and laterally into the armed forces and war production, organized labour in industries like shipbuilding often struggled to build memberships among an extremely diverse and fickle labour force.[28] The Halifax Shipyards was no exception. In 1938 the union was organized as Local 34 of the International Union of Shipbuilding and Marine Workers of America. Its affiliation with the All-Canadian Congress of Labour ended in September 1940, when Local 34 transferred to the newly-formed Canadian Congress of Labour, claiming 200 members.[29] On 28 April 1941, the union received a new charter as Local No. 1 of the Industrial Union of Shipbuilding and Marine Workers of Canada. In the interim, attempts to implement a check-off card system in the yard were frustrated. Union officials complained of "strong opposition...from the A.F. of L." and much "dissatisfaction among our... members".[30] Nevertheless, Local No. 1 was "the first industrial union in the country to have sole bargaining rights for all occupations in a single shipyard".[31]

From the outset Halifax Shipyards Limited flatly refused to consider any form of automatic dues deduction.[32] Negotiations for a new contract completely broke down in July 1941, partly because management insisted that the union "take no steps whatsoever to compel the Company to check-off for Union dues". With the help of a Board of Conciliation, an agreement was signed in August which contained an unusual clause:

> If it be determined that the provisions of the Trade Union Act of Nova Scotia relating to check-off for Union dues apply to this Company and the Union establishes its legal position, the Company agrees to conform with the relevant provisions of the legislation. The Company, however, contends that such provisions of the statute have no application to this Company....[33]

27 The Rand Formula contains an enlightened discussion of the check-off and the issues surrounding it. See *Canadian Labour Law Cases: Canada Wartime Labour Relations Board 1944-1948* (Don Mills, 1966), pp. 159-68.

28 By lateral movement I mean from other economic sectors, such as agriculture, fishing and mining, as well as the integration of formerly unpaid workers — unemployed males, married women, etc. — into the industrial labour pool.

29 Millard to Dowd, 9 September 1940, Industrial Union of Marine and Shipbuilding Workers of Canada (IUMSWC), Local 1, 1940-41, MG28 I 103, vol. 64, file 11, CLC, NA.

30 Meech to Dowd, 28 November 1940, *ibid.*

31 Cruikshank, "Politics of Unionism", p. 64.

32 Meech to Dowd, 14 May 1941, MG28 I 103, vol. 64, file 11, CLC, NA.

33 IUMSWC Local 1, 1941-42, Board of Conciliation Proceedings (Part 1), file 13, *ibid.*

This 12-month contract was renewed in November 1942. Negotiations reopened the following year but soon bogged down over the same demands: the check-off and a union shop.[34] Finally, in February 1944, an application was once again made for a Board of Conciliation under the Industrial Disputes Investigation Act. At a hearing in early April, the Conciliation Board, consisting of Judge John S. Smiley, C.B. Smith, K.C., legal counsel to HSL, and labour representative D.W. Morrison, upheld the union demand for the check-off, but not the closed shop.[35] HSL management ignored the majority recommendation of the Board; indeed the company was under no legal obligation to abide by the ruling. Worse still, HSL began to employ tactics designed to incite worker discontent. Pat Shea complained that "they [HSL] are changing conditions of work and closing canteens and doing everything they can to agitate the workers, deliberately. I have been trying to keep the workers quiet and have them stay on the job...but...the agitation by the Company [is]...making the workers very restless and difficult to handle".[36]

Shea knew well in advance that Dosco company policy opposed the check-off. During contract negotiations in October 1943 at another Dosco subsidiary, the Clare Shipbuilding Company in Meteghan, Nova Scotia, he had been given a rude shock, when after first agreeing to a check-off-clause, "the Company sent me a wire withdrawing the Check-off and stating they would agree on the rest of the contract.... There seems to be no sincerity on [their] part...to promote Industrial harmony in the plant and only a desire...to do everything in their power to create trouble".[37] The misunderstanding at Meteghan arose when the president of Clare Shipbuilding briefed his superiors in Montreal about the settlement. Corporate lawyers balked at the inclusion of the check-off, because it would set a precedent "not heretofore recognized by Eastern Shipyards".[38] Local No. 1 thus approached the prospect of battling HSL with no illusions.

The attitude of Dosco toward the check-off probably stemmed from its desire to undermine the authority of an industrial union which sought across-the-board concessions on behalf of all shipyard trades. As long as HSL continued to negotiate with distinctive trades, it could keep labour costs down by piecemeal

---

34   Canada, Department of Labour, *Report and Findings of the Board of Conciliation and Investigation in re a dispute between Halifax Shipyards Limited...and members of the Industrial Union of Marine and Shipbuilding Workers of Canada, Local No. 1* (Ottawa, 1944), p. 18.

35   Mr. Smith dutifully recorded a dissenting opinion in the Conciliation Board ruling. J.L. Cohen papers, MG30 A 94, vol. 42, file 3123, NA.

36   Shea to Conroy, 6 May 1944, H.A. "Pat" Shea Correspondence, 1942-44, part 2, MG28 I 103, vol. 163, CCL, NA.

37   Shea to Conroy, 9 October 1943, H.A. "Pat" Shea Correspondence 1942-44, part 3, *ibid.*

38   Clark to Shea (telegram), 8 October 1943, *ibid.*

bargaining and preserving the division between the skilled and unskilled. From Dosco's point of view, the check-off was an unwelcome harbinger of its labour troubles in the Cape Breton coalfields, where, many years before, miners had secured the check-off. When the general manager of Dosco's coal operations appeared before a Royal Commission investigating the Canadian coal industry in January 1945, he stated that deducting union dues from company payrolls "was of debatable value and it had not resulted in building up a union membership which accepted responsibilities nor had it tended to provide the union with the best leadership".[39] This supercilious pronouncement was typical of a managerial mindset that always blamed unions and workers for corporate setbacks. In fact, Dosco mining interests did not perform well during the Second World War, whereas HSL was one of the few credits on the company ledger.[40] It is thus conceivable that Dosco viewed the check-off not as a panacea for poor labour relations, but as a dangerous viral infection threatening to spread to healthier regions of the body corporate.

Not to be dissuaded, Shea convinced the negotiating committee of the Halifax local that a strike over the check-off issue was necessary as both a guarantee of financial security and a badge of credibility.[41] But the local was wracked with political turmoil. Charley Murray, business agent for Local No. 1 and the only Communist on the union executive, supported Shea but angered others by encouraging friendly relations with HSL management.[42] The Communist Party of Canada "adopted an official policy of cooperating with the government and promoting the war effort.... Strikes, slowdowns, and absenteeism were considered the weapons of fascism".[43] Communist shop steward Alex "Scotty" Munroe opposed resorting to strike action on those grounds, according to one witness.[44]

---

39 *Herald*, 23 January 1945.

40 The combative CCF Member of Parliament for Cape Breton South, Clarence Gillis, claimed that the corporation received more than $40 million from the government from 1939 to 1944, even though Dosco still showed a loss of $2,225,000 on coal operations in 1942 alone. See *ibid.*, 15 August 1944. The extraordinary corporate insensitivity of Dosco was never more evident than in a full page advertisement which appeared in the Halifax *Chronicle* on 8 April 1942. The notice — directed at the "miners of Cape Breton" — contained an itemized list of shortfalls in total productive capacity for the previous month. Among the causes enumerated were "Mines knocked off due to fatal accidents", and "Mines idle on day of funeral of victims of fatal accidents". Dosco accused miners of "not pulling their weight in Canada's war effort".

41 Interview with Doug Margerson, a former IUMSWC shop steward, by Michael Earle, 9 July 1986, p. 2. I am indebted to Michael Earle for kindly furnishing me with a transcript of this interview.

42 This was ironic, since Murray himself had been interned in 1940 for his labour activism. See William Repka and Kathleen M. Repka, *Dangerous Patriots* (Vancouver, 1982), p. 128.

43 Cruikshank, "Politics of Unionism", p. 108.

44 Margerson interview, p. 22.

Yet he was acknowledged by Shea as being the "spark plug inside the Yard".[45] In a letter to CCL president A.R. Mosher, Shea confirmed that Munroe "may have some connection with the Reds, this I know to be the truth...but...he can and will perform valuable work for us, for when he was working [at HSL]...he did not let his political ideas come before Union Duties".[46] Regardless of his feelings or politics prior to the walkout, Munroe staunchly supported the strike with militant rhetoric like this excerpt from a West Coast labour publication:

> We, as workers of the Halifax Shipyards Limited, are not on strike for higher wages or better working conditions, but to retain the democratic right of the trade union movement to play its part in bringing about a new era in which workers in this country and all over the world shall have the right to full employment and decent wages.[47]

As chief shop steward in the yard, Munroe routinely criticized wasteful company procedures. For his trouble, HSL management labelled him an "undesirable" and barred him from returning to work in the aftermath of the strike.[48] Pat Shea's CCF leanings did not carry him quite so far to the left, but he, like Munroe, willingly softened his political stance when necessary. Though respected by union stalwarts, some were suspicious. "You couldn't help but like [Shea], no matter what side you were on", remembers Doug Margerson, an IUMSWC shop steward, "[though] you never knew where he was going to stand at meetings, or what kind of a policy he would take. But he was the most persuasive type of man that I ever saw at a union meeting".[49]

On the afternoon of 24 July 1944, Pat Shea and 13 other union and HSL officials sat in the board room of the Halifax Shipyards. A last-ditch effort to avert a walkout had been convened by Horace Pettigrove, formerly a Fair Wages Officer for the New Brunswick government, and now with the federal Department of Labour. Pettigrove, an imposing physical presence at six feet seven inches, had a reputation for being pro-labour — likely a product of 15 years working in the Whittaker cotton mill in Marysville, New Brunswick.[50] At the meeting, the

---

45 Shea to Conroy, 18 November 1944, IUMSW of C Local 1 Correspondence 1944-46, MG28 I 103, vol. 65, file 1, CLC, NA.

46 Shea to Mosher, 24 November 1944, *ibid.*

47 Newspaper clipping: *B.C. Lumber Worker*, 21 August 1944, in Department of Labour, Strikes and Lockouts, No. 134, RG27, vol. 437 (Micro T-4070), NA.

48 Murray to Conroy (telegram), 23 November 1944, IUMSW of C Local 1 Correspondence 1944-46, MG28 I 103, vol. 65, file 1, CCL, NA.

49 Margerson interview, p. 27.

50 "An Interview with Horace Pettigrove", 10 July 1974, p. iv, MG28 I 269, vol. 1, file 1, University of New Brunswick School of Administration, NA.

company was represented by R.J.R. Nelson, general manager of the Halifax Shipyards, C.B. Smith, legal counsel to HSL, and five other executives. On the union side were Shea, Silby Barrett, veteran Cape Breton labourite and Maritime director of the Canadian Congress of Labour, Local No. 1 president James O'Connell, Scotty Munroe, Charley Murray, and two others. Pettigrove began by appealing to their sense of duty: "You all know what [the ship yard]...means to the war effort of this country, and...to the future of this industry. Everyone has something vitally at stake in this decision".[51] Neither side voiced any concern about possible repercussions of a strike, but in the presence of the enemy, that would have been a sign of weakness. When Nelson indicated that no compromise was in the offing, Barrett responded that the union would stand on the majority report of the Conciliation Board. "You cannot get to heaven in one gasp", Nelson chided the union representatives. "We will wait a long time to get to heaven", Barrett exploded, "if we wait for Dosco to hand us the Union Shop and the Check-off on a silver platter. I have not worked for them for twenty seven years and walked the rods and picket lines for ten without knowing what kind of chaps they are. This is Dosco policy... [and] you are not looking for peace in this industry...[Y]ou are going to...force us into a fight".[52] Shea pointed out that the Union had demonstrated its readiness to compromise by accepting the Conciliation Board recommendation that the demand for a union shop be modified to the less rigid maintenance of membership. With the two sides agreeing to disagree, Pettigrove had no alternative but to adjourn the meeting. Two days later, 3,000 men and women at the Shipyards in Halifax and the Marine Slip and Windmill Pier on the Dartmouth side of the harbour failed to report to work for the morning shift.[53]

Prior to the walkout the union was beset with internal problems. In January 1942, charges of peculation rocked the local when it was discovered that nearly 900 dollars were missing from union coffers. The treasurer narrowly escaped prosecution when the membership decided at the last minute to let the culprit repay the money at the rate of $20 per month, "the limit he could afford".[54] That same year, the accounts of Local No. 1 were in such disarray that a bookkeeper from another union was sent in by the CCL to balance the ledger.[55] In late 1943 union finances virtually collapsed. Pat Shea glumly informed his superiors that the

51 "Minutes of the Meeting held in the Board Room, Halifax Shipyards...July 25, 1944", Department of Labour, Strikes and Lockouts files, No. 134, RG27, vol. 437 (Micro T-4070), NA

52 *Ibid.*

53 *Labour Gazette*, 45 (March 1945), p. 383.

54 Eighteen to Dowd, 23 January 1942, IUMSW of C Local 1, 1941-42, MG28 I 103, vol. 64, file 14, CLC, NA.

55 Conroy to Moir, 15 November 1943, *ibid.*, file 12.

local was "in very bad shape and...getting worse all the time. The members...will not pay dues...and frankly I am at a loss to know how to handle it. There is no money in the treasury and...we cannot go on like this any longer.... P.S. Frankly I feel like throwing up my hands in disgust".[56] Three weeks later, Shea wrote again to express his frustration at being unable to find suitable candidates for the upcoming election of officers, because of the "continuous unfair sniping and unjust accusations hurled at [the executive]".[57]

The tribulations of the CCL's flagship Maritime local bewildered Congress leaders in Ottawa. Given the troubled state of affairs within the union, it seemed a rash desire even to consider a direct challenge to the company. Pat Conroy had profound misgivings about the "queer state of affairs" whereby "members are trying to destroy their own union and also claiming to be able to fight a large corporation on the check-off question". He also criticized the bargaining strategy of the Halifax executive: "making an issue of a new contract one centring around the check-off is not the best policy...the local committee should try and find out how much the company will agree with and not try to select, right away, the things the company will not agree with". Conroy concluded that unless Local No. 1 changed its strategy, "the Company is going to win the issue hands down".[58]

Notwithstanding these difficulties, by the fall of 1943 union leaders were confident enough to adopt a more aggressive posture. In September, a union ultimatum threatened strike action unless the National War Labour Board gave shipyard workers vacations with pay.[59] Horace Pettigrove hurriedly arranged a meeting between HSL management and the union, resulting in an agreement that Pat Shea called "the best plan so far worked out for any shipyard".[60] Perhaps the time was ripe, Shea added, to tackle the check-off question with "vigour and determination". A vote taken at the plant a few weeks earlier strongly endorsed the check-off: 1,750 voting in favour versus 87 against, with 500 "not voting".[61] But when IUMSWC officials actually sat down with man-

---

56   Shea to Conroy, 16 October 1943, H.A. "Pat" Shea Correspondence, 1942-44, part 3, MG28 I 103, vol. 163, CLC, NA.

57   Shea to Conroy, 6 November 1943, *ibid.*

58   Conroy to Moir, 28 October 1943, IUMSW of C Local No. 1 Correspondence, 1943, file 12, MG28 I 103, vol. 64, CLC, NA.

59   Douglass to Conroy, 29 September 1943, *ibid.*

60   Shea to Conroy, 9 October 1943, H.A. "Pat" Shea Correspondence, 1942-44, part 3, MG28 I 103, vol. 163, CLC, NA.

61   McDonald to Conroy (telegram), 3 September 1943, IUMSW of C Local 1 (1943), file 12, MG28 I 103, vol. 64, CLC, NA. Among the number "not voting", the percentage of wilful abstentions as opposed to those merely absent on the day of the vote is unknown.

agement on October 20, Shea himself expressed disapproval of their bargaining style:

NEGOTIATING COMMITTEE VERY ANTAGONISTIC IN PRE-
LIMINARY DISCUSSION WITH COMPANY TODAY STOP DETER-
MINED TO FORCE CHECK OFF AND UNION SHOP AND THEY
WILL USE ANY METHOD TO OBTAIN [them] STOP SITUATION
VERY CRITICAL STOP SUGGEST ROBSON COME EARLY NEXT
WEEK IN INTEREST OF CONGRESS RETAINING GOOD RELA-
TIONS WITH COMPANY.[62]

Shea was clearly worried that a premature standoff might escalate into an illegal walkout, thus prejudicing the union's chances of winning over a Board of Conciliation should one be appointed. In addition, this intriguing message implies the existence of a relationship between Congress and HSL management that excluded local union leaders. Shea distrusted Local No. 1 president, James O'Connell, and knew that a renegade faction existed within the local.[63] But the CCL did not respond to Shea's plea; the national was shifting its attention away from shipbuilding toward workers in other industries. The Congress saw better organizing prospects elsewhere than in a declining wartime enterprise, and had virtually given up on unions like Local No. 1 that were hopelessly behind in their per capita payments.[64] Whether the local executive was cognizant of this CCL policy is uncertain, but the Congress was certainly aware of the discontent within many Maritime locals and the gathering support for J.K. Bell's rebel forces in Saint John.

The mood of shipyard workers in general was difficult to assess. Since its inception in May 1941, the local experienced wide fluctuations in numbers of paid-up members, even though the union reported steady growth overall. When concessions from management or a favourable ruling from a government Board resulted in material benefits for workers, general satisfaction with the local tended to rise. By the summer of 1943 active recruitment had stabilized, but low numbers of paid-up members continued to plague the local (see Table I).[65]

---

62 Shea to Conroy (telegram), 20 October 1943, *ibid.* Elroy Robson, an official of the Canadian Brotherhood of Railway Employees and Other Transport Workers (CCL), had been sent to Halifax in late 1942 to help Local No. 1 sort out its finances and combat the incursions of AFL unions.

63 Cruikshank, "Politics of Unionism", p. 94.

64 *Ibid.*, p. 134.

65 Cruikshank claims 1,900 members in October 1942 out of a total labour force of 6,000. These figures are rather high, but he does confirm that less than 800 were paying their dues on a regular basis. *Ibid.*, p. 82.

TABLE 1: SELECTED IUMSWC LOCAL NO. 1 MEMBERSHIP STATISTICS

		reported	*paid up*
1941	May		172
	June	870	239
	July	888	231
1942	May	605	494
	June	759	648
	July	855	769
1943	May	1250	633
	June	1250	635
	July	1250	428

Source: IUMSW of C Local 1, "PER CAPITA STATEMENT", files 12 (1941-42), 14 (1943), MG28 I 103, vol. 64, CLC, NA.

Obviously the temporary nature of wartime contracts discouraged worker expectations of long term employment. Postwar prospects looked bleak in an industry that had previously experienced slumps in peacetime.[66] Neither did the city have a reputation for being a crucible of militant labour. A recent illuminating analysis of labour activism (or, more accurately, the lack of it) among an earlier generation of Halifax shipyard workers notes the virtual collapse of the trade union movement locally in the interwar period.[67]

Despite less than ideal conditions, the strike opened with optimism running

---

66 A pessimistic, if partisan appraisal of Ottawa's attitudes regarding the Maritime shipbuilding industry appeared under the heading "Review of Possibilities in Shipping Industry" in the *Herald*, 17 February 1945. See also Ernest R. Forbes, "Consolidating Disparity: The Maritimes and the Industrialization of Canada during the Second World War", *Acadiensis*, XV, 2 (Spring 1986), pp. 3-27.

67 Suzanne Morton, "Labourism and Economic Action: The Halifax Shipyards Strike of 1920", *Labour/Le Travail*, 22 (Fall 1988), pp. 99-137. In a similar vein, Ian McKay paints a picture of Halifax workers in the construction industry in the period 1920-50 as being essentially powerless, controlled by 'absentee' business unionism, and increasingly regulated by legal statutes. See Ian McKay, *The Craft Transformed: An Essay on the Carpenters of Halifax, 1885-1985* (Halifax, 1985), esp. ch. 4.

high. On the second day of the walkout, the regular monthly meeting of Local No. 1 turned into a high-spirited strikers' rally. Hundreds crammed into the Oddfellows' Hall on Agricola Street on a steamy midsummer's evening to hear speakers proclaim that the walkout was just "a prelude to post-war Canada" and that "other union organizations were behind them".[68] Proof of the latter came from the Sydney Steelworkers Union, which forwarded a resolution supporting the strike to Prime Minister Mackenzie King and Minister of Labour Humphrey Mitchell. Marine and ship repair workers in Cape Breton promised financial aid. In Glace Bay, the Cape Breton Labor Council and Local 11 of the United Mine Workers of America, District 26, sent telegrams to the Prime Minister, the Minister of Labour and the Minister of Munitions and Supply, calling for immediate federal intervention.

"The union has shown its strength and the company has shown its teeth", Pat Shea declared to the meeting. "Our strike will pull out those teeth".[69] Shea also assured the rally (somewhat prematurely as it turned out) that the American Federation of Labor was behind the strike. This surprising revelation was based on the fact that two executives from the Allied Trades Council, the AFL organization in H.M.C. Dockyard, had visited Shea and privately pledged their "full support".[70] But only a few Halifax unions, CCL affiliates all, publicly endorsed the strike — mainly in the form of sympathetic resolutions and good wishes. The Halifax District Council of the C.C.F. also declared "solidarity with the workers and their objectives".[71] With this statement duly placed on the public record, little more was heard from the CCF, although H.L. MacIntosh, president of the new Dockyard carpenters union, and future CCF candidate, urged the AFL and CCL to "forget past differences and stand together in the strike".[72] On the whole, however, labour in Halifax was dominated by cautious craft unions, and most organized workers seemed as reluctant to get involved as the federal government.

Strike activity in the first week was confined to "hurling taunts and insults" at the 30 or so men and women who continued to report for work. At the outset, Halifax Mayor J.E. Lloyd and Police Chief Judson Conrod had announced that police protection would be provided to workers crossing the picket line. In Dartmouth, the strike was 100 per cent effective, including four foremen.

---

68 *Herald,* 29 July 1944.

69 *Ibid.*

70 Shea to Conroy, 22 July 1944, H.A. "Pat" Shea Correspondence, Part 1, MG28 I 103, vol. 163, NA.

71 Newspaper clipping: *Herald* 1 August 1944, from Department of Labour, Strikes and Lockouts, No. 134, RG27, vol. 437 (Micro T-4070), NA.

72 *Herald,* 2 August 1944. See also McKay, *The Craft Transformed,* pp. 98-9.

Strikebreakers congregated at the Halifax yard — one was a woman labourer who had been given the honour of christening the destroyer H.M.C.S. "Nootka" the previous April. On the other hand, another woman addressed her fellow strikers at the mass meeting, telling them that her job at the shipyard supported herself and four children, "and if I can stay out and get along somehow you should be able to also". Events at the shipyard gates soon escalated to cat-and-mouse harassment as striking workers milled about on the roadway, looking for scabs being smuggled in and out by automobile and surreptitious routes. Some strike breakers walked along the railway line into the yard; others were transported by water in company boats. One fellow was hauled from a foreman's car and hounded by a hostile throng. After he took refuge in a street car, someone "plucked the trolley from the wire, cutting off [its] power". Eventually, the man was "whisked away in a police car". The next day, a Sunday, 500 workers normally would have reported for work, but not a single employee entered the yards in either Halifax or Dartmouth.[73]

"The spirit is very high", Shea wrote optimistically on the third day, "and the men are determined to win this strike come Hell or high water".[74] But soon there were signs of wavering solidarity. Many workers sought permission from National Selective Service officials to take temporary jobs; others left the area to find employment elsewhere.[75] The strategy of the strike leaders — ironically calling themselves the Action Committee — was to do nothing. If a prolonged strike ensued, then Ottawa would simply take over the shipyards in the interest of the national war effort.[76] The latter course of action was in fact taken by the government just a few weeks later in the Montreal Tramways strike.[77] Numerous precedents existed for the federal government to intervene: the Hamilton Steel Car Company dispute in early 1941, the takeover of the Quebec Shipyards by the Department of Munitions and Supply after a huge strike in June 1943, and federal control of Dosco's own Sydney Foundry and Machine Company.[78]

73 Details of strike activity are drawn from the *Herald*, 28, 29 and 31 July 1944.

74 Shea to Conroy, 29 July 1944, Shea Correspondence 1942-44, part 1, MG28 I 103, vol. 163, CLC, NA.

75 Created in March 1942, the NSS strictly regulated the mobility and allocation of labour, particularly in war-related industries. MacDowell, *'Remember Kirkland Lake'*, p. 17.

76 *Ibid.*, 28 July 1944.

77 On 12 August 1944, Minister of Labour Humphrey Mitchell announced that an Order-in-Council had been authorized giving two federal civil servants absolute control over the Montreal public transportation system. Ironically, one of those controllers was E.L. Cousins, former Toronto Harbour Commissioner appointed by C.D. Howe as Wartime Administrator of Canadian Atlantic Ports. Cousins was in fact based in Halifax, and nearly all his duties were concentrated there. See *ibid.*, 15 August 1944.

78 Cruikshank, "Politics of Unionism", pp. 30, 52. See also Roberts and Bullen, "A Heritage of Hope and Struggle" in Cross and Kealey, eds., *Modern Canada*, pp. 113-4, and R.B. Mitchell,

Undoubtedly the closest parallel occurred in a dispute between the Electro-Metallurgical Co. of Welland, Ontario and Local 523 of the United Electrical, Radio and Machine Workers of America. The circumstances and issues involved virtually mirrored the Halifax situation, except for one crucial difference — a strike was successfully averted due to the persistent efforts of Department of Labour officials (including the Minister himself, Humphrey Mitchell, in whose riding the company was located).[79]

But the government would not interfere at Halifax. Unbeknownst to them, the strikers at HSL were caught in the ebbing tide of the war. The four Tribal class destroyers then building at the yards added to the political prestige of the Minister for Naval Services, Angus L. Macdonald, but there was little urgency attached to their construction. The earliest estimated completion date for the first destroyer was March 1945, the second was due the following August, and the last two were not anticipated until 1946. As it happened, none were completed before the war ended.[80] Moreover, the most important function of the shipyards — the repair of damaged vessels — had fallen off considerably over the Summer of 1944. By October, HSL employed more workers on new construction than on ship repairs — the first time this had occurred during the war.[81] In sum, the operations in Halifax were no longer a first priority with the Navy or the government. After weeks of fruitless effort, CCL officials who lobbied in Ottawa on behalf of Local No. 1 conveyed the discouraging news that "the Government is...not prepared to adopt any conciliatory process unless the men first return to work. The outstanding fact seems to be that there is not the demand for ships that prevailed prior to the strike, and the Government appears to be unconcerned about the whole situation".[82]

"Sydney Harbour — The War Years, 1939-1945" in R.J. Morgan, ed. *More Essays in Cape Breton History* (Windsor, 1977), pp. 42-8. When the government chose not to intervene, as in a notorious dispute at the Peck Rolling Mills (yet another Dosco subsidiary) in Montreal, the effect on the union had been devastating. See *ibid.*, p. 54.

79 See Webber, "Compulsory Conciliation", pp. 148-9.

80 "Return of vessels building in Canada, U.K. and U.S.A. to Canadian account, 1 June 1944. Fleet Tribal Class Destroyers", file COAC 13-1-6 (a), vol. 2, RG24, vol 11,028, Department of National Defence, NA. The first two destroyers were laid down in May, 1942. Hull No. 278 was christened H.M.C.S. "Micmac" on 18 September 1943; Hull No. 279 (H.M.C.S. "Nootka") was launched on 26 April 1944. They were in the water undergoing "fitting out" when the strike took place; the other two remained on the slips. For more information on the Canadian-built Tribals, see J.H.W. Knox, "An Engineer's Outline of RCN History: Part 1", in James A. Boutilier, ed., *The RCN in Retrospect, 1910-1968* (Vancouver, 1982), pp. 108-9, 114.

81 National War Labour Board, "Application for review of the Board's decision of May 2, 1944...", Proceedings of Public Hearing, Ottawa, 15 February 1945, p. 54, RG36 series 4, vol. 132, file 2N-488, NA.

82 Conroy to Shea, 21 August 1944, IUMSWC, 1944-46, MG28 I 103, vol. 65, file 1, NA.

The stalemate dragged on with no end in sight. A strike fund committee was formed to "seek financial assistance from other unions across Canada".[83] Messages of encouragement continued to pour in from shipbuilding locals and workers in other war industries, but promises outnumbered actual contributions to the union war chest.[84] Hundreds of applications for temporary work permits were now being processed by the National Selective Service — an indication perhaps that few workers thought a swift resolution was likely. NSS officials also authorized about 100 workers of Central Canadian origin to leave their jobs at the shipyards and return home permanently.[85] While momentum gathered for calling a provincial work holiday, the strikers continued to meet with lukewarm support closer to home. In a stormy debate at the Labor Temple, a motion backing the strike was voted down by the Halifax Trades and Labor Council (AFL) when six delegates, including the president of the Longshoremen's Union, threatened to resign if the resolution went through.[86] The Council decided to postpone a decision pending advice from national headquarters. They faced a dilemma because the AFL in the United States pledged its unions to refrain from striking for the duration, and there was a similar understanding among Canadian craft unions.

In contrast, militant exhortations emanated loudly from the mining and steelworking communities of Nova Scotia, where memories were still fresh of the "largest work stoppage in Nova Scotia history" — a one-day protest over the closing of the rolling mill at Trenton steelworks — the previous December.[87] Among an estimated 20,000 workers across the province, at least half of the 3,000 shipyard workers at HSL stayed off the job. Now, two representatives of the United Steelworkers of America had arrived in Halifax from Trenton to assist shipworkers in their hour of need. Discussions were held with the IUMSWC Action Committee to consider whether another general strike in Nova Scotia was necessary.[88] Meanwhile, Local 4481 of the United Mine Workers in Stellarton announced that they would participate in a work holiday if it were called. In Glace Bay, the executive of District 26, United Mine Workers of America also notified both Local No. 1 and the CCL president in Ottawa that mine workers in Cape Breton would give "very favorable consideration to any proposed work holiday of a national character". And in Sydney, the Industrial Union of Foundry and Machine Workers recommended increasing the holiday to two days in the second week, three days in the third, and so on until the government was forced

83 *Herald*, 5 August 1944.
84 Halifax *Citizen*, 4 August 1944.
85 See *Herald*, 5, 8, 9 August 1944.
86 *Ibid.*, 10 August 1944.
87 *Ibid.*, 29 December 1943. See also Forbes, "Consolidating Disparity", pp. 22-3.
88 *Herald*, 9 August 1944.

to act. Shipyard workers in other parts of the province were not as forthcoming in their support, probably because the smaller yards engaged in wooden ship-building and were thus more craft-oriented. A notable exception was the Pictou shipyard (which built 4,700-ton steel cargo vessels), where the IUMSWC Local leapt to the strikers' defence, appointing delegates to attend an upcoming conference of labour organizations in Halifax, and authorizing the delegation "to commit their local to [take] strike action on behalf of the Halifax workers".[89] The conference was ostensibly called to muster support for Local No. 1, and to decide whether to go ahead with the one-day sympathetic strike.

Held on August 16, the meeting of trade unions turned out to be a much smaller affair than anticipated. Delegates were supposed to attend from all three Maritime provinces, but in the event only about 40 representatives of "mine workers, steel workers and shipyard workers throughout Nova Scotia" participated. CCL organizers had promised as well that Halifax affiliates of the Trades and Labor Congress would send delegates, but only one showed up — from the Dockyard carpenters' union (Local 1405). While making it clear that he was there unofficially, the AFL representative declared that his union was "100% behind Local No. 1".[90] If the conference had hoped to present a united and militant labour front to the public and, more importantly, the government, it certainly fell short of the mark. The marathon seven-hour session at the Canadian Fishhandlers' Union Hall exposed the underlying conservatism of the strike leaders. Backing away from the idea of a provincial "work holiday", the conference instead decided to send a delegation to Ottawa to meet with the Minister of Labour. Any further consideration of a work holiday was postponed indefinitely. The strike committee was also promised that one day's pay would be deducted from each of the 21,000 workers represented at the conference to bolster the union's dwindling strike fund. It was suggested that the deductions continue on a weekly basis until a settlement was reached. I.D. MacDougall, a former Conservative M.P. for Inverness, Cape Breton, gave a rousing report of the conference proceedings to a mass meeting of strikers that night. A representative of IUMSWC Local No. 7, MacDougall hailed the conference as the "exemplification of [a]...new frame of mind", and predicted that defeat for the shipyard union would mean "organized labor will be through in Nova Scotia.... The United Mine Workers will support you to a man, not only financially but when and if the time comes that labor must show its strength". If the Ottawa delegation was unsuc-cessful, MacDougall warned, then "the fight will become the fight of every organized man from Cape Breton to Vancouver".[91]

89 Quotations from *ibid.*, 11, 12 and 17 August 1944.

90 "Minutes of joint conference held Aug. 16th, 1944, to discuss the best method of settling the strike at the Halifax Shipyards Ltd.", p. 2, MG28 I 103, vol. 65, file 1, CCL, NA.

91 Quotations and conference details from the *Herald*, 17 August 1944. See also 10 August 1944, *ibid.*

Although Silby Barrett, Pat Shea, and others saw the strike as a potential test case which might set a precedent for granting the check-off in other shipyards, the stamina of Local No. 1 was not sufficient to withstand the rigours of a lengthy deadlock. Back on the picket line the number of strikers continued to fall — after three weeks, nearly half the workers had taken part-time work elsewhere. Some of them reported being turned away from job assignments by hostile employers when it was discovered they were strikers. In an effort to maintain union leadership in the face of mass desertion, an employment committee was formed to aid those whose straitened circumstances forced them to seek employment.[92] At the same time, the strike fund committee mailed appeals for financial assistance to 700 unions across Canada, promising to use any proceeds to help needy strikers, provided, of course, that they were members in good standing of Local No. 1. The monetary aid promised by other unions did not materialize, however. Following the conference, canvassers went door to door in Halifax collecting donations for the strike fund — further evidence that the union was desperate for funds and time was running out.[93] Strike leaders advised the public to verify that the canvassers were authorized union members with proper identification. Some money did trickle in — $50 from the Vancouver Labour Council, $14 from the C.C.F. Riding Association of Ottawa West, and so on. A substantial sum of $250 arrived from the national CCL office, but in the main contributions were meagre.[94] Any lingering expectations of support from the rival labour federation were also quashed once and for all on August 23. Percy Bengough, president of the Trades and Labor Congress, declared: "There is no reason why the [TLC]...should get behind the shipyards strike".[95] The next day, Halifax Mayor J.E. Lloyd warned that the city was being hurt "irreparably" by the strike, and "the future economic welfare of [the] Port...is now being threatened". He recommended that a government administrator be appointed to run the shipyards until better relations between management and labour could be worked out.[96] Lloyd was sympathetic to the strikers — he even offered to go to Ottawa with the labour delegation — but his belated jump onto the union bandwagon had negligible impact. All hope of resolving the dispute was now invested with the Ottawa delegation.

92   *Ibid.*, 12, 14 and 15 August 1944.

93   *Ibid.*, 19 August 1944. On 18 August 1944, the Halifax *Chronicle* carried a notice that canvassers would have credentials signed by the president of the union.

94   O'Connell to Conroy, 25 August 1944; Murray to Conroy, 8 September 1944, IUMSW of C Local 1, 1944-46, MG28 I 103, vol. 65, CLC, NA.

95   Newspaper clipping: Washington *Labor*, 26 August 1944, from Department of Labour, Strikes and Lockouts files, No. 134, RG27, vol. 437 (Micro T-4070), NA.

96   *Herald*, 24 August 1944.

The union representatives met with Labour Minister Mitchell in Ottawa on 24 and 25 August 1944. The atmosphere was not congenial; one unionist referred to the introductory meeting as a "dog fight".[97] Some progress was made — at the union's expense. The inclusion of a maintenance of membership clause in the new contract fell by the wayside; but the strike leaders would not budge on the check-off. Since it was clear that the Department of Labour had no intention of forcing Dosco's hand by taking over the company, the whole ceremony of lobbying the government seemed to be tinged with futility. Suddenly, at a meeting of the Nova Scotia Cabinet on 24 August, the idea came forward of submitting the check-off question to the newly-formed Regional War Labour Relations Board, and then — should the board fail to settle the dispute — referring it to the courts.[98] The proposal did not surprise strike leaders: Pat Shea had predicted that the question would eventually go before the courts, although he hoped that government intervention would obviate this necessity. Indeed, when the strike began the company had proposed that the question of the check-off should be referred to the Nova Scotia Supreme Court for an interpretation of the 1937 Trade Union Act. The union had rejected that initial offer, calling it "an empty gesture" that HSL would circumvent by "appeals" or "legal technicalities".[99] The difference now, of course, was that the strike leaders had been told by Mitchell and Deputy Labour Minister Arthur McNamara that no government intervention would occur. Even though the strike would probably be deemed a failure, there seemed to be no other way to obtain a ruling upholding the check-off. To be sure, due process would entail months of deliberation and delay, thus giving Dosco ample time to undermine the authority of Local No. 1, but at the same time the salutary effect of P.C. 1003 would presumably cast the whole issue of union security in a more sympathetic light in the eyes of the court.

Even though the plan was forwarded to federal officials for their consideration and approval, Nova Scotia's Minister of Labour Lauchlin D. Currie — who all along had claimed that the province had no jurisdiction in the matter — received the credit for ending the strike.[100] Curiously, only one newspaper mentioned that the *deus ex machina* was also the chairman of the War Labour Relations Board that would review the case.[101] This fact does not seem to have

---

97   *Ibid.*, 25 August 1944.

98   *Ibid.*, 25, 26 August 1944. Not to be confused with War Labour Boards formed much earlier, the Regional War Labour Relations Boards were separate entities created under P.C. 1003, and thus just beginning to operate by the fall of 1944.

99   *Ibid.*, 29 July 1944.

100   *Ibid.*, 25, 28 August 1944.

101   *Citizen*, 8 September 1944.

unduly upset strike leaders at the time, except that two months later Charley Murray, harbouring an old grudge against Currie,[102] bitterly denounced the Labour Minister's "union busting tactics" in the aftermath of the strike and accused Currie of "consultation with the Company [HSL] as to the best way to smash us [Local No. 1]".[103] Murray had his reasons for disliking Currie; however the union had little choice but to accept the provincial intervention. The Ottawa delegation returned to Halifax relieved, if not triumphant. A mass meeting was called for 27 August, exactly one month after the strike had begun. The Action Committee presented the Currie plan to the assembled workers and recommended adoption. The majority of workers were not at all pleased with the proposed settlement, and neither were Shea's enemies on the Local No. 1 executive. President James O'Connell — who did not make the journey to Ottawa — denounced the CCL and Shea for engineering a "sell out" of the union.[104] The mood of the meeting "was one of uncertainty whether to return to work...until Charles Douglas, [Local No. 1] executive member, told the workers frankly that the finances of the union were insufficient to carry on the strike". Douglas "explained that the day's pay promised by a number of locals in the province had not materialized", and referenda would have to be held in every plant "before a day's pay from each worker could be checked off".[105] It was ironic that the strike (the object of which sought to free unions from that very chore) should end on such a note.

Predictably, the Regional War Labour Relations Board failed to resolve the issue when it convened early in September.[106] Besides chairman Lauchlin Currie, the Board consisted of Ralph P. Bell, a wealthy Halifax businessman, Sidney Mifflen, a Dosco official from Sydney, Doane Curtis, a Cape Breton steelworker, and Hugh Henderson, vice-president of the Halifax Trades and Labour Council.[107] Although the provincial government had promised an answer within 60 days, nearly four months went by before the Supreme Court heard the case (argued on the union's behalf by a brilliant Toronto labour lawyer, J.L. Cohen) and it was not until February 1945 that the judgment was handed down in the

---

102 Currie had been Labour Minister in 1939, when a protracted dispute over recognition of the Canadian Fishermen's Union paralyzed the tiny community of Lockeport, Nova Scotia. He was convinced, along with then-Premier Angus L. Macdonald, that "outside agitators" were responsible for labour unrest among the Lockeport fishermen. One of the "agitators" (i.e. organizers) singled out by Currie was Charlie Murray. See Sue Calhoun, *The Lockeport Lockout* (Halifax, 1983).

103 Murray to Conroy, 9 November 1944, MG28 I 103, vol. 65, file 1, CLC, NA.

104 Shea to Conroy, 12 September 1944, *ibid*, and *Herald*, 25 August 1944.

105 *Herald*, 28 August 1944.

106 *Ibid.*, 8 September 1944.

107 *Citizen*, 21 July 1944.

union's favour.[108] The decision reinterpreted the clause in the 1937 Nova Scotia Trade Union Act which stated that "In any industry in which by statute or by arrangement between employer and employees deductions are made from the wages of employees for benefit societies, hospital charges, or the like, deductions shall be made by the employer...for periodical payments to a trade union".[109] Under conditions stipulated in the Act, a majority vote of employees was needed to ratify a check-off plan, and "a signed written request" from each worker was also required.

At first the company argued that Halifax Shipyards Limited was not an industry within the meaning of the Act. This ridiculous assertion was quickly dismissed by the court. HSL then claimed that union dues could only be deducted if similar payments were taken for benefit societies. The court heard that deductions on behalf of the "Halifax Shipyards Employees' Mutual Benefit Society" had been made from December 1922 to 7 July 1941, whereupon they were discontinued by the company "without notice to the trade union or the employees".[110] Since the union application for the check-off followed the cessation of benefit society deductions, the company contended that the obligation to withhold union dues was no longer valid. Mr. Justice C.J. Chisholm and two other judges ruled otherwise. In their opinion, the rights conferred upon employees in the 1937 Act "could not be divested by unilateral action by the company". It did not go unnoticed that the company ended the benefit society deductions at the precise moment when the check-off question was being considered by a Board of Conciliation — the strategy of the company was too blatant to ignore. One judge, Mr. Justice Emmett Hall, did register a dissenting vote, but the premise of his argument was overly technical and convoluted, hence less convincing than the majority opinion. Even so, the court could easily have decided in the company's favour, since the legislation was by no means clear on precisely when the check-off was warranted. Upholding the union claim showed that, in a close legal fight between labour and management, the former might now receive the benefit of the doubt.

The Supreme Court decision vindicated Local No. 1, but the ordeal had been costly. The failure to procure an outright concession from the company seriously damaged the credibility of the union and the CCL. One month after the strike ended, a dejected Charley Murray informed Pat Conroy that "the Local is in a very definite crisis with a large section of the membership looking for a scapegoat.

---

108 *Herald*, 28 August, 8 September 1944. For arguments presented to the court on 21 December 1944, and its decision handed down on 10 February 1945, see *Maritime Provinces Reports* (Toronto, 1946), pp. 230-53.

109 *Maritime Provinces Reports*, p. 233.

110 *Ibid.*, p. 251.

There has been a strong tendancy [sic] to accuse the delegation that went to Ottawa, Pat Shea, and the Executive of the C.C. of L. for making a deal which was not too favourable to the Local". Murray then revealed the reason why the local was so far behind in remitting per capita dues to the national office:

> [S]ome of us became suspicious of the actions of Moir, the Secretary-Treasurer, during...the strike, at a time when it could not possibly be made public that there was even a fear of irregularities in the finances...quite a sizable amount of money — sufficient to have paid *all* per capita taxes — appears to be missing. The method seemed to be that shop stewards' collection lists were destroyed after the amounts were credited up on [sic] the members' accounts.[111]

Moir was forced to resign, promising, like his light-fingered predecessor, to make up the missing funds. But for Congress officials, the limit of their toleration had been reached. In October 1944, the union received word that it was not entitled to send a delegate to the upcoming CCL convention in Quebec City because no per capita dues had been submitted for four months.[112] A stern lecture was delivered to the membership in late December, when a CCL official "told them very plainly" to begin regular payments "from now on without any fooling".[113]

As mastermind and protagonist, Pat Shea was bitterly disappointed in the outcome, attributing the fiasco to the hasty retreat of Silby Barrett in the early days of the walkout.[114] But Shea must share some of the blame for insisting on strike action even though the timing was not right and the likelihood of a settlement

---

111 Murray to Conroy, 27 September 1944, IUMSW of C 1944-46, MG28 I 103, vol. 65, file 1, CLC, NA. Murray did not specify the amount missing, other than to state that $500 "does not begin to cover the suspected shortage".

112 Dowd to Murray, 6 October 1944, IUMSW of C Local 1 (1944-46), MG28 I 103, vol. 65, CLC, NA.

113 Shea to Conroy, 23 December 1944, *ibid.*

114 Shea to Conroy, 29 July and 16 September 1944, H.A. "Pat" Shea Correspondence, 1942-44, part 1, MG28 I 103, vol. 163, CLC, NA. Shea felt betrayed by the sudden departure of Barrett from Halifax only a few days after the strike began, but he probably overestimated the latter's influence. In fact, Barrett's credibility with Cape Breton miners had evaporated during a protracted work slowdown in 1941, resulting in his eventual ouster from the executive of the United Mine Workers. See Paul MacEwan, *Miners and Steelworkers* (Toronto, 1976), pp. 225-38. By April 1944, George McEachern, Communist president of the IUMSW of C Local in Pictou, opined that Silby Barrett had "no more prestige with the shipyard workers here than he has with his own union". See also Cruikshank, "Politics of Unionism", p. 130 and Morton, *Working People*, p. 174. The dependence on Barrett for moral support reflected the difficulty Shea experienced in getting other militant unionists to back the HSL strike.

being reached through direct confrontation was decidedly slim. Knowing that adjudication was the logical eventuality in resolving the dispute, Shea nevertheless led Local No. 1 in a futile assault on the corporate bulwarks. George Smith, president of the Halifax Trades and Labor Council, rubbed salt into the wound during an AFL organizing drive at the Halifax Shipyards in November 1944. Shipyard workers, he declared, had taken "an awful licking" that would never have occurred if they "had been in A.F.L. unions". Smith claimed that two years before, he had suggested to Shea that the check-off should be taken to the courts. "Had they done so [then]", he added, "I think we would have been able to help them out with funds". Shea was present at the meeting, but his spirited response was not recorded — although it is known that the word "liar" was "hurled across the floor as the altercation reached fever pitch".[115] Once the Supreme Court decision was announced, Shea recovered his composure somewhat, but he still advocated cutting CCL losses in Halifax and cultivating greener pastures across the harbour:

> [The Dartmouth workers] are the most stable members of the Industrial Union [and] they should be granted...a Charter and be in a position to take care of their own affairs. The feeling in Halifax is running very high against Bro. Silby Barrett and his wild promises which he neglected to try and carry out, and there is considerable talk against the Congress as the result of his actions. The Dartmouth workers are staunch in support of the C.C. of L. so [we should]... seperate [sic] the good apple from the bad one and save at least the Dartmouth membership.[116]

The Dartmouth branch of Halifax Shipyards Limited was soon rewarded for its loyalty, receiving a charter as Local 13 of the IUMSWC. Not long after, however, the CCL conceded that it alone could not hold the Eastern shipyards together, and in 1945, Congress reconciled with J.K. Bell. The Maritime Marine Workers' Federation became the parent body for yards in Nova Scotia and New Brunswick, joining three other regional federations chartered by the CCL to manage its affairs in the troubled shipbuilding industry. It was to be the first step towards the long-heralded establishment of a nation-wide industrial union of Canadian shipbuilders; however, in the cold light of postwar regional disparities and the

---

115 Newspaper clipping: *Chronicle*, 13 November 1944, in Department of Labour, Strikes and Lockouts, No. 134, vol. 437, RG27 (Micro T-4070), NA. On George Smith, see McKay, *The Craft Transformed*, pp. 95-6.

116 Shea to Conroy, 16 September 1944, H.A. "Pat" Shea, Correspondence 1942-44, part 1, MG28 I 103, vol. 163, CLC, NA. Conroy replied on 26 September that to grant a charter to the Dartmouth Local would "weaken the position of all concerned", and advised Shea to "await the decision of the Supreme Court of Nova Scotia on the check-off question".

gradual disintegration of the CCL, this wartime dream quietly faded away.

Five years of economic prosperity, rapid industrialization and increasingly rigid state regulation forever altered the relationship between labour, business and government. The campaign for union security focused public attention on the grievances of workers at a time when the cooperation of labour was an essential component of the war effort. Although business and government frequently alleged that strikes of any kind were subversive and unpatriotic in wartime, episodes like the walkout at Halifax projected an image of orderly worker protest: there was little violence, no overt radicalism, and union security issues appeared to be relatively innocuous and less selfish than the typical wages/benefits dispute. In November 1946, a national Gallup poll asked Canadians, "In a factory which has a union, should the workers who are not members be obliged to pay the regulation union fees [i.e. dues] if they are getting union rates of pay" ? Among the general population, 52 per cent of the respondents said yes, 33 per cent said no. With the sample split according to political affiliation, the CCF naturally registered a strong 70 per cent affirmative, but a sizable 48 per cent of Liberals and 43 per cent of Progressive Conservatives also replied yes.[117] While hardly conclusive, these figures do reflect generally softening public attitudes towards organized labour. By the end of the Second World War, it seemed to many that the unions wore the white hats.

On the other hand, the ordeal of Local No. 1 and Pat Shea's quixotic quest for the check-off belie the notion that P.C. 1003 transformed the conventions of labour-management relations overnight. The whole thrust of federal labour policy had always been to manage and minimize labour strife; yet here was a case where the government completely abandoned its supposed obligation to promote, in Mackenzie King's bland phraseology, "the partnership of management, of workers and the community".[118] Even though the government indirectly stimulated unions to press for the check-off and other security clauses, it also failed to establish a policy with regard to union security. When the Executive Council of the Canadian Congress of Labour convened early in 1945 to discuss the merits and flaws of P.C. 1003, they expressed concern that the grudging toleration by employers of union security provisions would vanish when the nation was no longer at war. The Council recommended that government boards set up to administer P.C. 1003 be given the authority to impose union security clauses in collective agreements, and "failure to comply with any such order or direction...[would] constitute an unfair labour practice".[119] However, when the

117 Jeremy Taylor, "The Rand Formula", *The Quarterly Review of Commerce*, XIV, 2 (1950), p. 154.

118 From an address to the American Federation of Labor in October 1942. See the Toronto *Globe and Mail*, 10 October 1942.

119 "Report of Special Committee of the Executive Council on P.C. 1003 and P.C. 9384", 15 January 1945, p. 4, MG28 I 103, vol. 195, file 5, CLC, NA.

government finally completed the conversion of the emergency Order-in-Council into peacetime legislation in 1948, there was no legislative endorsement of union security. Incorporating the rights of workers into postwar public policy was largely left to the discretion of provincial legislation.[120] To that end, at least, the Halifax Shipyards strike had not been staged in vain: it clarified an important section of the 1937 Trade Union Act, and it probably saved the Local No. 1 from annihilation at the hands of AFL organizers as well. Indeed, the union turned out to be a hardy perennial, outliving the CCL, Dosco and even Halifax Shipyards Limited.[121] Local No. 1 continues to represent shipyard trades in Halifax to this day.

But the episode also illustrated the hazards of launching a strike action with no reasonable expectation of a compromise settlement. Exercising the option of last resort had been an ill-conceived ploy to probe weaknesses in the government's hastily-erected wartime labour policy, rather than a bargaining tactic intended to put pressure on recalcitrant managers. The outcome clearly shows that the conciliation process formulated by the federal government during the Second World War seemed poorly designed to establish ground rules for future labour-management relations. It was simply a collection of expedient statutes which channelled labour strife into a bureaucratic labyrinth. A "damage control" approach to labour relations in war production had the ironic side effect of encouraging labour to undertake measured doses of damage — i.e. work stoppages — as one means of securing basic concessions. This was the impetus behind scores of wartime strikes where union security was the central issue — not because wartime workers were overly militant, but because the legal framework created by the government to deal with labour strife left few other avenues open to settling disputes of that kind. The Halifax Shipyards case illustrates how easily that conciliation process could collapse, and how unwilling the government was to accept responsibility for the consequences of that breakdown.

120 Morton, *Working People*, p. 197.
121 The TLC and CCL merged in 1955. Dosco was dismantled in 1968, and HSL became Halifax Industries Ltd., a consortium of CN Marine, Hall Steamships and AMCA International. HIL declared bankruptcy in 1985, and was acquired by a group of Halifax businessmen. See Hamilton *Spectator*, 12 June 1985.

E. JEAN NISBET

"Free Enterprise at Its Best": The State, National Sea, and the Defeat of the Nova Scotia Fishermen, 1946-1947*

FEW EVENTS IN THE 20TH CENTURY Nova Scotian labour history were as fateful as the defeat of trade unionism in the fishing industry in 1946 and 1947. Fishermen made up one of the most numerous and potentially one of the most powerful groups of workers in the province. Like many Canadian workers, they emerged from the Second World War with a long list of grievances to settle and a new confidence in their collective ability. Theirs was an industry that was pivotal to postwar regional development strategies; their inability to organize within it meant those strategies unfolded without labour's influence.

In 1944 the federal government enacted an Order-in-Council (PC 1003) that made it a legal right of workers to organize unions, to strike, and to bargain collectively with their employers. On 7 February 1946 the National War Labour Relations Board (NWLRB), by overturning an earlier decision of the Nova Scotia War Labour Relations Board, opened the door for the fishermen of Nova Scotia to enjoy these trade union rights. The NWLRB ruled that offshore fishermen were employees, not "co-adventurers". (A "co-adventurer" is one who is a partner in a joint venture, in this case with the vessel owners.) When the Nova Scotia Supreme Court in the "Zwicker Decision" of 14 January 1947 determined that the Nova Scotia fishermen were not employees, and when National Sea Products, through one of the most vigorous anti-union campaigns ever staged in Canadian history, managed to defeat the fishermen's strike, a crucial and, from labour's perspective, catastrophic turning point was reached. After 1947 the state effectively denied Nova Scotia fishermen the right to organize trade unions. Ironically, capital and the state, victorious in the short term, lost over the long term. They paid a high long term price for crushing organized labour, since this removed the major incentive for technological change and efficient management, and robbed the industry of the stable and skilled workforce modernization would have required. Labour's defeat in 1946-7 was a sign of the coming new anti-labour order in Nova Scotia, and its ramifications can be felt, in the fishing industry's recurrent crises and its enduring fragmentation, to this day.

The crisis of 1946-7 was the climax of a long tradition of conflict in the Nova Scotia fishing industry. None of the issues raised in this crisis — the fishermen's "co-adventurer" status, the "lay" system through which the proceeds of the catch were divided between capital and labour, the monopoly powers of the fish

* My thanks to Ian McKay, who supervised the work on which this essay is based.

companies — was new. All had been issues in the Nova Scotia fishing industry over many years. The concept of the fishermen as a "partner" or "co-adventurer" originated in a much earlier time, and up to the mid-19th century some fishermen were truly independent commodity producers. Gradually, however, the fisherman's position changed, as his dependence on merchants increased. Fishermen rarely had enough cash to pay for supplies, which they therefore obtained from local merchants on credit. The interest on the credit was usually high, so by the time the fishermen were paid, their wages went to pay off the debt. Fishermen were thus unable to save money, but instead often found themselves trapped in a vicious circle of incurring further debt for expensive fishing vessels, gear, and other supplies, in order to pay off past debt to merchants.

The image of the fisherman as an independent "co-adventurer" was revitalized to some extent by the "Lunenburg 64" system, which emerged in the late 19th century as a way of more evenly distributing the risks of maritime enterprise, in response to an intensified demand for fishing vessels. Under this system, the ownership of vessels was divided into 64 shares which were then sold, often to fishermen. Many fishermen bought shares in more than one vessel, because they would thus even out their chances of getting a return on their investment. In general the captains and fishermen owned most of the shares, while fish companies (or those supplying fishing gear) owned no more than four shares per vessel. Here, then, was the traditional role of the fisherman as "co-adventurer": he owned part of the fishing schooner in which he sailed to the Grand Banks, and he received a certain percentage or "lay" of the catch.

This way of organizing the fishery is easily idealized; but in fact even a functioning co-adventurer system confronted fishermen with a number of serious difficulties. From about 1870 to 1930 it was common for the fishermen to be paid only twice a year. Moreover, the Nova Scotia companies did not pay the fishermen until they themselves were paid by the West Indies buyers who took a high percentage of Nova Scotia's fish. Since payment for shipments could take a long time, fishermen seldom had the cash to buy necessities and supplies, and consequently bought on credit from local merchants, who charged interest. By the time the fisherman received his cash from the fish companies he usually owed most of it to the merchants. Frequently these same merchants were part owners of the fish companies, and the companies often owned the fishing gear stores.[1] Should the market for fish fail, the fishermen would lose all their wages before the profits of the merchants were touched.

After the First World War the fishing industry went into decline. As a result, many fishermen had to sell their vessel shares. By the mid-1920s only two or three shares per vessel were owned by the fishermen. Although the provincial government enacted legislation enabling fishermen to receive loans to buy fishing vessels, doing so was beyond most fishermen's financial means. It was not, however, beyond the resources of the companies. This eventually excluded the

---

1   See Harold Innis, *The Cod Fisheries* (Toronto, 1954); Gene Barrett, "Underdevelopment and Social Movements in the Nova Scotia Fishing Industry to 1938" in Robert Brym and R. James Sacouman, eds., *Underdevelopment and Social Movements in Atlantic Canada* (Toronto, 1979); and Barrett, "Development and Underdevelopment and the Rise of Trade Unionism in the Fishing Industry of Nova Scotia, 1900-1950", M.A. thesis, Dalhousie University, 1976.

fishermen from any ownership or control of the means of production. Because a fisherman could no longer afford to buy vessel shares, he was no longer a true "co-adventurer". But the co-adventurer myth lived on long after the reality of co-adventuring was dead.

The drab reality behind the romance of the Grand Banks fishery was a style of life that was Dickensian in its suffering and poverty. Fishermen stayed on the vessels in all kinds of weather, and every minute they were on the vessel they were in danger of injury or death. Sometimes their hands would be so raw from the cold and hauling on the ropes they would bleed, and severe bruises, sprains and strained joints were commonplace. One fisherman remembered when "it took seven of us to hoist one end of a dory into the vessel...when one fellow could do it when his hands ain't sore". Sometimes the men would work as long as 72 hours without sleep. Once the fish were loaded on board, the fishermen still could not rest, but had to take turns standing watch. Often fishermen had to do with two or three hours rest in a night. The wages the men received certainly did not compensate for these abysmal working conditions. Another fisherman quoted in Peter Barss' excellent oral history, *Images of Lunenburg County,* remembers one voyage when he ended up with a take home pay of only 29 cents after all expenses were deducted. He made just over $100 for the whole season that year.[2]

The lay system, fiercely debated in the 1947 strike, was a legacy of this long history. The "lay" was the time-honored and immensely complicated convention governing the division of the profits of the catch from each voyage. Under the lay system the crew shared one part of the catch's value and the vessel owners divided the other. The captains received shares both as vessel owners and as crew members. The system incorporated a form of incentive wage: the more fish caught, the more money crewmen took home. The other side of this, however, was that if the catch was small there would be very little money to take home. Before 1947 the lay was divided so that the crew received 40 per cent of the gross value of the catch and the owners 60 per cent. Several deductions were taken from the gross before this division, including port fees, ice, and the engineer's wages. Then, out of the crew's 40 per cent were deducted items such as fuel, water, supplies, food, and the cook's wages. The fisherman's take home pay, after being lowered by these deductions, was then further reduced by his outstanding debts to merchants.[3]

Let us take the example of an average fishing voyage in 1947, during which the men caught about $20,000 worth of fish. After deductions off the top, about $18,835 was left to divide between the two parties, the owners and the fishermen (the captain received a portion of both the owner's and the crew's share). The

2 Peter Barss, *Images of Lunenburg County* (Toronto, 1978), pp. 38, 40. By the 1930s many Nova Scotians had voted with their feet on these primitive conditions, and were replaced by Newfoundlanders who were given six-month immigration permits to work on the deep-sea vessels sailing out of Nova Scotia. Newfoundlanders working as fishermen on the Nova Scotia vessels were in a particularly difficult position in the 1946 and 1947 struggles. Because of the strike immigration officials debated whether or not the Newfoundlanders would be allowed to stay in Canada. It was decided that they could stay, but if any permits lapsed while the strike was on, the Newfoundlanders would not get extensions. Many of the men left for home. *Halifax Chronicle,* 17 January 1947.

3 Keith Reyes, "Some of the Problems of Collective Bargaining for Nova Scotia Fishermen", M.A. thesis, Dalhousie University, 1971, pp. 25-6.

owners' 60 per cent amounted to $11,301, and the crew's 40 per cent was $7,534. The crew also paid other expenses totalling about $2,800, leaving $4,734 to be divided among the 17 crewmen. This amounted to an individual take home pay of $278.47. Such a figure needs to be seen in the context of a voyage which might last as long as six weeks, and an enduring pattern of seasonal unemployment, and of debt incurred in obtaining the necessities of life. It represented an appallingly low level of income for a fisherman's family.[4]

The concentration of capital in the 20th century industry made the lay system all the more inequitable. By the end of the Great Depression, there were three major and 15 minor fish companies in Nova Scotia. The major firms were Lunenburg Sea Products, the Lockeport Company, and Maritime-National Fish. Probably the most important change in the east coast fishing industry after the Second World War was the absorption of all of these companies into one huge conglomerate: National Sea Products Limited.[5] This company became the largest organization on the Atlantic coast of North America engaged in the production and processing of fish. Its meteoric rise owed much to numerous grants and subsidies received from both levels of government, especially to build new trawlers and buy various fish plants.

Despite the monopoly status of National Sea, its president was a throwback to 19th century competitive capitalism. Ralph Pickard Bell had capitalized brilliantly on business contacts made during the war, when he had been a member of the Joint Defence Production committee of the United States and Canada, a member of the Department of Munitions and Supply, and director general of Aircraft Production. It was Bell's proud boast that when he first went into the fishing industry, he did not know a thing about it. He mastered it quickly, building National Sea to its commanding position. In outlook, he was a 19th century capitalist, a believer in the doctrine of the "survival of the fittest".[6] He saw the fishermen as the exemplars of his individualist doctrine. According to Bell they were "resourceful, intrepid, adventurous...all they ask is good weather, good luck, and a reasonable price. Here is rugged individualism and our much vaunted free enterprise at its best".[7]

For many fishermen the rise of the monopolies in the fishing industry suggested the need to rethink their traditional aloofness from trade unionism. Unions for fishermen had been talked about since the early 1900s, but had been largely circumvented by an officially recognized movement which, despite being called the Fishermen's Union of Nova Scotia, was in reality an ineffectual pressure group. In 1937 the first real fishermen's union in Nova Scotia, the Fishermen's Federation, was formed under the leadership of two men, Captain Ben MacKenzie and Captain James Whynacht. Captain Whynacht, originally from Lunenburg, had gained invaluable experience as an active trade unionist in the fishermen's union in Gloucester, Massachusetts. Captain MacKenzie was a native of Lockeport and a seasoned fisherman. As one reporter remarked, he "learned to fish before he learned

4   The figures given are taken from *Halifax Chronicle*, 28 October 1946.
5   Gene Barrett, "Capital and the State" in *Atlantic Fisheries and Coastal Communities* (Halifax, 1982), p. 85.
6   *Halifax Mail-Star,* 19 January 1972.
7   Ralph P. Bell, "Fisheries" in *Nation on the March* (Toronto, 1953), p. 90.

to chew".[8] Early in 1937 union fishermen's stations were organized in Riverport, LaHave, and Lunenburg, and by the end of the year six more stations had been organized. In December 1937 the union went on strike for an increase of one quarter of a cent per pound in haddock prices. The fish buyers, not unexpectedly, refused to negotiate with or recognize the union. This strike involved over 800 inshore and offshore fishermen, who were joined by Halifax fish plant workers. The settlement in January 1938 did not favour the union. The small price increase was won, but the buyers unanimously refused to recognize or bargain with the Fishermen's Federation, and the attempt to organize the fish plants was also defeated. Although the Nova Scotia government had passed a Trade Union Act in 1937, supposedly guaranteeing workers the right to organize, this legislation did not include fishermen. Legally they had no right to bargain collectively with the fish companies.

In the wake of this defeat the Fishermen's Federation crumbled everywhere except Lockeport, where Captain MacKenzie kept the fishermen united.[9] In 1939, Lockeport fishermen became Local No. 1 of the Canadian Fishermen's Union (CFU), affiliated with the then rapidly expanding Canadian Seamen's Union (CSU). When fish plant workers also organized and became Local No. 2 of the CFU, the result was one of the most remarkable struggles in Nova Scotia labour history. The plant workers were locked out by the two local companies, Swim Brothers and the Lockeport Company, and then formed a co-operative to handle the fish caught by the fishermen. Denied collective bargaining rights under the Trade Union Act by the Nova Scotia government, the fishermen and fish plant workers were defeated by the companies with the government's assistance.[10] Lessons had been learned, nonetheless, most notably that the idea of the "co-adventurer" was an outdated relic whose survival helped only the companies.

Like other workers throughout the country, fishermen became unified and acquired new energy during the war. Across Canada labour finally gained the legal means to force employers to deal with their organizations. Employees now had a say in how the industries they worked for would be run. "To that extent", Laurel Sefton MacDowell argues, "a degree of democracy in industry was achieved".[11] Models of successful militancy could also be found in other contexts. Nova Scotia fishermen, for example, could look to New England, where in 1945 there was a fishermen's union strong enough to paralyze the industry and push wages up by $100 a month. The Canadian Fishermen's Union was one prominent beneficiary of this wartime militancy, achieving certification as the bargaining agent for east coast fishermen. The president of the CFU was Captain Ben MacKenzie. During the sixth biennial convention of the Canadian Seamen's Union in Montreal in March 1946 Captain MacKenzie reported that the union was signing up hundreds of new members. He put the CFU's membership at 2,000, and added "We expect to

8   *Searchlight*, 18 February 1947.
9   For an account of the Fishermen's Federation and of the earlier Fishermen's Union see Barrett, "Underdevelopment and Social Movements in the Nova Scotia Fishing Industry to 1938", pp. 138-51.
10   Sue Calhoun, *The Lockeport Lockout* (Halifax, 1983), gives a good account of these events.
11   Laurel Sefton MacDowell, "The Formation of the Canadian Industrial Relations System During World War Two", *Labour/Le Travail*, 3 (1978), pp. 175-96.

make a great deal of progress in winning the demands of the fishermen".[12] These organized fishermen were offshore, not inshore, fishermen. While the CFU included inshore fishermen, no attempt was made to negotiate on their behalf for the same terms as the offshore men. Inshore fishermen worked in their own boats, not on a vessel owned by someone else, and sold their catches to the fish companies.

In April 1946 leaders of the CFU and the Canadian Fish Handlers' Union (CFHU), realizing the potential power they would have if they combined in one union, decided that a joint convention of the two unions should be held. More than 60 delegates, representing 29 locals with a total membership of over 5,000, attended the convention in Halifax in October 1946. The delegates voted to merge the two unions, so that all workers in the Nova Scotia fishing industry would be represented by the Canadian Fishermen's and Fish Handlers' Union (CFFU). The executive included experienced seamen and fishermen, and there was also a ten-member executive board elected to represent the three sections of the new union: the fish handlers (fish plant workers), the inshore fishermen, and the offshore or deep-sea fishermen.[13]

The battle lines were soon sharply drawn. From the side of labour, CFFU secretary H.C. Meade proclaimed the workers' determination "to gain a more equitable share of the profits from catches".[14] Fishermen were suspicious of National Sea, the new corporation which, thanks to state subsidies and favours, dominated the east coast fishing industry. The union urged the Nova Scotia government to "assume its proper responsibility for thoroughly investigating and continually supervising the operations and plans of the National Sea Products Limited". The CFFU demanded a 40-60 lay, 40 per cent for the company and 60 per cent for the crew of a vessel. The union's resolve was strengthened on 8 November 1946 when a large majority of the unionized fishermen rejected a company proposal for a 50-50 lay. Fishermen may well have felt that they had some powerful weapons in any struggle with the company. One of these was the perishability of their product. Earlier in the year fish handlers in Nova Scotia had gone on strike for an eight hour day and pay equity with other major industries in the province. In the course of this victorious strike, a lot of fish had spoiled.[15]

On the side of capital was a diversity of men but a unity of purpose: profits. Capital in the fishing industry was not easily intimidated by unions. At a meeting of vessel owners in Lunenburg on 18 January 1946 a resolution was passed that "unanimously agreed that the vessel owners represented here today will not recognize or negotiate with the so-called union any further". The key figures behind this resolution were such men as C. J. Morrow, Homer Zwicker, W. W. Smith, and Ralph P. Bell. Morrow and Zwicker were Lunenburg entrepreneurs, Smith was a prominent Halifax businessman and Bell the president of National Sea.[16] In February 1946 the National War Labour Relations Board confirmed that the CFFU

12 *Searchlight,* 21 March 1946.
13 *Searchlight,* 18 April, 14 November 1946.
14 *Halifax Chronicle,* 28 October 1946.
15 *Searchlight,* 14 November 1946.
16 Copy of resolution passed by various vessel owners at a meeting in Lunenburg on 18 January 1946, Zwicker Papers, File 1526, Dalhousie University Archives (DUA).

was the legal bargaining agent for the crews of three fishing vessels: the *Isabelle J. Corkum,* owned by E. Fenwick Zwicker, and the trawlers *Cape North* and *Cape LaHave,* owned by Lunenburg Sea Products (a subsidiary of National Sea). When the NWLRB ruled that fishermen were employees and as such entitled to form unions, Ralph Bell and the Zwickers launched an appeal to the Supreme Court of Nova Scotia.

Here, then, were two radically conflicting agendas: the fishermen demanding structural changes, particularly a new "lay" and recognition for their union; and capital, determined to resist these demands to the bitter end.

On 9 November 1946 CFFU secretary Meade sent a letter to C. J. Morrow, president of Lunenburg Sea Products, telling him that the fishermen had voted to reject the company offer of a 50-50 lay. The letter also informed Morrow that the union executive would meet on Friday evening, 15 November, to discuss any further proposals the company might have. If the company did not come up with another proposal or failed to contact the union by 5:00 p.m. on that date, the union would assume that "no purpose can be served by extending the period of negotiations", and the CFFU would take "whatever action it will be necessary to take towards obtaining a lay that will meet the needs and desires of our membership".[17]

Copies of this letter were sent to other vessel owners, and leading Lunenburg businessman Homer Zwicker wrote to Meade stating that neither he nor Fenwick Zwicker had given Morrow the power to negotiate for them. Yet the vessel owners had met together to discuss the fishermen's union, and were to maintain correspondence with each other throughout the strike. Also, these owners made no attempt to negotiate with the CFFU themselves, although the union had specifically asked them to do so if they were not going to honour settlements negotiated with Lunenburg Sea Products. On 12 November the union received a reply from Morrow. He said his company wanted to keep negotiating, and suggested the two sides meet again the following week.[18] When on 19 November union and company representatives met in Lunenburg to discuss the lay, no agreement was reached. The CFFU demanded the fishermen receive 60 per cent of the value of the catch after certain deductions from the total. The cost of the food and the cook would be taken from the crew's 60 per cent, but all other deductions from the owner's 40 per cent. Morrow wished to discuss matters with the directors of his company, and the two sides agreed on a further meeting the following week.[19]

By 6 December the negotiations were at a standstill. The union stood firm for a 60-40 agreement, and the company insisted it could offer only the 50-50 lay.[20] National Sea Products, in a "Notice to Fishermen", declared it was "surprised and shocked" to learn the union was considering a strike, and claimed it was the company's "sincere hope" strike action would not be used and that an agreement could be made. Immediately after this, the company announced that fishermen

17   H. C. Meade to C. J. Morrow, 9 November 1946, Zwicker Papers, DUA.
18   C. J. Morrow to H. C. Meade, 12 November 1946, Zwicker Papers, DUA.
19   *Progress-Enterprise* (Lunenburg), 1 January 1947.
20   *Halifax Chronicle,* 7 December 1946.

would no longer be paid for their catch until the fish were processed. Remembering events earlier in the year, when fish spoiled during a fish handlers' strike, National Sea argued that it needed insurance against fish being damaged during industrial unrest. It was stipulated that fish would not be paid for until it was collected and processed from all vessels, or at least put into cold storage. The company refused responsibility for any fish that spoiled on a vessel that returned before the others; the fishermen would have to suffer the losses. This procedure would continue indefinitely.[21]

The union executive reacted quickly to this notice. The day after the announcement union secretary H.C. Meade wrote a general letter to fishermen informing them that the company's decision was not "in any sense, binding on fishermen". "The fishermen are NOT employed by National Sea Products Ltd", he noted. (Subsequent events would show the irony of Meade's position at this time.) He emphasized that fishermen were employees of the vessel owners, and their concern was catching fish. What happened after the fish was sold had nothing to do with the fishermen. The union had notified all vessel owners that they would be responsible for ensuring the crews were paid as usual. Meade also told the men that this announcement of a change in the payment system was merely a ploy of National Sea to try and break the union. He assured the fishermen it would not work as long as the men stayed together.[22]

By mid-December a compromise seemed in the offing. Morrow informed the CFFU that Lunenburg Sea Products would agree to a 60-40 lay if five other items were deducted from the gross stock. These items were the captain's commission, the medicine chest, certain port charges, and sick mariners dues. This seemed like a fair offer. Even with these new deductions, each crew member would have an increase of about $200 for an average voyage. However, the CFFU executive said the additional deductions were unacceptable, and its members apparently concurred. At the Parish Hall in Lunenburg on Saturday 28 December, 350 fishermen listened to a report on the status of negotiations, and then voted unanimously to go out on strike.[23] The fishermen of Nova Scotia were about to plunge into a life and death struggle for their union.

The strike commenced quietly, the main activity being an exchange of letters. C.J. Morrow of Lunenburg Sea Products responded to a letter from the union by calling the strike "hasty and ill-advised", and quoted Section 21 (b) of PC 1003, which governed conciliation procedures. The union had broken the rules by striking without notifying the minister and failing to give the required notice of strike action so that conciliation could be attempted. Because the CFFU had not observed these regulations, Morrow stated, Lunenburg Sea Products would decline any further negotiations with it.[24] Although it had violated legal procedure, the union was otherwise very careful and restrained in the first days of the strike. Any vessel out fishing when the strike was called was assured by the CFFU that it would be allowed to land its catch without interference. One trawler, *Cape LaHave,* was ready

21 *Halifax Chronicle,* 6 December 1946.
22 H. C. Meade to "Brothers", 9 December 1946, Zwicker Papers, DUA.
23 *Halifax Chronicle,* 30 December 1946.
24 Lunenburg Sea Products (C. J. Morrow) to H. C. Meade, 4 January 1947, Zwicker Papers, DUA.

to sail when the strike notice went out, but its owners told the crew to unload the ship and leave it tied up. Many of the inshore fishermen began to slow down their work to support the offshore men. The union saw no reason for the establishment of picket lines in Lunenburg. The waterfront was quiet.[25]

In the first week of January, the struggle between the union and the companies became more heated. When the trawler *Sea Nymph* pulled into port on 2 January to land the first catch since the tie-up began, the *Halifax Chronicle* reported that a "verbal bombshell exploded". The vessel's crew unloaded her, and then tied her up. Representatives of A.M. Smith and Company, which owned the trawler, were furious that the vessel was not returning to the banks. Fletcher Smith, the co-manager of the company, railed at the CFFU, saying the union was forcing the men to stay off the vessel. He claimed the fishermen were anxious to return to fishing but were being intimidated by unionists who warned them that if they did so they would never sail on a Nova Scotia vessel again. H.C. Meade placed a different interpretation on the activities of union members. "Now is the time for the fishermen to stand up and be counted", he proclaimed unapologetically. "We want to know who is with us and who against us". The *Sea Nymph's* crew joined the union.[26] By 6 January the strike was made complete when the last two trawlers came into port, unloaded their catches, and were tied up.[27] The union seemed confident of complete victory, and secretary Meade refused to consider the services of a conciliation board. He refused to apply to the Regional Labour Board or the provincial labour minister for any help in settling the dispute. He expressed his belief that only National Sea Products and the union could achieve a settlement, because they were the parties involved.[28] He later changed this position, and told C. J. Morrow that the CFFU would be willing to submit the question of the lay to arbitration. Meade suspected, rightly, that National Sea and the other companies were stalling for time, while the case they had brought on the CFFU's certification was before the court.[29]

Ticking away in the background had been this legal case that fish companies had referred to the Nova Scotia Supreme Court. On 14 January 1947 this time bomb exploded when the court, in the "Zwicker Decision", ruled that offshore fishermen were not employees, and hence could not exercise union rights under PC 1003 or other labour legislation. The Supreme Court's decision was based on its belief that the National War Labour Board had no jurisdiction in this matter because this was acting in a judicial capacity, whereas it was only qualified to act in an administrative capacity, applying well defined regulations on behalf of the government. Therefore the Board had no right to make a decision concerning the status of fishermen as employees. Further, Supreme Court Justice Sir Joseph Chisholm argued, the fishermen who manned the vessels of the applicants were not employees of the applicants. The Labour Relations Board had no authority to apply to them the provisions of Order in Council PC 1003, and in their attempt to do so had acted without jurisdiction.

---

25   *Progress-Enterprise,* 1 January 1947.
26   *Halifax Chronicle,* 2 January 1947.
27   *Halifax Chronicle,* 6 January 1947.
28   *Halifax Chronicle,* 8 January 1947.
29   *Halifax Chronicle,* 11 January 1947.

The Supreme Court of Nova Scotia thus downgraded those sections of PC 1003 which outlined what would be done should a question arise as to whether a person was an employer or an employee. In such cases, according to PC 1003, the National War Labour Board should decide the issue, "and its decision shall be final and conclusive for all the purposes of these regulations".[30] The NWLRB, accordingly, did have the jurisdiction to decide if certain bodies of people were employees. According to the Supreme Court, however, the NWLRB had acted in a "judicial" rather than an "administrative" capacity, although this objection had not arisen when the Nova Scotia Labour Relations Board had acted in a similarly "judicial" manner in late 1945, when it had found the fishermen not to be employees.

The Supreme Court argued that where no employer-employee relationship existed, the Board had no jurisdiction, and that this relationship did not exist in the fishing industry because the fishermen were paid under special arrangements which, with some variations, had been custom in the industry for many years. The persons who were engaged in procuring fish, Justice J.J. Doull argued, were not doing it "for the owners or for the captain, but for the general account of all...The fish belonged to no one before it was caught and it never belonged to the owner of the ship unless and until he bought it — if in fact he did". Although the Court acknowledged that there were times when fishermen absorbed losses and wound up with almost nothing in their pockets after lengthy voyages, it claimed ship owners faced the same problem. The owner stood to lose the hire of the vessel and his provisions, and the men their time and the use of some equipment. Since, in this case, there were no profits to divide, how could it be said that the men were employees and the owners employers? Moreover, the Court argued, fishermen were not employees because they were only required to remain on the vessel for one voyage.[31]

Many of the Court's arguments seem remarkably weak. Perhaps in the 19th century fishermen were indeed "co-adventurers", but by the 1940s the idea was ludicrous. The companies and the fishermen were in no way equal partners. The fishermen did not own any vessels, nor did fishermen share equitably with capitalists in the profits. The fishermen had no way to control the price they received for the fish they caught, because the buyer had already set the price before the fish were landed. The Court was also in error when it assumed that the fishermen were paid soon after each voyage; a key point arising in the struggles of 1946-7 was the company's demand that men be paid only after all the fish had been processed. As for the argument that frequent crew changes somehow affected the substance of the employer-employee relationship, the NWLRB had earlier pointed out that a change in the personnel of the crew should make no difference to collective bargaining, for "changes occur in the personnel of every industry".[32] The contract was with the union and not with each individual employee. Perhaps the most succinct puncturing of the co-adventurer myth had come from this NWLRB

---

30 *Canada War Orders and Regulations,* Ottawa, 17 February 1944, Wartime Labour Relations Regulations (PC 1003).
31 *Dominion Law Reports* (1947), p. 204.
32 Wartime Labour Relations Regulations (National), Otawa, Decisions of Proceedings, 7 February 1946, p. 11.

ruling, which commented: "One can imagine how annoyed the owners would be if fishermen pledged their joint credit as a partner may do".[33] Deeply flawed in fact and in logic, the Zwicker Decision nonetheless had a deep impact on the post-war fishing industry.

The Zwicker Decision came as a terrible shock to Meade and to the union. The companies had refused to recognize the union, and now they had a legal decision to reinforce this position.[34] This turned a fight over the "lay" into a struggle for union recognition and the survival of trade unionism in the industry. As Gene Barrett notes, "The next three months were a life and death struggle for the fishermen's union".[35] The CFFU could respond to the Zwicker Decision in four ways: appeal to the Supreme Court of Canada, persuade the federal government to act on the matter of fishermen's inclusion under PC 1003, fight for voluntary recognition from the companies, or fight for a change in provincial laws.

On 15 January Meade announced the union was going to appeal the decision to the Supreme Court of Canada. Probably because of insufficient funds, it never launched this appeal. It had earlier been barely able to manage the cost of an appeal of the 1945 decision of the Nova Scotia Labour Relations Board to the NWLRB.[36] The union was now on strike, and even with financial support coming in from other unions, the CFFU could not afford a long legal challenge to the Zwicker Decision. Feeding 500 striking fishermen and their families posed a serious challenge to the union's finances as it was. By the third week of January the strike was affecting other sectors of the industry, most notably the fish processing plants. There was scarcely any fish coming in to the plants, and close to 1,000 workers were laid off in Halifax and Lunenburg. The workers applied for unemployment insurance, and there was some question if they were eligible for benefits. When on 18 January the regional office in Moncton decided they were eligible, this made a great difference to the CFFU.[37] But the fact remained that a Supreme Court appeal was simply financially beyond reach.

The option of persuading the federal government to take action proved no less frustrating, although there was a clear precedent. The NWLRB had ruled that workers of the Levis Ferry Company in Quebec were employees. When this was overturned by the Quebec Supreme Court, the federal Justice Department took the case to the Supreme Court of Canada, which upheld the ruling of the NWLRB.[38] In the case of the Zwicker Decision, however, there were important jurisdictional questions. The federal government was preparing to return jurisdiction to the provinces in most labour matters, terminating the sweeping powers it had assumed under the War Measures Act. If the CFFU's case was taken to the Supreme Court, this process of the orderly return of powers might be delayed, and conflicting decisions might create further problems.[39]

33   *Ibid.*, p. 7.
34   *Halifax Chronicle*, 15 January 1947.
35   Barrett, "Development", p. 195.
36   *Halifax Herald*, 15 May 1947.
37   *Halifax Chronicle*, 17, 20 January 1947.
38   *Sydney Post Record*, 15 January 1947.
39   Barrett, "Development", p. 197.

Since the option of voluntary recognition from the companies was wholly unrealistic, the union was forced to rely upon the good intentions of the provincial government. The Liberal government of Angus L. Macdonald had by this point lost its earlier interest in advancing the rights of trade unions. Premier Macdonald took the position that the government could do nothing to assist either the fishermen or the vessel owners. Because the Court had ruled the fishermen were not employees, the "matter is one that does not come within the scope of any existing law or regulation".[40] This position ignored the fact that it was fully within the government's power to amend the Trade Union Act to include fishermen, or to create new legislation covering them as employees.

If none of these four avenues promised survival for the union, could it not at least take its case to the public? The newspapers echoed and re-echoed with the debate over the fishery in the early months of 1947. Unfortunately for the CFFU, in this public debate the companies held all the high cards. National Sea Products had launched one of the most intensive anti-labour propaganda campaigns ever waged in Canada.

One theme stressed was the alleged illegality of the strike. Ralph Bell, president of National Sea, said that the strike was "entirely illegal", and that "so far as union officials are concerned, [it] is a deliberate, flagrant flaunting of the laws governing labour relations".[41] But the early company statements were relatively restrained assessments of the harm the strike was doing to a wide range of Nova Scotia interests. In one of many half-page newspaper advertisements, Ralph Bell appealed "To All Nova Scotians Interested In The Welfare Of The Fishing Industry In This Province". He discussed his belief that National Sea Products had responsibilities to "Fishermen, Employees, Shareholders and the Public", and stressed how much money the company had pumped into the province. The strike was robbing the province of its markets for fish and they might never be regained. Everyone was losing money in the strike: "...the storekeeper, the dory builder, the repair plant operator, the truck operator, the Doctor, the landlord, the box manufacturer".[42]

In the wake of the Zwicker Decision, however, restraint was thrown to the winds, as a new word came to dominate the anti-union campaign: "communism". Instead of attacking the fishermen for the damage their strike was inflicting on the fishing industry, the advertisements began to denounce the strike as a communist plot. National Sea used every variation on this theme that it could. The company stated it was always "ready and willing" to talk with the fishermen, but would have nothing to do with the communist-dominated CFFU. National Sea Products, the advertisements proclaimed, "believes in the common sense and good judgement of Nova Scotia fishermen and is quite content to wait until they have figured this thing out for themselves and have re-asserted their independence".[43]

In this way the company tried to sow doubt in the fishermen's minds, and divide them from the CFFU leaders. National Sea continually repeated that it would always deal with the fishermen, but never with "Communists".[44]

---

40 *Halifax Chronicle*, 15 February 1947.
41 *Evening Times-Globe* (Saint John), 6 January 1947.
42 *Halifax Chronicle*, 11 January 1947.
43 *Bridgewater Bulletin*, 12 February 1947.
44 *Halifax Chronicle*, 19, 27 January 1947.

The CFFU was not, in reality, a "communist union", although the Canadian Seamen's Union with which the CFFU was affiliated did have Communist leadership. H.C. Meade, the CFFU's secretary, was a Communist Party member, but neither Captain Ben MacKenzie, the president, nor Willis Parke, the treasurer, were Communists. This rather marginal involvement of communists in the CFFU did not deter National Sea from presenting the issue of the strike as the choice of "Communist Dictatorship or Freedom". As Ralph Bell lectured the fishermen:

> I agree completely and without reservation, your method of organization is no business of ours, BUT when the actions of some of your leaders threaten the entire fishing industry of this Province and the livelihoods of thousands of Nova Scotians THEN it is NOT your business alone but becomes our business and the business of EVERY Nova Scotian...WE BELIEVE IN FREEDOM, SOME OF THEM BELIEVE IN FORCE. WE BELIEVE IN TOLERANCE, SOME OF THEM BELIEVE IN TYRANNY.[45]

National Sea Products carried the anti-communist campaign to a new height when it printed a series of "Pamphlets on Communism". One was based on a sermon given by Reverend W. E. Cholerton of Berwick, Nova Scotia. He compared Christianity and communism, arguing "One offers freedom, the other slavery", and the choice is "Revolution or Revival". Articles from various news sources on the fishermen's strike were quoted, and the pamphlet stated:

> there is scarcely anything in Nova Scotia at this time of greater importance to the people of this province than the circumstances which have resulted in the cessation of production of seafoods for the past month or so...Communism...is fighting now to entrench itself in the Nova Scotia fishing industry. If it succeeds in its purpose to dominate that industry, through its influence over the fishermen, which will give it power to call further strikes at any time without reason, the Nova Scotia fishing industry will be doomed.[46]

The American magazine *Time* picked up the anti-communist theme in its coverage of the story which claimed the companies were fighting the union strongly not for economic reasons, but because they wanted to prevent the communists from "getting too solid a footing in the industry". The article focused on Meade's political affiliation with the Communist Party, ignoring completely the fact that no other member of the CFFU executive was a communist.[47]

Another powerful weapon used in National Sea's propaganda war was an appeal to the co-adventurer tradition. The company said the fishermen should be able to

---

45   *Halifax Chronicle*, 26 February 1947.
46   *Christianity or Communism?*, No 1 in a series of Pamplets on Communism printed and distributed by National Sea Products, Limited, Zwicker Papers, DUA.
47   *Time*, 13 January 1947.

fish whenever they wanted because they had "always been able to do so in the past".[48] National Sea expressed great admiration for the way the industry operated:

> Here is an industry that has grown through partnership in joint adventure that offers opportunity to all. One in which any man of courage, heart and ambition can rise to the top (AS MANY MEN HAVE), and one in which those who are content with a more modest role can and do live in comfort and security If ever there was a system providing stimulus for people with ambition and determination to succeed, this is it. All concerned — crew, captain, and owners — share the expenses as well as the net proceeds of each voyage. The result has been individual interest in each item of expense and maximum incentive to all concerned.
>
> Skippers rose from dory hands. Some of the more ambitious and enterprising ultimately became leaders in the industry ashore, or retired in comfortable prosperity. THAT IS THE LUNENBURG SYSTEM — a tried and proven one that has stood the test of generations...one finds that this community which has from time immemorial operated on a joint adventure basis, is, by all the odds, one of the most prosperous in the Maritimes.[49]

The company left the fishermen with a final message: "Whenever you want to talk things over, get in touch with your skippers. We'll sit down with you and them at any time and talk this thing out, and settle it sensibly like partners and men".[50]

This appeal to a romanticized past was bolstered by the emergence of the captains as players in the dispute. In past disputes the captains had sometimes sympathized with the fishermen and even helped organize collective protests, although they were paid four or five times the wages of crew members. On this occasion, however, the captains came out on the side of the company. Late in January the vessel captains held a meeting in Halifax and decided to revive the Lunenburg Master Mariners Association (MMA). This organization had been dead for years, and its revival was another blow to the union. At its first meeting the captains adopted two resolutions directed straight at the CFFU:

> 1. That skippers refuse to negotiate with any persons not a resident of Lunenburg County actively engaged in deep-sea fishing, or who has not shown ability to operate deep-sea vessels efficiently, or has not the confidence of owners and crews.
>
> 2. That skippers refuse to sail unless the agreement about the distribution of proceeds is based upon the principle of partners or co-adventurers.[51]

48   *Bridgewater Bulletin,* 5 March 1947.
49   *Bridgewater Bulletin,* 26 February 1947.
50   *Ibid.*
51   *Halifax Chronicle,* 29 January 1947.

These demands would eliminate full-time union organizers or indeed any kind of trade or industrial union for fishermen. Although Captain Angus Walters argued that the captains "weren't ganging up on the men", he said "that the MMA would not have anything to do with the leaders heading the fishermen's strike. We are not against the fishermen forming a union, but we can't see the necessity of bringing outsiders to dictate to fishermen, the skippers, and the firms".[52]

Against such a wave of anti-communist hysteria, the union had few resources. While National Sea's advertisements appeared daily, the union's replies came out only sporadically. They dealt with such themes as the unfairness of denying fishermen the trade union rights other workers took for granted, the restraint the workers had shown during the war, and National Sea's monopoly control of the industry:

> Why are fishermen different? We work at one of the hardest, most hazardous jobs on the face of the earth. The contribution we make — year in and year out — to the prosperity of this province is no small one. Thousands of shore-side workers and businessmen — even R. P. Bell himself — depend on the fishermen going to sea. Without the fish we bring in, there is no work — NO PROFITS — for any of them.
>
> The Workers in every other important industry in the province enjoy the right to organize and bargain collectively. WE ASK ONLY THE SAME RIGHT! WHY ARE WE DIFFERENT? WHY ARE WE REFUSED THAT SIMPLE RIGHT? If we had gone on strike during the war years — when fish was so desperately needed — the strike would never have lasted...the government would have compelled the companies to recognize our union...the whole issue would have been in the interest of the war effort.... BUT WE KEPT ON FISHING — and did it in the INTEREST OF THE WAR EFFORT. MUST WE PAY FOR OUR PATRIOTISM NOW?[53]

On 7 February union members staged their first demonstration. They were fired up with enthusiasm at a meeting in Lunenburg's Capital Theatre, where Harry Davis of the Canadian Seamen's Union proclaimed that "any attack on the CFFU is an attack on the CSU".[54] When the fishermen left the meeting they gathered into parade formation, and, carrying about 25 different banners, marched through Lunenburg to the offices of Lunenburg Sea Products and other fish companies. Many townspeople turned out to watch this orderly procession. There were no fights, scuffles, or threats.[55]

A few days later, representatives of the captains and vessel owners met Premier Angus L. Macdonald and his cabinet to discuss the strike. The discussion went on for several hours, and the result was not good for the union. The owners argued

52 *Halifax Chronicle*, 29, 30 January 1947.
53 CFFU Advertisement, February 1947, Zwicker Papers, DUA.
54 *Halifax Chronicle*, 3, 4 February 1947.
55 *Halifax Chronicle*, 8 February 1947; *Progress-Enterprise*, 12 February 1947.

they had not been contacted early enough by the union regarding negotiations for changes in the "lay", not mentioning that the CFFU had written to ship owner F. Homer Zwicker as early as August 1946 to propose a new contract.[56] The Premier announced that the government would assist neither side in this strike. Because of the Supreme Court ruling it could neither order the fishermen back to work, nor order the companies to recognize the union. The dispute, MacDonald added, would have to be worked out between the fishermen and the companies.[57] The *Searchlight,* the journal of the CSU, which had previously called the Nova Scotia government a "dead being" for its inaction in the strike, now accused it of being in league with big business to break the union.[58]

Frustrated with the federal and provincial governments, the union looked far afield in its search for political allies, for it had become clear that only state intervention and public support could keep the organization alive. The CFFU sent letters to every municipal council in Nova Scotia asking them to petition the provincial and federal governments to amend PC 1003 to include deep-sea fishermen. The CFFU claimed that if fishermen were given the legal rights of other workers, the strike would be quickly and easily settled. National Sea Products immediately mailed their own letters to municipal councils stating that the choice was between "Communist dictatorship or freedom". The city council of Sydney was the first to endorse the union's request, and others followed. There was a spirited disagreement in the Halifax council, but it too eventually agreed to support the CFFU.[59] Only two town councils did not support the resolution: those of Lunenburg and Mahone Bay. Yet there was little local governments could do in a dispute such as this. Ben MacKenzie, who was in Toronto to drum up support for the CFFU, summed up the union's frustration by commenting that he "might have to go to the United Nations because no one in Canada seems to have authority to deal with the question".[60]

By the first week of March strike solidarity was beginning to weaken. The fishermen had been out of work for over two months, and as much as they may have wanted a union and to stick with the strike, ideals did not buy food and clothing for their families. At this point the Master Mariners Association held a meeting at which the captains decided they would ask individual crews what they wanted to do — stay on strike or resume fishing. On 4 March Captain Angus Walters of the MMA said that more than half of the striking fishermen wanted to go back to work. Some of the tied-up vessels, he predicted, would be heading back to the fishing banks by week's end. The day before about 100 fishermen had rushed to the Lunenburg docks when they learned that crew members had boarded the *Cape North.* When they arrived at the vessel the captain, Napean Crouse, told them in no uncertain terms that they "had better leave...you have no business on board without my permission". He then went below to talk with his crew, and the strikers left.[61]

56 Willis Parke to F. Homer Zwicker, 6 August 1946, Zwicker Papers. DUA.
57 *Halifax Chronicle,* 15 February 1947.
58 *Searchlight,* 27 February 1947.
59 *Halifax Chronicle,* 27, 28 February 1947.
60 *Halifax Chronicle,* 27 February 1947.
61 *Halifax Herald,* 4 March 1947; *Evening Times-Globe,* 4 March 1947.

On 5 March the strikers held a mass meeting in Lunenburg at which the leaders tried to revitalize solidarity. When the meeting was opened for discussion, Captain Crouse advised the men to bargain with the owners as crews, instead of through the union, so they could get back to sea. The floor instantly came alive with cries of "chase him out" and "sit down". But another fisherman asked for a vote on whether or not to resume fishing, and a few others asked for a secret ballot. Secretary Meade said a secret ballot would be fine with him, but no one actually moved such a motion. When the meeting was over the fishermen stayed around the town for some time discussing the issue.[62]

Very early on the morning of 11 March, as the pickets changed shifts, the *Marie-Brenda* slipped out of Lunenburg harbour and headed for Liverpool to pick up a crew. Later that same morning the *Dorothy Irene* pulled out of Halifax harbour. She had a "full crew aboard and sailed for the fishing grounds".[63] Two days later fishermen, aided by some picketing miners, ran to the Halifax waterfront when rumours that another vessel was about to sail reached them. The union then decided to set up 24 hour pickets in Halifax and Lunenburg, and ten men were sent to Liverpool to keep an eye on the *Marie-Brenda*.[64]

The union's position became even more untenable in the days that followed. On 14 March all Ralph Bell's words of warning about the dangers of communism seemed to be confirmed when J. A. "Pat" Sullivan, the man who had been most influential in building up the Canadian Seamen's Union, resigned as its president. He denounced the CSU as "nothing but a front for communists", and urged union members "to get out and stay out until honest seamen can be found to represent you". H. C. Meade, who had been the main target of National Sea's red-baiting, was mentioned personally by Sullivan as one of the union leaders who took orders directly from Moscow.[65] CSU loyalists condemned Sullivan as a traitor, and stated his "walking out in the midst of the Nova Scotia fishermen's strike" was "perhaps the worst piece of treachery".[66]

Within a few days vessels were breaking from the tie-up and heading for the banks, and there were no picketers around to stop them.[67] The CFFU held a mass meeting in Lunenburg on 19 March, at which the 400 fishermen present passed a vote of confidence in their union leaders, and decided to return to work. Captain Ben MacKenzie voiced their reasons for this decision:

> We are terminating our strike because we have reached the limit of our ability to keep our families alive and well without earning. We are not doing this because we are any less determined than we were three months ago that we need and must have a union to protect our interests nor because we are any less convinced that this is our right and in the interests of the entire province.[68]

---

62   *Halifax Chronicle*, 6 March 1947; *Halifax Herald*, 4 March 1947.
63   *Halifax Chronicle*, 12 March 1947; *Progress-Enterprise*, 12 March 1947.
64   *Halifax Herald*, 13 March 1947.
65   *Halifax Chronicle*, 17, 18 March 1947.
66   *Searchlight*, 10 April 1947.
67   *Halifax Herald*, 19 March 1947.
68   *Halifax Herald*, 20 March 1947.

The union meeting also passed a motion calling upon delegates to present a brief to the provincial government asking for amendments to the Trade Union Act so that fishermen could have collective bargaining rights. The decision to end the strike was not taken without acrimony. Some of the fishermen said they had been "fools to vote for the strike". Others said ending the strike would end the CFFU, while still others maintained that they had made their point before the public and the union "would be recognized before the end of 1947".[69]

It soon became apparent that CFFU members were to be blacklisted. On 25 March Captain Walters of the MMA confirmed a rumour that had already swept the fleet: even if the present CFFU leadership resigned, the skippers would have nothing to do with the union. They would, however, he said, "recognize, support, and assist a local union headed by men who know and understand the fishing industry".[70]

On 1 April National Sea Products announced that its vessels were ready to go fishing, although they would not all be sent at once because the company wanted to avoid glutting the market. The company also announced that the fishermen would be working under a 60-40 lay. The captain's commission, engineer's pay, bait, ice, lubrication, and fuel would all be deducted from the gross stock, after which the fishermen would receive 60 per cent of the value of the catch. This "lay" was similar to the proposal the companies had made, and the union refused, prior to the strike. National Sea also unilaterally reduced, by one cent and one half cent per pound, the prices it was willing to pay for haddock and cod. Ironically, the company that had repeatedly stated throughout the strike that it was not in control of fishermen's wages, could now tell them how much they were going to be paid.[71]

An equally hard line was taken on the question of trade unionism. National Sea instituted "articles of agreement" which applied for only one voyage, and would involve only the vessel's crew, the captain, and the managing owner. These articles, specifically defining the fishermen as "co-adventurers", had to be signed by each crew member before the ship sailed, or they would not be able to work. The beaten union realized fishermen had no choice but to accede to these demands. Even though they realized they would have to capitulate, however, the strikers wanted the public to know they were by no means voluntarily accepting the system against which they had protested. In a petition drawn up on 2 April at a CFFU meeting in Lunenburg, the fishermen demanded collective bargaining rights under law, and stated:

> Whereas we have recently signed articles of agreement with the managing owners in which we are described as co-adventurers we hereby wish to make it clear that we have done so only to enable us to obtain employment. We have done so because of economic necessity and not

69   *Halifax Chronicle*, 20 March 1947.
70   *Progress-Enterprise*, 26 March 1947.
71   *Halifax Herald*, 1 April 1947; *Progress-Enterprise*, 2 April 1947.

because we are anyways satisfied with the status of co-adventurers as a permanent agreement.[72]

The defeat of the strike had one painful epilogue: the losing fight to change the provincial government's position on the status of fishermen. On 21 March a delegation of fishermen met with Labour Minister L. D. Currie to ask that they be included in the proposed new Trade Union Act. After the meeting, Currie stated that he would "recommend to the Government of Nova Scotia that some means be found to enable bona fide deep-sea fishermen to bargain collectively". He added to this promising statement such recommendations as preferential hiring of Nova Scotian over foreign fishermen, a mechanism for arbitration of disputes arising from the settlement of voyages, and non-discrimination against the former strikers.[73]

These reassuring recommendations were not pursued. Angus L. Macdonald was a fierce anti-communist and had, since his early days as a reformer, become less sympathetic to trade unionism. In the legislature on 6 May Premier Macdonald said he was "a little tired of people always trying to put the blame on the backs of management and foremen".[74] As the provinces resumed their central role in labour legislation, the business community mounted a strenuous anti-labour campaign. National Sea Products, for example, sent a telegram to the Premier saying "We strongly endorse proposal for labour legislation by Nova Scotia members Canadian Manufacturing Association outlawing closed shop, registering of unions, prohibiting industry-wide bargaining".[75] O. F. MacKenzie, President of Halifax Fisheries Limited, claimed that prosperity required that "one-sided labour laws be corrected and at least give management an equal basis in law with labour". Until Canada became a "slave state", he added, "no union leader should dictate as to who should and should not have the right to be employed".[76] It appears that Angus L. Macdonald was very susceptible to this climate of opinion. Throughout the strike, one reason the provincial government had advanced for doing nothing was that the federal government still had jurisdiction in labour matters. Macdonald reiterated this in the House of Assembly on 26 March, the day the Legislature opened. That same day a new Nova Scotia Trade Union Bill was introduced. It did not include fishermen.[77]

Fishermen were, however, to be found in a bill that was given its first reading on 23 April. Under the proposed Fishermen's Federation Act, fishermen were to be allowed to organize only by individual counties. If 40 or more fishermen in one county applied to the Minister of Labour stating that they wished to form a group to enable them to bargain collectively with vessel owners, they could then be registered by the Minister under this act. Any person who was "not an active

72 *Halifax Herald,* 3 April 1947.
73 *Halifax Herald,* 21 March 1947.
74 *Halifax Mail,* 6 May 1947.
75 National Sea Products to Angus L. Macdonald (telegram), 17 April 1947, Angus L. Macdonald Papers, MG 2, 917, 26-2, Public Archives of Nova Scotia.
76 O. F. MacKenzie to Angus L. Macdonald, *ibid.*
77 *Progress-Enterprise,* 2 April 1947.

fisherman" could not be an officer or representative of these county "stations".[78] Every county with such an organization would have an Inspector, appointed by the government, who was to ensure that the fishermen received a fair amount of the catch, and he would also have the power to "certify the county stations as bargaining agent for all the active fishermen of the county for the purpose of bargaining collectively".[79]

This bill was anathema to organized labour. It allowed fishermen to bargain collectively only through the Fishermen's Federation, and by restricting bargaining to county units it also put an end to any industry-wide bargaining. Since fishermen from one county often sailed on vessels from different counties, their bargaining rights would be extremely circumscribed. The bill also excluded inshore fishermen and processing plant workers from membership in a common union with deep-sea fishermen. J. K. Bell of the Nova Scotia Federation of Labour remarked that "if this bill is passed, then any reputation the government may have had as being friendly to labour will have passed also". Ben MacKenzie stated the bill was a "rank betrayal of the fishermen and a threat to the very existence of a free trade union movement in this province".[80] Over the cries of labour, on 12 May 1947 the Nova Scotia Legislature passed the Fishermen's Federation Act.

So ended the fishermen's struggle of 1946-7. The workers' defeat had immense consequences. When the state later initiated an intensive modernization campaign in the industry, fishermen had no united, forceful voice to make their interests and concerns known. Labour's complete absence in state planning probably injured the industry in the long term, and may have accounted for the overall failure of modernization in the industry. The need for more good quality fish on a regular basis could only be met if crews of fishing vessels were ensured good conditions and decent wages. In such circumstances regular, experienced crews could have been kept, instead of occasional, inexperienced crews. Such improvements demanded collective bargaining and secure trade unions. But capital and the state had beaten the fishermen and forced them into the narrow and outdated role of "co-adventurers". This short term victory perpetuated the deep seated problems of a fragmented and chaotic industry, whose long term costs, particularly for the Canadian state, have been enormous.

---

78 *Statutes of Nova Scotia,* 1947, Fishermen's Federation Act, Sections 3(1) and 3(2).
79 *Ibid.,* Section 6(1).
80 *Halifax Herald,* 3 May 1947.

C.H.J. GILSON and A.M. WADDEN

The Windsor Gypsum Strike and the Formation of the Joint Labour/Management Study Committee: Conflict and Accommodation in the Nova Scotia Labour Movement, 1957-1979

IN 1957 THE 400 EMPLOYEES of the Canadian Gypsum Company at Windsor, Nova Scotia, conducted one of the longest and most bitter strikes ever recorded in the province. This was a 13-month work stoppage which involved much of the provincial labour movement in support activity and which was not soon or easily forgotten. Indeed, the defeat of this strike triggered a chain of events of profound significance in terms of the character and direction of the labour movement in Nova Scotia. The gypsum strike had displayed with rare clarity a classic struggle between the forces of capital and labour, but in the decade that followed working class combativeness was supplanted by union efforts to accommodate capitalism, mainly by the establishment of the Joint Labour/Management Study Committee (JLMSC).

The gypsum strike and the JLMSC initiative neatly capture the paradox of trade unionism. On the one hand, trade unions engage in titanic clashes with the forces of capital, conflicts which lay bare the diverse and ultimately separate interests between capital and labour. On the other hand, trade unions in capitalist societies display a strong tendency to moderate their behaviour in order to accommodate capitalism. The paradox thus noted is not a recent phenomena, and has long concerned theorists of revolution and the class struggle. While the "early" Marx saw trade unions as combinations which contained the seeds of the radical transformation of society,[1] both he and Engels, in their later writings, began to question the revolutionary potential of trade union activities.[2] Later Marxists developed these ideas further. Lenin always stressed the need for revolutionaries to work within the unions, since that was where workers had their earliest mass experience of a form of the class

---

1 Marx wrote that "the first attempts of workers to associate among themselves always take place in the form of combinations" and that, "this mass is thus already a class as against capital, but not yet for itself. In the struggles, of which we have noted only a few phases, this mass becomes united, and constitutes itself as a class for itself. The interests it defends become class interests". Karl Marx, *The Poverty of Philosophy* (1847), 155 ed., p. 150.

2 Engels's Letter to Bernstein, 17 June 1892. "The trade unions exclude on principle and by virtue of their status, all political action and consequently also the participation in the general activity of the working class as a class", cited in R. Hyman, *Marxism and the Sociology of Trade Unionism* (London, 1971), p. 10.

struggle, but he attacked as "economism" the idea that trade union activity by itself could lead workers to a revolutionary class consciousness. This required the intervention of a party with an explicitly revolutionary political agenda. Without this perspective, Lenin wrote that "trade union politics of the working class is precisely *bourgeois* politics of the working class".[3] Lacking the leadership of revolutionary ideology, workers and their unions would conduct their struggles on the terrain of the bourgeoisie to the point where they would become naturally integrated with capitalism, accepting along the way the rationale of capitalist ideology. Developing these ideas of Lenin, Italian Marxist Antonio Gramsci argued that trade unions were governed by the search for "industrial legality" for the purpose of engaging in collective bargaining. This, he suggested, led trade union leaders to pursue initiatives which fractured the relationship between themselves and their general membership:

> The union concentrates and generalizes its scope so that the power and discipline of the movement are focussed in a central office. This office detaches itself from the masses it regiments, removing itself from the fickle eddy of moods and currents that are typical of the great tumultuous masses. The union thus acquires the ability to sign agreements and take on responsibilities, obliging the entrepreneur to accept a certain legality in his relations with the workers. This legality is conditional on the trust the entrepreneur has in the solvency of the union, and in its ability to ensure that the working masses respect their contractual obligations.[4]

For Gramsci, then, trade unions acquired "institutional needs" which necessitated some form of accommodation with the forces which they formally opposed and a corresponding moderation of demands amongst the general membership.

In Nova Scotia, and in Canada generally, unions have long displayed the tendencies Lenin and Gramsci had noted in Europe. Throughout the first half of the 20th century these tendencies had been opposed by radical forces within the unions who provided leadership which, at least in part, upheld concepts of an irreconcilable class conflict between capital and labour. In the 1920s, 1930s and 1940s these radical forces in the unions were led mainly by the Communist Party. However, during the latter years of this period, the communists themselves moved somewhat closer in their trade union policies to the practices of bureaucratic unionism. Then, during the immediate post war years, communists and other radicals were strongly attacked by the right wing union leaders, aided by the CCF, the American head offices of most unions, and the Canadian federal and provincial governments. In the early Cold War years radicals were driven from most positions of influence in the unions. By the 1950s, therefore, the union movement in Nova Scotia and in most of Canada was strongly dominated by right wing leaders wedded to concepts of industrial legality such as those described by Gramsci.

3   V. I. Lenin, *What Is To Be Done?* (1902), *Collected Works*, vol. V (London, 1961), p. 426.
4   A. Gramsci, *Soviets in Italy*, Institute for Workers' Control, Pamphlet Series No. 11 (London, 1976), p. 14.

Further, during the war years the Canadian government had adopted policies which went far towards providing mainstream union leaders with the union legality they sought. Order-in-Council PC 1003, in particular, had at last given legal force to workers' right to collective bargaining through trade unions, although in this legislation the trade unions were circumscribed by regulations limiting the use of the strike weapon.[5] In 1947, when the wartime regulations were ended and labour legislation again came under provincial jurisdiction, almost all provinces adopted trade union laws modelled on PC 1003. In Nova Scotia, where the 1937 Trade Union Act had already formally granted collective bargaining rights, it was replaced by the 1947 Act which incorporated most of the features of the federal Order-in-Council, including provisions forbidding work stoppages during the life of a contract and requiring conciliation prior to any strike. However, in Canada generally in the early post-war years, union leaders could feel that great progress had been made towards legal rights for unions and union security. A landmark in the search for union security had been the famous court decision which followed a six-month strike of the United Auto Workers union against the Ford Motor Company of Windsor, Ontario, in 1945. Chief Justice Ivan Rand of the Supreme Court recommended that although an employee retained freedom of choice regarding union membership, a financial (dues) contribution should be made to the authorised bargaining agent, as the employee was benefitting from the activities of the union. This "Rand Formula" had since been applied widely throughout the country. Encouraged by this, union leaders hoped to convince governments and enlightened employers that a system of collective bargaining with "responsible" and disciplined unions was the best means of ensuring labour stability and productivity, and thus no impediments should be placed in the path of further growth of the union movement.

In Nova Scotia, however, the power of the union movement had not grown in the post-war years. No substantial advances had been made in organizing non-unionized workers, and some provincial industries in which large and powerful unions were well established, such as coal and steel, were in drastic decline. Thus the situation when the gypsum strike began was one in which a weakened labour movement led by men committed to the path of legality and accommodation with capitalism confronted a large corporation which was intransigent in its opposition to any interference in the management of its operations by trade unions. This was also a time in which the

---

5   PC 1003 contained sections modelled on the much older Industrial Disputes Investigation Act, which required conciliation proceedings before a strike could legally be held. This type of regulation of unions has usually been regarded by Marxists as "incorporation" of unions by the state. For example, Trotsky viewed such government actions as deliberate attempts to embroil union leaders into relationships which would in effect emasculate the independent power of the labouring masses, writing: "Monopoly capitalism is less and less willing to reconcile itself to the independence of trade unions. It demands of the reformist bureaucracy and the labour aristocracy who pick the crumbs from its banquet table, that they become transformed into its political police before the eyes of the working class". Leon Trotsky, "Trade Unions in the Epoch of Imperialist Decay" (1940) in R. Hyman, *Marxism and the Sociology of Trade Unionism*, p. 11.

provincial economy was weak and government was extremely reluctant to oppose the interests of any large investor in the area, such as the U.S. Gypsum Company.

The Canadian Gypsum Company was a wholly-owned subsidiary of the U.S. Gypsum Company of Chicago. The company had begun operations in Nova Scotia in 1924 and had quickly become the largest single employer in Windsor and the surrounding area. Moreover, it acquired 65 per cent of Nova Scotia gypsum production. In these early years, the company recognized the Nova Scotia Quarry Workers Union as the bargaining agent for its plant employees despite the fact that most other U.S. Gypsum holdings were unorganized.[6] In order to deal with trade unions, U.S. Gypsum had developed policies which were to be followed by all subsidiaries. The company was against any union security agreement which compelled employees to join a labour organization as a condition of employment. Management also opposed any seniority system that would hinder the promotion of employees on the basis of skill or ability independent of the years worked at the plant. Moreover, the company did not feel that the deduction of union dues from wages was desirable.[7] Conceding the check-off of union dues was seen as being too close to admitting formal recognition of a union, and the Rand Formula was not an alternative which it was prepared to consider. The Company was unequivocally anti-union.

The ideology of the company was most evident in its Works Manager, Michael King, who introduced a personal style of bargaining which reflected the overall company philosophy. The majority of the workers who had been employed at the Windsor plant for a number of years perceived King as an instrument of the parent company in Chicago. A steadfast attitude on King's part helped to increase animosity and this ultimately contributed to unpleasant and difficult negotiations. Because his military background, personality, and attitudes fit well with the overall style of U.S. Gypsum's philosophy and policy, King personified the company and was willing to assume local responsibility for its policies. Moreover, the company was noted for being very frugal at the bargaining table — not pleading inability to pay, but lack of desire to pay. The workers believed that the company was attempting to break the union, following the same process that it had carried out south of the border. Many employees saw King as the problem, since he represented these policies. One worker expressed the view that "he was one American who didn't believe there was such a thing as a good Canadian".[8]

Hostility towards the company and its officers was not restricted to its employees alone. The community of Windsor in general was subjected to a controversial company land policy. In the area, land was often handed down through families by a "verbal will" without legally changing title in the Registry of Deeds. Canadian Gypsum would contact a distant relative and inform them that they had a claim against the land. The company would then offer to buy the claim from the relative for

6   Tom Shiers, Personal Interview, 20 May 1987.
7   Harold D. Burgess. Attorney, *Industrial Inquiry Commission* (1958), vol. II, pp. 69-70.
8   Benny McCullogh, Personal Interview, 15 May 1987.

a small sum of money and, if successful, use this position as registered owner to demand ownership of the land from the person who had received it through an informal transfer. In this way, the company bought up much of the local land and many of its houses, undermining the culture and social customs specific to the area. Although the company could thus acquire land through legal loopholes, it embittered the relationship between the community and itself. The unusable condition in which the land was left by the company caused further resentment. The provincial government helped to increase the community hostility towards the company when, through a secret Order-in-Council, it issued a deed for a public highway to the company without the knowledge of the people who lived on the road. This gave the company sole access and right-of-way privileges.[9] Also, until the mid-fifties, no taxes were paid on gypsum removed from the province because gypsum was not classified as a Crown mineral. This changed in 1953, when the Nova Scotia government enacted special legislation to impose a tax of 33 1/3 percent on the profits of the mining operation.[10] However, it was difficult for the government to assess the real value of this particular operation as the company was permitted to file reports as a company total, rather than broken down by subsidiary. Through complex accounting practices, the company could engage in price transfers, profit switching from one area to another non-profit area (thus avoiding taxation) and the re-direction of its profit earnings.[11] Thus, under this system, the gypsum resource yielded minimal benefit for Nova Scotians, while providing substantial capital earnings and accumulation for the company. Overall, it could be said that the policies of the United States Gypsum Company had aroused antagonism from its workers, among the community in which it operated, and to some extent from the provincial government.

The Nova Scotia Quarry Workers Union represented 400 workers at the plant. These were divided into various classifications: general laborers, drillers, mechanics, welders, electricians, power shovel operators, locomotive engine and brakemen, crusher attendants, and car shop employees. Surprisingly, union security in the form of a closed shop, meaning that "none but union men can be employed except when no union men can be supplied", existed as early as 1924.[12] However, the union was not certified. In 1928 the union broke away from a national affiliation to become known, rather misleadingly, as an "independent union". Although the closed shop provision was maintained through these early years, it was quite meaningless. The union could hire whoever they wanted but, "always with 'father' looking over your shoulder".[13] The "independent union" was in fact a "company union" — ineffective and unable to make headway in negotiations.

9   *Ibid.*
10   H. Kuusisto and R. Williams, *Round One* (Halifax, 1974), p. 3.
11   *Ibid.*, p. 4.
12   *An Application for Certification of Bargaining Agent Pursuant to the Trade Union Act* (no date), MS-9, 26, A 260, Dalhousie University Archives.
13   Hugh MacLeod, Personal Interview, 15 May 1987.

It was only after the election of Tom Shiers to the Presidency of the Local in 1952 that the Union began to develop an independent character. Shiers was very straight and forthright in his approach to King, the Works Manager, and showed him no servility. Under Shiers, the union hoped for more meaningful negotiations and over the next five years the Local succeeded in obtaining formal certification and affiliation with the Canadian Labour Congress (CLC).[14] This was not easily achieved. The company opposed every institutional manoeuvre which increased the union's relative strength. For example, when the union finally became certified, in 1952, the company withdrew the union security clause which it had used to its own advantage during the formative years of its operations.[15] On the other hand, the rejection of the paternal "independent union" shows that with increasing aspirations, the workers were no longer prepared to "knuckle under" in a servile relationship. Conflict was inevitable, and a serious strike almost occurred in 1955 before a two year settlement was reached through the intervention of a Conciliation Board.

On 15 June 1957, when the contract expired and negotiations began, the union wanted an increase in wages and an improvement in the fringe benefits package. According to their figures, the rates of pay at Windsor were well below the rates offered by another company in the same industry in a nearby area.[16] The company, however, intended to stand firm on the issue of wages, despite the fact that the cost of Nova Scotia gypsum was now 70 to 80 per cent less than American gypsum, so wages could be increased with no real threat to the company. More significantly, the union was prepared to strike over its demand for union security, which had become very important to the workers for many reasons. They feared that technological change in the form of mechanization would result in a gradual reduction of the work force. King had also informally told Shiers that he wanted to see the work force cut from 400 to less than 150.[17] Without union security, the workers felt that their jobs might be in jeopardy especially since the company was known for its anti-union policy. There were several non-members working at the plant who were vocal in their anti-union sentiments. This increased the sense of irritation felt by Shiers and the large majority of the workers who saw the union as the appropriate vehicle to improve pay and conditions. Union security was also tied into the seniority clause. The union argued that in the event of a layoff, the company could dismiss union members and maintain non-union members regardless of seniority or skill. The union wanted to avoid these problems by ensuring that all workers paid union dues. A seniority clause would then protect every worker, ensuring the security of those who had served the longest. In this way, the union saw union security and the seniority clause as defenses against possible arbitrary discrimination by the company.

14 J. K. Bell, Personal Interview, 15 May 1987.
15 *Industrial Inquiry Commission* (1958), p. 109. King stated in testimony that "as long as that relationship with the old independent union lasted, I don't think we would have disturbed the clause in the contract.".
16 Ben O'Neil, President, Nova Scotia Federation of Labour, *Halifax Chronicle Herald,* 29 November 1957.
17 Tom Shiers, Personal Interview, 20 May 1987.

The union also called for an increase in the provincial tax on gypsum, and this demand was supported by many members of the community. Despite the 33 1/3 per cent tax which the government levied in 1953, it was apparent that little or no tax was in fact being paid. The company had claimed that it was not possible to allocate profits for each of its subsidiaries. Moreover, its accounting procedures moved company profits to those countries which levied the lowest tax rate. In 1955, after long negotiations, the government agreed that a profit of 18 cents per ton would be assumed. Thus the tax rate of 33 1/3 per cent realised a tax of only six cents per ton.[18] And the actual tax paid was less than this amount, since the company could make deductions for municipal taxes, cost of power, and insurance protection.[19] To the community it seemed that the United States Gypsum Company also destroyed the land, leaving it totally unusable. Frequently, land which had been used by the company was left filled with cliffs, holes and mud, and with no compensation or repairs offered which would allow the land to be used again. The bitterness felt by the community was summed up by Shiers when he stated:

> The resources of this land as a whole belong to us and should be in some way used to our advantage. We're entitled to a fair return and deserve a better shake from the results of our resources. If we (the union) can't negotiate more for the people in the province, then the government should step in to get the money the company is robbing us of and put it back in the economy of the province.[20]

For the union and the community at large, an increase in the gypsum tax would cause the company to show more corporate responsibility toward the resources and the land of the province. They argued that if the company was more responsible to the land, then it might show more social responsibility to its employees — and treat them better. Thus, the gypsum tax became a key issue during the dispute. The government was conspicuously inactive in this regard, since they feared that greater tax pressure on gypsum tonnage might see United States Gypsum leave the province. Nevertheless, this inactivity increased the workers' anger and resentment still further.

By the late summer of 1957, the impasse in negotiations reflected the large gap between the positions of the two sides. Despite the appointment of a Conciliation Board, no meaningful progress was made. The union had established the terrain upon which the impending dispute would be fought — union security. The company had no intention of conceding anything, believing it occupied a position of strength since production lost due to a work stoppage in Windsor could be made up by increasing production at other locations. In this sense, the workers in Windsor were striking against the whole company and not just the local subsidiary. Moreover, at this time the gypsum industry was in a major slump, and thus a reduction in production was seen by the company as rather fortunate. There was no common ground on the issues

18   Kuusisto and Williams, *Round One*, p. 4.
19   Don Nicholson, CLC General Representative, *Halifax Chronicle Herald*, 30 November 1957.
20   Tom Shiers, Personal Interview, 20 May 1987.

of wages and fringe benefits,[21] but though the wage question was not insignificant, the ensuing dispute essentially concerned a fundamental principle, namely union security. As such it soon involved the wider labour movement of the province, represented by the Nova Scotia Federation of Labour. Moreover, the strike represented a community uprising against half a century of grievances. On 31 October 1957, 400 workers walked off the job and the strike was on.

In the first weeks of the strike, the bitterness towards King was very strong. There were calls for his dismissal, and the request that another Works Manager be appointed before further negotiations could take place. It was stated in the *Halifax Chronicle Herald* that "perhaps the company should recall King and send someone with a greater sense of fair-play, someone with more understanding and humility in his make-up, who, in the union's opinion, tries to understand and appreciate the problems of his employees".[22] Various unions, including the United Mine Workers, called for his deportation, labelling him a "very undesirable alien".[23] The personalization of the dispute meant that contact between the union and the company during the early part of the strike was in the form of letters, which were made public in local and provincial newspapers.[24]

On 30 November Stephen Pyke, the Minister of Labour, announced he would intervene in the strike. Pyke arranged for separate meetings with management and union representatives who were now assisted by officials from the Federation of Labour and the CLC. In late December, further offers were exchanged and on 7 January 1958, the union made its first concession. It announced that its stand was "flexible" on wages and working hours, but "firm" on union security. There was no response from the company. On 17 January the Nova Scotia Federation of Labour urged the government to increase the gypsum tax and the Halifax and District Labour Council passed a resolution asking for an investigation into mining operations in Nova Scotia to determine if the taxes paid were fair and adequate. There were also calls for a "value-added" tax, whereby the government would tax gypsum based on the expected added value of the mineral once it had been processed and finished in the United States.

In the meantime, it was a full month after the strike began before strike pay was received — at the rate of five dollars per week for a single man and 12 dollars per

21 In the negotiations the union demanded a 15 cents per hour wage increase, a decrease in the work week from 44 hours to 42 hours with the same take home pay, union security in the form of compulsory union dues check-off, and assorted fringe benefits including a contributory health plan and a pension plan. The company offered an eight cents per hour increase, and stated that the work week had already informally been reduced to 42 hours. No mention was made of other benefits. The union charged that the eight cents per hour increase offered actually amounted only to a two cents per hour increase in take home pay because it would take six of the eight cents offered to allow the worker to maintain the same take home pay with the work week reduced from 44 to 42 hours.

22 Letter to the Editor, *Halifax Chronicle Herald*, 4 October 1957 (Pro Bono Publico).

23 *Halifax Chronicle Herald*, 4 October 1957.

24 Examples in the *Halifax Chronicle Herald*, 18, 19, 24, 28, 30 December 1957.

week for a married man.[25] In addition to strike pay, various unions throughout the province and other jurisdictions pledged support to the striking workers. The CLC, although urging strike action, clearly did not consider the issue of national importance. This was reflected in the amount of financial support which was offered. Of the approximately $170,000 received over the length of the strike, only $40,000 came from the CLC. The bulk of the funds came from the various provincial union locals. It was generally felt by the strike leadership that the CLC did not understand the significance of the battle or do enough research into U.S. Gypsum to understand its policies. Shiers, in particular, felt that the CLC could have given more support.[26] Assistance from local unions helped, but it could not sustain an indefinite strike.

In February the strikers' wives became involved. They met with Premier Stanfield in Halifax, who told them that he could not impose a settlement in the form of compulsory arbitration. He argued that this was against the public interest. Although this initiative produced no visible results, it was significant in that the women's action showed the depth of the support which the strikers enjoyed.[27] There were also calls for representatives of all organized workers in the province to give support to the strikers through a protest to be made to the provincial cabinet.[28] By now, the effects of the strike had spread to the shipping terminals, causing curtailment of operations and lay-offs in some instances. Provincial labour organizations such as the Halifax District Trades and Labour Council and the Nova Scotia Federation of Labour came forward with support and held meetings in an attempt to find a settlement or establish some middle ground. They felt that the matter was important enough for an impartial investigation in the form of a Royal Commission which could conduct hearings, take evidence, make on-the-spot studies into the operations of the firm, and judge whether the tax of six cents per ton was fair and adequate. The provincial government resisted all these pleas.

At the beginning of March, Canadian Gypsum Company manager King himself addressed the workers in an effort to get them back to work. Another strike vote was taken and the workers voted, by an overwhelming 210 to 31, to stay on strike. Shiers stated that this vote demonstrated that the members were still determined to obtain a measure of justice from U.S. Gypsum. The next initiative occurred on 15 March with the appointment of Professor H.D. Woods, Director of Industrial Relations at McGill University, as a special mediator. Despite several meetings with both sides and lengthy discussions lasting until 25 March, he too was unable to find common ground. The head office in Chicago seemed to be ignoring the strike, as it had made no visible attempts to settle the dispute. The company appeared confident that a small group of workers in Windsor, Nova Scotia, could not stand up to a multi-

25 Hugh MacLeod, Personal Interview, 15 May 1987.
26 Tom Shiers, Personal Interview, 20 May 1987.
27 According to J. K. Bell, a long time leader of the labour movement in Nova Scotia, this was "one of the earliest occasions that women became active in an industrial dispute. It was a breakthrough in strikers finding an ally in their wives and female friends. The fact that they decided to help was a bit of history making". J. K. Bell, Personal Interview, 15 May 1987.
28 *Halifax Chronicle Herald,* 30 November 1957.

national. And by the late spring of 1958, despite the support which had been forthcoming throughout the locality and the wider labour movement, it was clear that new initiatives would be needed to break the deadlock. For this reason, the leaders of the strike approached politicians of all parties with a view to exerting influence on the government to persuade it to intervene.

In March, Michael McDonald, Co-operative Commonwealth Federation (CCF) MLA in the Nova Scotia Legislature for Cape Breton Centre, formally called for an industrial inquiry to be set up. He stated:

> The history of this company – the history between this company and the union, is such that a great deal of ill will has been felt between the two parties for the past number of years...this had been a situation which has grown up throughout the years and reached the explosive point this past summer...should the strike be ended tomorrow and the men return to work, the solution would not be reached, for we would once again have a recurrence in a very short time...there are not further policies [sic] granted to the Minister under the Trade Union Act other than that he might order an inquiry into the industrial dispute.[29]

His plea was supported by a resolution drawn up by 25 citizens, including businessmen. In April, Pyke finally responded to this pressure by setting up an Industrial Inquiry Commission headed by Judge Ralph Shaw which, after numerous meetings and discussions, reported on 27 June. Judge Shaw urged the signing of a 30 month contract containing a 42 hour work week for the first six months and 40 hours for the next 18 months, a 25 cents per hour wage increase spread over the 30 months, and a revised seniority clause. On the important union security issue, the Commission recommended an irrevocable check-off for all employees.[30] (Only one non-union employee objected to this.) The company and the union agreed to all aspects of the report, except the matter of union security. King reiterated his belief that "no employee should be compelled to join a union or maintain membership in a union or to support a union financially as a condition of employment".[31] Put simply, the company rejected the Commission's recommendations as a basis for settlement. Judge Shaw, in a remarkable attack, unequivocally condemned the company's rejection of union security: "the adamant stand of the company on this point has to my mind no merit or justification and it is not in line with the present accepted labour-management relations in the province of Nova Scotia".[32]

With the failure of the Shaw Commission to achieve a settlement the solidarity that had been visible in the strike up to this point began to crack. In early August, King sent letters to all employees inviting them back to work. It was now nine months since the strike began, and successive attempts to break the deadlock had

---

29 *Minutes from Legislative Debate*, 7 March 1958, J104.K2, Public Archives of Nova Scotia.
30 *Industrial Inquiry Commission* (1958), vol. III.
31 *Halifax Chronicle Herald,* 28 June 1958.
32 *Halifax Chronicle Herald,* 27 June 1958.

failed. Against the background of increasing desperation and impending poverty, 50 of the workers made the painful decision to go back to work. The union erected picket lines at the plant and, inevitably, violence erupted, although Shiers and the union threatened the withdrawal of strike pay should the workers engage in violent picketing or spontaneous demonstrations.[33] The RCMP were brought on site to escort the workers into the plant, and were charged by the union with strike-breaking. King himself led the parade into work, often getting his windshield broken by rocks thrown by angry strikers. Refusing to be intimidated, the company offered a $5,000 reward for information which would lead to the arrest and conviction of any person who had caused injury or damage to company personnel or property. By the end of August 40 arrests had been made. On 8 September there was a mysterious dynamite explosion at the plant which severely damaged a $60,000 diesel powered shovel. However, the company was succeeding in producing some gypsum, and on 17 September, in a highly charged atmosphere, the first gypsum ship since the previous autumn sailed out of Hantsport destined for New York, further sapping the morale of the strikers. With their jobs being filled by non-union workers and more union men breaking ranks the remaining strikers began looking for a settlement. On 26 September the union announced that it was prepared to drop the issue of union security.

Tom Shiers later claimed that one of the most important reasons for the decision to back down on union security was the CLC's lack of support for the strike, both morally and financially.[34] A second key factor was the possibility of achieving the aim of union security through provincial legislation. This had been the topic of conversation between union leaders and politicians of all parties after the demise of the Shaw Commission. The Federation of Labour (which Shiers was about to join as an elected officer) also had the union security issue on its legislative agenda with the cabinet.[35] With a voluntary dues check-off already part of the Trade Union Act the legislative route looked promising. In any case, the issue of union security was now surrendered by the Windsor strikers.

Surprisingly, this offer by the union did not immediately end the strike. There remained the issue of how the 100 or so workers who had crossed the union picket lines would be dealt with, and the company refused to guarantee that there would be no disciplining of the strikers who had been arrested. In an effort to bring pressure on the company, Hugh MacLeod and Ben O'Neil, representatives of the Nova Scotia Federation of Labour, met with Premier Stanfield and threatened a general strike throughout the province in support of the gypsum workers. Stanfield reacted strongly and accused MacLeod of trying to ruin the province.[36] This threat, although not followed through, succeeded in mobilising the Minister of Labour to become involved in negotiations once again. On 15 October, in an attempt to reach a

33 *Halifax Chronicle Herald*, 15 August 1958.
34 Tom Shiers, Personal Interview, 20 May 1987.
35 *Labour Gazette* (1959), p. 973.
36 Hugh MacLeod, Personal Interview, 15 May 1987.

settlement, he started a series of meetings with King and CLC Director Jos MacKenzie. At first, the contents of the meetings were kept confidential. Finally, on 17 November, the company issued an offer that was placed before the strikers. It contained a voluntary dues check-off, a 42-hour work week reduced to 40 hours after six months, and a general increase of 25 cents per hour to be implemented in stages.[37] The employee seniority existing at the time of the strike was to be restored and the company agreed with the union on the procedure for the re-employment of workers following the end of the strike. Other fringe benefits which the union had tabled earlier in the strike were left out of the settlement. The union membership was not happy with this final offer, but voted 147 to 52 to accept it.

On 20 November 1958 the strikers returned to work. Thirty employees who had been convicted of violence on the picket line were fired but were to have their cases submitted to arbitration to determine if they were to be re-employed. The 13 month strike had finally ended in what must be considered a serious defeat for organized labour in Nova Scotia. The local had failed in its attempt to get the key demand of union security written into its contract. However, it should be pointed out that the strike took place in a rural community with little or no labour tradition, and that the Quarry Workers Union was isolated from the mainstream of the labour movement, including the full support of the CLC. The workers faced a determined anti-union multi-national corporation and a government unwilling to act firmly for fear of losing a significant tax-paying provincial employer. Any assessment of this strike cannot simply dwell on the failure to win union security, but must record this as a remarkable example of a struggle by rank-and-file workers to obtain job security. But in the conduct of the Windsor strike a close relationship between the local leadership and Federation and CLC Officers was also displayed. The importance of this development cannot be overestimated. The Gypsum strike can be identified as a watershed simply because it marks an important stage of the transition whereby rank-and-file struggle was almost totally replaced by the activities of a self appointed labour elite which saw accommodation with employers as the only viable means of maintaining an effective presence in the province. The potential for this dispute to encourage the development of wider forms of consciousness and awareness amongst similarly placed workers was thereby curbed. This strike, in which the power of the international company was considerably greater than the local strikers, could only have been won if the government had been brought to intervene through the fear of a general upsurge of the workers of the province. It had been the activity of masses of workers and the potential for greater mobilization that had won the concessions to unions gained in earlier periods from governments and employers. But the leadership of the union movement by this time discouraged any militant mass action, reflecting the relative passivity of trade union politics and the accommodationist tendencies which had developed during the post-war period. Purges of communist leadership, the

---

37   Twelve cents per hour immediately, eight cents per hour after six months, and five cents per hour after 18 months.

development of a more complex legal system of trade union law, the existence of new state social welfare provisions, had all helped to integrate the unions into the fabric of the capitalist system. While falling short of obsequious behaviour, the union bureaucrats of the day were not the men to lead or promote the militant involvement of large numbers of workers in the struggle for union rights.

American sociologist C. Wright Mills, writing in this period, characterised union leaders somewhat unflatteringly as "managers of discontent" who, in order to secure collective bargaining rights, held that:

> the interests of labour and business are complementary rather than contradictory, [and] that labour and business must co-operate in the actual process of production and in the conduct of the political economy as a whole. To ensure peaceful plants and profitable enterprises in a stable economy, the leaders of labour will deliver a responsible, which is to say, a well-disciplined, union of contented workers in return for a junior partnership in the productive process, security for the union and higher wages for the workers of the industry.[38]

But such "managers of discontent" have difficulty in maintaining balance over a long period. Their usefulness to government and employers sharply diminishes if they cannot, in fact, control workers' militancy; but their success in winning any concessions for workers becomes limited if they are too successful in repressing militancy. In periods in which the potential for workers' discontent to lead to a large scale disruption of production has been undermined by a leadership unwilling to risk its already tenuous relationship with employers and government, a strike such as that of the Gypsum workers posed only a limited threat to capital. For the leaders, the demand for basic union recognition through a union security clause was, in itself, essentially an attempt to gain industrial legality within the capitalist system, and this demand was pursued entirely within the framework provided by the legal system. Accordingly, a plethora of government appointed conciliators, mediators, and Courts of Inquiries were employed in order to try and break the deadlock. Despite the intensity of the conflict, the sanctity of these legal parameters was never questioned, and all attempts to settle the strike took place within the prevailing ideology of established dispute resolution procedures. As to the national labour movement, although the question of union security was a universal one for trade unions, this was treated by the CLC as a strike on a simple plant-based grievance. Lack of support from the CLC placed greater demands upon Maritime unions to make up the shortfall so that the strike could be continued. Moreover, almost all external trade union support consisted of financial aid, never solidarity action to mobilize other workers who faced aggressive anti-union employers. In this way, despite the broad support offered by many trade union locals, the dispute remained a sectional one entangled in the web of established procedures. Thus the Gypsum strike could not emerge as a

38   C. Wright Mills, *The New Men of Power* (New York, 1948), p. 119.

broader challenge to the way capital was operating in the province, even though it was on an issue that was of crucial importance to all trade unionists.

This committment of the union leaders to industrial legality also explains the seeming paradox of the fact that the failure of the strike led directly to efforts by the union bureaucracy to establish better relations with employers and tacitly with the government, the formation of the Joint Labour/Management Study Committe being one result. There can be little doubt that the failure of the Gypsum strike to win union security from the United States Gypsum Company exercised a dramatic affect on the trade union leaders and the labour movement of the day. At the least, the strike's defeat effectively drained combativity out of the leadership which had mobilised around the conflagration. Put simply, militant forms of industrial action seemed largely discredited to the principal leaders of the Nova Scotia Federation of Labour, and it would be more than a decade before working class militancy in the province would again take the form of large scale industrial conflict. In the meantime, in contrast to the experience of the previous 14 months, the labour leaders who had brought the Gypsum strike to an end were busy constructing an entirely new initiative which was to rely on accommodation and reason for the purposes of "managing" provincial union/management relations.

The shift towards legislative lobbying on the critical issue of union security hinged upon the relationship between the trade union officials and progressive politicians. Meetings between strike leaders and selected politicians had already taken place with a view to encouraging government intervention to bring the strike to a conclusion. Now a new set of meetings crystallized around the notion of introducing a Bill to guarantee union security. On 21 November, as the strike was concluding, Tom Shiers had summed up the situation by saying:

> Tension has been eased, but the big issue remain union security and we will never feel there has been complete settlement until we get it. We are looking to the government for new legislation in this matter. [39]

The mantle of responsibility here fell upon Michael McDonald, MLA for Cape Breton Centre, who as a representative of the CCF was already seen as a strong ally of labour, since the Nova Scotia CCF was largely sponsored and supported by District 26 of the United Mine Workers, themselves pressing for greater union security. The Federation of Labour Convention in the October of 1958 also carried a unanimous resolution calling for legislation on the union security issue. Support for this resolution was reiterated at the 1959 and 1960 Conventions.[40] In addition, the Federation's annual brief to the provincial government in January 1960 urged the incorporation of a union shop provision in the Trade Union Act. The Federation argued that such a clause would "go a long way towards stopping the industrial strife

39   Tom Shiers, *Halifax Chronicle Herald*, 21 November 1958.
40   *Labour Gazette* (1960), p. 135.

caused by the attempts by employers to entice employees away from duly certified unions".[41]

The culmination of these activities was the introduction of Bill 116 by McDonald, on 29 March 1960. The aim of the Bill was to alter Section 67 of the existing Trade Union Act by including the following clause:

> It shall be a condition of employment that all employees who are eligible within the scope of the bargaining unit shall become and remain members of the union in good standing. All future eligible employees must, as a condition of employment, become and remain members of the union in good standing.[42]

During the second reading on 12 April, McDonald claimed that the Bill before the Assembly represented a new departure in terms of the manner in which the trade union movement was attempting to change the labour laws. He noted that "this is the first time that organised labour used their influence by way of having a Bill introduced...the first time they have ever requested any amendment to any Act".[43] McDonald was certainly wrong in this claim, since organized labour had frequently so used its influence in earlier years. However, this type of intervention did mark a fundamental shift in the policies of the Nova Scotia labour movement. Its primary reliance had now moved away from industrial action and towards political lobbying for the purposes of legislative change.

Despite McDonald's exhortations, the Assembly agreed with the Chairman of the Committee on Law Amendments when he warned, "It is clear that widely divergent views on the subject matter of the Bill are held by large portions of the public".[44] This prompted the Conservative government to adopt the Amendment Committee's recommendation to set up a study of the Trade Union Act. This study, the Chairman argued, "should be made as soon as reasonably possible, and that the best way of making such a study is by a legislative committee assisted by some competent, independent, fact-finding body".[45] What is clear from the debates over Bill 116 is that the government of the day was unwilling to accept the arguments of the trade union movement and legislate in favour of union security against the wishes of provincial employers. It seems evident also that the subsequent setting up of a "Fact Finding Body on Labour Legislation" was a not-so-subtle attempt to sidestep or postpone consideration of the union security issue.

The result was the appointment of Judge Alexander H. McKinnon as a one man committee who began his work in the summer of 1960. Broadly, McKinnon's task was to make inquiries concerning "existing legislation", canvass the opinions "of

---

41 *Ibid.*
42 Act to Amend Chapter 295 of the Revised Statutes, 1954, the Trade Union Act, No. 116 Bill (1960), pp. 5-6.
43 *House of Assembly*, Minutes of Debate, 12 April 1960, p. 2268.
44 *Ibid.*, p. 2264.
45 *Ibid.*, p. 2265.

experts in the field", and, finally, "to assess the extent to which the said legislation promotes industrial peace".[46] Although McKinnon was expected to submit his findings within the year, it was not until February 1962 that the Report was made public. By this time the impetus for obtaining union security through legislative change, born out of the struggles of the Gypsum workers, had been diluted by the passage of time, even supposing any number of mainstream politicians had earlier supported this idea. It was now some three and a half years since the end of the Gypsum strike, and the "Introduction" to the McKinnon Report offered little encouragement to any notion that the government would now be prepared to discuss Bill 116 in a favourable light. On the contrary, the Report argued "that such industrial peace as exists within this country has occurred in spite of, rather then because of, the existence of legislation".[47] Accordingly, McKinnon recommended that the "compulsory union shop should not be made a legislative provision because it is one of the most important issues which should be decided by mutual agreement resulting from collective bargaining".[48] The prospects for mutual accord on this matter were, however, almost non-existent. In their briefs to the Mckinnon Report, eight employers and 12 trade unions made their feelings known, and there was no common ground. The unions advocated making union security a statutory obligation, and the employers all expressed strong opposition to this.[49]

The McKinnon Report's basis for rejecting a union security provision in the law was indicative of its overall philosophy, which was to encourage a voluntary approach to industrial relations based on the Swedish system. This makes the McKinnon report an historical oddity in that it called into question the whole direction and thrust of contemporary industrial relations, not only in Nova Scotia but in Canada as a whole. State intervention in the form of regulatory legislation aimed at reducing industrial disputes had long been the practice in Canadian labour relations, but McKinnon concluded "that restrictive legislation has driven an ever-deepening wedge between management and labour and has made much more difficult the voluntary co-operation which is vital to the welfare of industry and its employees".[50] The report also reasoned that "a continuation of this trend could well mean an ever-widening rift between the parties and not a remote possibility of a renewal of the class struggle which besmirched the record of the last century".[51] The solution proposed by McKinnon was to set up a joint Union/Management "Labour Market Board" similar to that existing in Sweden. This body would then set about the task of "developing greater understanding and trust". It was argued that "the mutual understanding between unions and management at the top level reaches down to the manager's desk and the worker's bench".[52]

---

46   *Report of Fact-Finding Body Re Labour Legislation* (1962), p. 5.
47   *Ibid.*, p. 15.
48   *Ibid.*, p. 51.
49   *Ibid.*, pp. 61-77.
50   *Ibid.*, p. 19.
51   *Ibid.*
52   *Ibid.*, p. 27.

The pluralist rhetoric in the McKinnon Report held obvious attractions for right wing union leaders, yet the analysis put forward was fundamentally flawed. In the first place, the die had already been firmly cast in Nova Scotia in terms of the development of a highly legalised framework responsible for directing the behaviour and attitudes of the parties. Second, the Swedish model was not an appropriate comparison in that union density was substantially greater there (90 per cent of the workforce was unionized in Sweden, and less than 30 per cent in Nova Scotia). In other words, trade unions in Sweden were much stronger and more able to meet employers on equal terms. Moreover, the structure of collective bargaining in Sweden was highly centralised whereas in Nova Scotia it was (and remains) fragmented and localised with no significant employers' federation. Nevertheless, despite the naivety of its analysis, the McKinnon Report laid down the conceptual foundation used to justify the collaboration and integration of the trade union bureaucracy in Nova Scotia into the fabric of provincial capital development. The idea of an institutional solution to confrontational bargaining and possible strikes attracted some labour leaders and some "progressive" employers who had, in the previous two years, been experimenting with joint meetings with labour. The result was that, following a number of visits to the province from the Swedish Labour Attache in Washington, the Institute of Public Affairs at Dalhousie University helped to established the Joint Labour-Management Study Committee (JLMSC) in the Spring of 1962.

The founding of the JLMSC was seen by the leaders of the Nova Scotia Federation of Labour as a major initiative representing a new era of co-operation between management and labour, and a decisive break with the bitter conflicts of the past. For them the JLMSC legitimized the voice of labour and represented a new sphere of influence which might facilitate progressive legislation. For labour leaders such as Ed Johnston, Federation of Labour President at this time, the JLMSC offered the prospect of an improved image for labour. Johnston later observed that, because of the JLMSC, "we do not have to fight constantly for labour representation on Boards, Commissions and other agencies, functioning through the community as we had to do prior to the 1960's".[53] Thus, for the Federation leaders, the JLMSC was a substantial opportunity and the embodiment of a resolution which was passed at the 1961 Convention which envisaged a "committee on which organized labour, management and government would be equally represented".[54] Nevertheless, some opposition to labour's role in the JLMSC was orchestrated by hard-line leftwingers such as J.K. Bell and George MacEachern, who cogently argued that there had been no rank-and-file endorsement of the Federation's support for the JLMSC, and that, more importantly, the whole initiative was based on the erroneous assumption that the interests of capital and labour could be distilled into a joint venture. Despite these criticisms, the floor at successive Federation Conventions lacked support for any radical ideas. The vision of co-operation and accommodation was clearly in the

53   Ed Johnston, *Report to the Nova Scotia Federation of Labour, 1970,* p. 18.
54   *Labour Gazette* (1962), p. 1254.

ascendence in Canadian organized labour in this period, and this ideological dominance by the right has much to do with the Nova Scotia Federation's eagerness to go into the JLMSC.

However, there were reasons why the concept of co-operation with employers was especially attractive to labour leaders in Nova Scotia at this time. The formation of the JLMSC must be seen in the context of the weak condition of the union movement in the province. Trade union membership was standing lower than 20 years earlier, the general economy of the province was in decline, and, as far as the leaders of the unions were concerned, the defeat of the Gypsum strike had turned them away from any belief that they could gain major advances through industrial action. It is also apparent that some of the province's labour leaders were now sympathetic to the argument that strikes had to be "sat on" in order to attract investment and hence jobs. This had been a preoccupation of Nova Scotian governments for years, with their idea that only heavy outside investment could revive the flagging regional economy. Further, in the early 1960s Nova Scotia, like other provinces, was eager to obtain as much as possible of the federal infrastructure money being made available to alleviate regional disparity. From this perspective, the historical tradition of labour militancy in the province, particularly in the Cape Breton coal mining areas, was seen as an impediment to new investment, and it was important to publicize the notion that such union militancy was a thing of the past, that Nova Scotian workers no longer deserved such a reputation. Many union leaders were prepared to co-operate with government and employers in creating a new image of labour stability and "responsibility" in Nova Scotia.

For the trade union leaders who were centrally involved with the operations of the JLMSC, there was no contradiction or conflict of interest. The JLMSC was seen as a natural extension of existing collective bargaining relationships, another legitimate sphere of influence, just as collaboration with government ministers through the JLMSC was seen as an opportunity to strengthen the legal status of trade unions. These ideas of union acceptability and accommodation with employers were explicitly recognised when the first JLMSC conference in November 1962 adopted a set of guiding principles. These included a moratorium on unilateral labour or management appeals to the Legislature to alter existing legislation "until all approaches to closer union-management action have been examined"; an unequivocal recognition by employers of the right for all workers to organise and of the contribution of collective bargaining to the economy; a condemnation by the employers of unfair labour practices during the certification process; and recognition by unions that "management is entitled to a fair return on its investment".[55] The institutional recognition which these accords gave to organised labour was seen as a significant development within the context of a province which to a large degree had

---

55 *First Agreement, Joint Labour-Management Study Conference* (Halifax Institute of Public Affairs, Dalhousie University, 1962).

been dominated by employers who had placed little faith in the process of collective bargaining and hence acceptance of trade unionism in general.

By early 1963 the JLMSC consisted of seven members from each side of industry, plus two members from the Institute of Public Affairs, which provided the chairman. The employers' side was made up of companies which in total had over 25,000 employees and the labour side of union officials who represented over 35,000 members.[56] This Executive met on a monthly basis and, until 1969, refused to follow the usual practice of taking and circulating formal minutes of their meetings, nor for the first two years of its existence was there a formal agenda. From these beginnings, the JLMSC sponsored an annual Study Conference of up to 130 people, consisting of 50 representatives from both sides and 30 as observers. In keeping with the spirit of the McKinnon Report, the second Study Conference adopted the following agreement:

> The Labour-Management Study Committee of the Institute of Public Affairs, Dalhousie University, predicates its activities on the belief that joint, voluntary, active cooperation between labour and management will bring respect and understanding required for the achievement of Committee objectives.[57]

The objective was "To promote a sound and harmonious relationship between employers and unions and the employees they represent".[58]

In order to act upon these principles, the JLMSC adopted a structure which was designed to influence the legislative process. Invariably four steps were used to develop a consensus on issues of concern which had been identified by either party. First, a meeting of the total committee would identify problem areas where consensus might be reached and this would be developed further by a sub-committee who would then report back to the whole committee for purposes of decision making. Second, these decisions would be communicated to an annual study conference for further discussion and eventual ratification by the JLMSC. Third, once

---

56   The first Chairman was Guy Henson. Four outstanding business members were: R. G. Smith, General Manager of National Sea Products, who was also the Chair of the Dalhousie Bureau of Industrial Relations and a Board member of the Institute of Public Affairs; Frank Covert, President of Moirs, Ben's, Atlantic Building Materials and Maritime Paper Products, and widely believed to be one of the most influential businessmen of the day; Gordon Stanfield, President of Starr Manufacturing, V. P. of Nova Scotia Light and Power, past Chair of the Canadian Manufacturers Association, and brother of the Premier, Robert Stanfield; Russell Harrington, President of Nova Scotia Light and Power, prominent member of the Halifax Board of Trade and management representative on the Nova Scotia Labour Relations Board. The most prominent labour members were: Joseph Gannon, President of the Halifax-Dartmouth District Labour Council and a past-president of the Federation of Labour; Ed Johnston, President of the Federation; Hugh MacLeod, CLC Representative; and Dwight Storey, Canadian Legislative Director of the United Steelworkers of America.

57   K. Antoft, *Harnessing Confrontation: A Review of the Nova Scotia JLMSC 1962-1979* (Brown's Flat, N.B., 1981), p. 107.

58   Institute of Public Affairs, *The Second Nova Scotia Labour-Management Study Conference* (Halifax, 1964), p. 6.

the JLMSC had formally adopted the Study Conference resolutions, the decisions were then communicated openly to the labour and management bodies throughout the province represented on the JLMSC. Finally, after completion of this process, the matter was placed before a special legislative committee of the JLMSC which invited the Minister of Labour to attend as an observer. A brief was then prepared with the expectation that this would be translated into the form of an amendment to existing legislation.[59]

During the 1960s the JLMSC can be seen to have directly influenced the amendments made to the Trade Union Act, since each of the specific changes made between 1963 and 1969 reflected the recommendations made by the previous year's Study Conference. In 1964, the Act was amended to proscribe unfair labour practices by employers who communicated with their employees in forms of "coercion, intimidation, threats or undue influence".[60] A new clause was added which permitted the signing of a union security agreement if both parties were in agreement on the matter — surely a final residue (if much diluted) from the Gypsum strike.[61] Employers were also prohibited from altering wages and conditions of employment during the certification process up to and including the point at which a first contract would be signed.[62] Perhaps of greater importance were changes which introduced new guidelines for the operation of Conciliation Boards. The upshot of these changes was that the parties would be free to lock-out or strike 21 days after the Conciliation Officers' report had been filed with the Minister of Labour. The setting up of a Conciliation Board now became less attractive and as a result the incidence of such Boards being used almost disappeared during the 1960s.[63] In 1965 the JLMSC successfully persuaded the government to guarantee the continuation of collective bargaining rights where "the sale or transfer (of a business) has not resulted in a substantial change in the plant property, equipment, procedures, working force and employment relations of the business".[64] Another addition that year established bargaining rights for employees of "any (provincial) Board, Commission or similar body".[65] In 1969 these rights were extended to municipal policemen.[66] There is little doubt that these changes were of advantage to trade unions, and the JLMSC's coinage increased in value accordingly, effectively stifling radical criticism for a time.[67]

---

59 Guy Henson,"The Nova Scotia Labour-Management Agreements", *Relations Industrielles*, 24, 1 (January 1969), p. 104.
60 Act to Amend Chapter 295 of the Revised Statutes, 1954, the Trade Union Act. Chapter 48, S. 4(5) (1964), p. 144.
61 *Ibid.*, S. 6(1).
62 *Ibid.*, S. 14(b), p. 145.
63 *Ibid.*, S. 17, 21, 22(2), pp. 146-8.
64 Act to Amend Chapter 295 of the Revised Statutes, 1954, the Trade Union Act, Chapter 53, S. 20 (1965), p. 233.
65 *Ibid.*, S. 68, pp. 234-5.
66 Act to Amend Chapter 311 of the Revised Statutes, 1967, the Trade Union Act, Chapter 79, S. 68A (2) (1969), p. 357.
67 Even one writer in general severely critical of the JLMSC, Brian MacLean, recognises that the amendments sought and obtained by the JLMSC, "improved the (Trade Union) Act for labour".

However, the process for initiating amendments to the Trade Union Act, as described above, proved to be somewhat tortuous, and there was a substantial risk that each step in the process might dilute the original intention. In this way, important legal principles were effectively subjected to a piecemeal bargaining process. Longtime labour activist J.K. Bell has recently argued that the results of the JLMSC's deliberations probably "secured less than what could have been achieved through the normal process of submitting a legislative shopping list independent of the employers".[68] It is also clear that the entrance of some of the more intransigent employers of the province into the JLMSC during the 1970s made the passing of legislation favorable to unions still more difficult.

Aside from the JLMSC's role on legislation, it also aimed to promote stable and peaceful labour relations in the province. Attempts were made to establish an employers' federation, not only to achieve better co-ordination with respect to collective bargaining, but to encourage moves towards industry-wide and province-wide bargaining. In 1967, Matts Larssen from the Swedish Metal Workers Employers Association addressed the annual Study Conference in support of this idea. However, there was no advance in this direction, and the reasons for the lack of progress in setting up an employers' federation reveal some of the weaknesses of the JLMSC. Those employers who were represented on the JLMSC were in no position to claim they represented all provincial employers. Establishing a coherent employers' federation throughout the province was therefore unlikely, and JLMSC agreements in general had the problem that they could not be "policed" as far as the employers' side was concerned. Moreover, a move to centralised bargaining, the likely upshot of formalising bargaining relationships through an employers' federation, might well have exacerbated an already acute problem for the JLMSC — that of the incidence of wildcat strikes.

By 1966 the JLMSC was tentatively claiming that its work had resulted in a decline in industrial conflict.[69] Yet in the following year the explosion of wildcat strikes in the construction industry (widely believed to have been caused by the cost-plus nature of the contracting process) forced the JLMSC to recognise that its influence in terms of day to day workplace conflicts was tenuous at best. This led the JLMSC to set up a special sub-committee on the construction industry, which successfully persuaded the government to pass legislation allowing certification of building trade unions in only three days and an accreditation procedure which encouraged construction employers to bargain in geographic areas.[70] These changes had the effect of formalising the bargaining process, thus fixing the wage rates of each of the various building trades. The practice of "leap-frogging" wage demands

---

Brian MacLean, "Nova Scotia Labour and the JLMSC 1962-1975", Honours thesis, Dalhousie University, 1979, p. 25.

68 J.K. Bell, Personal Interview, 15 May 1987.
69 G. Henson, "The Nova Scotia Labour-Management Agreements", *Relations Industrielles,* 24, 1 (January 1969), pp. 87-128.
70 *Ibid.,* p. 119.

through wildcats was effectively reduced, and a "compliance agreement" with the employers provided contract continuity with new jobs and new contractors. The result was that, from 1972 on, there was a dramatic fall in the number of wildcat strikes in the construction industry.[71] Despite this apparent success, strike frequency increased dramatically throughout the 1970s. From 1963 to 1973, 331 strikes were recorded in the province, and 70 per cent of these were unofficial wildcats.[72] In the absence of "official" direction, rank-and-file workers were taking militant action on their own.

While workers were thus displaying by their actions the distance between their thinking and that of the labour officials represented on the JLMSC, there soon began to be indications that government support for the concept was not as great as it had once been. Through the 1960s, government officials professed great faith in the JLMSC, as in the speech of a Minister of Labour at a regional JLM Conference in July 1968:

> We in the Department of Labour want to establish a formal relationship with the JLMSC as the organization representing labour and management in the Province to whom we can look for guidance and advice not only in the legislative field, but in all areas in the field of collective bargaining.[73]

Addressing the 1971 Federation Convention, the Minister of Labour noted that, "some managements appear unwilling to communicate with labour" and that even the most enlightened legislation will fail "if management continues to take a narrow view of what they can discuss with employee representatives".[74] However, by the time of the 1973 Nova Scotia Federation of Labour Convention, Ed Johnston saw the situation as changed, accusing the Liberal government of showing favour to "the demands of multi-national corporations, who had their own industrial relations policies and techniques and were not ready to subscribe to the committee's co-operative approach". He added that, "local anti-union people who were in league with them have set out to by-pass the committee and destroy it". [75]

In fact, government interest in the Committee appears to have been contingent and ultimately unpredictable. The first signs that the new Liberal government of Gerald Regan was marching to a different tune came in an unexpected alteration to Section 24 of the new 1972 Trade Union Act. "Independent" management representations had convinced the government to legislate "that in every case where there is an application for certification by a union, a vote of employees should take place".[76] Although some discretion was left with the Labour Relations Board in terms of when votes were to be conducted, this amendment had the unequivocal impact of making it harder to achieve certification. It also showed that the JLMSC moratorium

---

71   C. H. J. Gilson, *Strikes: Industrial Relations in Nova Scotia 1957-87* (Hantsport, 1987).
72   *Ibid.*, p. 15.
73   G. Henson, "The Nova Scotia Labour-Management Agreements", p. 121.
74   *Labour Gazette* (1972).
75   *Labour Gazette* (1973), p. 693.
76   M. Belliveau and B. deMarsh, *The Five-Legged Sheep* (Halifax, 1977), p. 9.

on employers or unions unilaterally lobbying for changes to the Trade Union Act was no longer effective. A second and more public display of the JLMSC's impotence came in June of the following year, when an Order-in-Council made two changes to union certification procedures. One change made it impossible for a craft based union to be certified in an industrial plant, and the other provided that the Labour Relations Board would order a secret ballot if a single employee requested it, even if the number of signed cards had reached over 50 per cent of the workers in a defined bargaining unit. These regulations were obviously brought in so that the Michelin Tire Company could defeat an organising drive being conducted by the craft-based International Union of Operating Engineers, and Michelin and other anti-union employers could more easily resist the unionization of their employees. In the aftermath of these government actions, the JLMSC nearly collapsed. Nonetheless, the leaders of the Federation were still wedded to the idea that the Committee was useful to them, and it continued in existence until the "Michelin Bill" of 1979 was passed. This change to the Trade Union Act has helped the Michelin Company defeat several successive attempts to unionize its plants, by requiring that all employees of one industrial concern, although in widely separated geographical locations, take part in the one certification vote. This was so blatantly a case of the government passing legislation in order to cater to the anti-union policies of a large multi-national firm that it was impossible for the labour representatives to remain in the JLMSC. It had, however, been made clear in 1973 that government support for the JLMSC, and any government reliance on it for determining the content of labour law, would be continued only as long as this was expedient.

For provincial governments, the JLMSC had initially presented substantial opportunities. Government ministers could hope that the Committee would help provide stable and peaceful industrial relations. Moreover, unions would be embroiled in an exhaustive process of piecemeal bargaining with employers before changes in labour law were proposed, thus making it unlikely that any highly controversial legislation would be called for. Not only this, but the government also retained the luxury of constructing its own agenda independent of the JLMSC, leaving organised labour with little or no opportunity to mount effective opposition to anti-labour legislation. In effect then, it could be argued that the JLMSC created the illusion of progress for labour when in fact the government was generally going in the same legislative direction which had already been established by other provinces. This applied to governments of both the Liberal and the Conservative Parties. It was the Liberal government of Gerald Regan which introduced the anti-labour regulations in 1973, and the Conservative government of John Buchanan which brought about the "Michelin Act" of 1979. This certainly shows that, for the purposes of attracting and holding industrial investment in the province, provincial governments were more interested in responding to the whims of a multi-national corporation than cementing co-operative forms of co-existence between progressive employers and the representatives of organised labour. Presumably the political analysis involved was that, for winning votes, job creation was much more important than placating organized labour. By the late 1970s the provincial government had decisively shifted its focus away from embracing unions. Instead, it showed itself to be openly hostile towards the interests of unions. The leadership of the labour movement, which had put all its energy into supporting the JLMSC, could only respond by withdrawing from the Committee, and no possibility existed in 1979 of labour mounting a stronger attack on the passing of the "Michelin Bill". Rank-and-file opposition to anti-union legislation could not be effectively mobilised by a labour leadership which had long since departed the terrain of class struggle.

Thus, it can be argued that the JLMSC created expectations which damaged the combativity and independence of the trade union movement. Yet it cannot simply be asserted that the labour movement of the post Gypsum strike era was "side-tracked" or "incorporated" into a soporific relationship with both employers and government. By that time the leadership was already strongly committed to ideas of trade union accommodation with capitalism, to industrial legality, and to the notion that "enlightened" employers could be brought to understand that it was in their interests to work with labour unions for industrial peace and stability. Most crucially, it must be recognised that the JLMSC initiative was a product of the defeat of the Gypsum strike. It is within this context that the post-strike developments — from Bill 116 to the McKinnon Report and finally to the JLMSC itself — should be analyzed. Direct confrontations with employers to demand union security and other benefits formed a strategy which, in the minds of the dominant leadership of the Nova Scotia labour movement, essentially had been discredited and abandoned by the fall of 1958. It is perhaps not surprising then that an attempt would be made to replace such conflicts with an institutional initiative which reflected a labour movement on the defensive.

The JLMSC, in the ultimate analysis, was an effort to ensure a compliant workforce which could guarantee greater rates of return and an increase in investment in the province. Labour leaders were prepared to co-operate with employers and the government to achieve this aim. Presumably one reason for this was the belief of these leaders that only expanded industry in Nova Scotia would lead to an increase in union memberships. It was also true that provincial governments in the 1960s were prepared to accept some mildly pro-union legislative changes to the Trade Union Act put forward by the JLMSC. Since the edifice of corporatism already existed in the form of union certification, dispute resolution procedures, and other regulations, it was not difficult for governments to go along with suggested modifications to the established framework.

Despite getting these slight concessions for labour, the JLMSC could not repress manifestations of worker discontent. The distance between the trade union representatives on the Committee and the rank-and-file workers was revealed by the wave of unofficial strikes which took place. According to R.F. Hoxie, "government and leaders are ordinarily held pretty strictly accountable to the pragmatic test. When they fail to deliver the goods both are likely to be swept aside by a democratic uprising of the rank and file".[77]

It is sometimes argued that, as it is the natural tendency of unions to seek industrial legality and to become integrated into the capitalist system, it is inevitable that the relationship between rank-and-file union members and trade union leadership becomes fractured and any democracy within unions ceases to exist. Robert Michels, in his famous work *Political Parties*, described this phenomena as the "iron law of oligarchy". He noted that established union leaders became entrenched in their positions of authority and power and were able to manipulate policies due to the apathy and ignorance of the general membership. As a result, he observed that, "the leaders lose all true sense of solidarity with the class from which they have sprung".[78] In this way, Michels saw union leaders as invariably pursuing policies which did not reflect the interests of the broad mass of workers who they claimed to represent. But, as one critic of Michels' theory of the inevitable defeat of democracy has argued,

> If oligarchical waves repeatedly wash away the bridges of democracy, this eternal recurrence can happen only because men doggedly re-build them after each inundation...There cannot be an iron law of oligarchy...unless there is an iron law of democracy.[79]

The wildcat strikes that began in the late 1960s showed that the combativity of the Nova Scotia working class had not vanished with the defeat of the Gypsum strike, but had been merely displaced to another theatre which the JLMSC could not influence directly. According to Richard Hyman,

> The explanation is, essentially, that the institutionalization of industrial conflict does indeed achieve a *provisional* containment of disorder; but where workers' grievances and discontents are not resolved, they give rise eventually to new forms of conflict, perhaps involving new types of demands and a new means of action.[80]

By the early 1970s, both employers and government had become impatient with the JLMSC's inability to deliver labour peace. Increasingly, then, the government's corporatist overtures became scarcely veiled attacks on the right to organise, culminating in the 1979 "Michelin Bill". This made of the JLMSC an empty proposition even for those who had seen it as an opportunity to create permanent security for trade unions. For a period of 16 years, however, trade union leaders in Nova Scotia who embraced the JLMSC saw close relations with employers and government, rather than with their own memberships, as the way in which progress could be made.

77   R. F. Hoxie, *Trade Unionism in the United States* (New York, 1923), p. 46.
78   R. W. E. Michels, *Political Parties* (1915) [New York, 1962], pp. 81-2.
79   A. Gouldner, "Metaphysical Pathos and the Theory of Bureaucracy" in L. A. Coser and B. Rosenburg, eds., *Sociological Theory* (New York, 1964), p. 507.
80   R. Hyman, *Industrial Relations: A Marxist Introduction* (London, 1975), p. 199.

The experiences of the Gypsum strike and the JLMSC clearly displayed features which reflect classical Marxist and neo-Marxist analyses of trade unions under capitalism. Despite the tenacious struggle of the gypsum workers, the strike of 1957-58 was defeated. Such a strike revealed the contradiction between capital and labour without seriously threatening the institutions — the "earthworks and fortresses" — of capital. Yet the subsequent rise of the JLMSC shows that attempts to construct accommodative relations with employers and the government yield precarious results for workers. The unmistakable conclusion must be that the true interests of workers clearly transcend policies which remain rooted within the formal structures and influence of capitalism.

ANTHONY THOMSON

From Civil Servants to Government Employees: The Nova Scotia Government Employees Association, 1967-1973

BETWEEN 1967 AND 1973 the character of the Nova Scotia Civil Service Association (NSCSA) underwent a significant change in the direction of more fully developed trade unionism. The process entailed a change in the members' conception of their relationship to the government. A key event bringing about this changed outlook was the imposition of selective wage controls on government workers in 1972. Rather than opposing these controls the leadership of the NSCSA acted in the interests of the government, convincing the membership to acquiesce to what were really wage cuts, given the escalation in the cost of living. This action, in the face of substantial pockets of militancy in the association and the successes achieved elsewhere in Canada by public sector workers, marked a low point in the association's history. During this time the leadership of the NSCSA passed from the hands of the supervisory staff to those of senior employees who adopted a more unionist frame of reference, in keeping with the dissatisfactions and alienation of increasing numbers of government employees. If conservatism still prevailed among civil servants, it became less the traditional subservience to legitimate authority and the service ethic and more a cynicism about the possibilities of militant action and progressive change.

The transformation over time of the Civil Service Association in Nova Scotia can best be represented as a change from traditional paternalism to contemporary unionism, partly symbolized by changes in name: first Nova Scotia Civil Service Association; then Nova Scotia Government Employees Association; then the present Nova Scotia Government Employees Union. In the course of this evolutionary development, three milestones stand out. The first was the passing of the Civil Service Joint Council Act in 1967. During and following the debate which culminated in this legislation, two groups emerged within the association. One favoured retention of this Act as a structure within which reforms could occur, the other wanted to supersede the Joint Council and win full trade union rights, particularly signed collective agreements. This article is concerned with an analysis of the confrontation between these two groups, which resulted in the second milestone, a wholesale change in the leadership of the association and the ascendancy, by 1973, of more union-oriented members to positions of dominance in the association. The third milestone came five years later when a new Civil

Service Collective Bargaining Act was passed marking the culmination of the union group's efforts and establishing the present framework of employee-employer relations in the Nova Scotia civil service. The change in leadership in 1972 and 1973, precipitated by provincial wage controls, was the key facilitating factor in the development of a more union-like relationship with the government.

Traditionally, the civil service was small and positions were obtained by government patronage. In 1933 there were only about 1,600 civil servants in Nova Scotia. As the scope of government intervention into the economy grew and government services proliferated, civil service reforms were instituted to undermine patronage and create a professional body of public servants. In 1935 the Liberal government of Angus L. Macdonald proclaimed the Civil Service Act which instituted a merit system of appointment to the civil service. The Civil Service Commission (CSC), which was created to oversee the Act, was responsible for personnel management in the service. With the CSC, the government took one step back from direct, paternal control of the civil service. But governments still determined the parameters within which the CSC operated, and, at times, the government would engage more directly in decisions affecting its employees.

Fundamentally, employment was still at the pleasure of the government and there was no legal recourse for civil servants whose employment was terminated. However, traditional patronage was declining and many civil servants were employed in positions which were not subject to easy dismissal following a change in the governing party, as were the employees in the liquor stores. But the shadow of government paternalism persisted and contributed to the maintenance of a conservative ethic among civil servants as it was re-shaped by the new professional ideology of the CSC into a service ethic which was inimical to unionization. Unions were perceived to be special self-interest groups while government workers were expected to serve all interests equally and neutrally.

It was easy to maintain this image in the 1930s when government jobs were relatively secure and the development of an independent employee organization was not a consideration. This consciousness of special employment has not entirely disappeared, but events have considerably eroded it in the period since the Second World War. During the first two post-war decades, in Nova Scotia as well as in Canada generally, the public sector was a growth industry. In the proliferating bureaucracies, positions were relatively easy to obtain and qualified candidates could reasonably expect promotions. The traditional security of government employment continued to be the rule. Public employees represented a special case within a general commitment to maintain relatively high levels of employment. With real wages increasing nationally, the public sector was only one example of relatively secure and reasonably paid employment during the comfortable growth years of the 1950s and 1960s. This security was matched by complacency: civil servants in Canada generally remained aloof from the labour movement and eschewed militancy. This virtual absence of militant struggle, although subject to considerable regional and temporal variations, had deep roots in the specific nature of government employment, which afforded benefits which surpassed those of white-collar workers in the private sector.[1]

1   Adolf Sturmthal, *White Collar Trade Unions* (Chicago, 1967).

The calm surface of government employment, however, masked some deeper turbulence. Structural changes in the political economy were occurring which would propel some workers in the public sector to the forefront of class struggle in the country. The growth of the public sector, which was contingent upon the expanded role of the government in the national economy, undermined some of the traditional disparities with private industry. Large numbers of government employees were being brought together in more concentrated work settings. Old classification procedures, management techniques and practices were obsolescent and the cause of much friction and grievance in the government departments, emphasizing the need for reforms. The resulting attempts to rationalize the service were accompanied by the usual problems associated with these procedures in any workplace, problems which are as intense in non-manual as in manual settings. Rationalization in the government sector brought about significant changes in the conditions of work and raised to consciousness issues concerning the direction of the changes and the control over the procedures. The formation of the Nova Scotia Civil Service Association in 1958 resulted from dissatisfaction over the absence of procedures which employees could use to influence their conditions and terms of work. Further, attempts to rationalize the service by the hiring of an American consulting company had been important in consolidating acceptance among government employees of the need for collective representation. Opposition was engendered by the process of developing job descriptions, which employees feared would be narrow and limiting, and by the increasing specialization which accompanied the growth of bureaucracy. As government turned to a more professional management model, some of the traditional differences which had seemed to separate public from private employment were eroded.[2]

In addition to the transformation of work in the civil service itself, the spread of full collective bargaining in the private sector meant that organized workers were making gains in wages and also closing the gap with the civil service in the area of benefits.[3] Government employees had traditionally been paid a lower salary than that prevailing for equivalent work in the private sector, but had better benefits and job security.[4] With the winning of equivalent fringe benefits by unionized non-government workers and the general full employment in an expanding economy, some of the traditional benefits lost their saliency and contributed less to the maintenance of a conservative outlook. The wage gap was increasingly regarded as an injustice providing not only an impetus to demand salary adjustments but also to seek the best means for the improvement of the terms of labour contracts – collective bargaining. The differing mechanisms through which salaries were

2   A. Thomson, "The Nova Scotia Civil Service Association, 1956-1967", *Acadiensis*, XII, 2 (Spring 1983), pp. 81-105.
3   C. Balfour, *Incomes Policy and the Public Sector* (London, 1972); S. Frankel, *Staff Relations in the Civil Service* (Montreal, 1967); L.W.C.S. Barnes, *Consult and Advise: A History of the National Joint Council of the Public Service of Canada* (Kingston, 1975); S. Jamieson, *Industrial Relations in Canada* (Toronto, 1973); J. Anderson and T. Kochan, "Impasse Procedures in the Canadian Federal Service: Effects of the Bargaining Process", *Industrial and Labor Relations Review*, XXX, 3 (1977).
4   R. M. Bird, "The Growth of Government Expenditures in Canada" in B. S. Kierstead *et al.*, eds., *Economics Canada: Selected Readings* (Toronto, 1974).

determined in the private and public sectors was thrown into sharp relief. As a result, throughout the 1950s a growth of collective consciousness was emerging among public employees, a change which was reflected in the development of employee associations and bargaining strategies.

Trade union membership in Canada had declined in the late 1950s, but following the end of the recession in 1963, union growth and worker militancy revived. Both were fueled by mid-decade price increases which were inflationary by post-war standards. Beginning in the 1960s and continuing into the early 1970s, many public sector workers across Canada demanded and won collective bargaining rights, including in some instances the right to strike, and immediately became involved in catch-up campaigns to redress the wage inequalities and recover losses in their purchasing power.[5] Collective bargaining legislation was passed for federal civil servants as well as for provincial employees in Quebec and New Brunswick.

Among public employees in Nova Scotia the most significant early advances were made by the provincial teachers, who during the 1950s engaged in some strikes and emerged with better contracts, more secure employment and a stronger union. This early promise of militancy, which was largely confined to Cape Breton, has not been maintained in the Nova Scotia Teachers' Union. While they possess all the structural formalities of labour unions, teachers remain apart from organized labour and confine their activities to protecting their members' economic interests.

For the civil servants of Nova Scotia, a province which during the 1950s was enduring serious dislocations of primary industries and which at the best of times never escaped from perpetual underdevelopment, the security of government employment was an especially prized perquisite of the job. The absence of any form of influence over the conditions of employment had only recently become a source of grievance and the traditional practices of the civil service continued to shape employer-employee relations. In no other sector was the tradition of union conservatism, belief in the neutrality of the state, and absence of militant unionism as apparent as in provincial government employment.

Despite this traditional subservience, there were significant changes in the trade union orientations of provincial civil servants reflected in the complex interplay between membership attitudes and leadership during the late 1950s and early 1960s.[6] Civil servants in Nova Scotia had received permission from the government to form an association, and did so in 1958. The Nova Scotia Civil Service Association was founded with the expressed aims of developing higher standards of service for the public, maintaining good relations with the government, and furthering the interests of civil servants.[7] Its independence was nominal. The association was very much under the thumb of the government which controlled the constitution and maintained all the prerogatives of sovereign power. In short, the NSCSA began as a classic "company union".

---

5   L. Katz, "The Attack on the Public Sector: Counter Strategy", *This Magazine*, XIII, 1 (1979), p. 43.
6   Thomson, "The Nova Scotia Civil Service Association, 1956-1967".
7   *Civil Servants by the Sea* (Halifax, 1977).

Organized primarily by middle-management and supervisory personnel, during the first decade of its existence the association slowly established some limited degree of effectiveness. The culmination of this early period of growth was the Civil Service Joint Council Act (Bill 111), proclaimed in 1967. But by the time it was passed, Bill 111 was already an anachronism. While it provided a forum within which employees could help to shape some of the conditions of employment, this Act was still a long way from the formal equality of collective bargaining and the only voices heard were those of the senior supervisors in the service. The Act had been accepted by the NSCSA over the objections of a vocal minority which was attempting to push the association further in the direction of unionism or, alternatively, felt the employees should withdraw from the association and affiliate with a trade union. The actual experience of the Joint Council Act provided this union group with further ammunition for its cause. Negotiations under the Act consisted of closed discussions between the Civil Service Commission and the executive of the NSCSA, who together formed the "Joint Council". Resulting agreements were then recommended to the government and legislated into effect by order-in-council. This cooperative labour-management approach proved unsuitable to the more antagonistic labour relations of the 1970s.

The paternalism characteristic of government service was replicated in the structure of the association as well as in the Joint Council. The NSCSA was governed by a highly centralized administration. At the top was the president, elected at annual conventions, who headed the provincial executive and the smaller executive committee. At all levels of the association, from the president through the divisional executives, the dominant figures were supervisory civil servants. As the association's relationship with the government evolved towards collective bargaining, a change in leadership became inevitable, not only because the interests of supervisors often differed from those below them, but because the upper levels would be excluded from the association.

Alex Buchanan became president of the NSCSA in 1962. Unlike his predecessor, George Burnham, who had been more at home with trade union rhetoric, Buchanan was obviously conservative. In 1962, however, Buchanan was reasonably representative of the membership. The prevailing wind in the civil service was still quite conservative, and provided the currents of change were moderate, Buchanan could accommodate to some developing trends. Much of the business of the association was handled by the president, who exercised a preponderant role in the executive.

However, none of the executive positions were full-time and consequently the association hired an executive secretary who attended to the day-to-day business. Increasingly playing the role of expert at the centre of the NSCSA, the executive secretary became a key individual in shaping the character of the organization. At first, the NSCSA had hired a public relations specialist for this position, but by 1967 the executive secretary was Tom Shiers, a long-time unionist in Nova Scotia. Shiers had led the Windsor Gypsum workers in their 1957 strike and had been an executive member of the Nova Scotia Federation of Labour. In many ways Shiers was responsible for shaping the character of the association in a unionist direction, but, as events unfolded, he became identified with the conservatives in the executive. In fact it was these two men, Shiers and Buchanan, who more than any others came to represent the conservative policy of the association.

Among the membership, militant opposition to this leadership could be found in significant numbers only in three divisions and the militants, overall, were in a considerable minority. Much of the pro-union sentiment in the association was in Cape Breton (Division One), and was given voice in the provincial executive by Sidney Vickers. The explanation for this is largely historical, rooted in the regional experience of Cape Breton unionism. The other significant pocket of militancy was among medical technicians working in Halifax in the Victoria General Hospital (Division Eleven) and in the Pathology Institute (Division Thirteen). Among this vocal minority, Ken McKenzie was the most prominent representative on the NSCSA council. Although an explanation for the higher degree of trade union consciousness among these technicians is beyond my purpose here, it should be noted that hospital workers were in the forefront of public employee militancy throughout Canada, and Nova Scotia was no exception.[8]

It is not possible to tar all the remaining civil servants with the brush of conservatism. During the decade of Buchanan's presidency there was a growing dissatisfaction with what the association was able to achieve on behalf of its members. The gains may have been significant, but they fell far short of the heightened expectations of the late 1960s and early 1970s, expectations which it took compulsory wage restraint legislation to curb. This dissatisfaction among members surfaced in a growing opposition to the old executive, in demands for more collective bargaining rights, and in demands for a greater role for employees in decisions affecting them. Overall there was a growth of trade union consciousness across all classifications in the civil service. But just as different classifications began with distinct degrees of commitment to the tenets of unionism, so too the newer stages of consciousness and militancy varied according to the employment situation of the workers.

Under the leadership of Shiers the NSCSA evolved in the direction of formal trade unionism in a number of ways. Although the original legislation which gave permission for the founding of the association in 1956 explicitly declared that the constitution of the NSCSA could only be changed by the government, the executive resisted this vestige of company union status. A constitution committee was struck and, in 1970, a new constitution was adopted for the association during the convention. An order-in-council in 1971 amended the original law to allow the changes. The structure of the association was altered by the elimination of councilors and the creation of shop stewards. The "divisions" were re-named "branches". Horizontal "components" were created (of similar occupations) for the purposes of bargaining, a change which formalized a process which had already been occurring in practice under the Joint Council Act. Some improvements were made through the gaining of a check-off privilege, and more attention was paid to grievances, although a formal grievance procedure was still to be won. The association formally claimed to be engaged in collective bargaining under the Joint Council Act. Just as significantly, the association staked out a broadened

8   R. Mahon, "Canadian Labour in the Battle of the Eighties", *Studies in Political Economy*, 11 (Summer 1983), p. 153; R. Laxer, *Canada's Unions* (Toronto, 1976).

jurisdiction, claiming the right to organize government employees of Boards and Commissions and to bargain for these employees under the Trade Union Act. To formalize this widened scope of potential membership, the name of the association was changed in 1971 to the Nova Scotia Government Employees Association (NSGEA). In addition, serious consideration was given to joining the Canadian Labour Congress. These measures indicated the growth of the association as a union, although some were more contentious than others. The issue of the new jurisdiction, for example, passed by a very slim margin. Overall, then, there was movement but not a wholesale change in the character of the association and in the union consciousness of the members.

But the central and most divisive issue in 1969-70 was the question of whether to replace the Joint Council Act with full collective bargaining rights. This Act was the most significant achievement of the Buchanan-Shiers period and dissatisfaction with the results of the Joint Council Act inevitably meant conflict with the executive. All factions in the association claimed to be in favour of "collective bargaining", but much hinged on different conceptions of what this process entailed.

The Joint Council Act had done nothing to quiet the demands of the trade union group in the association. The practice and disappointing results of the Joint Council provided them with ammunition. In addition, other provinces, including neighboring New Brunswick, were implementing procedures which gave employees a greater independent role in collective bargaining. Consequently, in January 1969, the provincial executive appointed a committee to look into the New Brunswick legislation. In its "Preliminary Report", the committee recommended that a similar Act should be introduced in Nova Scotia. The provincial executive voted to accept the report and the committee was authorized to continue discussions.[9]

However, the executive's opposition to the principles embodied in the committee's recommendations was soon revealed. Executive Secretary Shiers opposed the New Brunswick model, noting first the aspect of the New Brunswick legislation which opened bargaining units in the civil service to organization by any union, while in Nova Scotia the NSCSA had exclusive jurisdiction. Shiers explained that the union movement in New Brunswick wanted to represent civil servants and the Collective Bargaining Act had resulted from union lobbying of the Legislature. The same thing would probably follow in Nova Scotia, he warned, and it was not in the interests of the NSCSA to abandon exclusive jurisdiction.[10] Shiers also claimed that the Joint Council legislation in Nova Scotia was better than most other provisions for collective bargaining in Canada. In fact, however, little of significance was accomplished at the Joint Council level. Most negotiations, such as they were, were carried out informally between Shiers and the CSC Commissioner prior to the Joint Council stage. Trade unionist Shiers had

9   Minutes of Executive Committee Meeting, 10-11 January 1969, NSGEA Papers, 7: 3.6A, Dalhousie University Archives (DUA). The committee included former Executive Secretary Hugh MacLeod and four members who were not on the Executive: Charles Crowell (Chairman), Leo LeFort, Amos Stephens and David Campbell.
10   Minutes of Executive Committee Meeting, 10-11 January 1969, NSGEA Papers, 7: 3.6A; NSCSA "Press Release", 13 January 1969, NSGEA Papers, 22: 16.3A, DUA.

adapted himself to joint consultation. While he had earlier in some forums claimed not to be wedded to this form of paternalism, he argued for only "slight amendments" to Bill 111. [11]

President Buchanan also opposed the committee's recommendations, expressing his desire to retain the basic principles of the Joint Council which, he claimed, were working fairly well, but required improvement. Buchanan adopted a morally high-minded stance, arguing that the New Brunswick legislation was insufficient for full bargaining rights since some employees could be "designated" in the event of a strike. On the other hand, he claimed there was too much free collective bargaining in a statute that permitted both associations and unions to operate in the public service field.[12] Buchanan thus wrapped himself in the cloak of collective bargaining while implicitly arguing against it, and agreed with the Civil Service commissioner who had praised the procedures of joint consultation which had evolved during his tenure.[13]

Given the committee's recommendation in favour of a new Act, and the leadership's opposition, debate became increasingly fractious at division meetings.[14] A motion at the 1969 Fall Council to leave the matter to the executive committee to "take whatever action they think best" was challenged by a proposed amendment that a membership referendum on the question be held. Both the amendment and the original motion were defeated, and a compromise motion was passed which directed the executive to report back to the council.[15] Charles Crowell, chairman of the collective bargaining committee, charged that Bill 111 was not collective bargaining and that the members had demanded full bargaining rights.[16] He wanted the civil service to come under the Trade Union Act and have the strike option, and no alternative was acceptable that provided only for arbitration. The majority of provincial executive members disagreed with Crowell and held to the traditional outlook that maintaining the good will of the government was paramount. Both the Crowell committee and Executive Secretary Shiers, who favoured only slight amendments to Bill 111, were instructed to put their recommendations in writing. These would then be taken to the premier, and a report brought back to the provincial executive. [17]

---

11 Minutes of Meeting of CAPE, 25 July 1969, NSGEA Papers, 5: 3.1.3, DUA; Report of the Executive Secretary, 1969 Fall Council, 14 November 1969, NSCSA *Newsletter*, 7, 8 (December 1969). These arguments produced considerable disagreement after Crowell left the meeting early. According to the recording secretary — who was unequal to the task of recording — "a good cross fire discussion developed" on Crowell's recommendations versus "the collective bargaining we now have". Minutes of the NSCSA Division President's Meeting, 25 June 1970, NSGEA Papers, 2: 2.5.1C, DUA.

12 Minutes, CAPE Meeting, 1-2 February 1969, NSGEA Papers, 5, 3.1.3, DUA; President's Report, 1969 A. G. M. , NSCSA *Newsletter*, 7, 4 (April-May 1969).

13 Civil Service Commission *Report* (1968).

14 NSCSA *Newsletter* , 8, 2 (February 1970).

15 "Fall Council Session", NSCSA *Newsletter*, 7, 8 (December 1969).

16 Minutes of the NSCSA Division President's Meeting, 25 June 1970, NSGEA Papers, 2: 2.5.1C, DUA.

17 Minutes of Executive Committee Meeting, 16-17 January 1970, NSGEA Papers, 18: 13.1C, DUA.

The special committee struck for the purpose[18] met with Premier G. I. Smith, claimed to have been very well received, and came away with the verbal assurance that the cabinet approved in principle the proposal for minimal changes in Bill 111, and this is what the executive committee therefore decided to recommend to the upcoming special council meeting.[19] Two proposals were put to the council: Crowell's, to seek amendments bringing civil servants under the Trade Union Act; and the executive's, to "improve on the present legislation and that it be tested before a wholesale change in our negotiations be sought". The Crowell proposal was defeated in an 18-15 standing vote,[20] and the council opted to request the slight improvements to Bill 111 recommended by Shiers and Buchanan. At this point the issue had become tied to confidence in the leadership, and most civil servants were still willing to give the provincial executive the benefit of the doubt. Dissension remained, however, particularly in Cape Breton where Division One representative Vickers claimed that "the Association was not being run well and that there was a conspiracy by Mr. Buchanan and Mr. Shiers for their own good". He objected to "the way the question on collective bargaining was presented at the Special Council meeting and he felt that [Buchanan and Shiers] had not wanted collective bargaining".[21]

Division also existed within the provincial executive.[22] Dissatisfaction centered around the two key figures, Buchanan and Shiers. Some members felt that decisions taken by the association, whether at the provincial executive or convention levels, were not subsequently carried out by the president or executive secretary. A discussion on forming an investigative committee split the executive, especially when it was implied that Buchanan should be excluded. As he pointed out, under the constitution the president was "ex-officio on all committees". The culmination of this debate came in 1971 when Buchanan requested a vote of confidence: he "felt he could not continue to act as President with the comments going around about his actions".[23] The motion of confidence was passed, although the meeting was held *in camera,* with Shiers and Buchanan absent.[24]

At the 1971 Fall Council meeting, objections were raised that the provincial executive had too much authority, that a quorum of one third was too small, that members should vote annually on the post of executive secretary "so that we know whether our members are satisfied or not", and that the provincial executive met too infrequently, further centralizing authority in the hands of the executive

---

18   Buchanan, Shiers, Puchyr and Norah Stephen.
19   Minutes of Executive Committee Meeting, 20 February 1970, NSGEA Papers, 18: 13.1C, DUA. Moved by John Samson and seconded by LeRoy Zwicker; opposed by Sidney Vickers and John MacCormick. Passed by a vote of 13 to two.
20   NSCSA *Newsletter*, 8, 3 (March 1970). The vote was reported in the Minutes of Division Eleven Monthly Meeting, 18 March 1970, NSGEA Papers, 4: 2.5.2. (11)A, DUA.
21   The first comment was minuted in a Division One meeting. Called to task by the Executive Committee, the second was his explanation. Minutes of Executive Committee Meeting, 21 March 1970, NSGEA Papers, DUA. Moors (Division Thirteen) asked whether it was necessary for persons to account to the executive for Division meetings.
22   Stanley Curtis to F. T. Gay, 19 January 1971, NSGEA Papers, 7: 3.7.4.C, DUA.
23   Moved by Noel Johnston and seconded by Cyril Reddy. They were to become, respectively, the third and fourth Presidents of the Association.
24   Minutes of Executive Committee Meeting, November 1971, NSGEA Papers, 18: 13.1D. DUA.

committee. The most vocal opponent was Division Thirteen Councillor Ken McKenzie, and Buchanan was his chief target.[25] The issue was executive accountability and the rights of members to participate in decision-making. At one point Buchanan attempted to reverse the practice of having observers attend meetings of the provincial executive. As a councillor at the time, McKenzie wanted the right to observe these meetings and report to the technicians in Division Thirteen. Buchanan, however, interpreted calls for accountability as implying that the executive committee, and himself in particular, were not acting in the best interests of the association.

Although it had been decided to retain the Joint Council, in practice important changes in negotiation procedures were being engineered by the Civil Service Commission and Executive Secretary Shiers, ignoring the framework of the existing legislation. The Civil Service Commission's salary reviews were increasingly based on "components", horizontal groupings of similar occupations. Early in 1969 the association had held its first meeting of an employee group for whom negotiations were being conducted, in order to obtain their response to the proposed salary revision. The meeting marked the beginning of development of a formal ratification procedure.[26] Through these changes in practice, a negotiation procedure was developing outside the constitution.

The new procedures allowed the membership some voice in negotiations, to at least express their acceptance or rejection of recommended settlements. However, binding arbitration was the only mechanism for dispute resolution contained in the Civil Service Joint Council Act. The arbitration board consisted of one member from the CSC, one from the association, and a mutually acceptable chairman. It was only in 1970 that the association began to push negotiations to the arbitration stage. In the face of a recent inflationary spiral, members were increasingly displeased with government offers. The first components to go to arbitration were the clerical grouping and the technical workers. In a June 1970 mass meeting 350 clerical workers met to hear a discussion on the salary negotiations and to approve the decision to refer the dispute to arbitration. According to the *Newsletter,* dissatisfaction was caused by the growing disparity between the wages of organized labour outside the civil service who were receiving substantial increases, and those of the civil servants who were "being asked to practice wage restraint" as part of the government's plan to reduce inflation.[27] The change in attitude did not go unnoticed by the Civil Service Commission, which reported that civil servants had become increasingly militant.[28]

The executive committee's support for arbitration seemed justified when the first four simultaneous awards granted increases between nine and 15 per cent, more than the government had offered, results that received banner headlines in the *Newsletter.*[29] This 1970 round of arbitration decisions had two major effects. It

25 Minutes of Fall Council, 12-13 November 1971, NSGEA Papers, 1: 1A, DUA. At one point Buchanan refused him the floor, a ruling which was accepted following a show of hands when McKenzie asked the Councilors to overrule the chairman's decision.
26 NSCSA *Newsletter,* 7, 4 (April-May 1969).
27 *Ibid.*
28 Civil Service Commission *Report* (1971).
29 NSCSA *Newsletter,* 8, 7 (July 1971).

seemed to support the view that arbitration was, to quote Shiers' editorial, "the only workable method for resolving...government employee-employer disputes". Second, it exposed the inadequacies of the Civil Service Joint Council Act. The arbitration board had concluded that the Joint Council had become merely a formality prior to arbitration and that nothing of a meaningful nature was accomplished at that level: "references to the Joint Council are most unlikely to be fruitful as the Council is presently constituted".[30] By implication, the conservatives in the association were defending a dinosaur. Nevertheless, a new adversarial relationship was developing with the government to which the executive had to respond. There was no going back to mutual consultation and the association was adapting to a more union-like rhetoric without any reference to its own recent past of supporting "good relations".

Although the first experience with arbitration was generally positive for the employees, government policies were soon to change this. While inflation fostered a more militant work force, it also legitimated the government's anti-inflation drive which, in part, acted to discipline the employees. As elsewhere in Canada, in 1971 the provincial government in Nova Scotia called for voluntary wage restraint. The government intended to break the link between market prices and free collective bargaining and "make provincial government employees scapegoats in the battle against inflation".[31] The call for restraint was accompanied, the association claimed, by manipulation of the arbitration process. This involved such tactics as delays in appointing arbitrators, in reaching agreement on a neutral chair, as well as in setting agendas and meeting times. Even when agreements were reached or decisions rendered, memoranda of agreement between the association and the government were delayed further at the order-in-council stage. By late 1971, dissatisfaction with the arbitration procedures was increasing among association members. At the 1971 Convention, Divisions One and Thirteen put forward resolutions complaining about delays and postponements and requesting time limits in mediation and arbitration processes. In response to the tactics of the official side the *Newsletter* reported growing employee anger and warned that civil servants "are talking about mass booking off for sickness; about 'working to rule'...and even to the extent of picketing the Provincial Building".[32] The executive of the association charged the new Liberal government (elected in October, 1970) with "doing everything in its power to wreck the excellent collective bargaining relationship" established with the previous government.

For opponents of arbitration, the manipulations practiced by the government added fuel to the campaign for full bargaining rights. The most outspoken opposition to arbitration was in Division One. A motion from Cape Breton at the 1973 Convention referred to compulsory arbitration as "an unwarranted interference in the process of collective bargaining" which "make[s] a sham" of bargaining. It was of a piece with "discriminatory legislation" which "makes public employees

30 Civil Service Arbitration Board, "Salaries of Clerical and Related Classifications", June 1970, NSGEA Papers, 1: 1.1.3B, DUA.

31 Telegram to Chairman, Prices and Incomes Commission, reprinted in NSCSA *Newsletter*, 8, 6 (June 1970).

32 Editorial, NSCSA *Newsletter*, 9, 6 (July-August 1971).

second class citizens".[33] In the period between the 1969-70 debate about the New Brunswick collective bargaining bill and 1972 many of the members of the NSGEA had modified their stand on collective bargaining, and the distance between the membership and the executive committee had widened.

The provincial executive, which still argued for only slight modifications of the existing legislation,[34] was being left behind not only by many members but by the Civil Service Commission as well. In the view of the CSC, change was essential because what they called the "personnel function", including collective bargaining, had not kept pace with other changes in government management. The CSC called for new legislation: "New personnel policies must be drawn and these cannot be based on experience gained with earlier civil servants, which, of course, will not meet the needs, interests and characteristics of the present Civil Service".[35] It was clear that the association's executive officers, "the earlier civil servants" mentioned, were not equal to the changes which were required.

Under pressure from these differing quarters in 1972 the executive established another special committee to review civil service collective bargaining legislation and recommend changes. The draft report of this committee again included provisions for the dual option: arbitration, or conciliation and strike.[36] The executive committee decided that it would put forward this draft of a new Collective Bargaining Act at the council meeting on the following day. Overnight, however, a transformation in thinking occurred. At a special executive committee meeting held 15 minutes prior to the special council meeting, material was circulated by Shiers describing the undesirable features of strikes in the public sector. The point of this extraordinary meeting was to amend the agreement of the previous day by removing the strike option and leaving arbitration as the only mechanism for dispute resolution. Consequently, the motion of the previous day was rescinded.[37] The executive committee decided that "the Legislation Committee be empowered to seek improvements and the necessary refinements to the system of arbitration terminating in a signed collective agreement through legislation". The new resolution was carried in the special council meeting by a 32 to 6 vote. The material outlining the arbitration/strike option, which had been distributed at the meeting, was collected back, since it "could possibly now lead to confusion".[38]

As long as the issues in dispute involved trade union rights at the level of negotiation with their own employer – with the important exception of the right to strike – civil servants in Nova Scotia were adopting a more independent stance *vis-à-vis* the government and displaying some growth of trade union consciousness. Issues which involved an identification with other employees, particularly those in the private sector, were more contentious. This was partly because government employees believed themselves to be significantly different from those in the

---

33   Minutes, NSGEA Annual Convention, 1973, NSGEA Papers, DUA.
34   Minutes of Special Legislation Meeting, 16 December 1971, NSGEA Papers, 8: 3.7.15, DUA.
35   Civil Service Commission *Report* (1972).
36   Minutes of Executive Committee Meeting, 14 January 1972, NSGEA Papers, 18: 13.1D, DUA. No vote was recorded, but Vickers requested that his name be recorded against the motion — he favoured the Trade Union Act.
37   Minutes of Special Executive Meeting, 15 January 1972, NSGEA Papers, 19: 13.1H, DUA.
38   Minutes of Special Council Meeting, 15 January 1972, NSGEA Papers, 19: 13.1H, DUA.

private sector, and partly because of status differences characteristic of many white-collar employees. The crucial issue which distinguished civil servants in Nova Scotia from other unionized workers continued to be their rejection of the strike, the strongest weapon in the arsenal of conventional trade unionism, and the most potent expression of independence from the employer and recognition of the inherent conflict of interests.

The issue of the right to strike continued to smolder among some groups in the association, but the evidence suggests that only a minority of employees really desired this right. The right to strike was not an issue in most divisions and received minimal support during conventions. Most civil servants responded to a service ethic which united them with their employer in the provision of services for the public. According to the ideology of public service, the interests of the government and the employees were the same. The withdrawal of labour was not something that civil servants did. This was only in part because public employment, according to the service ethic, was regarded as different from working in the private sector. The anti-strike sentiment was particularly strong among white-collar employees whose status consciousness hindered the development of an identification with manual workers. Even among blue-collar civil servants, many of whom had experience in the private sector, union consciousness was weak. Some were building second pensions while others had sought government employment for the security it afforded in contrast to the more lucrative but volatile private sector. Feminization of the civil service was well under way, but many new employees were less concerned with comparative wages and benefits than with the advantages of an earned income, and the threat of a strike induced feelings of insecurity. The result of these factors was that the level of union consciousness was still relatively low, and effective arbitration seemed preferable to the withdrawal of services. The spectre of the picket line was useful for eliciting support for a non-conflictual option. The provincial executive would soon use it to advantage in its attempts to smother the flames of discontent. These flames, however, were being fanned by a government which increasingly emphasized its role as an employer. While negotiations were undertaken by the Civil Service Commission, the role of the government was partly obscured, but in the climate of restraint which was emerging in the early 1970s the government as employer was about to step out from behind the screen.

In February 1972, the provincial Liberal government announced that it was imposing a five per cent ceiling on salary increases for government employees. This restraint policy effectively nullified any provision for the arbitration of salary adjustments. Just prior to this the *Newsletter* had been playing up the new found militancy of the association, claiming that the old approach of an individual dealing directly with management had "gone by the board". In his editorial, Shiers claimed that the members of the NSGEA had undergone an attitude change and had learned that the exercise of power could reap great benefits. Since organized private sector workers had caught up in wages and benefits which "at one time were the exclusive property of civil servants", government employees were becoming more militant. They now realized that the old arguments, "Lack of money, higher taxes, and on, and on, and on", only end with "the boss gleefully rubbing his hands together". The editorial concluded:

But...all is not lost....[I]t is a lot more difficult to convince six thousand employees that they should take a smaller increase than it would be to convince one. In fact, judging by the militancy that is becoming prevalent in the civil service, it will be next to impossible to convince any of the groups that they should take a smaller increase....[A]s long as...prices continue to rise, the civil servant must and will continue to press the employer for a better share of the national income.[39]

It is ironic that the provincial executive was soon to attempt this "next to impossible" task, and that the weakness in the association's response to the wage ceiling finally undermined confidence in the executive and led to the change in leadership which solidified the move to collective bargaining.

The day following the government's announcement a special provincial executive meeting was called to consider possible protest action against the freeze. At this meeting it was noted that a similar policy in Ontario had been reversed only after the Civil Service Association of Ontario had threatened a strike. Consequently, direct confrontation was advocated by many of the association's members at the special meeting.[40] The provincial executive "voted overwhelmingly to reject the principle of a 5% ceiling", but added that there were many unanswered questions concerning increments, reclassification, previously negotiated scales and those in negotiation, and so on. A letter was written to the premier "strongly deploring his announcement", and a press release was also drafted.[41] The letter was sent to the premier, but no press release appeared in the newspapers. When the executive council met ten days later, Division One representative Vickers led an attack on the staff for this failure to carry out association policy. Shiers replied that he had not acted "contrary to the wishes of the Executive members", having interpreted the decision to send out the press release as contingent upon receiving no reply from the premier. Buchanan, more openly to the point, argued that the draft press release was "too strong action to take at this time". He cited the loss of the check-off and the disastrous result of the 1959 strike in British Columbia as arguments which compelled moderation. It was agreed not to publicize the press release until after the meeting with Premier Regan, if it should be necessary. This question of tactics aside, a motion that the association was not going to accept the five per cent guideline was carried.[42]

After meeting with the premier, Buchanan reported to the executive committee that Regan was adamant in his stand and, furthermore, that he had "good reasons". "The government could not afford to give more", and "the Premier had stressed how poor the Province was". At this meeting Premier Regan had used both promises

39   Editorial, NSCSA *Newsletter*, 9, 5 (June 1971).
40   NSGEA Press Release, 8 February 1972, NSGEA Papers, 7: 3.7.4C; NSGEA Press Release, 21 February 1972, NSGEA Papers, 22: 16.3B, DUA. The Ontario action was cited by the less senior staff in a letter which was an implicit recommendation. They were Cliff Boudreau, Rita Lucas, Bill McMullin, Jim Vance and Alan MacLeod. NSGEA Papers, 18: 13.1C, DUA.
41   Minutes of Emergency Session, Provincial Executive Committee, 9 February 1972, NSGEA Papers, 7: 3.7.4C, DUA.
42   Minutes of Executive Committee, 18-19 February 1972, NSGEA Papers, 19: 13.1H, DUA.

and threats to secure executive compliance. His argument was conciliatory: he hoped the ceiling would not be in place for long and promised that when the economic situation improved the civil service "would be the first to be considered". The government, he had said, must "think of Nova Scotia not just the civil servants". However, Regan held out the promise of granting the association those requests which were outstanding which would not require the expenditure of government revenue – early closing and 26 paydays were cited as examples. Finally Regan declared "that if [the association] did proceed to arbitration and thereby demonstrate its rejection of the guideline, he would take action to legislate the removal of the right to arbitration by legislation and give us the right to strike". [43]

This was a remarkable moment in the history of the association. The government was making an offer, the right to strike, which would meet the demands of the most union-conscious group in the association. It was, however, a very calculated manoeuver. For most members of the executive committee of the NSCSA, it could only be regarded as a threat, and presumably this is how Premier Regan intended it. Some were ideologically opposed to the use of the strike in government service, and concluded that, henceforth, the government would negotiate in a confrontational manner. Others claimed that, principles aside, civil servants would not strike or could not strike successfully. They had just won an internal union battle to retain the right of arbitration. With the restraint legislation this had been lost temporarily and now the government was threatening to make the loss permanent. The executive committee concluded that, for the next year or so, the association would concentrate on issues which were not concerned with remuneration.[44] The premier was informed of the motion [45]which, although it did not explicitly say so, was an acceptance of the guidelines and rescinded two earlier motions. It was generally agreed that the association not go to arbitration for the time being.

The most vocal opponents of this weak response came from members in Cape Breton and the hospital divisions. Ken McKenzie, representing Division Thirteen, argued in favour of taking as much action as possible and complained that the result of singling out the civil servants, who were the first to be considered when restraint was imposed, was that they were "going to bear the burden of somebody else's increase". He requested that the members who were present at the meeting with the premier sign the report on the statements so that he could take it back to the members who "would be asking us about this".[46] The executive was making an important decision on behalf of the membership without consultation.

A *Newsbulletin* was quickly drafted to explain the decision of the executive to the membership. In capital letters, the bulletin stressed that the five per cent limit was firm and that the government would not negotiate this point. Having given the government's position the status of immutable law, the bulletin requested that no dispute be referred to arbitration. If an arbitral award exceeded five per cent, the bulletin added, then the government will nullify the award by legislation and cancel

---

43 Minutes of Special Executive Meeting, 25 February 1972, NSGEA Papers, 19: 13.1H, DUA.
44 *Ibid.* Moved by Settle and seconded by Morehouse. Ken McKenzie and Allan James were opposed; Vickers was not present.
45 *Ibid.* Moved by Anthony and seconded by Amiro. McKenzie opposed.
46 *Ibid.*

the arbitration process. The provincial executive – "which is the association's governing body between conventions" – had decided to concentrate on non-monetary fringe benefits.[47]

The publication of this bulletin brought a mixed reaction. Speaking from the point of view of "those in the higher income brackets", one member noted that "we cannot continue to receive increments and increases ad infinitum".[48] Condemnation of the executive's stand, however, was more frequently voiced. One letter declared that the *Newsbulletin* seemed to represent the employer rather than the employees, and protested "vigorously the action of our Executive and the publishing of this newsletter which must be of much comfort to our employer". A "Commentary" claimed that "many of our so-called association representatives are supporting 'the party' and making no bones about it", and suggested turning to "a non-partisan organization for support and representation": "If this is the best the Association can come up with then I say let's get rid of the Association and at least give a fighting organization a chance to come in and organize us in the proper manner".[49]

A petition circulated in Branch Nine to protest the manner in which the provincial executive had handled the imposed five per cent guideline was signed by three quarters of the branch members.[50] At an angry Branch Eleven meeting – which had earlier recommended a substantial public relations campaign against the ceiling [51]– the association was charged with not doing enough and Buchanan's public comment that the civil servants were being "good citizens in accepting the 5%" was criticized. One member "felt that too few people spoke for too many people". A motion which reprimanded Buchanan was carried, along with a motion that the executive retract acceptance and carry out a referendum of the membership.[52]

In the light of the contradictory public responses of the provincial executive and some of the divisions, it was not completely clear whether or not the association had accepted the five per cent ceiling. Branch Thirteen wanted the matter settled by a membership referendum, but McKenzie's first effort to have a referendum was defeated in March.[53] The request for a referendum was a direct challenge to the right of the executive committee to conduct association business. The opposition was sufficiently intense, however, to compel the executive to adopt this more democratic method of determining the association's response to the wage controls. During the April meeting of the executive committee a decision was taken to hold a membership referendum.

This was, however, a very stormy meeting, and momentous with regard to the composition of the leadership. In the context of debate over the ceiling and the

47   NSGEA *Newsletter*, 10, 5 (28 February 1972); NSGEA Papers, 9: 3.8.0.1A, DUA.
48   Donald M. Levy to T. Gay (Secretary-Treasurer, NSGEA), 7 March 1972, NSGEA Papers, 9: 3.8.0.1A, DUA.
49   George E. Goodwin to NSGEA, 6 March 1972, NSGEA Papers, 9: 3.8.0.1A, DUA.
50   Annette Aucoin to NSGEA, 8 March 1972, NSGEA Papers, 9: 3.8.0.1A, DUA.
51   Minutes of Branch Eleven Monthly Meeting, 16 February 1972, NSGEA Papers, 4: 2.5.2(11)B, DUA.
52   *Ibid.*, 15 March 1972. Bob Beckwith was the principal spokesperson at this meeting.
53   Minutes of Provincial Executive Meeting, 24-25 March 1972, NSGEA Papers, 19: 13.1H, DUA.

proper role of the executive committee, other contentious matters arose. During this meeting, Buchanan unexpectedly resigned as president. The immediate issue precipitating the resignation was Buchanan's falling out with First Vice-President Stanley Curtis, who was charged by Buchanan with having mishandled a meeting. When Buchanan refused to retract his charge, Curtis resigned. A motion that the president apologize was defeated by a vote of ten to six.[54] While he believed his criticism just, Buchanan expressed his regret and then tendered his resignation, effective immediately. Buchanan "said that he had worked hard for the association and he had been condemned and crucified on many occasions. He said that this had been coming for a long time". Buchanan remained on the executive, holding the post of past-president, and at the next executive committee meeting, McKenzie tried three successive resolutions to have Buchanan resign from all executive offices. The first two were ruled out-of-order and the last was defeated. Although there had been very vocal opposition to Buchanan, a motion requesting him to reconsider his resignation was passed nine to five. The majority of the executive committee, therefore, still indicated some confidence in his leadership. Subsequently, Noel Johnston and Ken McKenzie were nominated for president. McKenzie had led the fight against Buchanan but, given the majority sentiment in the executive committee, the more middle-of-the-road Johnston won the election. Since Curtis had also resigned, vice-presidential elections were held. Vickers was elected second vice-president having declined to run for first vice-president, a post which was won by a relative newcomer, Cyril Reddy, over McKenzie. Reddy had championed the referendum and represented the union the NSCSA was becoming more than the former association. He would use his new position in the executive committee to campaign for the presidency, centering his campaign on criticism of Shiers' interventions in the referendum campaign.

Once the executive committee decided that a referendum was appropriate, debate centered around the information which should be circulated to the members prior to the vote. Shiers proposed that "the referendum include the concessions that the Government is prepared to give us and the losses we may suffer by rejecting it". The extent of mistrust within the executive committee was evident when a three-member committee, including Buchanan, was delegated to write the letter. A motion that the draft of the letter should be circulated to the provincial executive members before being sent to the membership was carried by the margin of one vote.[55] The final draft of this letter to the members offered two choices:

> Acceptance – If you accept the 5% guideline the Government shall be advised that should the guideline be broken on behalf of other Government Employees, Civil Servants shall be demanding equal adjustments.

---

54 Moved by Ken McKenzie, seconded by John Hacquoil, Branch Eleven, NSGEA Papers, 19: 13.1H, DUA.

55 Minutes of Special Executive Committee Meeting, 5 April 1972, NSGEA Papers, 19: 13.1H, DUA. Several changes in the draft were made before the letter was sent to the members. Rather than the phrase "the Premier announced that the Government would impose", the revised letter stated: "the Premier announced that due to the financial position of the Province the Government had found it necessary to impose".

Rejection – If you reject the 5% guideline the Government will enact legislation granting the right to strike, subject to the Essential Services provision.

The first choice left the battle against the five per cent ceiling in the hands of other public service unions, only indicating that, should another organization succeed in breaking the guidelines, the association would no longer be bound by them. The second choice implied that the government would enact, simultaneously, the right to strike in the civil service and essential services legislation which would negate this right in practice.

Under Shiers' editorship, the *Newsletter* added two arguments of a more directly ideological nature: The first noted that a civil servant was also a citizen and a taxpayer concerned about "the Province's financial exigencies". This induced a sense of responsibility; the civil service should "do its part to ease the Province's financial burden". "For the time being, militarism has given way to patience...and to a sympathetic appreciation of the Province's financial position. The executive's acceptance of the five percent wage freeze is an act of good faith".[56] Second, arbitration was defended on the grounds that it was in the forefront of the progressive labour movement. The editorial praised George Meany, the leader of the American Federation of Labour, who "favoured binding arbitration...as a substitute for strikes". In contrast, most of the leaders of the Canadian Labour Congress adopted the "traditional attitude" and opposed arbitration – an indication of "the inability of most of Canada's labour leaders to accept change". However, "there is hope!" because government employees, a large part of the Canadian labour force, have accepted arbitration which has "become a workable and acceptable way of life". Strikes have "become out-moded weapon[s]" because of their expense, because of the opposition to organized labour widespread in the labour force, and because public service strikes affect the public and members alike as consumers.[57]

What Shiers saw as the progressive labour movement, however, was nothing of the kind. While Buchanan and Shiers referred to the unsuccessful civil service strike in British Columbia in 1959, the collective bargaining climate had changed radically in the 1960s. In the wake of a highly successful illegal strike by postal workers, federal civil servants had been given the right to strike in 1967. In 1972, the same year Shiers was writing his editorial praising the timid leadership of the AFL-CIO, the Common Front in Quebec was about to demonstrate the potential power of public sector strikes and the potential unity which could be achieved with private sector employees. In Nova Scotia even such an essential service as police forces were granted the right to strike and used the weapon successfully to improve the wages, benefits, and working conditions of municipal police officers in the province. Under the leadership of Reddy and his successors, the association would take major steps in its transition towards union status, joining the Canadian Labour Congress, sponsoring a new Collective Bargaining Act and formally requesting the right to strike.

56   NSGEA *Newsletter*, 10, 1 (Spring 1972)
57   Editorial, *ibid*.

These developments, however, were still a few years in the future. In 1972, many civil servants in Nova Scotia were still responsive to traditional images and fearful of militant action. It was this fear which Shiers utilized in his campaign for acceptance of the ceiling. To add to the pressure on the membership, Shiers issued a *Newsbulletin* in April entitled "Quit or Strike", boiling the matter down to two options should the employees reject the government's ceiling.[58] Shiers defended his actions by stating the bulletin was written "in reply to the questions being asked by many members respecting further effective action if the 5% guideline was rejected by referendum vote".[59] In his view, if the ceiling was rejected, dissatisfied civil servants could only go on strike or quit the service. This line in the *Newsbulletin* was too blatant even for the relatively moderate opposition in the provincial executive, which ordered Shiers to retract the bulletin, thereby isolating the executive secretary. Even those employees most in fear of the strike option objected to being told how to vote. Vice-President Cyril Reddy emerged as one of the most vocal opponents of Shiers during this campaign, and at the 1972 Spring Convention he was elected president of the association.

On the referendum ballot the issue had been defined as the right to strike rather than as a protest against the discriminatory legislation, and this was reinforced by Shiers' last-minute letter. Opponents of Shiers complained that he had "tried to push [his] conclusions through along with the facts".[60] In Branch Eleven, (Victoria General Hospital) Bob Beckwith felt that "Civil Servants who received the letter with their ballot had no choice but to vote to accept the 5%, especially those who did not regularly attend the monthly meetings and were unaware of the situation".[61] John Puchyr, the assistant to the executive secretary, distanced himself from Shiers by placing the responsibility for the last *Newsbulletin* entirely on Shiers' shoulders. Drafting this letter "was the responsibility of the Executive Secretary", he said, deflecting responsibility from the executive committee and himself. It was primarily on the basis of this issue that a motion was carried "that Branch 11 support any vote of non-confidence which may come up at the Provincial Executive meeting or the Spring Convention against the Executive Secretary of the NSGEA".[62]

However, Shiers' intimidating campaign was effective, and the membership voted to accept the guideline. The vote was 2,868 for acceptance and 920 against. The government was informed that the civil servants had agreed to accept the five per cent ceiling.[63]

While the association members had acquiesced, other groups of government employees were less willing to accept the government's rationalizations. In its negotiations with other unions the government found it increasingly difficult to maintain the ceiling. When the CBRT&GW negotiated an agreement for a raise in

---

58   NSGEA *Newsbulletin*, 13 April 1972.
59   NSGEA Press Release, 24 April 1972, NSGEA Papers, 22: 16.3B, DUA.
60   Frank Gervais to Shiers, 21 April 1972, NSGEA Papers, 9: 3.8.0.1B, DUA.
61   Minutes of Branch Eleven Monthly Meeting, 19 April 1972, NSGEA Papers, 4: 2.5.2(11)B, DUA.
62   *Ibid.* Moved by Morash and seconded by Verge.
63   Johnston to Riley, 28 April 1972, NSGEA Papers, 9: 3.8.0.1B, DUA. Of those who voted, 75.7 per cent accepted the guidelines.

pay of over five percent on behalf of workers at the Victoria General Hospital who were not in the civil service, opposition in Branches Eleven and Thirteen was solidified. The fact that others were able to successfully break the guidelines placed in sharp relief the weakness of the NSGEA. In the face of the heavy-handed campaign persuading them to accept the government's word, civil servants felt they had been deceived. The association's response to the imposed ceiling would become a well-spring of resentment throughout the early 1970s, a period in which there were two illegal strikes in the hospital.

Following the CBRT agreement, President Reddy informed the government that the guideline had been broken and that therefore the NSGEA would refer any unresolved matters to arbitration.[64] By then the government had become conciliatory. The minister assured the executive committee that no changes in arbitration would be made without prior consultation.[65] It was obvious that the previous executive had over-reacted to government threats. By this point, the damage to the credibility of those responsible for the campaign to accept the wage ceiling was irreparable.

With Buchanan out of the executive committee – after the election of Cyril Reddy as president at the 1972 convention, Noel Johnston became past-president – the focus of the opposition shifted to Shiers. Over the course of many changes in the membership and of the provincial executive, Shiers had alienated many people. Foremost was his controversial role during the debate on the five per cent ceiling.[66] In opposing Shiers, however, the new executive chose not to debate concrete policies and practices. Rather, the only explanation offered was that Shiers' positions did not reflect the wishes of the new executive committee. The first direct evidence of these differences of opinion came when an effort was made to gag the executive secretary. It was decided "that all public statements be made through the President" – if Shiers was asked a question by the media he should say: "No comment".[67] This was a clear expression of a lack of confidence in Shiers, but the executive committee was unwilling to follow this through to its logical conclusion. A motion in May 1972 that Shiers' contract be terminated was defeated.[68]

However, this decision was reversed in February 1973 when a motion to relieve Shiers of his post passed unanimously.[69] Because some branches were upset by Shiers' firing and the failure to consult the membership on the matter, Reddy wrote

---

64 Reddy to Regan, 28 June 1972, NSGEA Papers, 9: 3.8.0.1B, DUA.
65 Reddy, Shiers and Dave Peters indicated that NSGEA would not be willing to accept arbitration only by government consent as in New Brunswick. NSGEA *Newsletter*, 10, 6 (15 September 1972).
66 One other issue was his mishandling of the organizing drive with the highway workers, a drive which brought media attention to alleged collusion between Shiers and the Canadian Union of Public Employees.
67 Moved by Vickers, seconded by Sage. Minutes of Provincial Executive Committee, 26 May 1972, NSGEA Papers, 19: 13.1H, DUA.
68 Moved by Hacquoil and Foran. Minutes of Provincial Executive Committee, 26 May 1972, NSGEA Papers, 19: 13.1H, DUA.
69 Moved by Reddy, seconded by Annette Aucoin. NSGEA Papers, 19: 13.1J, DUA.

an explanatory letter. The dismissal, he argued, was not because of "any wrong-doing or incompetence" and, to avoid this suggestion, the dismissal had been done with as little publicity as possible. It was neither a question of integrity nor Shiers' "devotion to his job as he saw it".

> There had, however, developed a wide difference of opinion between the Provincial Executive and Mr. Shiers on policy matters. These differences had developed over the past several years....It was the culmination of many months of frustration caused by the disagreements over Association policy and direction that led to the decision.[70]

Reddy did not specify the details of the disagreements over policy. The letter, he said, was designed to undercut the rumours and "improper assumptions" which had been made. Nevertheless, Shiers complained about the negative publicity which had surrounded the event, making it difficult for him to find alternative employment. He requested that the decision to dismiss him be decided by an arbitrator, but this request was ignored and the decision to fire him subsequently confirmed by the provincial executive.[71] There was some criticism of this in the association. Members in some branches were reported to be unhappy with the explanation received, especially because Reddy's letter had not explained what the divergences in policy were.[72] In the end, the new executive maneuvered Shiers out of office and weathered the protests.

Less than one month after the firing, a special convention was held to approve the recommendation of the housing committee to purchase a building on Spring Garden Road at the cost of $525,000. The debate over the purchase of land for the association had been especially bitter and had involved Buchanan as well as Shiers. The new building was expected to enhance the association's status, among members and negotiating parties alike.[73] Opponents considered it to be a white elephant.

With the matter of Shier's removal completed, Reddy and the new executive secretary, John Puchyr, were in positions of power in the association. Under their control the formal procedures and structure of the association continued to develop in the direction of trade unionism. The new executive seemed to have polished up the image of the association. To consolidate his hold on the presidency, Reddy visited each branch. In his rhetoric, however, he provided an insight into the continuity between the new and the old ideology of the Civil Service Association when he asserted: "This is your Association. You are the stockholders".[74]

Thus by 1973 there had been a wholesale change in the provincial executive and structure of the Nova Scotia Government Employees Association. This was not, however, simply a case of new people bringing new policies. While by 1972 developments had swirled past President Buchanan and Executive Secretary Shiers,

70   Reddy to Branch Presidents, 7 March 1973, NSGEA Papers, DUA.
71   Minutes, Executive Committee, 26 February 1973, NSGEA Papers, 19: 13.1J, DUA.
72   Minutes, Provincial Executive Meeting, 9-10 March 1973, NSGEA Papers, DUA.
73   NSGEA *Newsletter*, 11, 2 (23 March 1973).
74   President's Report, A. G. M., 3-5 May 1973, NSGEA Papers, 1: 1C, DUA.

swallowing up the old supervisory leadership, it should be noted that considerable changes had taken place during their period in office, particularly with respect to the structure and functioning of the association. Despite their different backgrounds, Shiers and Buchanan worked closely together and shared similar fates. Shiers' position, however, was more enigmatic than that of Buchanan. Opposition to Shiers had come from two opposing quarters. For some, Shiers had always been tainted with too much unionism and he was held responsible for the drift towards union status in the association. For others, Shiers had been a road-block in the way of progressive development towards full union status. Therefore, from his perspective, he was caught between a majority sentiment in the civil service favouring accommodation and a militant faction demanding full bargaining rights.

Shiers, however, was more than just an employee responsive to a conservative executive. He exercised his independent influence to advance the cause of arbitration and oppose the right to strike in the civil service. In particular, it was Shiers' strong preference for non-conflictual options – and the lengths he was willing to go to gain compliance for them – that undermined his credibility in the association. His campaign against the strike option was coloured by his previous experience in the Windsor Gypsum strike which had been long and bitter and was ended by neutral arbitration. He readily accepted the arguments against strikes in the public sector, despite evidence to the contrary elsewhere, and estimated the union consciousness in the association to be at a low level.

To be sure, there were important developments during Shiers's tenure. The association had a new constitution, along with the power to amend. It claimed a wider jurisdiction which was reflected in the change of the name of the organization to the Nova Scotia Government Employees Association. In the association's structure the position of councillor was eliminated and internal functions, particularly the handling of grievances, were to be handled by "shop stewards". The divisions were re-named branches and a parallel structure of "components" was set up for which separate collective agreements would be negotiated. The provincial executive was still the chief governing body, but it was expanded to include representatives from the 13 branches and from the ten components. While a president and secretary-treasurer were elected at the convention, the provincial executive elected other members of the executive committee from its own members.[75] The association had also bought a prominent building in Halifax and used it to house a growing body of staff workers and employee relations officers to service the needs of the membership. In all these ways, the NSGEA was becoming a *bona fide* trade union.

The assumption of office by President Reddy and Executive Secretary Puchyr did not mark a radical break with the past. They consolidated some of the trends which were coming to fruition under Buchanan and Shiers but, at the same time, took those further steps which the old leaders had resisted. The leadership of the association had passed from the old guard not to the more radical trade union group, but to representatives of the senior non-supervisory employees. They inherited a bargaining structure which was anachronistic and a bargaining climate which was propelling workers – especially public sector and white-collar workers – in the

75   Minutes of 1970 A. G. M., May 1970, NSGEA Papers, 1.1B, DUA.

direction of labour militancy. In 1973, nurses employed in the Victoria General Hospital adopted a mass resignation tactic in the absence of the right to strike to press their salary demands. A longer and less successful resignation by hospital technicians occurred in 1975. Between these dates, the provincial executive under President Reddy approved affiliation with the Canadian Labour Congress (although opposition from the Canadian Union of Public Employees prevented the NSGEA from joining until 1975), and also succeeded in having a special convention adopt a resolution calling for civil servants to be brought under the Trade Union Act. This had been the most radical of the proposals brought forward and rejected in the association's recent past. Ultimately, the government passed a Civil Service Collective Bargaining Act in 1978 which was an improvement on the previous Joint Council Act, but was still relatively weak compared to similar legislation in Canada. For example, civil servants, despite the demonstrated willingness of some components to withdraw their labour, were still denied the right to strike. In contrast to the past, however, the association was on record as requesting this right. Later, still, the association would become a "Union" in name as well as organizational structure.

There was still a gap between what the most militant employees wanted and what the association was able to achieve. Reddy was accused of autocratic practices by the hospital technicians who conducted the mass resignation in 1975. Executive Secretary Puchyr would subsequently cross the line and become the chief negotiator for the Hospital Commission. This leadership was still far from militant.

Despite the apparent commitment to the principles of trade unionism in the organization this did not necessarily translate into changed membership attitudes. Trade union ideology among members is not a simple thing but a fluctuating index of structural contradictions, class consciousness and leadership. If some circumstances compel passivity and complacency, other circumstances provide fertile ground for more assertive action. In the case study presented above, the old leadership responded to changes which they did not initiate, in ways which reflected an interpretation of the "best interests" of the employer and the senior staff more than the interests and potential of the general membership. Yet the changes in the organization under the new leadership should not necessarily suggest that members' consciousness had changed dramatically. The more formal the structure of the association, the more developed and independent the service staff, the more may the leadership be remote from the membership. Ironically, the old regime of Buchanan and Shiers may have been more in touch with membership sentiment, prior to 1970, than the new executive of Reddy and Puchyr subsequent to their assumption of office. The fractious debate during Buchanan's presidency was, at least, indicative of the difference of opinion among the membership. In contrast, in 1974 Reddy called a special convention to debate a motion that the NSGEA be brought under the Trade Union Act. The convention was the culmination of a well-orchestrated campaign carried to each branch. The motion passed without debate and almost without dissent. Such an outcome may indicate some change in members' trade union consciousness. The year 1974 was the high point of public sector and trade union militancy in Canada and Nova Scotian civil servants were reacting to the widening gap caused by inflation and government efforts at restraining employee salaries. But the absence of overt opposition at the special convention also reflected the professional organizational ability of the new executive. Even in the more militant components, for example, evidence suggests that only a minority of employees expressly supported CLC affiliation, the right to strike, coming under the Trade Union Act, or the change in the name of the organization from "Association" to "Union".[76]

Furthermore, while the change in leadership over the 1967-1973 period was crucial for the consolidation of the union trend in the NSGEA, and there is evidence indicating some change in members' perceptions of their employment status, it is important to recognize the changing context of unionism. The Canadian Labour Congress in 1975 was considerably different from what it had been during the founding of the NSCSA. Three of the four largest unions in the Congress during the 1970s organized workers in the public sector. The Canadian Union of Public Employees, which organized largely among municipal employees and workers employed by Boards and Commissions, was becoming the largest union in the country. Gone were the days when civil service unions had tried to form a separate union central expressing the interests of government employees, interests which were deemed to be sufficiently separate from the private sector to warrant a separate labour central. The affiliation of the NSGEA to the Canadian Labour Congress, then, represented as much a change in the character of the central body as it did the evolution of the association to union status.

Just as the relationship of the association to the Congress is affected by changes in both, so too the relationship among membership, leadership and formal policy is complex. Members' consciousness is neither uniform nor linear. In many ways, the notion of a general membership was superseded by components and bargaining units. The consciousness of the membership varied, as elsewhere, according to occupational group and local traditions. In addition, consciousness is situational. Circumstances, such as the five per cent ceiling and the executive's conciliatory response to it, create real changes in response as well as the potential for a sustained alteration of consciousness. In this circumstance, the evolution of the NSGEA in the direction of more developed trade unionism was consolidated by a new executive which, in turn, was made possible by a partial transformation of the consciousness of many civil servants in Nova Scotia.

76 A. Thomson, "Trade union consciousness in the para-public sector", Unpublished Report prepared for the NSGEA and the Victoria General Hospital, 1980.

CRAIG HERON

Afterword:
Male Wage-Earners and the
State in Canada *

A MALE WORKER MEETS many faces of the state. Few of them seem friendly. One afternoon, he is handed a leaflet advising him that his union's negotiators have met with a provincial mediator but have been unable to work out a settlement. The next morning he joins a picket line where he confronts a phalanx of policemen trying to keep the company's gates open. By angrily resisting the police, he is arrested and meets in succession the jail keepers and then the judge, who fines him heavily and orders him to stay away from the picket line. Arriving home that night, he sees on television the stern face of the premier deploring the picket-line violence and the inconvenience to the public. His daughter informs him that her teacher had made similar comments at school. Eventually opening his mail, he finds a letter from the workers' compensation board rejecting his longstanding claim for help as a result of a back injury at work. As the strike drags on for several weeks, he lines up first in the unemployment insurance office and then at the welfare department trying to convince tightfisted administrators that he needs help in paying his rent and feeding his family. The next spring, he will curse more loudly than usual the taxes he has to pay to support these various state apparatuses.

These many faces of the Canadian state are not always closely connected and, on occasion, can even present contradictory messages. Yet there is an overall consistency in their approach to workers in Canada that allows us to sketch a collective portrait. In doing so, we enter into the hotly contested terrain of theories of the state. Most Marxists agree that the state in a capitalist society plays a role that facilitates the process of capital accumulation and the maintenance of capitalist power. The debate is over precisely how to conceptualize that role. It is not argued that the state is directly at the beck and call of capitalists, or that its activities are shaped purely in response to expressed capitalist concerns. Rather, the institutions, policies, and programs of the capitalist state evolve with some autonomy, though always within a broad consensus that private ownership of the means of production and the subordination of other classes to the dominant capitalist class are good for society. State activity tends to promote capital accumulation directly (through tariffs, development of the infrastructure, tax write-offs, and so on), but also works

*   I am grateful to the members of the 1988-89 Advanced Seminar on Law and Labour in the Commonwealth at York University for helpful comments and criticisms on an earlier draft of this paper.

to legitimize the social order in the eyes of the citizenry. In particular, it encourages the consent of subordinated classes to their place in the structure of wealth and power and attempts to keep all social conflicts within acceptable bounds. State officials can rarely claim any particular clarity of social vision — often their activity amounts to little more than political opportunism by governing parties — but sometimes they play a creative role in identifying and attempting to eliminate the sources of major social tensions.[1]

In Canadian history the state has had to deal with workers as a problem for both accumulation and legitimization. First, they had to be marshalled into a well-stocked capitalist labour market if industrial development (and thus capital accumulation) were to proceed in the country. Second, as one of the two major subordinate classes in Canada (alongside the once much larger numbers of independent commodity producers), the working class has not always "consented" to the terms of its subordination and has posed repeated challenges to the structure of accumulation. Over the past 150 years the Canadian state has intervened in workers' lives in an ongoing, dynamic process of anticipating and responding to their activity. Initially that intervention reflected a concern with controlling individual workers, but by the last quarter of the 19th century, industrial militancy and working-class political pressure prompted more vigorous state action. The focus of this discussion will be primarily on male wage earners, for the simple reason that during most of the period under examination public life has been defined as a masculine sphere from which women were completely excluded. The state, in the person of male politicians, judges, civil servants, and so on, helped to define women's appropriate role as "private" and domestic, and to circumscribe tightly the female wage-earning experience.[2]

The first workers whose behaviour brought state attention were those at the dawn of large-scale capitalist development in Canada who appeared unwilling to integrate themselves compliantly into an emerging capitalist society. As colonial officials noted with consternation in the first half of the 19th century, many seemed more interested in the independence of backwoods farming than in making themselves available for regular wage earning. State land granting policies were subsequently tightened up to make land less accessible and thus to create a pool of landless labour that incipient industrialists could employ.[3] When potential workers

---

1   See Leo Panitch, "The Role and Nature of the Canadian State" in Panitch, ed., *The Canadian State: Political Economy and Political Power* (Toronto, 1977), pp. 3-77; Paul Craven, *"An Impartial Umpire": Industrial Relations and the Canadian State, 1900-1911* (Toronto, 1980), pp. 157-207; and, for a review of much of the debate over theories of the state, Bob Jessop, *The Capitalist State* (Oxford, 1982).

2   A full discussion of the state and the Canadian working class would have to address the impact of the unpaid domestic work carried out by women, especially the work of reproduction, including state intervention through schooling, public health, child welfare work, medical regulation, and much more beyond the scope of this paper.

3   Leo A. Johnson, "Land Policy, Population Growth, and Social Structure in the Home District, 1793-1851" in J. K. Johnson, ed., *Historical Essays on Upper Canada* (Toronto, 1975), pp. 32-57; Gary Teeple, "Land, Labour, and Capital in Pre-Confederation Canada" in Teeple, ed., *Capitalism and the National Question in Canada* (Toronto, 1972), pp. 43-66. Note that encouraging the development of a "free" labour market did not prevent the continuation of "unfree" indentured labour where labour shortages required it, notably among young farm workers and Chinese labour in British Columbia. See Joy Parr, *Labouring Children: British*

continued to flow into the rural hinterland or out of the country, the state undertook to promote and facilitate extensive immigration, especially from Britain, Europe, and Asia.[4] In later years, the problem was mainly the supply of sufficient numbers of skilled workers. Despite some pioneering programs in technical education aimed at upgrading Canadian labour to meet changing economic needs in the early 20th century, it was not until 1960 that Canada moved decisively (though never completely) away from immigration as the main mechanism for meeting new skill requirements, and introduced much more elaborate vocational training programs in a vastly expanded public education system.[5] Throughout its history the Canadian state has thus taken a major role in establishing and maintaining the capitalist labour market.

Men and women might be coaxed and cajoled into making their labour power available to Canadian employers, but, as newcomers to capitalist social relations, they often resisted the self-discipline expected in a bourgeois social order. Concerned merchants, industrialists, lawyers, clergymen, and others in the upper and middle classes believed that many workers were too often drunk and disorderly, too resistant to the punctuality of clock time, and too ready to avoid the discipline of the capitalist labour market by living off charity or crime. Alongside voluntaristic campaigns to encourage personal moral regeneration such as evangelical Protestantism and temperance, and intellectual "improvement" through mechanics institutes and the like, they promoted a variety of state initiatives, beginning as early as the 1830s and 1840s, designed to reshape the attitudes and behaviour of this first generation of Canadian workers into a form compatible with and supportive of capitalist development — that is, industry, diligence, sobriety, punctuality, and general respect for property. New laws appeared to restrict and even criminalize a wide range of public behaviour, especially leisure activities — from Sunday observance to controls on ball playing in the streets to restrictions on the sale and consumption of alcohol.[6] New professional police forces appeared in many towns to curb inappropriate social and moral behaviour, and police courts became colourful new arenas for punishing recalcitrant workers.[7] In the early 20th

---

Immigrant Apprentices to Canada, 1869-1924 (London, 1980), and Edgar Wickberg, ed., *From China to Canada: A History of the Chinese Communities in Canada* (Toronto, 1982).

4   Norman MacDonald, *Canada: Immigration and Colonization, 1841-1903* (Toronto, 1966); Donald Avery, *"Dangerous Foreigners": European Immigrant Workers and Labour Radicalism in Canada, 1896-1932* (Toronto, 1979); Freda Hawkins, *Canada and Immigration: Public Policy and Public Concern* (Toronto, 1972).

5   Robert Miles Stamp, "The Campaign for Technical Education in Ontario, 1876-1914", Ph.D. thesis, University of Toronto, 1970; and *The Schools of Ontario, 1876-1976* (Toronto, 1982); Donald MacLeod, "Practicality Ascendant: The Origins and Establishment of Technical Education in Nova Scotia", *Acadiensis*, XV, 2 (Spring 1986), pp. 53-92.

6   J. R. Burnet, "The Urban Community and Changing Moral Standards" in Michiel Horn and Ronald Sabourin, eds., *Studies in Canadian Social History* (Toronto, 1974), pp. 298-325; Christopher Armstrong and H. V. Nelles, *The Revenge of the Methodist Bicycle Company: Sunday Streetcars and Municipal Reform in Toronto, 1888-1897* (Toronto, 1977).

7   Nicholas Rogers, "Serving Toronto the Good: The Development of the City Police Force, 1834-84" in Victor Russell, ed., *Forcing a Consensus: Historical Essays on Toronto* (Toronto, 1984), pp.. 116-40; Paul Craven, "Law and Ideology: The Toronto Police Court, 1850-80" in David Flaherty, ed., *Essays in the History of Canadian Law, Volume 2* (Toronto, 1982), pp. 248-65; Allan Greer, "The Birth of the Police in Canada" (paper presented to the

century the state stepped up its moral regulation with such experiments as complete prohibition of liquor and the censorship of movies — creating in the process some of the most straight-laced urban cultures in the western world.[8]

Parallelling these repressive initiatives were efforts to reform rather than simply punish workers who resisted orderly self-discipline. State-funded charitable institutions were reorganized to teach the poor new habits for the new age. The Kingston Penitentiary was opened with a great flourish as a reformatory for criminals, and "lunatic asylums" similarly promised to cure the disruptive behaviour of those designated insane. Perhaps most important, beginning at mid-century, a state-run public school system emerged to begin inculcating the new discipline and "correct" knowledge at an early age.[9] Most of these institutions ran into difficulties as the zeal of the reformers dissolved into the narrow-mindedness of the administrators, and as workers continued to elude or subvert their influence (for example, by sending their older children out to work rather than to school). The regular influx of new workers from non-industrial backgrounds threw up the same problems for successive generations of social engineers in Canada. Many new programs were launched in the early 20th century to accomplish essentially the same old goals, notably through a more far-reaching compulsory school system and the growing fields of social work and public health.[10] A wide range of state institutions still works away at restraining the disruptive behaviour of individual workers (absenteeism, alcoholism, drug abuse, and so on) and instilling the appropriate self restraint. It is, in part, the extension of state activities into these areas of moral regulation that has prompted some writers to talk about state formation as "cultural revolution".[11]

Few of these initiatives touched workers directly on their jobs. It was judges who set the first and most important parameters for workers' behaviour in a capitalist workplace. Through their evolving interpretation of the common law, British jurists and their colonial cousins implemented the concept of the contract of employment between workers and employers ("masters and servants"), which could be enforced in the courts. Central to this notion was the assumption that the two parties to the contract participated equally and freely in forming the terms of the

interdisciplinary workshop, "Social Change and State Formation in British North America, 1830-1870", 1989).

8   E. R. Forbes, "Prohibition and the Social Gospel in Nova Scotia" in Samuel D. Clark et al., *Prophecy and Protest: Social Movements in Twentieth-Century Canada* (Toronto, 1975), pp. 62-86; Gerald A. Hallowell, *Prohibition in Ontario, 1919-1923* (Ottawa, 1972); Malcolm Dean, *Censored! Only in Canada: The History of Film Censorship — The Scandal Off the Screen* (Toronto, 1981).

9   Judith Fingard, "The Relief of the Unemployed Poor in Saint John, Halifax, and St. John's, 1815-1860" in P. A. Buckner and David Frank, eds., *Atlantic Canada Before Confederation: The Acadiensis Reader, Volume One* (Fredericton, 1985), pp. 190-211; Dan Francis, "The Development of the Lunatic Asylum in the Maritime Provinces", *ibid.*, pp. 245-60; Richard B. Splane, *Social Welfare in Ontario, 1791-1893* (Toronto, 1965); Susan E. Houston and Alison Prentice, *Schooling and Scholars in Nineteenth Century Ontario* (Toronto, 1988); Bruce Curtis, *Building the Educational State: Canada West, 1836-1871* (London, 1988).

10   See, for example, Neil Sutherland, *Children in English-Canadian Society: Framing the Twentieth-Century Consensus* (Toronto, 1976).

11   Philip Corrigan and Derek Sayer, *The Great Arch: English State Formation as Cultural Revolution* (Oxford, 1985); Curtis, *Building the Educational State*.

contract, just as any two parties might in arranging any other kind of contract. Yet, in practice, employers normally had the upper hand in these deals. Not only could they frequently rely on competition in a well-stocked labour market to keep down wages, but what they got from workers in return for the payment of wages was open-ended service, obedience, and loyalty. Judges readily supported this employer control over his worker with legal sanctions. In Canada West the legislature strengthened the judge's hand with a Masters and Servants Act in 1847 and later with similar legislation governing railway employees. Until 1877, then, a disobedient worker in Canada could be a criminal.[12]

A set of assumptions and structures that insisted on treating workers as individuals in a capitalist labour market ran into difficulties, however, when the workers responded with collective assertions of their own needs and concerns. First they challenged their employers on the jobs with strikes and other disruptions of production and, occasionally, disturbed public order. By the late 19th century, many were joining increasingly well-organized unions to carry out these workplace confrontations. Canadian workers also had political rights in a liberal-democratic state that forced politicians to take heed of their concerns lest their disaffection lead them toward political options that threatened the status quo. These industrial and political challenges thus prompted some creative statecraft to prevent collective resistance from disturbing the central processes of capitalist accumulation in Canada, and to restore workers' consent to their subordination within the social order.

These were pressures felt throughout the western world, but state intervention in the lives of Canadian workers took its characteristic shape from two overriding considerations: the particular structure of the Canadian state itself, and the relative weakness of workers' movements in Canada. The Canadian state developed within the liberal-constitutionalist mould established in Britain by the mid-19th century. Politicians and state officials kept close touch with policy initiatives within the British state and frequently adopted these as models for Canadian legislation. The legal systems were closely integrated through the common law and the final appellate jurisdiction of the Judicial Committee of the Privy Council (until 1950). But state structures and policy evolved according to the specific economic and social conditions of the Canadian context, notably a heavy emphasis on resource export and the proximity of a powerful southern neighbour, the United States. Particularly important for considering the state's policies towards workers were strong regional divisions, which were entrenched in the British North America Act and strengthened by the courts in subsequent decades. Through their constitutional responsibility for "property and civil rights", the provinces got the power to legislate in labour relations (scarcely imagined in 1867) and thus eventually produced an uneven legal patchwork reflecting major regional differences in

---

12   Harry J. Glasbeek, "The Contract of Employment at Common Law" in John Anderson and Morley Gunderson, eds., *Union-Management Relations in Canada* (Don Mills, 1982), pp. 47-77; Paul Craven, "The Law of Master and Servant in Mid-Nineteenth Century Ontario" in David H. Flaherty, ed., *Essays in the History of Canadian Law: Volume 1* (Toronto, 1981), pp. 173-211; Paul Craven and Tom Traves, "Dimensions of Paternalism: Discipline and Culture in Canadian Railway Operations in the 1850s", in Heron and Storey, eds., *On the Job*, pp. 49-52.

industrial structure and development and in working-class power. All workers have not been treated the same in Canada.

Within Canadian capitalist society, moreover, workers' movements remained relatively weak within industrial life and thus within the body politic. Workers had difficulty holding together permanent organizations for a variety of reasons. They faced seriously divisive forces. A relatively small working population was strewn across a vast expanse of land in small clusters of industrial activity that varied significantly between regions and shared few common concerns. The contrast between the many craftsmen in the factory towns of Ontario and Quebec and the miners and transportation workers in the west is probably the most striking. Workers in each region often had more regular contact and affinity with their counterparts south of the American border than with other Canadian workers far across the country. Even within their own workplaces and communities workers faced forces that undermined the potential for solidarity and collective action. Transiency was one problem. The widespread seasonality of production and employment, especially in the resource industries, and the frequent booms and busts of the business cycle in most sectors of the Canadian economy prompted many workers to move on, either to another city or region or out of the country altogether. Transiency must also be seen within a context of intense competition for jobs within frequently over-stocked labour markets, particularly as a result of heavy immigration. Furthermore, over the past century and a half, the Canadian working class has gone through a series of major recompositions resulting from the transplantation and wholesale reorganization of production processes and from new recruitment practices. The Canadian state facilitated these transformations through state-sponsored research on science and technology, tax incentives for "modernizing" plants, and so on.[13] These changes dissolved pre-existing patterns of cohesion at the workplace, and required workers to learn new modes of solidarity and community within new mixes of occupation, ethnicity, race, and gender.

Canadian employers added to Canadian distinctiveness by striking a vigorous anti-union posture from the start. In the large and important sectors of the Canadian economy based on resource extraction and semi-processing for export, two groups of employers with considerable political clout — farmers and resource corporations — were determined to keep down labour costs on the products that had to compete internationally. They therefore insisted on heavy immigration to stock the labour market and resisted any concessions to labour. These concerns were shared by those provincial governments, such as that of Nova Scotia, whose tax revenues rested heavily on royalties from resource extraction. At the same time, many manufacturers imitated American models of powerful, large-scale corporations, which utilized mass-production techniques to help them escape heavy

---

13 I have discussed these factors at greater length elsewhere: see "On the Job in Canada" (co-authored with Robert Storey), in Heron and Storey, eds., *On the Job*, pp. 3-46; "Labourism and the Canadian Working Class", *Labour/Le Travail*, 13 (Spring 1984), pp. 45-76; *Working in Steel: The Early Years in Canada, 1883-1935* (Toronto, 1988); "The Second Industrial Revolution in Canada, 1890-1930" in Deian Hopkin and Gregory S. Kealey, eds., *Class, Community, and the Labour Movement in Canada and Wales, 1890-1930* (Aberystwyth, 1989); "The Great War and Nova Scotia Steelworkers", *Acadiensis*, XVI, 2 (Spring 1987), pp. 3-34.

reliance on scarce, high-priced skilled workers, and adopted aggressive union-busting practices.

Under these circumstances, few unions in Canada survived in the century before the Second World War, huge sectors of industry remained untouched by unions, and the first substantial labour parties appeared only at the end of the First World War and died quickly.[14] Even where workers were able to organize, they most often felt outnumbered: the Canadian working class was a minority within the total social structure until after the Second World War, when the number in the previously largest class, the independent commodity producers, began to decline precipitously.[15] As a minority, workers could more easily be ignored within the political process. All these particular features of the Canadian situation produced a set of state policies towards the working class with predominantly repressive and miserly overtones.

Meeting the Challenge of Militancy

Militancy erupted in Canadian workplaces from the earliest days of capitalist employment. In the mid-19th century canal labourers, miners, and other groups of workers often organized themselves informally but effectively in defense of common interests and traditional practices that they believed their employers had violated. The state's only involvement in these frays was repressive: whenever crowd action seemed threatening to social peace, or likely to succeed, troops were sent in to put down the "riot".[16] By mid-century, journeymen craftsmen in the larger towns and cities had also begun to organize, though they created more permanent, and more respectable, craft societies whose tactics were less riotous.[17] While some employers came to terms with these new organizations informally, many were still unwilling to tolerate any collective efforts to effect the terms or conditions of employment. The workers' tactics of striking and picketting brought criminal prosecutions, and the very existence of a union was construed in some circles as an illegal conspiracy in restraint of trade under the common law, although, in Halifax and Toronto at least, no workers were ever successfully prosecuted purely for membership in a union.[18]

14 For a brief sketch of the fortunes of Canadian unions, see Craig Heron, *The Canadian Labour Movement: A Short History* (Toronto, 1989).

15 Leo A. Johnson, "The Development of Class in Canada in the Twentieth Century" in Teeple, *Capitalism and the National Question*, pp. 141-84.

16 Ruth Bleasdale, "Class Conflict on the Canals of Upper Canada in the 1840s",, *Labour/Le Travailleur*, 7 (Spring 1981), pp. 9-39; C. B. Fergusson, *The Labour Movement in Nova Scotia Before Confederation* (Halifax 1964), pp. 19-21; James M. Cameron, *The Pictonian Colliers* (Halifax, 1964), pp. 141-3; K. G. Pryke, "Labour and Politics: Nova Scotia at Confederation", *Histoire sociale/Social History*, 6 (November 1970), pp. 33-5; Bryan D. Palmer, "Labour Protest and Organization in Nineteenth-Century Canada, 1820-1890", *Labour/Le Travail*, 20 (Fall 1987), pp. 62-7.

17 Eugene Forsey, *Trade Unions in Canada, 1812-1902* (Toronto, 1982).

18 Pryke, "Labour and Politics", pp. 34-40; Paul Craven, "Workers' Conspiracies in Toronto, 1854-72", *Labour/Le Travail*, 14 (Fall 1984), pp. 49-70. In both Britain and the United

It is worth emphasizing that the state's first repressive framework for dealing with organized workers was never completely dismantled. New elements were simply grafted on, although often fitting uncomfortably. Judges continued to uphold the primacy of the contract of employment until the Second World War, when new collective bargaining legislation was passed that superseded the common law. But the postwar jurisprudence in labour law still tried to keep the key concepts of the individual employment contract alive in the new collective bargaining regime.[19] Similarly, the armed force of the state was mobilized repeatedly in industrial disputes involving mass pickets and displays of strong working-class consciousness, usually in order to allow employers to maintain production with scab labour. The militia was sent into numerous struggles, especially in the resource, transportation, and construction industries, including the Sydney steel strikes of 1904 and 1923, the coal miners' strikes in Nova Scotia in 1909-11 and on Vancouver Island in 1912-14, and numerous street railway strikes across the country. These troops rolled into their last strike in Stratford, Ontario, in 1933, but by that time the Royal Canadian Mounted Police and provincial police forces had taken over this responsibility, often acting as little more than goon squads in the service of anti-union employers. Sydney steelworkers met these toughs in 1923, as did Lockeport fishery workers in 1939 and the women striking at Fleck Manufacturing in small-town Ontario in 1978.[20] Frequently, it should be noted, the use of armed force backfired, in that wider sympathy for the strikers and anger at the state violence spread through the community and boosted the workers' morale.

Repression also took on a political dimension. It was never uncommon for local police forces to dispense with free speech and break up street-corner meetings of radical workers,[21] and, after socialism became a matter of international politics in 1917, the federal government became much more deeply involved in the battle to prevent the spread of radical ideas in Canada. During the First World War the

---

States, the courts were slowly working out a legal distinction between the mere existence of a workers' organization, which was tolerable, and its activities in interfering with other workers' fulfillment of their contract of employment, which was not. See Henry Phelps Brown, *The Origins of Trade Union Power* (New York, 1986), pp. 23-44; and Christopher L. Tomlins, *The State and the Unions: Labor Relations, Law, and the Organized Labor Movement in America, 1880-1960* (New York, 1985), pp. 32-59.

19 Glasbeek, "Contract of Employment".
20 Desmond Morton, "Aid to the Civil Power: The Canadian Militia in Support of Social Order, 1867-1914" in Horn and Sabourin, eds., *Studies in Canadian Social History*, pp. 417-34; and "Aid to the Civil Power: The Stratford Strike of 1933" in Irving Abella, ed., *On Strike: Six Key Labour Struggles in Canada, 1919-1949*, pp. 79-92; Donald MacGillivray, "Military Aid to the Civil Power: The Cape Breton Experience in the 1920s" in MacGillivray and Brian Tennyson, eds., *Cape Breton Historical Essays*, pp. 95-109; Heron, *Working in Steel*, pp. 154-6; Jim Green, *Against the Tide: The Story of the Canadian Seamen's Union* (Toronto, 1986), pp. 68-70; Julie White, *Women and Unions* (Ottawa, 1980), pp. 95-103.
21 David Frank and Nolan Reilly, "The Emergence of the Socialist Movement in the Maritimes, 1899-1916" in Robert J. Brym and R. J. Sacouman, eds., *Underdevelopment and Social Movements in Atlantic Canada* (Toronto, 1979), pp. 89-90; A. Ross McCormack, *Reformers, Rebels, and Revolutionaries: The Western Canadian Radical Movement, 1899-1919* (Toronto, 1977), pp. 105-7; W. Craig Heron, "Working Class Hamilton, 1895-1930", Ph.D. thesis, Dalhousie University, 1981, pp. 654-5.

Borden government developed a network of spies to report on working-class radicals and militants, and after the war consolidated this espionage work in a permanent new branch of the RCMP.[22] During the Winnipeg General Strike, the federal government also introduced an amendment to the Criminal Code to outlaw radical activities, which allowed for the prosecution of strike leaders in Winnipeg and, in 1931, for the banning of the Communist Party and the jailing of its leaders.[23] While the Mackenzie King government repealed this draconian measure in 1936, it used the War Measures Act five years later during the Second World War to outlaw communist activity and to intern the party's leaders.[24] Also, throughout the period from the First World War to the Cold War, immigration policy was used to expel foreign-born radicals from their working-class communities, where they were seen to be dangerous troublemakers.[25] The racist overtones of conflating "foreigner" with "radical" also served to divide workers and discourage the development of a cohesive class consciousness. The Criminal Code thus remained a potent resource for repressing working-class resistance.

Workers in Canada, therefore, had good reason to see the state as a set of frequently hostile institutions. They were not deterred, however, from coalescing, as early as the 1850s, 1860s, and 1870s into occupationally based unions and cross-occupational councils, federations, and congresses. They developed structures of solidarity, often stretching across the 49th parallel, which allowed them to sustain more effective battles with employers, although most unions had a tenuous and brief existence before the Second World War. In the face of persistent militancy from these organized workers, successive administrations at the federal and provincial levels soon learned that outright repression alone would not work. Smashing workers' organizations might only breed deeper resentment and more serious industrial or political challenges to the existing order. It was necessary to cultivate the consent of organized workers to their subordinate status within capitalist society. The Canadian state therefore set out to find a new framework for tolerating but tightly regulating union activity. Four times in Canadian history the state intervened with a legal restructuring of industrial relations. Each time the new regime so established was a response to workers' demands for better negotiating relationships with their employers, but the state's response never took the precise form labour wanted. Each time the government's intention was to use state regulation to channel the exercise of collective working-class power so as to limit its destructive impact on capital accumulation and the larger social order. Unions were to be placated with some formal recognition and increased responsibility, but the basically repressive intent was evident in the repeated efforts to restrict the use

22 S. W. Horrall, "The Royal North-West Mounted Police and Labour Unrest in Western Canada, 1919", *Canadian Historical Review*, 61, 2 (June 1980), pp. 169-90.
23 David Jay Bercuson, *Confrontation at Winnipeg: Labour, Industrial Relations, and the General Strike* (Montreal, 1974), pp. 163-75; Lita-Rose Betcherman, *The Little Band: The Clashes Between the Communists and the Political and Legal Establishment in Canada, 1928-1932* (Ottawa, 1981).
24 Reg Whitaker, "Official Repression of Communism During World War II", in *Labour/Le Travail*, 17 (Spring 1986), pp. 135-66.
25 Avery, *Dangerous Foreigners*; Barbara Roberts, "Shovelling Out the 'Mutinous': Political Deportation from Canada Before 1936", *Labour/Le Travail*, 18 (Fall 1986), pp. 77-110.

of the strike weapon. While the state took these initiatives in the interests of stabilizing the capitalist system, this was not always with the complete agreement of all capitalists; often, in fact, there was considerable resistance until employers discovered how the new regime could work to their benefit. The Canadian state thus had a semi-autonomous role in alleviating class conflict.

The first explosion of working-class organizing peaked in 1872 when craft unionists in several central Canadian towns and cities launched the Nine-Hours Movement and thus brought the legal ambiguities regarding workers' organizations to a head. The Toronto printers, who took the lead in striking for shorter hours, found their leaders arrested for criminal conspiracy in restraint of trade at the instigation of the bellicose George Brown and his fellow employing printers. Before they came to trial, however, Brown's wily political foe in Ottawa, Sir John A. Macdonald, brought the prosecutions to an end with a new Trade Unions Act. Macdonald's coup was a brilliant political maneuver for shoring up working-class support for his party and its emerging policy of stimulating industrialization. Yet there was little substance to this apparently dramatic stroke freeing unions from the criminal taint. The Tories had borrowed an elaborate legislative package enacted in Britain the year before, which was much more restrictive in intent than some latter-day commentators have assumed. Unions were to be tolerated legally only if they formally registered. Moreover, under a Criminal Law Amendment Act passed as part of the package, their activities in striking and picketting were to be restrained just as harshly as they had been under the common law. The few cases heard under this new legislation in the mid-1870s continued the repression that had been imposed over the previous 20 years. In short, legal recognition within this new regime would come at the cost of any effective power to confront employers. This first attempt to place a legal straightjacket on Canadian unions failed, however, when unions refused to register under the Trade Unions Act, and when a persistent labour movement used its limited political clout to win federal laws in 1876-7 permitting non-obstructive picketting and decriminalizing breaches of the contract of employment.[26] Henceforth, the legislatures assumed that workers and their bosses could proceed with "private ordering" of the employment relationship without the criminal sanction. In practice, the courts no longer entertained the notion that unions were criminal conspiracies, but refused to recognize them in common law.

Over the last quarter of the 19th century, the Canadian state made no dramatic new departures to curb industrial militancy beyond making available mediation services, which were seldom used. In 1888 Nova Scotia introduced the country's first compulsory arbitration legislation, but it proved unworkable and was quietly abandoned.[27] The explanation for this inactivity undoubtedly lies in the general

---

26 John Battye, "The Nine-Hour Pioneers: The Genesis of the Canadian Labour Movement", *Labour/Le Travailleur*, 4 (1979), pp. 25-56; Donald Creighton, "George Brown, Sir John A. Macdonald and the 'Workingman'" in *Towards the Discovery of Canada: Selected Essays* (Toronto, 1972), pp. 174-93; Gregory S. Kealey, *Toronto Workers Respond to Industrial Capitalism, 1867-1892* (Toronto, 1980), 124-53; Craven, *Impartial Umpire*, pp.167-74.

27 Ian McKay, "'By Wisdom Wile or War': The Provincial Workmen's Association and the Struggle for Working-Class Independence in Nova Scotia, 1879-97", *Labour/Le Travail*, 18 (Fall 1986), pp. 46-9; Margaret E. McCallum, "The Mines Arbitration Act, 1888, Compulsory

weakness of organized labour in late 19th century Canada and the regular failure of so many of the strikes launched in the period (in contrast to the growing web of collective bargaining spreading through several British industries).[28] An overstocked labour market and capitalist intransigence were restraining militancy quite adequately without any help from the state. By the early 1900s, however, industrial conflict was escalating quickly in many parts of the country, most alarmingly on the railways and in mining communities that were closely tied to the government's economic development plans. The Canadian judiciary became much more active in penalizing militant strike activity in civil actions under common law, especially in the wake of the Taff Vale decision in Britain, which allowed employers to sue unions for damages and encouraged similar actions in Canadian courts. British unionists got legislative relief from this legal constraint in 1906, when the new Labour Party exerted its increased parliamentary pressure on the Liberals, but, in the absence of any comparable labour representation, no Canadian provincial legislature made a similar move in this period except in British Columbia, where a socialist MLA with the balance of power managed to push a measure through the house in 1902.[29]

The potential dissonance between state institutions became more evident when the federal government passed the federal Conciliation Act in 1900 and thereby declared, in contrast to the courts' union-busting animus, a willingness to use mediation to promote industrial peace. In fact, implicitly the federal government was announcing its predominance over the provinces in dealing with industrial conflict (though not other matters of labour policy) in the national interest — a role that would last for half a century with only a minor interruption in the mid 1920s. The architect of what was to become the second major state initiative into containing workers' industrial power was the young deputy minister of labour (and chief conciliator under the 1900 legislation), William Lyon Mackenzie King. Building on the already emerging practice of the federal government, King's solution to the "labour problem" took the form of compulsory conciliation. This was embodied in special legislation for railway workers in 1903, and then in the Industrial Disputes Investigation Act of 1907, which remained the most important Canadian legislation governing industrial conflict until 1944. The law required workers and employers in resource, transportation, and utilities industries to postpone strikes or lockouts until a three-person board of conciliation had heard the issues, deliberated, and issued a report, and until an appropriate "cooling-out" period had allowed the two sides to consider the report and to feel the weight of public opinion. Jumping the gun could make a party liable to criminal prosecution, though the government virtually never used that penalty. Despite the rhetoric about the restraining power of public disapproval, in practice the boards were expected to work more quietly to mediate a settlement of the dispute without issuing a report — indeed, often by threatening to expose the parties' positions to public scrutiny if they did not settle. The advantage of this new set of procedures

Arbitration in Context" in P. Girard and J. Phillips, eds., *Essays in the History of Canadian Labour Law, Volume 3* (Toronto, 1989).

28   C. J. Wrigley, ed., *A History of British Industrial Relations, 1875-1914* (Amherst, 1982).

29   Craven, *Impartial Umpire*, pp. 196-207.

was clearly that production would continue without disruption while some settlement was attempted. Unfortunately, many workers found that the delays could undermine the momentum that new unions built up and that employers were still free to dismiss union leaders and in various ways prepare for a strike. During the First World War, the act was extended to cover all munitions workers and eventually any unionized work force. Paradoxically, many union leaders came to support this compulsory conciliation law by the end of the war for its implicit support of recognition from employers. In 1925 the Industrial Disputes Investigation Act was successfully challenged in the Judicial Committee of the Privy Council as beyond the federal government's constitutional powers, but most provinces soon enacted legislation allowing the law to be extended into their jurisdiction. At the outbreak of the Second World War all war-related industries once again came under the act.[30]

The third major state initiative designed to contain collective working-class activity arose out of the dramatic wave of union organizing and militant strikes that peaked in 1943 and that threatened to overflow into support for the social-democratic Co-operative Commonwealth Federation. Early in 1944 the Mackenzie King government passed an order-in-council, PC 1003, which introduced a set of procedures for recognizing union representatives and guaranteeing that employers would have to sit down with them at a bargaining table. Like some parallel initiatives at the provincial level in the same period, this emergency legislation borrowed several of its essential provisions from the Wagner Act passed in the United States in 1935, especially the creation of a labour relations board to oversee union representatives' certification and to monitor "unfair labour practices", but it never formally recognized unions and built in numerous constraints on aggressive union organizing techniques. The act also incorporated the key concepts and practices of the Industrial Disputes Investigation Act, including the compulsory conciliation procedures. It took a huge wave of successful strikes immediately after the war to convince state officials to make the legislation a permanent feature of postwar Canadian industrial relations, this time, however, decentralized to the provinces.

The new structures assumed that labour and capital would continue to work out most of their differences and the contents of their agreements on their own — the state guaranteed no specific outcome. Backed by a federal government promise to stimulate a full-employment economy, organized workers were expected to be able to wrench significant concessions from their corporate employers. But the state had tied unions' hands in numerous ways. Most important was the severe restriction on the right to strike. Not only did workers have to wait out the familiar "cooling-off" period during and after conciliation before they could strike, but they were also forbidden to strike for union recognition or during the lifetime of a collective agreement, when disputes were to be settled by a grievance-arbitration system. The

---

30 Craven, *Impartial Umpire*; Jeremy Webber, "Compulsion and Consent in Canadian Labour Law: Canada's Choice of Conciliation over Arbitration, 1900-1907" (paper presented to the York University Advanced Research Seminar on Labour and Law in the Commonwealth, 1989); Judy Fudge, "Voluntarism and Compulsion: The Canadian Federal Government's Intervention in Collective Bargaining From 1900 to 1946", Ph.D. thesis, Oxford University, 1987.

traditional forms of direct action that workers had used spontaneously to resist management pressure on the job were now to be replaced by slower, more impersonal, more bureaucratic procedures that were most often controlled by lawyers and wrapped in a mystifying new legal language. Sympathy strikes were now almost impossible, since workers' contracts bound them to stay on the job, and, as employers and labour relations boards soon insisted on single-plant bargaining units, workers' collective power was divided into tiny, isolated fragments across the country. The Winnipeg General Strike could never again happen legally. And there was now less chance of the rapid leftward politicization that so often resulted from major strike waves, when workers had found common cause in shared and parallel struggles.[31]

This new regime of tightly structured industrial legality took deep root in the mass-production, resource, and transportation industries, and between 1965 and 1975 was extended to public-sector workers, including Nova Scotia provincial government employees.[32] Cracks had begun to appear by that point, however, as new generations of workers facing tougher management, disruptive technological change, and rapid retail price inflation found the system too cumbersome and insensitive to their concerns. A massive explosion of militancy across the country in the decade after 1965, sometimes in defiance of union officials and generally spearheaded by newly unionized public-sector workers, reached unprecedented proportions that were allegedly surpassed internationally only by Italy.[33] In 1975 the Canadian state made its fourth major structural effort to constrain workers' collective power. The wage control program introduced that year by the federal government and supported by all the provinces, along with a simultaneous turn to tight-money monetarist policies, inaugurated a new era of curbing working-class incomes and constraining workers' collective power. Federal and provincial governments also undermined workers' bargaining strength by deliberately stimulating unemployment and weakening the "safety net" of social security programs. They disrupted and limited collective bargaining with increasingly frequent use of back-to-work legislation and other controls on public-sector unions. Following the example of Nova Scotia's so-called "Michelin Bill", which undercut union organizing drives in the province's new tire plants, some provinces made moves in the 1980s to weaken permanently unions' legal room to maneuver.

---

31 Laurel Sefton MacDowell, "The Formation of the Canadian Industrial Relations System During World War Two", *Labour/Le Travailleur*, 3 (1978), pp.175-96; Jeremy Webber, "The Malaise of Compulsory Conciliation: Strike Prevention in Canada During World War II" in Bryan D. Palmer, ed., *The Character of Class Struggle; Essays in Canadian Working Class History* (Toronto, 1986), pp. 135-59; Judy Fudge, "Voluntarism and Compulsion: The Canadian Federal Government's Intervention in Collective Bargaining From 1900 to 1946" (paper presented to the Australian-Canadian Labour History Conference, Sydney, 1988); Peter J. Warrian, "'Labour is Not a Commodity': A Study of the Rights of Labour in the Canadian Postwar Economy, 1944-48", Ph.D. thesis, University of Waterloo, 1986; Heron, *Canadian Labour Movement*.

32 Allen Ponek, "Public-Sector Collective Bargaining" in Anderson and Gundarson, *Union-Management Relations*, pp. 343-78; Anthony Thomson, "The Nova Scotia Civil Service Association, 1956-1967", *Acadiensis*, XII, 2 (Spring 1987), pp. 81-105; and "From Civil Servants to Government Employees: The N.S.G.E.A., 1967-1973" in this volume.

33 Heron, *Canadian Labour Movement*.

Workers have not found, in general, that their organizations were attacked and destroyed on the model of American union-busting, but that their unions have nevertheless been severely weakened in the Canadian industrial relations system.[34]

In Canadian history, also, state regulation rather than repression of unions has been a policy applied only to the most organized and most vocal, excluding large groups of workers who were less well organized, who were more vulnerable to employer retaliation, or who were employed in areas considered too sensitive. Until late in the 20th century, domestic servants and farm labourers were explicitly exempted from collective-bargaining legislation in most jurisdictions in deference to upper-class householders and farmers. These workers consequently remained enmeshed in private, patriarchal work relations with little or no recourse to state assistance. Fishermen were another group of vulnerable workers facing legal restraints. In Nova Scotia, once they had begun to organize collectively to resist their abjectly dependent status as producers and wage-earners, the courts excluded them from the collective bargaining regime in 1947 on the grounds that they were "co-adventurers" with the corporations controlling the fishing industry and therefore not employees under collective-bargaining legislation.[35] And employees of the federal and provincial governments were consistently denied collective-bargaining rights until the 1960s and 1970s, when new legislation generally still limited their right to strike or to negotiate over such important issues as job classifications or pensions. Since the mid-1970s, moreover, these workers have had even those limited rights drastically reduced.

To win the widest possible support for new forms of labour regulation, the state began in the early 20th century to justify its intervention with some definition of the "public interest" separate from the interests of the specific workers involved. Mackenzie King was an early ideological architect of a distinct public interest in labour relations, in practice in the operations of the Industrial Disputes Investigations Act, and in long-winded theory in his *Industry and Humanity*.[36] By the 1970s and 1980s the state's public-interest rhetoric had turned nastier, describing unionized workers as greedy, selfish, and threatening to the economic well being of all Canadians. The highly fragmented structures of postwar collective bargaining that isolated the struggles of individual groups of workers and inhibited sympathetic actions of solidarity made it harder for workers to link their immediate interests with those of a larger public (some public sector workers have been struggling to make these connections in recent years, most notably the beleaguered postal workers).[37]

---

34   David A. Wolfe, "The Rise and Demise of the Keynesian Era in Canada: Economic Policy, 1930-1982" in Michael S. Cross and Gregory S. Kealey, eds., *Readings in Canadian Social History, Volume 5: Modern Canada, 1930-1980's* (Toronto, 1984), pp. 46-78; Allan M. Maslove and Gene Swimmer, *Wage Controls in Canada, 1975-78; A Study in Public Decision Making* (Montreal, 1980); Leo Panitch and Donald Swartz, *The Assault on Trade Union Freedoms: From Consent to Coercion Revisited* (Toronto, 1988).

35   E. Jean Nisbet, "'Free Enterprise at its Best': The State, National Sea, and the Defeat of the Nova Scotia Fishermen, 1946-1947" in this volume.

36   Craven, *Impartial Umpire*.

37   R. A. Sample, "Struggle '88: Postal Workers' Vision of an Improved Canada Post", *Canadian Dimension*, 23, 1 (January/February 1989), pp. 33-6.

At the same time, the Canadian state has regularly reached out to managers and union leaders to deepen their commitment to industrial peace. During the 20th century the Canadian state added to its new forms of regulation some programs to encourage new managerial methods aimed at promoting harmony between workers and bosses. Before the First World War, Mackenzie King's Department of Labour publication, the *Labour Gazette,* broadcast the early, scattered experiments in company welfare programs for workers, and after the war that department actively promoted the expansion of such management "with a human face". Department officials also pushed another King solution to labour problems, developed for the Rockefeller interests in the United States — the industrial council of employee and employer representatives in one workplace, which was to discuss issues without the conflictual relations brought by unions. Half a century later, federal and provincial governments began to promote a program with a similar goal, most often known as "Quality of Working Life", which encouraged worker participation in low level decision making on the shop floor. New provincial and federal legislation introduced in the 1970s and 1980s also sought to promote the settlement of disputes regarding occupational health and safety in committees outside the framework of collective bargaining. In practice, of course, these programs were exercises in convincing workers to reduce or abandon their own class interests in the face of their employers' need for more productivity and profitability. Relative to other approaches to working-class militancy, however, these state initiatives to encourage workplace harmony had an extremely limited impact.[38]

Ultimately more important were the Canadian state's efforts to cultivate the support of apparently trustworthy, responsible labour leaders, who seemed to share a common interest in industrial peace. Almost invariably these have been the bureaucrats of the labour movement — full time officials and staff concerned about the respectability and political and financial stability of their organizations. Most often these men (and more recently women) have also been politically cautious and resistant to any radicalism and militancy that emerged within their unions. In Nova Scotia the coal miners' unions produced a series of these men — Robert Drummond in the 1890s, John Moffat in the 1910s, Silby Barrett from the 1920s to the 1940s.[39] The headquarters of international unions and the executive offices of the Trades and Labour Congress of Canada were often fertile breeding ground for such unionists. They usually had a clear enough sense of their independent union interests that they seldom became complete dupes of politicians or civil servants, but they were generally willing to co-operate in any new state framework that guaranteed them and their organizations recognition and some semblance of power.

---

38   Craven, *Impartial Umpire*, pp. 101-5; Bruce Scott, "'A Place in the Sun': The Industrial Council at Massey-Harris, 1919-1929", *Labour/Le Travailleur*, 1 (1976), pp. 158-92; James Naylor, "The New Democracy: Class Conflict in Industrial Ontario, 1914-1925", Ph.D. thesis, York University, 1988, pp. 373-442; Don Wells, *Soft Sell: "Quality of Working Life" Programs and the Productivity Race* (Ottawa, 1986); Victor Levant, *Capital and Labour: Partners? Two Classes — Two Views* (Toronto, 1977).

39   McKay, "Wisdom, Wile, or War"; Paul MacEwan, *Miners and Steelworkers: Labour in Cape Breton* (Toronto, 1976); Michael Earle and Hebert Gamberg, "The United Mine Workers and the Coming of the CCF to Cape Breton" in this volume.

Since the Second World War many of these union leaders have been social-democrats who have looked longingly at the active role of their counterparts under social-democratic administrations in western Europe.

Since the turn of the century, federal and provincial departments of labour have most often been the agencies for building these relationships with reliable union bureaucrats. Mackenzie King was among the first to cultivate union leaders when he strung together his network of *Labour Gazette* correspondents across the country after the creation of the federal Department of Labour in 1900. Since King's day as well, state officials have courted the leaders of "legitimate" unions and excluded from their embrace the heads of more radical or militant organizations. As secretary of a 1903 royal commission on industrial conflict in British Columbia King penned the first denunciation of irresponsible radicalism, making charges that would be repeated in ever more vigorous forms against the One Big Union and communist-led unions from the 1920s to the 1950s.[40] Yet, despite the flirtations with individual union bureaucrats, formal experiments in corporatist integration of labour leaders were rare in Canadian history, probably because so few Canadian capitalists would sit down with unionists and because unions were so comparatively weak before the Second World War. After refusing to involve union leaders in any significant wartime administrative bodies, Robert Borden's government made a stab at a corporatist solution to labour unrest in 1919 when it convened a large National Industrial Conference of labour, employer and "public" representatives, intended to advise the government on labour policy and carefully chosen to exclude any "reds". It resolved nothing and was never reconvened.[41]

For the next half century, labour leaders continued to complain that they were excluded from all significant advisory and administrative boards beyond those narrowly focussed on such specific labour matters as unemployment insurance. In 1962 the Nova Scotia government gestured in a corporatist direction when it began to respond to the advice of the privately sponsored Joint Labour-Management Study Committee.[42] Thirteen years later, federal Labour Minister John Munroe sponsored a short-lived tripartite Canadian Labour Relations Council in 1975 seeking solutions to some of the major problems that had cropped up in the industrial relations system. But the next year, when the Canadian Labour Congress leadership proposed European-style tripartite bodies to engage in social and economic planning, federal officials gently deflected such ideas into new discussions of some more limited kind of corporatism, which soon involved the Business Council on National Issues. The CLC and the Business Council eventually launched the bipartite National Labour Market and Productivity Centre in 1984 with federal government support. In the same period, labour leaders joined businessmen on several departmental committees for long-range economic forecasting. However, as a major state solution to labour-relations problems, corporatism never really got off the ground in the 1970s and 1980s. Constitutional

---

40   Craven, *Impartial Umpire*; David Jay Bercuson, *Fools and Wise Men: The Rise and Fall of the One Big Union* (Toronto, 1978); Whitaker, "Official Repression"; Green, *Against the Tide*.
41   Naylor, "New Democracy", pp. 443-504.
42   C.H.J. Gilson and A. M. Wadden, "The Windsor Gypsum Strike and the Coming of the Joint Labour-Management Study Committee: Conflict and Accommodation in the Nova Scotia Labour Movement, 1957-1979" in this volume.

power over industrial relations is too spread out through the provinces for national structures to have any real impact. Moreover, neither capital nor labour had a central organization with the mandate to carry out the negotiations that would be necessary to make such a system work. In any case, most capitalists seemed more interested in a get-tough approach to organized labour, rather than in polite dialogue with union bureaucrats.[43] Federal officials nonetheless have never underestimated the importance of seeking a friendly rapport with labour leaders who were uncomfortable with militancy and who craved some political recognition for themselves and their organizations. Their commitment to the legitimacy of the social order could help to discipline their membership.

Overall, then, the Canadian state's response to collective working-class resistance in the workplace has been repressive regulation. Union organizing and striking were consistently hampered by court and military repression until they appeared to threaten serious disruption of production processes, public order, or workers' faith in the capitalist system in general. At the first seriously menacing point, in the early 1900s, the federal government began to put together a subtler alternative that tried to promote industrial peace through interventionist mediation. Federal labour officials subsequently played a key role in industrial relations through the first half of the 20th century, often in the face of continuing belligerence from courts and provincial administrations (witness Mackenzie King's discomfort at the heavy-handed use of militia and police force in Sydney in 1923, which prompted him to set up a royal commission to investigate). The legal recognition that the federal government granted to unionized workers was nonetheless always highly restrictive in that it tightly constrained both the use of the strike weapon and the scope for broadening workers' struggles beyond a particular workplace. These forms of regulation were introduced most often when workplace militancy and the overall labour movement seemed unusually powerful, notably in 1907 and 1944, but when unions lacked sufficient real strength to press successfully for legislation more favourable to the workers' interests. Other state initiatives to encourage personnel management policies or corporatist integration of union bureaucrats were too sporadic and limited in their impact to change the fundamentally repressive pattern of state action against working-class organization and workplace struggles in Canada.

The Politics of Labour

One of the ironies of a liberal-democratic capitalist society is that workers have more egalitarian rights in the political than the economic sphere. Of course, unlike their counterparts in the United States, Canadian male workers did not enjoy full electoral rights at the dawn of industrial capitalism in the mid-19th century. It would take steady pressure to win the right to vote and hold office for all white

43　Roy J. Adams, "The Federal Government and Tripartism", *Relations industrielles/Industrial Relations*, 37, 3 (1982), pp. 606-17; K.G. Waldie, "The Evolution of Labour-Government Consultation on Economic Policy" in W. Craig Riddell, ed., *Labour-Management Co-operation in Canada* (Toronto, 1986), pp. 151-201; Don Wells, "Ontario's Quality of Working Life Centre Dies, But Co-optation of Labour Thrives", *Canadian Dimension*, 22, 7 (October 1988), pp. 26-7.

men (generally by the turn of the century), women (during and after the First World War, though not until 1940 in Quebec), and Asians (in the late 1940s in British Columbia).[44] Nor, given the defeat of the 1837-8 insurrections, could workers appeal to any specific revolutionary traditions within Canada such as existed in several European countries and in the United States to guarantee the "rights of man". However, as "free-born Englishmen", Anglo-Canadian workers had some idea that they had a right to influence state policy (even if most often they cynically denied that their voice had any impact and often did not bother to vote — the most industrialized parts of the country have seen abysmally low voter turnouts at several points in the 20th century).[45]

Politicians who controlled the elected branches of the state had to pay at least some attention to placating working-class voters, lest they vote for the opposition or, worse yet, form a new party of their own with an anti-capitalist ideology and program. The latter possibility was generally strongest when the size, power, and anger of the labour movement was on the rise.[46] Typically in such circumstances, a royal commission or special investigation was set in motion to indicate sympathy without definite commitment. Ultimately, modest reforms became an alternative to both the untrammelled capitalist labour market and the bogey of socialism.[47] Legislation intended to ameliorate the working and living conditions of workers and their families was introduced in spurts that corresponded to upsurges of labour organizing and militancy — the 1880s, the 1910s, the 1940s, and the mid 1960s through mid 1970s. The Tories made a few sympathetic gestures in the 1870s,[48] but for several decades it was mainly Liberal administrations that took the reform initiative. In fact, the Liberals' success in placating labour leaders in Nova Scotia, Quebec, and the Prairies in the early 20th century helped to delay the emergence of a substantial labour party in most of these regions until the First World War, and enabled them to tug back the independent-minded Liberal-Labour types (the "Lib-Labbers"). Seldom could direct representatives of the labour movement or labour parties carry their own legislative program through a Canadian legislature. Before the Second World War, Canadian labour parties were directly involved in provincial governments only in Ontario from 1919 to 1923 and, marginally, in Alberta from 1921 to 1935. The postwar record was slightly better but still limited: the CCF's breakthrough into government in Saskatchewan in 1944 was not matched until

---

44   Norman Ward, *The Canadian House of Commons: Representation* (Toronto, 1950); Catherine Cleverdon, *The Women's Suffrage Movement in Canada* (Toronto, 1950); W. Peter Ward, *White Canada Forever: Popular Attitudes and Public Policy Toward Orientals in British Columbia* (Montreal, 1978).

45   See, for example, Michael J. Piva, "Workers and Tories: The Collapse of the Conservative Party in Urban Ontario, 1980-19", *Urban History Review*, 3-76 (1977), pp. 23-30; Heron, "Working-Class Hamilton", pp. 493-508.

46   Heron, "Labourism"; MacDowell, "Formation of the Canadian Industrial Relations System".

47   The International Labour Organization, created at a peak of labour unrest in 1919, was supposed to be the worldwide rallying point for this reformist alternative, but Canadian governments ignored most of the ideal labour standards enunciated there. John Mainwaring, *The International Labour Organization: A Canadian View* (Ottawa, 1986).

48   Pryke, "Labour and Politics", pp. 48-53; Kealey, *Toronto Workers*, pp. 124-72.

1969 in Manitoba and 1971 in British Columbia.[49] Small wonder, then, that Canada's "social wage" has remained much more limited than that in most other advanced capitalist countries (excepting the United States and Japan) and that postwar federal governments preferred the indirect approach of the Keynesian full-employment economy to a European-style welfare state.

The measures introduced by all these administrations covered many aspects of workers' lives, especially occupational health and safety, minimum wages, shorter hours and paid holidays, and other employment standards, as well as such income-security measures as mothers' allowances, unemployment insurance, pensions, health insurance, and so on. Most of it differed from the regulatory measures discussed above in that it attempted to intervene in the contract of employment to limit an employer's freedom of action, either by forbidding certain employment practices or by providing alternative forms of income to that available purely through wages. For the most part, however, such legislation did not constrain capital nearly as much as state regulation bound labour.

In each case, labour was usually first to put such reform issues on the political agenda. Without much working-class representation in the legislatures, however, the eventual legislation often reflected some departure from labour's stated goals. Almost invariably some substantial body of capitalists opposed the measures, and politicians were wary about upsetting business sentiment too profoundly. But key business leaders did occasionally recognize that more economic and social stability might well result from laws easing workers' conditions. Once workers were organized and mobilized successfully enough to be taken seriously, two forces generally shaped the outcome of demands for this kind of legislation: the convergence of diverse social interests on a particular demand, and the ideology of the labour movement itself.

Other groups often shared an interest in a particular reform for quite different reasons. Labour's demands were only part of the chorus of concern about the impact of rapid industrialization and urbanization. For example, upper and middle-class activists, especially the women, were particularly anxious to protect idealized notions of fragile femininity and precious childhood that seemed to be threatened in the new factories and sweatshops. They found common cause with labour leaders, who operated on their own patriarchal views of women and children (and fears about the erosion of their own skills), but were also concerned about the degradation and exploitation of labour evident in the patterns of women's employment. The factory acts of the 1880s and the minimum wage legislation of the early 1920s both reflected this combination of interests.[50] In a similar way, the unemployment insurance scheme that emerged in 1941 bore the stamp not only of

---

49   Heron, "Labourism"; Naylor, "New Democracy", pp. 312-72; Anthony Mardiros, *William Irvine: The Life of a Prairie Radical* (Toronto, 1979); Ivan Avakumavic, *Socialism in Canada: A Study of the CCF-NDP in Federal and Provincial Politics* (Toronto, 1978).

50   Lorna F. Hurl, "Overcoming the Inevitable: Restricting Child Factory Labour in Late Nineteenth Century Ontario", *Labour/Le Travail*, 21 (Spring 1988), pp. 87-122; Margaret McCallum, "Keeping Women inTheir Proper Place: the Minimum Wage in Canada, 1910-25", *ibid.*, 17 (Spring 1986), pp. 29-58. On the specifically working-class notions of womanhood, see Bettina Bradbury, "Women's History and Working-Class History", *ibid.*, 19 (Spring 1987), pp. 35-6.

labour demands, but also of bankers' and politicians' concerns about the solvency of municipal governments required to dole out relief during the depressions.[51]

Once the legislative initiative was underway, the intervention of capitalist lobbyists could be crucial in limiting the scope of reform, to prevent it from dramatically threatening capital-accumulation processes. Through such pressure the factory acts were tamed to prevent officious inspectors from disrupting production. The Canadian Manufacturers' Association seems to have bungled similar attempts to shape Ontario's workers' compensation legislation just before the First World War, but in Nova Scotia the corporate fish-packers managed to get their workers out from under the protection of such legislation in 1928.[52] Also, the actual administration of the acts, which generally lay beyond any direct democratic control, could alter the effect of a law from the original intention. The reluctance of factory inspectors to prosecute employers for violating the factory acts and the turn-of-the-century violations of the Alien Labour Act were glaring examples.[53] Similarly, any legislation that involved payments to workers — workers' compensation, old-age pensions, unemployment insurance, and so on — was marked by the suspicions of working-class "pauperism" that had dominated charity and social-welfare administration since the early 19th century. As a result, economic assistance to workers often came wrapped in means tests and other demeaning red tape and was invariably kept well below normal earnings from wages. Industrial discipline (the "work ethic"), based on the threat of poverty, was not to be undermined by these programs. The treatment of the working-class victims of the 1917 Halifax explosion provides a good example of the suspicions workers had to confront when they applied for relief.[54]

The residue that accumulated on the statute books from these initiatives was particularly constraining for women workers. Only in the past 15 years have women begun to challenge the assumption built into most legislation that men should earn a "family wage" on which the women, relegated to the domestic sphere, should be dependent. Much of the early labour legislation was primarily concerned with restricting the employment of women, setting special hours and other working conditions for them. The first minimum wage boards similarly reinforced women's limited labour-force participation by pegging female wages far below those of men. The limited mothers' allowances introduced in the 1920s and the "baby bonus" in the 1940s were income supplements paid only for mothering responsibilities. Other welfare schemes were structured on the assumption of the family wage.

51 James Struthers, *No Fault of Their Own: Unemployment and the Canadian Welfare State, 1914-1941* (Toronto, 1983).

52 Eric Tucker, "Making the Workplace 'Safe' in Capitalism: The Enforcement of Factory Legislation in Nineteenth Century Ontario", *Labour/Le Travail*, 21 (Spring 1988), pp. 45-86; and "The Determination of Occupational Health and Safety Standards in Ontario, 1860-1982: From the Market to Politics to . . . ?", *McGill Law Journal*, 29 (March 1984), pp. 260-311; Michael J. Piva, "The Workmen's Compensation Movement in Ontario", *Ontario History*, 67 (March 1975), pp. 39-56; Fred Winsor, "'Solving a Problem': Privatizing Workers' Compensation for Nova Scotia's Offshore Fishermen" in this volume.

53 Avery, *Dangerous Foreigners*, pp. 32-3.

54 Suzanne Morton, "The Halifax Relief Commission and Labour Relations during the Reconstruction of Halifax, 1917-1919" in this volume.

It must be said, however, that the ultimate shape of this labour legislation also reflected what the labour movement expected from the state. Perhaps the most important difference between Canadian and many continental European unions in the 19th century was that, like their British and American counterparts, they won some limited freedom to operate in capitalist society without the sponsorship of a socialist party. Labour leaders thus came to believe that amelioration of working-class life was possible through the slow and fragmented processes of union organizing (especially craft unions) and negotiations with employers — in short, collective self-help. In effect, they promoted a form of working-class liberalism that maintained a rigid separation of state and civil society. The American Federation of Labor, to which so many Canadian craft unionists hitched their stars at the turn of the century, was led by men committed to winning labour's battles solely through industrial action, without state intervention. The Catholic labour movement that had taken shape in Quebec by the end of the First World War was similarly dedicated to voluntarism, rather than state action. In the early 20th century, many Canadian craft unionists were more ambivalent. It was their frustrations with the "unfair" lopsidedness of the state's support for capital, especially in the courts, that pushed these men into an independent political stance, first on the edge of the Liberal Party (as "Lib-Labbers"), and then in Independent Labour Parties. These labourists were most often craft unionists who urged democratization of government (through an unrestricted franchise, proportional representation, abolition of the Senate, and so on), but they remained slightly suspicious of the state. They still put more faith in free association of workers, and fair, voluntary agreements with capitalists within the general rule of law, than they did in any fundamental transformation of capitalist social and economic structures. Their calls for state intervention were generally limited to demands for legislation to curb monopolies and other sources of ill-deserved and privileged power, to protect voluntary union activity, and to support those incapable of supporting themselves — women and children, the sick and aged, the unemployed.[55] The heyday of labourism was over by the 1920s, and Canadian craft unionists henceforth followed the preference of the AFL and the Catholic unions for keeping a distance from politics.

There has seldom been complete ideological unanimity in the House of Labour. Two other political tendencies, Marxism and social-democracy, attempted to win over Canadian unionists. Compared to labourism, both were advocates of a larger social vision and of a more active role for the state in working-class liberation. In contrast to the labourists (whom they regularly denounced), the early Marxists' analysis of workers' problems brought them to the conclusion that capitalism had to be replaced with some version of a socialist society controlled and managed by workers themselves. These radicals attempted to convince their fellow unionists that politics mattered much more than narrow union interests, and that the state could be an effective instrument for ending workers' exploitation and oppression by seizing control of the means of production, distribution, and exchange. Before the First World War, the Marxists in the Canadian labour movement were members of small socialist parties, who found their strongest support in coal mining towns,

---

55 Heron, "Labourism".

where a handful of them were elected to seats in the British Columbia and Alberta legislatures. Elsewhere their influence was minimal.[56] For a brief period at the end of the First World War these radicals found much wider audiences within the general working-class revolt of the period, notably in the One Big Union, and helped to sharpen the vision of workers' movements.[57] For the next forty years, it was the communists who carried the banner of Marxism in the labour movement under the inspiration of the Soviet Union and the always-shifting Bolshevik road to social transformation. They had a significant, though fluctuating following, through their leadership of the Workers' Unity League in the early 1930s and later some of the CIO unions, but the repression of the Cold War era pushed them to the margins of the labour movement.[58] Today their political heirs can be found within the minority opposition caucuses in the provincial federations and the Canadian Labour Congress.

The social-democrats first emerged as a distinct political tendency in the 1920s and in 1933 coalesced into the Co-operative Commonwealth Federation. They were slower to win a following in the labour movement, but by the 1940s were engaged in a head-to-head confrontation with the communists for control of the new industrial union movement in Canada. By the early 1950s they had maneuvered themselves into command of most of the large new labour organizations in the country. In the CCF, social-democratic labour leaders were junior partners in a formal alliance with radicalized professionals, other middle-class Canadians, and, in the west, farmers. Initially their program shared with the communists a moral rejection of capitalism and projected a stirring vision of an alternative society based on considerable state ownership, centralized planning, and extensive social-security programs. Their soaring popularity during the Second World War that so frightened Mackenzie King was based on their calls for an extensive "welfare state" to take the insecurity out of workers' lives. By the time of the creation of the New Democratic Party in 1961, the social-democrats had jettisoned nationalization and extensive state planning in favour of Keynesian regulation of the economy and concentrated on a package of reforms for making capitalism more humane.[59] The dominance of social-democratic politics in the postwar labour movement and the partial implementation of a social-democratic program (often by the Liberals) nonetheless created an expectation of "social rights" to economic security guaranteed by the state that went beyond the concepts of "liberty, equality, and fraternity" carried forward from the 18th century revolutions by the old labourists. The modern labour movement is thus loud in its defense of the social programs that late 20th century Canadian governments seem so eager to slash.

56 Frank and Reilly, "Socialist Movement"; McCormack, *Reformers, Rebels, and Revolutionaries.*

57 Gregory S. Kealey, "1919: The Canadian Labour Revolt", *Labour/Le Travail*, 13 (Spring 1984), pp. 11-44; Heron, "Labourism".

58 Norman Penner, *Canadian Communism: The Stalin Years and Beyond* (Toronto, 1988).

59 Walter D. Young, *The Anatomy of a Party: The National CCF, 1932-61* (Toronto, 1969); Irving M. Abella, *Nationalism, Communism, and Canadian Labour: The CIO, the Communist Party, and the Canadian Congress of Labour, 1935-1956* (Toronto, 1973); Desmond Morton, *NDP: Dream of Power* (Toronto, 1974).

Yet Canadian unionists never lost the old suspicion of the state. Social-democratic politicians envisioned major social change proceeding only through elections and parliamentary acts, and major social policy being set by elites of enlightened experts. Workers would benefit from this kind of society, but only as passive recipients. The politicians recognized workers' right to organize and bargain collectively, but assumed that these rights would be subordinated to centrally planned incomes policies (all three NDP governments supported wage controls in the mid 1970s). That statist perspective inevitably created tensions with the labour leadership, which remained suspicious of too much state intervention in industrial relations, preferring voluntarism and free association for both unions and private enterprise corporations (the unions participating in the New Democratic Party have repeatedly used their power to curb left-wing enthusiasm for public ownership). They are also still prepared to use more direct action in the form of strikes than social-democratic politicians are normally comfortable with; hence the often chilly relations between provincial labour movements in Manitoba, Saskatchewan, and British Columbia and their New Democratic governments in the 1970s. More importantly, the NDP's failure to elect a national government, or a provincial government in central or eastern Canada, has left the labour movement little choice but to continue its emphasis on industrial action (or, in a few cases, tripartism).

The Canadian labour movement also never abandoned its patriarchal assumptions about women workers. It was probably the first social group to raise the demand of women's right to vote and run for office, but male workers collaborated in the creation of protective legislation for women and the defense of the family wage. Only in the 1970s and 1980s did women workers begin to break down some of these prejudices among their fellow unionists.

The politics of labour, then, has been a mixed bag. Not only has labour seldom been close enough to state power to carry out its own agenda and thus has seen its concerns watered down and twisted in unanticipated ways, but the mainstream Canadian labour movement has never completely abandoned the labourist faith in voluntarist relationships outside the state as the most appropriate way to improve workers' conditions. Labour still harbours some uneasiness about too much state intervention. Limitations in the scope of the labour legislation that entered the state books reflected at least in part labour's limited focus on freedom of association for workers' organizations and on the economic well-being of working-class families attacked by crises with which they were unable to cope on their own. More radical alternatives that envisioned aggressive state action to transform Canadian society into a workers' republic were jettisoned in the Red Scares that followed each World War. The defeat of radicalism within the labour movement was reinforced by state repression and by the creation of tightly controlled, fragmented collective bargaining structures, which limited the political solidarity that could grow out of industrial struggles. Labour's ideological caution developed in a position of beleaguered weakness, as capital used its considerable power to undermine a series of labour movements and to blunt their political achievements, and as the state quite effectively constrained the exercise of collective working-class power in industrial life.

In the end, then, Canadian workers have most often encountered the state as a check or deterrent on their individual and collective behaviour. It was certainly not neutral in the fundamental conflicts that erupted in industrial capitalist society. The many branches of the Canadian state have not always marched in lock-step in their approach to the "labour problem" — the courts and the legislatures have often followed their own tunes, and the various provincial administrations have dallied and straggled according to their own rhythms. But, on balance, the institutions of the Canadian state saw the "labour problem" as one of order, not equity or justice. The overriding concern was always the efficient functioning of capitalist industry in Canada, especially its labour markets and labour processes. Workers' ability to organize collectively and challenge the terms of their subordination in Canadian capitalist society was consistently restricted by state action, and consequently their ability to mobilize political movements to use the state for their own interests was severely limited. Where workers organized they were carefully regulated to avoid serious disruptions; otherwise they were left to work out the best deals they could through uncertain private negotiations with their employers. The only state programs intended to improve workers' living and working conditions directly were those introduced under pressure from labour and its occasional allies, and, owing to labour's industrial and political weakness and ideological ambivalence, those remained incomplete and comparatively parsimonious. The state thus remained more a stern disciplinarian than a kindly paternalist for the Canadian working class.

To suggest that workers found the state in Canada fundamentally constraining is not to suggest that those workers have been consistently on the verge of open revolt, held in check only by coercion. The existence of repressive mechanisms, the historical memory of their use, and the thorough extinction of alternative possibilities can limit expectations, whether through fear or fatalism; but repression alone is never very successful. Coercion, to be most effective, must interact with positive reassurances of good intentions from politicians and others that are aimed at making workers feel comfortable with their place in the social order (though in Canada the payoff for workers' compliance has been a lower "social wage" than in most industrialized countries). Workers' consent also reflects the successful inculcation of normative values, beliefs, and habits of deference by the schools, the mass media, and other agencies. The unequal divisions of power and wealth in capitalist society and the appropriately limited expectations for workers come to seem natural and inevitable. The particular blend of coercion and consent that emerged in Canadian state practice has thus helped to give the working class its own "Canadian identity".

THE CONTRIBUTORS

KIRBY ABBOTT, who received an M.A. in history at Carleton, has recently completed his law degree at Dalhousie.

MICHAEL EARLE is a Ph.D. student in history at Dalhousie University.

HERBERT GAMBERG is a member of the Sociology Department at Dalhousie University.

C. J. H. GILSON is Associate Professor of Industrial Relations at Saint Francis Xavier University.

CRAIG HERON is a member of the History Department at York University.

IAN McKAY is a member of the History Department at Queen's University.

SUZANNE MORTON is a Ph.D. student in history at Dalhousie University.

E. JEAN NISBET is a researcher who lives in Saint John, New Brunswick.

ANTHONY THOMSON is a member of the Sociology Department at Acadia University.

A. M. WADDEN is at present working towards a combined Master of Business Administration/Bachelor of Law degree at Dalhousie.

JAY WHITE is a Ph.D. student in history at McMaster University.

FRED WINSOR is a Ph.D. student in history at Memorial University.